T0329968

A Quantitative Approach to Commercial Damages

The National Association of Certified Valuators and Analysts (NACVA) supports the users of business and intangible asset valuation services and financial forensic services, including damages determinations of all kinds and fraud detection and prevention, by training and certifying financial professionals in these disciplines. NACVA training includes Continuing Professional Education (CPE) credit and is available to both members and non-members. Contact NACVA at (801) 486–0600 or visit the web site at www.NACVA.com.

A Quantitative Approach to Commercial Damages

Applying Statistics to the Measurement of Lost Profits

MARK G. FILLER
JAMES A. DiGABRIELE

WILEY

John Wiley & Sons, Inc.

Published by John Wiley & Sons, Inc., Hoboken, New Jersey.
Published simultaneously in Canada.

Microsoft and Excel are registered trademarks of Microsoft Corporation.

For general information on our other products and services or for technical support, please contact our Customer Care Department within the United States at (800) 762-2974, outside the United States at (317) 572-3993, or fax (317) 572-4002.

Wiley also publishes its books in a variety of electronic formats. Some content that appears in print may not be available in electronic books. For more information about Wiley products, visit our web site at www.wiley.com.

Library of Congress Cataloging-in-Publication Data:

Filler, Mark, 1942–
    A quantitative approach to commercial damages : applying statistics to the measurement of lost profits / Mark Filler, James DiGabriele.
        p. cm.
    Includes bibliographical references and index.
    ISBN 978-1-118-07259-2 (cloth/website); ISBN 978-1-118-22244-7 (ebk);
    ISBN 978-1-118-23637-6 (ebk); ISBN 978-1-118-26104-0 (ebk)
    1. Lost profits damages–Valuation–Statistical methods.   I. DiGabriele, James A., 1962–   II. Title.
K837.F55 2012
347'.077–dc23

                                                                    2011050886

Printed in the United States of America.

10 9 8 7 6 5 4 3 2 1

To my children, Joshua David and Rachel Leah, who have exceeded my hopes and expectations.

—MGF

To my wife Lori, my sons, Daniel, James, and John. I thank them for their encouragement, love, support, and patience during this journey.

—JAD

A Quantitative Approach to Commercial Damages

Contents

Preface

From years of presenting at conferences and seminars, participating in roundtable discussions and case study analyses, and mentoring fellow practitioners, it became obvious to us that the typical ABV, CBA, ASA, or CVA who was attempting to calculate economic damages either as a stream of lost profits or as lost value of the business using the direct market data method had little knowledge of either statistical methods or the advantages to be obtained by applying them to the task at hand.

This book is intended for practitioners who have some experience in the field of calculating economic damages and who are looking to acquire some new tools for their toolkit—tools that are more sophisticated and flexible than simple averaging techniques. These typical practitioners will remember little from their college statistics course and will not have access to or be capable of using stand-alone statistical packages such as SAS, SPSS, Stata, and so on. But they will be familiar with Excel, and our pedagogical approach is to demonstrate the use of the statistical tools that come either built into Excel or as add-ins that are freely or inexpensively available.

The level of knowledge that is required to get the maximum benefit from this book does not exceed that needed for an introductory statistics course. Therefore, this book is not designed for trained statisticians or PhDs in economics or finance whose education, knowledge, and training far exceed the fundamentals expounded herein.

Is This a Course in Statistics?

The simple answer is no! This book is intended to be an introduction and a "how-to" of some basic statistical techniques that can be useful in a lost profits analysis. It is not, however, meant to replace a statistical text or give the reader an in-depth understanding of statistics.

We have provided a glossary of terms as they are defined by standard statistical textbooks, and a bibliography that provides the reader with sources to study for a more in-depth analysis of the concepts introduced in this book.

While the book focuses on the basic statistical applications as found in Excel or its add-ins, readers are encouraged to undertake a more thorough understanding of the conceptual underpinnings of the techniques by referring to the textbooks recommended in the bibliography.

At a minimum, we suggest the following three Excel add-ins. First, there is the StatPlus add-in that comes with Berk and Carey's book, *Data Analysis with Microsoft*

Excel. Second, there is the popular free downloadable add-in, Essential Regression. And last, if you can find it on the Internet, Gerry LaBute's downloadable add-in, Gerry's Stats Tools. The latter two add-ins come with handbooks that not only serve as instruction manuals for the software, but are primers for regression and statistics in general, respectively.

How This Book Is Set Up

The organizing principle that motivates this book is the attempt to match up Excel's and its add-ins' statistical tools with common, quotidian problems and issues that damages analysts face in their day-to-day practices. We approached the subject matter from both sides of the matchup.

First, we examined the statistical tools available in Excel's Analysis ToolPak, its statistical formulas, and the specialized tools available in the add-ins and asked ourselves: In what ways can we apply any of these tools to commercial damages cases? Second, we reviewed the literature looking for typical commercial damages cases and asked: Is there a statistical solution to this problem? The results of our back and forth approach are the 16 case studies in this book, with each (as the Contents listing shows at the front of this book) presented as its own chapter.

Case Study 1 demonstrates how to use the standard deviation to determine if some number, say, a period's gross margin or a month's sales, falls within an expected range based on past performance.

Case Study 2 concerns itself with testing the sales history of the XYZ Motel to determine if there is an upward trend in the data as asserted by the claimant.

Case Study 3 is an introduction to regression analysis in the context of measuring damages for lost profits as the value of a business destroyed by the actions of the defendant.

Case Study 4 returns to the XYZ Motel and the forecasting of expected sales during the period of restoration using an econometric regression model.

Case Study 5 uses the XYZ Motel data once again to forecast expected sales during the period of restoration using a time series regression model.

Case Study 6 demonstrates the forecasting of sales using an econometric regression model, the determination of saved expenses using a simple linear regression model, and introduces the idea of interrupted time series analysis.

Case Study 7 involves the comparison of pre- and postincident sales and demonstrates techniques to answer the question: Did sales really fall off after the incident?

Case Study 8 demonstrates the forecasting of sales using a time series regression model and tests the significance of an intervening event with the use of interrupted time series analysis.

Case Study 9 involves the issue of cost behavior and estimation.

Case Study 10 presents a problem concerning the determination of saved expenses and introduces the issue of statistical significance vs. practical significance.

Case Study 11 presents the plaintiff's and the defendant's expert's reports in a breach of contract action, points out the flaws in each, and offers a reconciling resolution to their differences.

Case Study 12 is about the application of forensic accounting principles to a lost profits case.

Case Study 13 shows how to set up and use a nonstatistical method for accounting for trend and seasonality when forecasting expected sales.

Case Study 14 involves techniques used to analyze historical sales data searching for trend and seasonality.

Case Study 15 displays nonregression techniques for forecasting sales when the historical sales data is stationary.

Case Study 16 displays nonregression techniques for forecasting sales when the historical sales data is nonstationary.

The Job of the Testifying Expert[1]

According to Federal Rule of Evidence 702, an expert will be allowed to testify in the form of an opinion if,

1. The testimony is based upon sufficient facts or data.
2. The testimony is the product of reliable principles and methods.
3. The witness has applied the principles and methods reliably to the facts of the case.

In addition, the opinion given must be "within a high degree of (economic or financial) certainty." In other words, a trier of fact, either a judge or jury, is looking for an opinion that will help them to "understand the evidence or to determine a fact in issue." An academic treatise that increases the storehouse of knowledge might meet that requirement, but given the amount, accuracy, and verifiability of the facts and data available to the expert in a litigation matter, will generally not be forthcoming. Therefore, given the different purposes of the researcher and the testifying expert, different methods of analysis and different uses of the traditional research tools is to be expected.

In the course of this book we will be demonstrating selected statistical techniques to be applied in lost profits cases, where the end result is to form an opinion as to the amount of economic damages, even if there are limits to the facts and data and all the supporting documentation you want is not available. The testifying expert, while using research tools familiar to academics, is attempting to assist the trier of fact, and therefore is not engaged in an "exhaustive search for cosmic understanding but for the particularized resolution of legal disputes."

About the Companion Web Site—Spreadsheet Availability

There is a companion web site to this book—found at www.wiley.com/go /commercialdamages—that contains all the spreadsheets for the case studies in this book. So, you have a choice—you can create the spreadsheets from scratch, following the instructions contained in each chapter, or you can simply download them from the web site and start your analysis immediately. For pedagogical purposes, we recommend that you create your own spreadsheets—there's something about putting them together yourself that leads to a quicker understanding of their purpose.

Note

1. Adapted from the paper "To Infinity and Beyond: Statistical Techniques Appraising the Closely Held Business," presented by Drs. Tom Stanton and Joe Vinso at the 20th Annual IBA Conference, San Antonio, TX, January 1998.

Acknowledgments

The authors wish to express their gratitude and appreciation to the following individuals who served as readers and reviewers of this book.

David H. Goodman, MBA, CPA/ABV, CVA
J. Richard Claywell, CPA/ABV, ASA, CBA, CVA, CM&AA, CFFA, CFD, ABAR
John E. Barrett, Jr., CPA/ABV, CBA, CVA
James F. McNulty, CPA

We would also like to thank Nancy J. Fannon, CPA/ABV, ASA, MCBA, for first suggesting the idea of this book and for initially reviewing the introduction and the first six chapters.

The Application of Statistics to the Measurement of Damages for Lost Profits

To get the most out of the case studies in this book, the reader needs to attain a minimum amount of statistical knowledge.

The Three Big Statistical Ideas

There are Three Big Statistical Ideas: variation, correlation, and rejection region (or area). If we can build sufficient intuition about these interrelated concepts, then we can construct a raft for ourselves upon which we can explore the bayou of statistical analysis for lost profits. Therefore, what follows is a very broad introduction to statistics, which does not allow us to explain or define every technical term that appears. To assist you, we have included all those technical terms in a Glossary at the end of the book where they are defined or explained.

Variation

The first Big Idea is that of variation, which means to vary about the average or mean. It deals with the degree of deviation or dispersion of a group of numbers in relation to the average of that group of numbers. For example, the average of 52 and 48 is 50; but so is the average of 60 and 40, 75 and 25, and 90 and 10. While each of the sample data sets has the same average, they all have different degrees of dispersion or variances. Which average of 50 would you have more confidence in—that of 52 and 48, or that of 90 and 10—to predict the population mean?

Variance can also be depicted visually by imagining two archery targets, with one target having a set of five arrows tightly grouped around the bull's-eye and the other target with the five arrows widely dispersed about the target. Not only will the average score of each target be different, but also so will their variances. One could then conclude that based on the widely diverging variances, two different archers were involved.

For statistical purposes, variances are calculated in a specific way. Since some of the numbers in a data set will be less than the average, and hence will have a negative

TABLE I.1   Deviations Squared, Variance, and Standard Deviation

Row #	Annual Sales	Average	Deviation	Deviation^2	Operator
4	58	130	−72	5,184	
5	105	130	−25	625	
6	88	130	−42	1,764	
7	118	130	−12	144	
8	117	130	−13	169	
9	137	130	7	49	
10	157	130	27	729	
11	169	130	39	1,521	
12	149	130	19	361	
13	202	130	72	5,184	
Average	**130**			**15,730**	Sum
Sample Variance				**1,748**	Sum/$n - 1$
Sample Standard Deviation				**41.81**	Square Root of Variance
Excel Functions:					
Deviations Squared				**15,730**	DEVSQ(B4:B13)
Sample Variance				**1,748**	VAR(B4:B13)
Sample Standard Deviation				**41.81**	STDEV(B4:B13)

deviation from the mean, we need to transform or convert these negative numbers in some way so that we can compute an average deviation. This transformation consists of squaring each deviation. For example, if the mean is 10 and the particular number is 8, then the deviation is −2. Squaring the deviation gives us 4. Summing the squared deviations of all the numbers in the data set gives us something called, surprise, sum of squared deviations. Dividing this result by the number of observations in the data set minus 1 ($n - 1$) gives us the sample variance.[1]

Taking the square root of the sample variance produces the sample standard deviation, or the average amount by which the observations are dispersed about the mean.

Table I.1 expresses the relationship among the sum of deviations squared (DEVSQ), variance (VAR), and standard deviation (STDEV).

As we shall see in the case studies, how far a particular number is from 0, a mean, or some other number, measured by the number of standard deviations, comes into play in every parametric statistical procedure we will perform. Nonparametric tests rely on the median, not the average, and therefore have no need of a standard deviation.

Correlation

The second Big Idea is correlation, and to survey that concept we need to go back to the notion of variance and express it in a common-size or dimensionless manner by standardizing the deviations about the mean. For example, in a preceding paragraph we mentioned a mean of 10, a number of 8, and a deviation of −2. If the standard deviation of the data set is 1.5, then by dividing −2 by 1.5 we have standardized,

TABLE I.2   Coefficient of Correlation

Trans. #	Actual		Standardized[2]		
	SDE ($000s)	Price ($000s)	SDE	Price	Product
1	13,457	94,769	2.34	2.22	5.19
2	7,448	52,000	.84	.72	.60
3	5,884	48,400	.45	.59	.27
4	5,846	47,000	.44	.54	.24
5	2,888	33,740	−.30	.08	−.02
6	4,600	33,715	.13	.08	.01
7	2,855	21,100	−.31	−.36	.11
8	1,088	7,500	−.75	−.84	.63
9	133	3,700	−.99	−.97	.96
10	661	2,550	−.86	−1.01	.87
11	166	1,800	−.98	−1.04	1.02
Mean, or Average	4,093	31,479	0.0	0.0	
Std. Deviation	4,005	28,524	1.0	1.0	
Sum					9.876
$n - 1 = 11 - 1$					10
Average = Sum/$(n - 1)$ = R					.9876
R^2 =					.9754

or common-sized, the −2 deviation to be −1.33 standard deviations from the mean. This process would be repeated for each observation in the data set.

For example, assume you have information from 11 purchase and sale transactions that provides you with the selling price of each company's fixed and intangible assets as well as the seller's discretionary earnings (SDE) of each company. To determine the degree of correlation between selling price and SDE, we would first standardize each number in both sets of variables using Excel's STANDARDIZE function. We would common-size the 11 selling prices based on the mean and standard deviation of selling prices. Then we would repeat the process for the 11 SDE values, but using the mean and standard deviation of SDE.

By matching up the corresponding standardized selling price and SDE, we can see how closely they tally with each other. The tighter the match between standardized values, the higher the degree of co-variance, or co-relatedness. To develop a metric that measures the strength of the linear relationship between selling price and SDE, we multiply each set of corresponding standardized values for price and SDE in the Product column, sum the Product column, and then divide by $n - 1$. The result is known as the coefficient of correlation, symbolized as either r or R. An example is provided in Table I.2.

From Table I.2 we can see that the closer the matchup between the variances of the two variables, expressed as the common-sized deviations from their respective means, the higher the correlation coefficient and the stronger the linear relationship between the two variables. This is what is meant when R^2 is defined as the metric that measures how much of the variation in the dependent variable is "explained," or accounted for, or matched up with the variation in the independent variable.

From the above, we can conclude that correlation summarizes the linear relationship between two variables. Specifically, it summarizes the type of behavior often observed in a scatterplot. It measures the strength (and direction) of a linear relationship between two numerical variables and takes on a value between −1 and + 1. It is important in lost profits calculations as a summary measure of the strength of various sales and cost drivers.

THE CONCEPT OF THE NULL HYPOTHESIS   An outcome that is very unlikely if a claim is true is good evidence that the claim is not true. That is, if something is true, we wouldn't expect to see this outcome. Therefore, the statement can't be true. For example, a picture of the earth taken from space showing that it is round is not likely to happen if the world is flat. Therefore, that picture is very good evidence that the claim of flatness is not true. Or if the defendant in a criminal trial is not guilty; that is, is no different from or is just like everyone else, then finding gunpowder residue on his hands and the victim's blood on his shoes is strong evidence that he is not innocent, but is in fact guilty of the crime.

These claims, that the earth is flat or not round and that the defendant is not guilty, are called, in statistical terms, null hypotheses. In order to reject these null hypotheses strong evidence has to be produced by the scientist and the prosecutor to convince others to accept the alternative hypotheses, that is, the world is round and the defendant is guilty. In lost profits cases, we too have to deal with claims of null hypotheses—that there is no difference between pre- and postincident average sales; that there is no difference between sales during the period of interruption and the preceding and succeeding periods; or that the slope of our sales forecasting regression line is no different from zero. Rejecting these null hypotheses or accepting their alternatives leads us to the next Big Idea of statistics.

Rejection Region or Area

The final Big Idea is the rejection region or area. In statistics, when we say that we are 95 percent confident of something, we are implying that we are willing to be wrong about our assertion 5 percent of the time. So, how do we set forth the boundaries that measure this 5 percent? The answer to this question flows from our understanding of standardized data. From Table I.2, we can see that a distribution or list of standardized data has a mean of 0 and a standard deviation of 1, calculated in the same manner as previously described. Assuming that the distribution is also near–bell shaped, or normally distributed, then the empirical rule would come into play, and we would find that about 68.1 percent of the values lie within ± 1 standard deviation from the mean and that about 95.3 percent of the values lie within ± 2 standard deviations from the mean. This is demonstrated on the bell-curve shown in Figure I.1.

Therefore, when we choose a confidence level of 95 percent, we are saying that if our test statistic falls within approximately ± 2 standard deviations from the mean, or within the 95 percent acceptance area, we cannot reject the null hypothesis, for example, that there is no difference between our number and the sample average, and we must accept the status quo. But if our test statistic falls outside approximately ± 2 standard deviations from the mean, or inside the 5 percent rejection area, then we must reject the null hypothesis and accept the alternative hypothesis that things are different because it is very unlikely to find a test statistic and p-value this extreme

Figure I.1
Normal Distribution

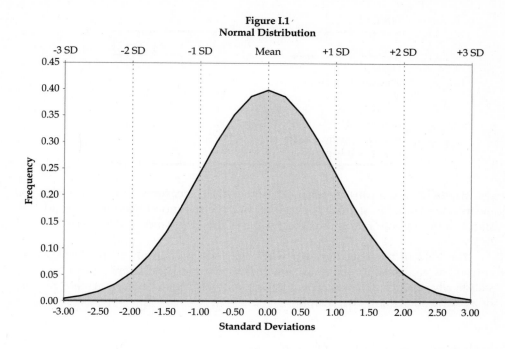

if there is no difference between our number and the sample average. Therefore, the claim of no difference must not be true and can be rejected.

The rejection region on the right-hand side of the distribution is called the upper tail, and the rejection region on the left-hand side is called the lower tail. If we are asking, for example, if our calculated number is greater than, say, 10, then we would look for our answer in the upper tail alone, prompting the name "one-tailed" test. The same is true if our question about the calculated number concerned it being less than 10. The answer would be found in the lower tail alone, also indicating a "one-tailed" test. However, when we are interested in detecting whether our calculated number is just different from 10; that is, either larger or smaller, we can locate the rejection region in both tails of the distribution. Hence the name "two-tailed" test.

In order to test a null hypothesis we need to create a statistical test that has four elements:

1. A null hypothesis about a population parameter, often designated by the symbol H_0. For example, "There is no difference between A and B." Or, "The difference between A and B is zero, or null."
2. An alternative hypothesis, which we will accept if the null hypothesis is rejected; often designated by the symbol H_a.
3. A test statistic, which is a quantity computed from the data.
4. A rejection region, which is a set of values for the test statistic that are contradictory to the null hypothesis and imply its rejection.

Two examples of a statistical test are demonstrated in Table I.3. In each case, the null hypothesis is that the difference between the mean and X is zero, or null; the alternative hypothesis is that there is a difference between the mean and X; the

TABLE I.3

	Example 1	Example 2
Mean	100	100
Standard Deviation	25	25
X	135	175
Test Statistic	1.4	3.0
Critical Value	1.96	1.96
Is t-stat > critical value	No	Yes
Reject null hypothesis?	No	Yes

test statistic is $(X - \text{mean})/\text{standard deviation}$, which measures how far X is from the mean as measured in standard deviations; and the rejection region lies beyond 1.96 standard deviations (1.96 is the actual value of the ± 2 standard deviations referred to above).

The idea of the rejection area will come into play in all of this book's case studies, as we use it to determine whether or not the conclusions of our tests are statistically significant; that is, whether the results happened because of mere chance, or because something else is afoot.

Introduction to the Idea of Lost Profits

Recovery of damages for lost profits can take place in either a litigation setting if the cause of action is a tort or a breach of contract, or under an insurance policy following physical damage to commercial property. In both situations there has been an interruption of the business's revenue stream, causing it to lose sales and eventually to suffer a diminution of its profits. In a tort, lost profits are generally defined as the revenues or sales not earned, less the avoided, saved, or noncontinuing expenses that are associated with the lost sales. For business interruption claims the policy wording is "net income plus continuing expenses." This is a bottom-up calculation that ought to deliver an equal amount of damages as the top-down calculations used for torts if the fact patterns are the same.

In the top-down approach, the costs of producing the lost sales that do not continue or are avoided or saved might include sales commissions, cost of materials sold, direct labor, distribution costs and the variable component of overhead, or general and administrative expenses. To a damages analyst using this approach, the computation of damages is typically concerned only with incremental revenue and costs, that is, only that revenue that was diminished by the interruption and only those costs and expenses that vary directly with that revenue. The idea of lost profits in a tort or breach of contract situation can be presented schematically, as follows:

> lost revenues
>
> − avoided saved or noncontinuing expenses
>
> = lost profits
>
> + "extra" expense due to interruption
>
> = economic damages

Fixed costs are usually ignored as the injured party would generally have to incur those costs regardless of the business interruption.

The schematic for the bottom-up approach, typically used for business interruption insurance claims, is as follows:

expected net income

+ continuing expenses

= lost profits

+ "extra" expense due to interruption

= actual loss sustained

Saved, avoided, or noncontinuing expenses are usually ignored as the purpose is to recompense the injured party for the net income they would have earned plus reimbursement for those expenses that continued during the period of interruption, including those such as leases, which might continue due to contractual obligations.

An implication of both these approaches is that the measurement of damages is a multistage process that begins with forecasting sales and then proceeds to indirectly compute lost profits, rather than forecasting lost profits directly. This is so because, as we have explained already, the idea of lost profits is more than the idea of net income—it also includes a component of expense, whichever approach we use. As such, there is no line item on the income statement that is an exact representation of our concept of "lost profits." Therefore, a lost profits calculation needs to begin with a forecast of expected revenue and then proceed to the examination and classification of expenses into continuing and noncontinuing categories, and then on to those necessary additional steps depending on the chosen approach, before finally arriving at an amount of lost profits.

This section of the introduction will present an overview of the damages measurement process. The second section will introduce various sales forecasting methodologies and will describe the situations that are appropriate for their use.

Stage 1. Calculating the Difference Between Those Revenues That Should Have Been Earned and What Was Actually Earned During the Period of Interruption

Determining what sales would have been during the period of interruption "but for" the actions of the defendant or casualty is the first stage of computing lost profits. For both tort cases and business interruption claims, the damages analyst must rely on a wide range of data and facts to project the expected level of sales. Since the best estimate of the interruption period revenue is related to a variety of factors concerning the capacity to produce and the capability of the market to buy a service or product, the damages analyst needs financial and statistical tools that are capable of incorporating all those factors into a sales forecast. A starting point for measuring the degrees of capacity and capability is to examine what has actually transpired before and after the period of interruption. The business's performance on both sides of the interruption period ought to help identify what the business could have done but for the tort or covered peril, absent other intervening causes. Subtracting actual sales earned from expected sales will produce lost sales or incremental revenues for the period of interruption.

Stage 2. Analyzing Costs and Expenses to Separate Continuing from Noncontinuing

Those costs that vary directly with sales during the pre- or postloss period are good evidence of the saved costs to the firm of not obtaining the "lost" revenues claimed in stage 1. Statistical models can also be useful here to help determine how certain types of costs vary with different levels of service or production. If using a top-down approach, variable costs and expenses should be included in the lost profits calculus, while those that do not vary with sales or production (i.e., fixed or continuing costs) should be excluded from the computation. An example of a variable or saved cost is the income statement line item called "cost of goods sold." Most or the entire amount of selling expense ought to be variable, and therefore saved, as well. Because financial statement categorization does not necessarily distinguish which costs are variable and which are not, the damages analyst must often use professional judgment and statistical tools to separate continuing from noncontinuing expenses. Regressing costs and expenses on sales can be very effective in this situation if certain requirements are met, as we shall see in future chapters.

In a bottom-up approach, the steps involved are slightly more numerous and include preparing an income statement for the period of interruption that includes all expenses, both fixed and variable. Regression is typically not used in creating the income statement—rather, the analyst's judgment coupled with trends and percentages of sales derived from historical financial statements are used to forecast expected costs and expenses that would have been incurred against expected sales. The next step is to determine what expenses would have continued, based on how costs have behaved in prior periods or actually did continue during the period of interruption.

Stage 3. Examining Continuing Expenses Patterns for Extra Expense

Often certain expenses may increase and new costs may be incurred during or after the business interruption period as a result of the tort or casualty. Management may indicate, for example, that the company had to incur overtime expense to make up lost production, or that temporary office or production space had to be leased. Inquiries of management and the examination of postloss month-to-month changes in wages, overtime, and overhead accounts can identify these costs.

Stage 4. Computing the Actual Loss Sustained or Lost Profits

In the top-down approach, lost profits are the incremental revenues the plaintiff would have earned "but for" the actions of the defendant, less those expenses related to the lost revenues that are saved or avoided. In the bottom-up approach, adding those continuing expenses computed in stage 2 to the expected net income before taxes during the period of interruption and then subtracting any gross profit realized during the same period will give us the business's actual loss sustained. Extra expense incurred by the damaged party resulting from the interruption should be added to the damages. The calculation of each of these elements can be aided with statistical methods.

Choosing a Forecasting Model

The damages measurement scheme not only begins with a sales forecast, but is also, we believe, the critical step in the whole process. Since all the cost and expense considerations that affect lost profits are ultimately dependent on the level of forecasted sales, if we get the sales forecast wrong, even if our expense allocation procedures are correct, the final damages conclusion will still be incorrect. Therefore, we will spend considerable time and effort explaining and in later chapters demonstrating how to get that sales forecast right. To begin, as there are many forecasting models available, how do we choose the most appropriate one for our situation? The one we pick will depend upon five characteristics of the damages measurement question:

1. Type of interruption.
2. Length of period of interruption.
3. Availability of historical data.
4. Regularity of sales trends and patterns.
5. Ease of explanation.

Type of Interruption

Business interruptions can be characterized as "closed," "open," or "infinite."

Closed = business interruption is over (i.e., only actual or past lost profits will be calculated).

With a closed interruption, the period of interruption has ended before the damages analyst gets involved. The damages analyst has actual sales data from both before and after the loss period to use in forecasting expected sales.

Open = losses continue into the future (i.e., both past and future lost profits will be calculated).

With an open interruption, the company is still in business, but sales have not yet returned to normal by the time the damages calculations are made. The damages analyst has sales data only from before the loss period to work with and, in addition, will have to determine when the loss period will end, as well as the amount of damages. The question of when to end the period of interruption is as much a legal as a financial issue in a tort, while the typical business interruption policy caps the loss period to the estimated time necessary to rebuild, repair, or restore the damaged property.

Infinite = the business has ceased operations (i.e., lost value may be the best measure of economic damages).

An infinite interruption is one where the business suffers through a period of operating losses, then declares bankruptcy or is sold for less than its value at the date of loss. There are only preloss sales data available, and the sales forecast can be used both to compute losses up to the date of sale or bankruptcy and to value the company at the time either of those events takes place. This would be a situation where total losses would entail both a lost profits element and a valuation element.

As there would no longer be any cash flows from a business that had ceased operations due to the actions of the tortfeasor, the measure of damages becomes the present value of those lost future cash flows plus the lost profits suffered up to the point of sale or bankruptcy. For a business interruption claim, the same rule applies to an infinite loss as an open loss with the additional limit on the period of interruption to typically not exceed one year.

Length of Period of Interruption

Sales forecasting techniques that are readily applicable to longer-term interruptions, such as multiple months, quarters, or years, are too cumbersome and complicated for short-term losses measured in days or weeks. In those cases, comparison with the same number of days or weeks just prior to the interruption and/or the same time period one year before may be sufficient to determine lost sales as long as there is either no or a minimal upward or downward trend in sales.

Availability of Historical Data

The amount and type of sales data available may force the choice of a forecasting method. If only two or three annual sales figures are obtainable, the options are much narrower than if you have 36, 48, or 60 months' worth of daily, weekly, monthly, or quarterly data. Another consideration is the duration of the loss period—whether it is measured in days, weeks, or months will decide what type of sales data will be needed. A special problem is job shops and construction contractors who record their sales on an irregular basis.

Regularity of Sales Trends and Patterns

Almost all quantitative forecasting methods begin by looking for and discerning patterns in historical sales data, then projecting those patterns into the future as a forecast. The two most important factors of a pattern are trend (upwards or downwards, and straight or curved), and seasonality (e.g., motel sales in the Northeast are high in July and August but lower in January). New products and additional locations can affect sales patterns, and the damages analyst needs to be on the lookout for their appearance in historical sales data, as well as random outliers (abnormally large or small nonrepeating sales figures). A significant amount of noise, or random error, in the sales data will also bear on the choice of forecasting method.

Ease of Explanation

Because the forecasting method and its results might have to be described to someone not familiar with statistical forecasting procedures, such as a judge, jury, or claims manager, the ease with which the method can be explained is important. If you can derive the same sales forecast using multiple techniques, choose the one that is the easiest to explain and understand.

Whichever forecasting model is ultimately chosen, the accuracy of the resulting forecast should be a concern of the damages analyst. In the business world a forecaster can make a projection, wait to see how accurate the forecast turns out to be, and then modify the forecasting model if accuracy is below some acceptable level. Such is not the case in forecasting sales that might have been earned during the period of interruption—those sales will never be observed. However, by performing a "hold back"[3] forecast, which we will demonstrate in one of the case studies, the damages analyst can achieve credibility and demonstrate goodness of fit for the ultimate forecast. In addition, the forecast model should be one that is widely known and used in the litigation support arena.

Conventional Forecasting Models

Keeping the previous cautions and provisos in mind, we can ask which sales forecasting models are likely to work well in lost profits cases. While we have our favorite models, each of the following models has at least one particular situation in which it has proven useful. For now we simply introduce and describe them, while, later in the book, we will present their usage in various case studies.

Simple Arithmetic Models

There are a number of forecasting computations that can be made that involve no more than the four arithmetic functions; for example, computing a simple daily average of the days' sales in any month prior to the injury, and multiplying that daily average by the number of days of expected interruption to arrive at estimated lost sales for the period. Another type of simple arithmetic model is to take the average of the prior and succeeding four weeks' daily sales for those days in question, for example Wednesday to Friday, and use that three-day average as the estimate for lost sales for the missing three days.

Simple arithmetic models are appropriate to use when the period of interruption can be measured in days or weeks and when there is neither a trend nor seasonality present in the historical sales data.

More Complex Arithmetic Models

Given enough historical sales data—say, 60 consecutive monthly sales figures up to the month of injury—two computations can be made that when averaged together will produce forecasted sales. For example, if sales through May (five months) are $865,000, then annualized sales will be $ 2,076,000 ($865,000 ÷ 5 × 12). If June is the interrupted period, and the five prior Junes averaged 10 percent of each year's annual sales, then forecasted sales for this June would be $207,600 ($2,076,000 × 10%).

The second computation compares year-to-date sales for the current year with that of the immediately preceding year and calculates the percentage increase or decrease. This percentage is then applied against last year's same month's sales as this year's interrupted month, and the result is the expected sales for this year's interrupted period. For example, if last year's sales through May were $850,000, then the percentage increase for this year is 1.76 percent (($865,000 ÷ $850,000) − 1 = .0176). If June's sales for last year were $201,500, then this year's expected sales for June would be $205,046 ($201,500 × 1.0176).

Averaging these two results gives June's expected sales of $206,323. Of course, the damages analyst must ensure that such a model accurately reflects the company's sales patterns, both historical and anticipated.

This model, while nonstatistical, affords a highly accurate result as it can be adjusted through the use of weighted and/or different multiyear averages to be sensitive to trends and seasonality. However, it is best limited to those situations when the period of interruption does not exceed 9 months.

Trendline and Curve-Fitting Models

Trend and curve-fitting models, using time as the predictor or independent variable and pre- and/or postloss sales as the response or dependent variable, are more sophisticated but still lucid forecasting techniques. The idea is to estimate the equation of a line or curve that fits (i.e., lies close to) the historical sales figures before the interruption period, and if available, to those actual sales after the interruption period.

If the historical sales figures lie in a roughly horizontal line (a "flat" pattern), the arithmetic mean of those sales can be used as a forecast of probable sales during the interruption period, as described previously. However, where historical sales show a rising or falling trend, ordinary least squares (OLS) regression can be used to define the equation of a straight line or a polynomial curve that best "fits" the actual sales in the pre-interruption periods. Projecting the line or curve over the loss period produces the required sales forecast. If sales trends are changing at increasing or decreasing rates, then the use of logarithms or exponents applied to sales and/or time can be used to fit the trendline to the data.

When using curve-fitting techniques, one should be careful not to forecast impossible situations, such as negative sales or sales that exhibit infinite growth characteristics. Sales forecasts that have an exponential factor included in the model can quickly grow to outlandish size, such that the sales of Mom & Pop's Sandwich Store quickly rival those of Wal-Mart! In those situations where exponential growth is called for, models with a reasonable upside limit can be called upon, such as the Gompertz and logistic curves that work very nicely when the sales of a new company or new product are expected to exhibit an S-shaped pattern.

Seasonal Factor Models

This method is really just an add-on to trend and curve-fitting methods in cases where sales show monthly or quarterly seasonal variation. The historical sales data are smoothed or averaged out to remove the seasonal variation and place sales on a trendline basis, which are then compared with the original sales numbers to estimate the seasonal factors. A trend curve is fitted to the smoothed sales data and projected over the loss period. These projected sales trend figures are then adjusted by the appropriate monthly or quarterly seasonal factors to obtain the appropriate seasonal forecasts.

Smoothing Methods

There are a number of ways of averaging out the highs and lows in a set of historical monthly or quarterly sales data, either with moving averages and weighted moving averages, or with exponentially weighted and centered moving averages. A plot of the resulting smoothed sales history may more clearly reveal the underlying patterns than the original sales data, thereby facilitating the choice of an appropriate forecast model. Used in this way, smoothing can be an antecedent of any forecast method. In certain circumstances, however, smoothing can generate the forecasts themselves. Exponential smoothing models available to the sales forecaster are Brown's one-parameter model, Holt's two-parameter model, and Winters's three-parameter model. The first two are applicable to sales patterns that exhibit no seasonality but have an approximate linear trend, and the third model can be used when both trend and seasonality are present.

Multiple Regression Models

The curve-fitting models just mentioned typically involve a simple linear regression of sales or an exponent of sales on time or some function of time. These simple linear regression models can be easily extended to multiple regression models where several variables are used to explain the pattern in sales. One common multiple regression specification is the "seasonal factor" model, in which sales are regressed on both a time trend and on monthly or quarterly seasonal indicator variables. The result is a combination of curve-fitting and seasonal factor models; it is easy to estimate and explain and can be quite accurate. An advantage of these time-series regression models is that they do not depend on either leading or lagging economic indicators whose values may not be known at the time the forecast is being prepared.

A different form of multiple regression methodology is employed when a forecaster uses independent variables other than time and seasonal factors to identify and measure the strength of relationships among sales and other economic factors. These are called econometric models, and they might be used in the context of loss estimation when the sales variable depends heavily on other external economic variables and does not exhibit a clear pattern of its own when plotted over time. For example, the sales of an aftermarket auto parts dealer may depend heavily on new automobile sales during the previous quarter and on the average price charged per part, but show no particular trend or other pattern when graphed in isolation. A second example of an external economic predictor variable is that of total motel sales in any one of a state's Economic Summary Areas (ESA). Pre- and postloss sales of any motel in that particular ESA can be regressed against ESA sales, allowing us to forecast lost sales during the period of interruption once we have total motel sales for that ESA for the period in question. Another example, one of an internal economic variable, is where revenue was suspected of being underreported at a campground by newly installed management, but a regression of prior sales against electricity usage allowed expected sales to be accurately predicted and matched against reported sales. Economic variables can also be combined with seasonal factors in a multiple regression model. Econometric modeling is the most complicated kind of forecasting discussed in this book, and it requires some knowledge of regression analysis theory and practice. In contrast to time series models, econometric regression models that rely on leading or lagging economic indicators for the period of interruption may not be able to be used if the interruption is still open. This could lead to an unenviable situation where the independent variables in an econometric regression model themselves have to be forecasted.

The following point should be kept in mind when selecting from the forecast models discussed previously. While any of the models listed here can handle a simple assignment, most extended interruption periods require that trend and trend dampening, seasonality, economic variables, and outlying events be controlled or accounted for. Multiple regression methods, either time-series or pure econometric models, are flexible enough to handle all of these situations very well and are therefore our usual models of choice.

Other Applications of Statistical Models

Very often in lost profits cases, the first task is to establish that the damaging event actually had a statistically significant impact on the plaintiff's monthly revenues, and therefore the decrease in revenue was not the result of some random event. One way to accomplish this is to apply a methodology known as interrupted time series analysis (ITSA), which is a specific application of multiple regression analysis. In an ITSA model, after typically accounting for growth in sales over time and any seasonality in the data, the next two elements to be accounted for are two types of possible interventions that could occur, starting when sales are interrupted. An intervention occurs when there is some outside influence at a particular time that affects the dependent or forecast variable, which in this case is revenue. One of those interventions could have caused a new trend in sales, and the second intervention could have caused a shift in sales, either upward or downward. We can account for both of these interventions in a model by the use of number sequences and dummy variables, as demonstrated in a future chapter.

Conclusion

As future chapters will show, the calculation of economic damages in lost profits cases can be quite simple. We have had quite satisfactory results using only simple arithmetic sales projection models. On the other hand, most of our cases have called for more sophisticated modeling techniques to handle seasonality and exponential trends. As we will demonstrate, the search for the best model is often one of trial and error. We hope to ease that process by making available to you our Excel spreadsheets, both in this book and on the Web, as well as detailed instructions as to their choice and in their use.

This book explains and demonstrates the various methods a damages analyst can use to estimate business interruption losses during some specified loss period. However, we will not be discussing certain problematic issues, such as how to discount damages to present value and then bring damages forward to a current amount necessary for trial testimony, how income taxes fit into the picture, and *ex ante* vs. *ex post* models.

The following chapters will demonstrate, through the use of case studies, the application of the various statistical forecasting and analytical models described in this chapter.

Notes

1. Why divide the sum of squared deviations by $n - 1$ rather than n? In the first step, we compute the difference between each value and the mean of those values and then square that difference. We don't know the true mean of the population; all we know is the mean of our sample of 11 transactions. Except for the rare cases where the sample mean happens to equal the population mean, the data will be closer to the sample mean than it will be to the true population mean. So the value we compute by summing the squared deviations will probably be a bit smaller (and can't be larger) than what it would be if we used the true population mean in step 1. To make up for this, we divide by $n - 1$ rather than n. This makes the sample variance a better, unbiased estimator of the true population variance.

   But why $n - 1$? If you knew the sample mean and all but one of the values, you could calculate what that last value must be. Statisticians say there are $n - 1$ degrees of freedom as we use one degree of freedom to calculate that last value.

2. For example, to standardize SDE for transaction #1, the formula is $((13,457 - 4,093)/ 4,005) = 2.34$; and to standardize price the formula is $((94,769 - 31,479)/28,524) = 2.22$. Their product is 5.19 (2.34 × 2.22).

3. A "hold back," or *ex post* forecast is one in which all values of the dependent and independent variables are known and therefore can be used as a means to evaluate a forecasting model. For example, if we construct a forecasting model based on 36 months of historical sales data, we can test the accuracy of that model by "holding back," say, the last five months and input 31 months of those sales back into the model to forecast the "held back" five months. We would then compare the fit of the actual sales to the predicted sales for the five months in order to assess the forecast's accuracy.

CHAPTER 1

Case Study 1—Uses of the Standard Deviation

I n this and all the other case studies in this book, you will come across statistical terms that will be unfamiliar to you. Rather than explain each term in the body of the case study, or populate each case study with explanatory foot- or endnotes, we have provided a glossary at the end of the book to facilitate your understanding of the text.

The Steps of Data Analysis

An important step in data analysis, and hence forecasting, is to determine the shape, center, and spread of your data set. That is, how are the data distributed (normally, uniformly, or left- or right-skewed), what is its mean and median, and to what degree is it dispersed about the mean? The answers to these questions are important, as they will determine what statistical tools we can use as we attempt to determine lost profits. The questions can be answered graphically with histograms, stem and leaf plots, and box plots as well as computationally through the use of various Excel descriptive statistical functions such as AVERAGE, STDEVP, SKEW, and KURT. Knowing a data set's distribution (normal, or at least near–bell shaped), its center (mean), and its spread (standard deviation), we can begin to draw conclusions about it that will allow us to meaningfully compare it with other contemporaneous data points.

Our first case, while not strictly on the subject of lost profits, is about an issue our readers see all the time in their practices. The case concerns the value of a business on June 30, 2010, for shareholder buyout purposes. The subject company's year-to-date (YTD) gross margin of 14.4 percent at the June 30 date of loss was substantially below its nine-year historical average. We want to know if this difference is statistically significant and if so, what the probability of its occurrence is. In order to run the tests to help answer these questions, we need to assure ourselves that the distribution of the nine years'[1] gross margins is, if not normal in shape, at least near–bell shaped. We begin this process with the following calculations and charts.

	B	C	D	E
2	**Table 1.1**			
3		**Year**	**Gross Margin**	
4		2001	26.6%	
5		2002	21.3%	
6		2003	26.7%	
7		2004	27.1%	
8		2005	28.4%	
9		2006	22.4%	
10		2007	24.7%	
11		2008	21.1%	
12		2009	24.2%	
13		June 30, 2010	**14.4%**	
14				
15	Mean		24.7%	
16	Population Standard Deviation		2.5%	
17	Kurtosis		-1.5	
18	Skewness		-0.2	
19	Median		24.7%	
20	Test statistic (14.4% - 24.7%/2.5)		-4.1	
21	p-value		0.35%	

Shape

As shown in Table 1.1, the nine-year average gross margin is 24.7 percent; its standard deviation is 2.5 percent (we are treating the nine years as the population, not a sample, so the Excel function is STDEVP); it is symmetrical,[2] as its median of 24.7 percent equals its mean; and it is near–bell shaped, as both KURT and SKEW return results that are between –1.5 and +1.5. While there are too few data points to construct a meaningful histogram to informally test for normality, we can create a normal P-plot, or probability plot, where we match up our nine observations with the normal scores that we would expect to see if the data came from a standard normal distribution. If our nine observations follow a general straight line on the normal probability plot, especially at both ends, we can feel assured that the data are near–bell shaped.

Figure 1.1 demonstrates four methods for producing the expected values for a P-plot, with no one method being superior to the others. The reader can choose any one method he or she prefers. Since two of the methods require that the data be ranked, we first sorted the gross margins from smallest to largest, and then applied the particular formula for each method and charted the results.

For ease of understanding, we have also shown the formulas for each method in Figure 1.2. But a nagging question remains: If all the observations do not lie directly on the trendline, how do we know that the data are still near–bellshaped? The answer to that question is shown in Figure 1.3, where we have substituted nine numbers created by using Excel's random number generator, which is found in the Analysis ToolPak. Selecting normal distribution from the analysis tool's drop-down menu, and then filling in the rest of the dialogue box with the mean and standard

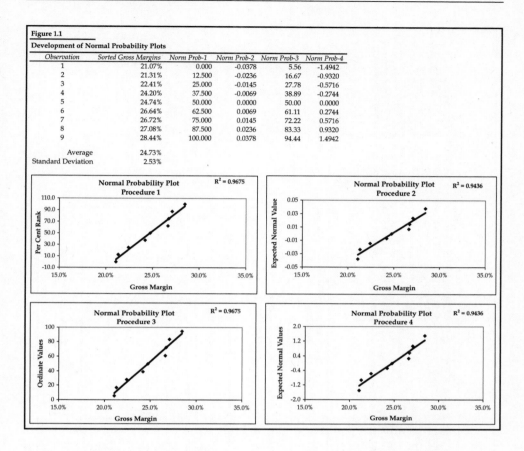

Figure 1.1

Development of Normal Probability Plots

Observation	Sorted Gross Margins	Norm Prob-1	Norm Prob-2	Norm Prob-3	Norm Prob-4
1	21.07%	0.000	-0.0378	5.56	-1.4942
2	21.31%	12.500	-0.0236	16.67	-0.9320
3	22.41%	25.000	-0.0145	27.78	-0.5716
4	24.20%	37.500	-0.0069	38.89	-0.2744
5	24.74%	50.000	0.0000	50.00	0.0000
6	26.64%	62.500	0.0069	61.11	0.2744
7	26.72%	75.000	0.0145	72.22	0.5716
8	27.08%	87.500	0.0236	83.33	0.9320
9	28.44%	100.000	0.0378	94.44	1.4942
Average	24.73%				
Standard Deviation	2.53%				

deviation of the original nine observations, produces nine random numbers that are normally distributed with approximately the same mean and standard deviation as the original nine gross margin numbers.

Comparing the two sets of charts in Figure 1.1 and Figure 1.3, we can see that both data sets have the same degree of deviation about the trendline, indicating that the original data set can be considered near–bell shaped. This near–bell shape of the distribution allows us to use parametric tests that involve the use of the two parameters of the distribution, its mean and standard deviation. Absent this shape, we would have to turn to nonparametric methods, a subject we leave to another book.

Spread

The next step is to create a test statistic that measures how far June 30's 14.4 percent is from the nine-year average gross margin. The test statistic is: $(X - \text{mean})/\text{standard deviation}$, or $(14.4 - 24.7)/2.5$. The resulting statistic, called a z-score, of -4.1 indicates that 14.4 percent is 4.1 standard deviations below the nine-year average. Is this too far from the average for our purposes? We know from the empirical rule that if a data set is near–bell shaped, then approximately 95 percent of its observations will fall within ± 2 standard deviations from the mean, and 99.7 percent of its observations

Figure 1.2
Development of Normal Probability Plots (with formulas showing)

Observation	Sorted Gross Margins	Norm Prob-1	Norm Prob-2	Norm Prob-3	Norm Prob-4
1	0.210734195128272	=PERCENTRANK(C$6:$C$14,C6)*100	=NORMSINV((B6-0.375)/(COUNT($C$6:$C$14)+0.25))*$C$17	=100*(B6-0.5)/COUNT($C$6:$C$14)	=NSCORE(C6,$C$6:$C$14)
2	0.213050581127736	=PERCENTRANK(C$6:$C$14,C7)*100	=NORMSINV((B7-0.375)/(COUNT($C$6:$C$14)+0.25))*$C$17	=100*(B7-0.5)/COUNT($C$6:$C$14)	=NSCORE(C7,$C$6:$C$14)
3	0.224100289593413	=PERCENTRANK(C$6:$C$14,C8)*100	=NORMSINV((B8-0.375)/(COUNT($C$6:$C$14)+0.25))*$C$17	=100*(B8-0.5)/COUNT($C$6:$C$14)	=NSCORE(C8,$C$6:$C$14)
4	0.242049070081447	=PERCENTRANK(C$6:$C$14,C9)*100	=NORMSINV((B9-0.375)/(COUNT($C$6:$C$14)+0.25))*$C$17	=100*(B9-0.5)/COUNT($C$6:$C$14)	=NSCORE(C9,$C$6:$C$14)
5	0.247413026402897	=PERCENTRANK(C$6:$C$14,C10)*100	=NORMSINV((B10-0.375)/(COUNT($C$6:$C$14)+0.25))*$C$17	=100*(B10-0.5)/COUNT($C$6:$C$14)	=NSCORE(C10,$C$6:$C$14)
6	0.266356952685531	=PERCENTRANK(C$6:$C$14,C11)*100	=NORMSINV((B11-0.375)/(COUNT($C$6:$C$14)+0.25))*$C$17	=100*(B11-0.5)/COUNT($C$6:$C$14)	=NSCORE(C11,$C$6:$C$14)
7	0.267173096624755	=PERCENTRANK(C$6:$C$14,C12)*100	=NORMSINV((B12-0.375)/(COUNT($C$6:$C$14)+0.25))*$C$17	=100*(B12-0.5)/COUNT($C$6:$C$14)	=NSCORE(C12,$C$6:$C$14)
8	0.270835225360009	=PERCENTRANK(C$6:$C$14,C13)*100	=NORMSINV((B13-0.375)/(COUNT($C$6:$C$14)+0.25))*$C$17	=100*(B13-0.5)/COUNT($C$6:$C$14)	=NSCORE(C13,$C$6:$C$14)
9	0.284385977190271	=PERCENTRANK(C$6:$C$14,C14)*100	=NORMSINV((B14-0.375)/(COUNT($C$6:$C$14)+0.25))*$C$17	=100*(B14-0.5)/COUNT($C$6:$C$14)	=NSCORE(C14,$C$6:$C$14)

Average =AVERAGE(C6:C14)

Standard Deviation =STDEVP(C6:C14)

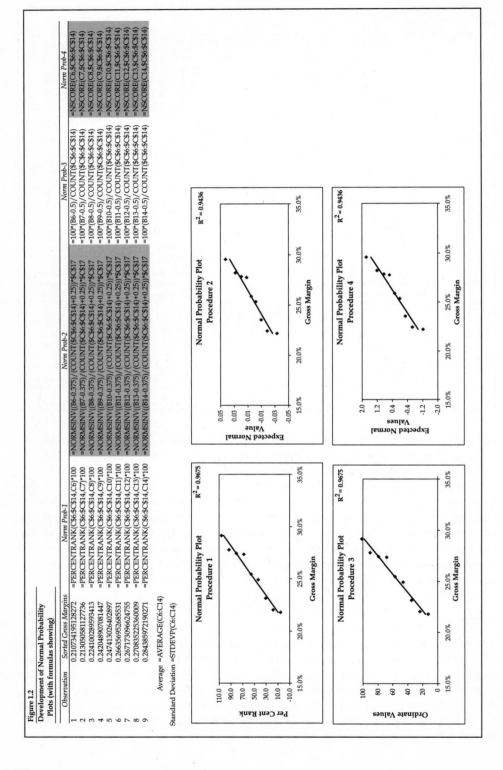

Normal Probability Plot Procedure 1 — $R^2 = 0.9675$

Normal Probability Plot Procedure 2 — $R^2 = 0.9436$

Normal Probability Plot Procedure 3 — $R^2 = 0.9675$

Normal Probability Plot Procedure 4 — $R^2 = 0.9436$

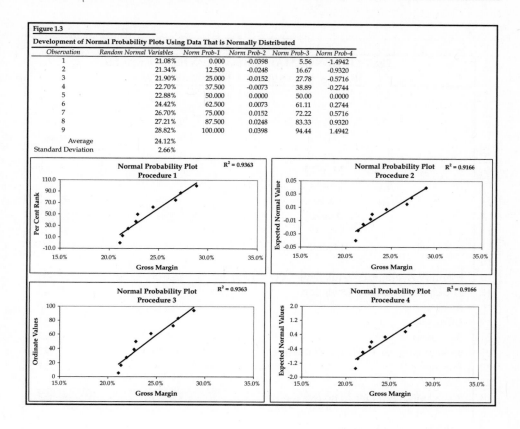

Figure 1.3

Development of Normal Probability Plots Using Data That is Normally Distributed

Observation	Random Normal Variables	Norm Prob-1	Norm Prob-2	Norm Prob-3	Norm Prob-4
1	21.08%	0.000	-0.0398	5.56	-1.4942
2	21.34%	12.500	-0.0248	16.67	-0.9320
3	21.90%	25.000	-0.0152	27.78	-0.5716
4	22.70%	37.500	-0.0073	38.89	-0.2744
5	22.88%	50.000	0.0000	50.00	0.0000
6	24.42%	62.500	0.0073	61.11	0.2744
7	26.70%	75.000	0.0152	72.22	0.5716
8	27.21%	87.500	0.0248	83.33	0.9320
9	28.82%	100.000	0.0398	94.44	1.4942
Average	24.12%				
Standard Deviation	2.66%				

will fall within ±3 standard deviations from the mean. At 4.1 standard deviations below average, June 30's gross margin is literally off the charts. In fact, using Excel's NORMDIST function, we can show that there is only a 0.35 percent chance that the gross margin on June 30 of 14.4 percent was drawn from the same pool as the nine year-end gross margins.

Once this, and its implication that they were deliberately cooking the books to lower the value of the company, was pointed out to the other side, they immediately increased their buyout offer by 50 percent.

Our second situation involves a car dealership that experienced a small fire in its parts department in early August 2010, and then claimed lost sales for weeks afterwards. Are the decreases in parts and service departmental sales during the month of August 2010 greater than 1.645 or more standard deviations of the historical average, and therefore statistically significant, or are the decreases in the normal course of business? Our procedure is essentially the same as that just described in the first situation. We begin by analyzing the previous six and succeeding two months of sales and find that both data sets are near–bell shaped—the median approximates the mean, and kurtosis and skewness measures are between −1.5 and +1.5 as shown in Table 1.2. Unlike situation 1, where the question posed was whether June 30's sales were different in either direction, that is, greater or lesser, from the nine-year average, in situation 2 we only want to know if August's sales

	A	B	C	D	E	F	G
1			Table 1.2				
2			TEST OF ABNORMALLY BELOW AVERAGE SALES				
3			PARTS AND SERVICE DEPARTMENTS				
4				Sales			
5				Parts		Service	
6			Feb-10	84,195		84,010	
7			Mar-10	96,404		94,483	
8			Apr-10	85,947		101,376	
9			May-10	83,634		92,268	
10			Jun-10	78,590		91,981	
11			Jul-10	84,336		97,762	
12			Aug-10	57,845		75,511	
13			Sep-10	92,091		87,610	
14			Oct-10	103,750		100,907	
15							
16		Monthly Average, Feb–Jul, Sept–Oct		88,618		93,800	
17		Population Standard Deviation		7,682		5,743	
18		Median		85,142		93,376	
19		Kurtosis		0.21		(0.86)	
20		Skewness		0.92		(0.27)	
21		Critical value of z - 95%, one-tail test		1.645		1.645	
22		+- range		12,636		9,447	
23							
24		95% Confidence Level - no less than		75,983		84,353	
25							
26		August sales fall into the 5% rejection range					
27							
28		Test Statistic:					
29		Average Sales		88,618		93,800	
30		August Sales		57,845		75,511	
31		Delta		30,773		18,289	
32		Critical value of z - 95%, one-tail test		1.645		1.645	
33		No. of Std Devs from Average		4.006		3.184	
34		Greater than 1.645?		Yes		Yes	
35		Unusual Event?		Yes		Yes	

are less than the average—statistically speaking, situation 1 called for a two-tailed test and situation 2 calls for a one-tailed test.

The cutoff point for a one-tailed test is 1.645 standard deviations if we are willing to be wrong about our conclusions 5 percent of the time. That is, we enter the 5 percent rejection area at 1.645 standard deviations, rather than the 1.96 standard deviations of a two-tailed test. Multiplying the population standard deviation by 1.645 and subtracting the product from the eight-month average sales for both departments gives us the lower limit of our 95 percent confidence level. For example, in the parts department, average sales equaled $88,618, and the standard deviation was $7,682. Multiplying $7,682 by 1.645 gives us $12,636. Subtracting this from average sales gives us $75,983, an amount greater than August's sales of $57,845. Since actual sales for August are less than $75,983, we can say with 95 percent confidence that those sales did not decrease in the ordinary course of business—that there was some intervention that caused them to be this far below average. As such, after subtracting avoided costs, the insured's claim for lost profits was honored.

Conclusion

In this chapter we demonstrated how the standard deviation can be applied in situations where the data set you are working with is the population, and not a sample. How does one know whether the data set is a sample or a population? The answer lies in whether or not you make inferences outside the data set. For example, a classroom of 30 students is a population if all your statistical tests and inferences are about the 30 students. But if you are going to use the statistical test results of those 30 students to make inferences about other students in other classrooms, then you are working with a sample.

In the next chapter we introduce you to various data analysis techniques that should precede any selection of a sales forecasting methodology.

Notes

1. Generally speaking, in statistics, the larger the sample size, the better the results. However, in damages cases, the analyst has to work with what is given. Therefore, while for academic research a sample size of 9 would probably be considered too small, for litigation purposes it will have to do.
2. If folded over at the midpoint, its left side would be a mirror image of its right side.

CHAPTER 2

Case Study 2—Trend and Seasonality Analysis

May 31, 2010, was a dark and stormy night. The 18-wheeler turned off the interstate and roared down the sloping off-ramp, heading for the town of Brunswick on Route 1. At the base of the off-ramp, at the point where it curves into and merges with Route 1, sits the XYZ Motel, eagerly awaiting guests for Memorial Day weekend and the start of the tourist season. Just before midnight, it got the biggest guest it ever had, as the tractor-trailer combo failed to negotiate the curve and plowed right into the building that housed the motel office and the manager's quarters, effectively demolishing it. Fortunately, there was no loss of life and no personal injuries, nor were any rental units damaged, as the office is a stand-alone building. But the claimant insisted that there was lost income as a result of the manager losing her on-site living space and the office having to be replaced with an unsightly temporary trailer.

Claim Submitted

The complete text of the claim submitted by the XYZ Motel follows:

In December 2001, negotiations with the franchiser were finalized. This resulted in approximately $60,000 in capital outlay to acquire the franchise, the equipment updates and changes required by the franchiser to meet their standards for operation.…

Generally, it takes four to five years to realize the results of a large capital outlay like this. All indications were that 2010 was going to be one of their best years. Subsequent to [calendar year] 2005, through [calendar year] 2008, revenues had increased an average of 12.8 percent per year. [Calendar year] 2009 revenues increased 10.9 percent over 2008.…

In order to determine lost revenues due to the accident, we have assumed that 2010 would have increased 10.9 percent over 2009 revenues. We then compared anticipated 2010 revenues to actual 2010 receipts (subsequent to the accident) to calculate the shortfall that is due to the accident.

The claimant submitted the information shown in Table 2.1.

TABLE 2.1

Month	2009 Actual Receipts	2010 Anticipated Receipts	2010 Actual Receipts	Lost Revenues
June	$ 32,038	$ 35,530	$ 25,346	$10,184
July	57,112	63,337	43,217	20,120
August	59,838	66,360	55,136	11,224
September	46,981	52,102	41,151	10,951
Totals	$195,968	$217,329	$164,850	$52,479

Claim Review

Let's examine the claimant's assertion that receipts would have increased by 10.9 per-cent in 2010 over the same period for 2009. While usually advising the reader to first graph the data in any damages case, in this instance we initially need to rearrange our 36 months of data from a calendar year presentation to a fiscal year presentation so that the trailing 12 months end in the month preceding the incident. This allows for a more meaningful and accurate analysis of past performance as it relates to future expectations. Once this rearrangement is performed, the actual increase for 2008 to 2009 over 2007 to 2008 for the 12 months ended May 31 is only 9.9 percent, not 10.9 percent, and for 2009 to 2010 versus 2008 to 2009, there is a −3.2 percent decrease from the prior year (see Table 2.2). But the whole year is not the period of interruption; June through September is. The percentage increase for 2008 to 2009 over 2007 to 2008 is 1.6 percent (see Table 2.2), and for 2009 to 2010 over 2008 to 2009 the percentage increase is 3.7 percent (see Table 2.2).

Next, we created two run-up periods—October to May and December to May—as the months of October and November still attract tourists to the motel, thereby allowing for a potential difference between the two periods. A look at the run-up months to the period in question for all years shows that the periods October 2008 through May 2009 and December 2008 through May 2009 have increases over the same periods of the prior year of 25.0 percent and 50.1 percent, respectively. But the same periods for the next year, October 2009 through May 2010 and December 2009 through May 2010, show decreases of −13.5 percent and −32.1 percent, respectively, from the prior year (see Table 2.2). These are hardly good omens for a 10.9 percent increase in the succeeding summer months.

Occupancy Percentages

Occupancy percentages for the 36-month period are shown in Table 2.3. This table shows increases for 2008 to 2009 over 2007 to 2008 and decreases for 2009 to 2010 over 2008 to 2009 in total rooms sold, average annual occupancy percentage, and av-erage room rate. What is critical here is that for the period of June to September 2009, total rooms sold decreased but total dollars received increased when compared to the prior year, indicating that room rates were raised to offset declining occupancy rates. Since room rates, due to competitive forces in the marketplace, are only elastic

Table 2.2
XYZ MOTEL
HISTORICAL RECEIPTS

	2007–2008			2008–2009			2009–2010			2010–2011	3-YEAR AVERAGE	
	$	%	CUM %	$	%	CUM %	$	%	CUM %	$	MONTH	CUM %
JUNE	27,241	9.5%	9.5%	31,249	9.9%	9.9%	32,038	10.5%	10.5%	25,346	9.96%	9.96%
JULY	55,473	19.3%	28.8%	57,299	18.2%	28.1%	57,112	18.7%	29.2%	43,217	18.73%	28.70%
AUGUST	58,073	20.2%	49.0%	56,579	17.9%	46.0%	59,838	19.6%	48.8%	55,136	19.26%	47.95%
SEPTEMBER	45,159	15.7%	64.8%	43,827	13.9%	59.9%	46,981	15.4%	64.2%	41,151	15.01%	62.96%
OCTOBER	37,917	13.2%		35,490	11.3%		41,902	13.7%		164,850	-15.88%	
NOVEMBER	11,902	4.1%		13,967	4.4%		15,232	5.0%				
DECEMBER	5,268	1.8%		10,362	3.3%		7,642	2.5%				
JANUARY	4,995	1.7%		6,788	2.2%		5,015	1.6%				
FEBRUARY	6,816	2.4%		14,940	4.7%		5,378	1.8%				
MARCH	6,073	2.1%		14,490	4.6%		7,332	2.4%				
APRIL	9,152	3.2%		11,951	3.8%		9,540	3.1%				
MAY	18,966	6.6%		18,409	5.8%		17,338	5.7%				
	287,035	100.0%		315,352	100.0%		305,347	100.0%				
% CHANGE FROM PRIOR YEAR				9.9%			-3.2%					
OCT–NOV %	53.4%	52.5%		53.0%			54.9%					
TOTAL, JUNE TO SEPT	185,945			188,954			195,968			190,289		
% CHANGE FROM PRIOR YEAR				1.6%			3.7%					
THREE-YEAR AVERAGE												
TOTAL, OCT TO MAY	101,090			126,398			109,379					
% CHANGE FROM PRIOR YEAR				25.0%			-13.5%					
TOTAL, DEC TO MAY	51,271			76,941			52,244					
% CHANGE FROM PRIOR YEAR				50.1%			-32.1%					

CHANGE FROM PRIOR YEAR

RECEIPTS DURING PERIOD OF INTERRUPTION

27

A Quantitative Approach to Commercial Damages

	B	2007–2008 ROOMS OCCUPIED		2008–2009 ROOMS OCCUPIED		2009–2010 ROOMS OCCUPIED		2010–2011 ROOMS OCCUPIED	

Table 2.3
XYZ MOTEL
OCCUPANCY PERCENTAGES

TOTAL ROOMS AVAILABLE PER NIGHT = 29
TOTAL ROOMS AVAILABLE PER 30-DAY MONTH = 870
TOTAL ROOMS AVAILABLE PER 31-DAY MONTH = 899

	2007–2008 ROOMS OCCUPIED		2008–2009 ROOMS OCCUPIED		2009–2010 ROOMS OCCUPIED		2010–2011 ROOMS OCCUPIED	
	NO.	%	NO.	%	NO.	%	NO.	%
JUNE	593	68.16%	655	75.29%	606	69.66%	518	59.54%
JULY	850	94.55%	890	99.00%	851	94.66%	670	74.53%
AUGUST	889	98.89%	886	98.55%	874	97.22%	783	87.10%
SEPTEMBER	841	96.67%	866	99.54%	835	95.98%	743	85.40%
OCTOBER	750	83.43%	704	78.31%	778	86.54%		
NOVEMBER	303	34.83%	358	41.15%	383	44.02%		
DECEMBER	125	13.90%	334	37.15%	197	21.91%		
JANUARY	125	13.90%	207	23.03%	134	14.91%		
FEBRUARY	175	21.55%	487	59.98%	152	18.72%		
MARCH	157	17.46%	514	57.17%	185	20.58%		
APRIL	239	27.47%	347	39.89%	238	27.36%		
MAY	433	48.16%	392	43.60%	372	41.38%		
TOTALS	5,480	51.58%	6,640	62.72%	5,605	52.74%		
AVG ROOM RATE	$ 52.38		$ 47.49		$ 54.48			
TOTAL, JUNE TO SEPT	3,173	89.57%	3,297	93.10%	3,166	89.38%	2,714	76.64%
% CHANGE			3.9%		-4.0%			
AVG ROOM RATE	$ 58.60		$ 57.31		$ 61.90		$ 60.74	
TOTAL, OCT TO MAY	2,307	32.59%	3,343	47.53%	2,439	34.43%		
% CHANGE			44.9%		-27.0%			
TOTAL, DEC TO MAY	1,254	23.74%	2,281	43.47%	1,278	24.14%		
% CHANGE			81.9%		-44.0%			

within a limited range, this represents a Band-Aid solution to the problem. Considering that the run-up period(s) to the 2010 summer season shows such dramatic decreases in occupancy percentages from the year before (–27.0 percent and –44.0 percent), it could be expected that the 2010 summer season would, at worst, also show a similar decrease and, at best, show some slight improvement. It is hard to believe that any future decrease in occupancy percentage could have been offset by another price increase. In fact, room rates were dropped 1.9 percent to $60.74 for the 2010 summer season.

The essence of the claim is that there is an upward and continuing trend to the claimant's receipts over the immediate past few years. However, if we look at the chart in Figure 2.1, we see an obvious seasonal cycle to the XYZ Motel's business. The variation in this seasonality can distort the overall trend of a set of data. Therefore, some tests need to be carried out that can help determine the strength of the trend, if any, and the degree of seasonality in the data set.

Trend, Seasonality, and Noise

The graph in Figure 2.2 shows the degree of trend, calculated as the variance across years; the degree of seasonality, calculated as the variance within years; and noise, calculated as what's left over when we subtract trend and seasonality variance from

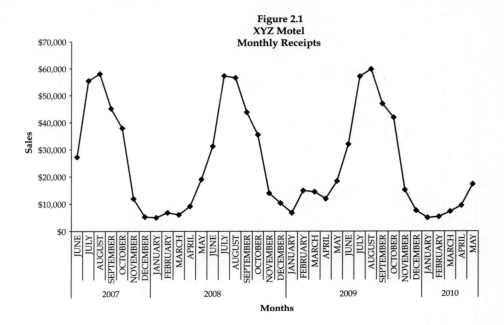

Figure 2.1
XYZ Motel
Monthly Receipts

total variance, in a summary fashion. A quick glance at Figure 2.2 effectively deals with to the claimant's assertion that revenues would have trended upward during the period of interruption by more than 10 percent over the prior year, as there is no history of an upward trend.

Here is a quick rundown of the calculations as shown on Table 2.4. First, compute the average sales for each of the twelve months as shown in column (A).

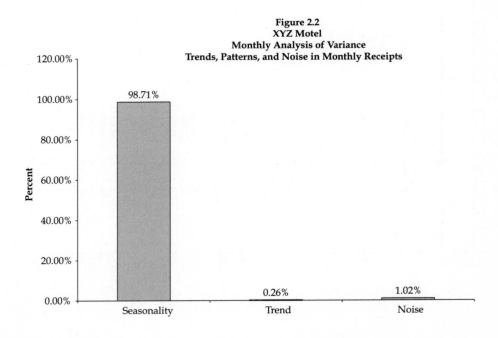

Figure 2.2
XYZ Motel
Monthly Analysis of Variance
Trends, Patterns, and Noise in Monthly Receipts

Table 2.4
XYZ MOTEL
ANALYSIS OF VARIANCE

Year	Month	Period	Historical Receipts
2007	6	1	27,241
	7	2	55,473
	8	3	58,073
	9	4	45,159
	10	5	37,917
	11	6	11,902
	12	7	5,268
2008	1	8	4,995
	2	9	6,816
	3	10	6,073
	4	11	9,152
	5	12	18,966
	6	13	31,249
	7	14	57,299
	8	15	56,579
	9	16	43,827
	10	17	35,490
	11	18	13,967
	12	19	10,362
2009	1	20	6,788
	2	21	14,940
	3	22	14,490
	4	23	11,951
	5	24	18,409
	6	25	32,038
	7	26	57,112
	8	27	59,838
	9	28	46,981
	10	29	41,902
	11	30	15,232
	12	31	7,642
2010	1	32	5,015
	2	33	5,378
	3	34	7,332
	4	35	9,540
	5	36	17,338

SOURCE OF VARIANCE	PERCENT
TREND	0.3%
SEASONALITY	98.7%
NOISE	1.0%
TOTAL	100.0%

Month	Year			(A)
	2007–2008	2008–2009	2009–2010	AVG
6	27,241	31,249	32,038	30,176
7	55,473	57,299	57,112	56,628
8	58,073	56,579	59,838	58,163
9	45,159	43,827	46,981	45,322
10	37,917	35,490	41,902	38,437
11	11,902	13,967	15,232	13,700
12	5,268	10,362	7,642	7,757
1	4,995	6,788	5,015	5,599
2	6,816	14,940	5,378	9,045
3	6,073	14,490	7,332	9,298
4	9,152	11,951	9,540	10,214
5	18,966	18,409	17,338	18,238
(B) AVG	23,920	26,279	25,446	

SEASONAL VARIANCE OF THE MONTHLY AVERAGES - (A)   4,286,716,983
TREND VARIANCE OF THE YEARLY AVERAGES - (B)   2,864,026
TOTAL VARIANCE OF THE 36 MONTHS - (C)   13,027,828,380

	A	B	C	D	E	F
1				Table 2.5		
2				XYZ MOTEL		
3				SET-UP SHEET FOR		
4			ANALYSIS OF VARIANCE OUTPUT			
5				SHOWN IN FIGURE 2.6		
6						
7				Historical Receipts		
8			2007–2008	2008–2009	2009–2010	
9		June	27,241	31,249	32,038	
10		July	55,473	57,299	57,112	
11		August	58,073	56,579	59,838	
12		September	45,159	43,827	46,981	
13		October	37,917	35,490	41,902	
14		November	11,902	13,967	15,232	
15		December	5,268	10,362	7,642	
16		January	4,995	6,788	5,015	
17		February	6,816	14,940	5,378	
18		March	6,073	14,490	7,332	
19		April	9,152	11,951	9,540	
20		May	18,966	18,409	17,338	
21						

For example, the monthly average receipts for June is $30,176, (AVERAGE(27241,31249,32038)), for July it is $56,628 (AVERAGE(55473,57299,57112)) and so on for the next ten months. The twelve monthly averages occupy cells Q6:Q17.

Next, compute the average annual monthly receipts for each year as shown in row (B). For example, average monthly receipts for fiscal year 2007 to 2008 is $23,920 (AVERAGE (N6:N17)), for 2008 to 2009 it is $26,279 (AVERAGE (O6:O17)), and for 2009 to 2010 it is $25,446 (AVERAGE (P6:P17)). The annual averages of monthly receipts occupy cells N18:P18.

Then calculate the total variance of the 36 months (C) using Excel's DEVSQ function (DEVSQ (N6:P17)). Next, compute the trend variance by using the DEVSQ function for row (B) (DEVSQ (N18:P18)). The trend ratio (12 × trend variance)/(total variance) is then defined as the proportion of variance due to trend. The next step is to compute the seasonal variance by using DEVSQ for column (A) (DEVSQ (Q6:Q17)). The seasonality ratio (number of years of data × seasonal variance)/(total variance) is defined as the proportion of variance due to seasonality. Since the proportion must add up to 1.0, the proportion of noise is taken to be 1.0 − (proportion due to trend + proportion due to seasonality). These ratio calculations are found in cells J10:J12.

This result can also be obtained using the Excel tool known as Anova: Two-Factor Without Replication, which is one of the analysis tools found in Excel's Data Analysis ToolPak. The setup sheet for this analysis is found in Table 2.5, with the output shown in Table 2.6. Please note that both worksheets shown in Tables 2.4 and 2.6 will only work with complete fiscal years of data; that is, with at least 36, 48, 60, 72, and so on months of data.

Table 2.6
XYZ MOTEL
ANALYSIS OF VARIANCE OUTPUT

Anova: Two-Factor Without Replication

SUMMARY	Count	Sum	Average	Variance
June	3	90,528	30,176	6,615,853
July	3	169,883	56,628	1,009,421
August	3	174,490	58,163	2,660,372
September	3	135,966	45,322	2,507,071
October	3	115,310	38,437	10,482,002
November	3	41,101	13,700	2,825,900
December	3	23,272	7,757	6,496,871
January	3	16,798	5,599	1,059,534
February	3	27,134	9,045	26,585,773
March	3	27,895	9,298	20,611,978
April	3	30,643	10,214	2,299,566
May	3	54,714	18,238	684,374
2007–2008	12	287,035	23,920	411,287,094
2008–2009	12	315,352	26,279	328,855,057
2009–2010	12	305,347	25,446	441,081,491

ANOVA

Source of Variation	SS	df	MS	F	P-value	F crit
Rows	12,860,150,949	11	1,169,104,632	192.94	3.16E-19	2.26
Columns	34,368,312	2	17,184,156	2.84	0.08	3.44
Error	133,309,119	22	6,059,505			
Total	13,027,828,380	35				

Source of Variation	Per Cent
Seasonality	98.71%
Trend	0.26%
Noise	1.02%
Total	100.0%

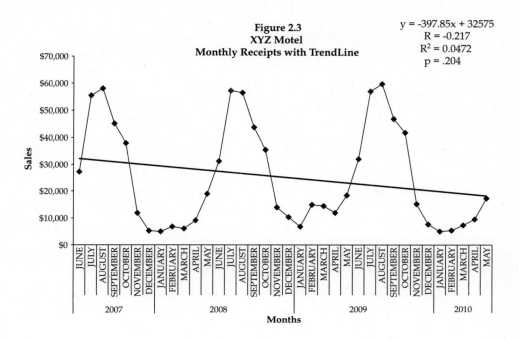

$$y = -397.85x + 32575$$
$$R = -0.217$$
$$R^2 = 0.0472$$
$$p = .204$$

Figure 2.3
XYZ Motel
Monthly Receipts with TrendLine

Trendline Test

A second test is to compute and show the linear trendline for the 36 months of data, with time as the independent variable and monthly receipts as the dependent variable. If we refer to the chart in Figure 2.1, right click on any data point, select "Add Trendline.." from the menu, then select "Linear" as the type, and check the "Display Equation on Chart" and "Display R-Squared Value on Chart" boxes, Figure 2.3 will appear. We can see that if there is a trend to the data, it is not only very slight but also negative at the rate of $398 per month. With an R-square of .0472, an R-value of −.217, and a p-value of .204[1] for R (remember, p-values less than .05 at 95 percent confidence place the test statistic in the rejection area), we cannot reject the null hypothesis that room receipts have no significant relationship with time, either statistically or practically.

Cycle Testing

Of course, for forecasting purposes we would like to know if this downward trend is expected to continue, or whether the worst is over and it has bottomed out and is now headed upward. We can find the answer to this question by computing and graphing sets of values that show how receipts for a given period compare with the same period a year earlier. Figure 2.4 shows a graph for 1/12 comparative receipts. The number 1 means that the index, or ratio, numbers are based on single-month totals, and the number 12 means that the totals are separated by 12 months. The other four charts can be interpreted the same way, for example, the 6/12 comparative

Figure 2.4

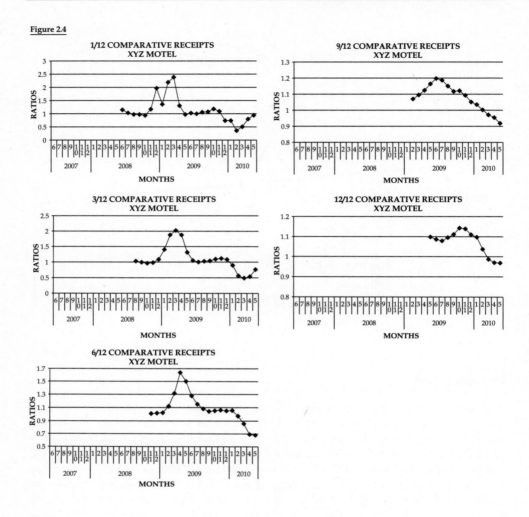

receipts graph compares six months of receipts ending on any particular month with a six-month total ending in the same month but a year earlier, and so on for the three-month, nine-month, and 12-month charts. A review of the five charts for the XYZ Motel indicates that at worst, the decline in receipts that began in mid-2009 and accelerated in early 2010 is still headed downward. At best, it has turned around, but even so, by May 2010, receipts had still not equaled the same amount in the prior year's time period, no matter whether it was 1/12 or 12/12. The worksheet that supports the charts is shown in Table 2.7.

Conclusion

In this chapter you were introduced to several data analysis techniques that you should always apply, along with a chart of your data, to all the lost profit situations you encounter where the period of interruption is measured in months.

Table 2.7
COMPARATIVE SALES ANALYSIS OF VARIOUS PERIODS
XYZ MOTEL SALES
2007–2010

Year	Month	Period	Actual Sales	1/12 Ratio	3-mo. Total	3/12 Ratio	6-mo. Total	6/12 Ratio	9-mo. Total	9/12 Ratio	12-mo. Total	12/12 Ratio
2007	6	1	27,241									
	7	2	55,473									
	8	3	58,073		140,787							
	9	4	45,159		158,704							
	10	5	37,917		141,148							
	11	6	11,902		94,978		235,764					
	12	7	5,268		55,087		213,791					
2008	1	8	4,995		22,166		163,314					
	2	9	6,816		17,080		112,058		252,844			
	3	10	6,073		17,885		72,972		231,676			
	4	11	9,152		22,041		44,207		185,355			
	5	12	18,966		34,191		51,271		146,249		287,035	
	6	13	31,249	114.7%	59,367		77,252		132,340		291,044	
	7	14	57,299	103.3%	107,514		129,555		151,721		292,869	
	8	15	56,579	97.4%	145,127	103.1%	179,318		196,399		291,376	
	9	16	43,827	97.1%	157,705	99.4%	217,072		234,957		290,044	
	10	17	35,490	93.6%	135,896	96.3%	243,410		265,452		287,617	
	11	18	13,967	117.4%	93,284	98.2%	238,411	101.1%	272,602		289,682	
	12	19	10,362	196.7%	59,819	108.6%	217,524	101.7%	276,891		294,776	
2009	1	20	6,788	135.9%	31,117	140.4%	167,013	102.3%	274,528		296,569	
	2	21	14,940	219.2%	32,090	187.9%	125,374	111.9%	270,502	107.0%	304,693	
	3	22	14,490	238.6%	36,218	202.5%	96,038	131.6%	253,742	109.5%	313,110	
	4	23	11,951	130.6%	41,381	187.7%	72,498	164.0%	208,395	112.4%	315,909	
	5	24	18,409	97.1%	44,850	131.2%	76,941	150.1%	170,224	116.4%	315,352	109.9%
	6	25	32,038	102.5%	62,398	105.1%	98,616	127.7%	158,435	119.7%	316,140	108.6%
	7	26	57,112	99.7%	107,559	100.0%	148,940	115.0%	180,058	118.7%	315,954	107.9%
	8	27	59,838	105.8%	148,988	102.7%	193,838	108.1%	225,928	115.0%	319,212	109.6%
	9	28	46,981	107.2%	163,931	103.9%	226,328	104.3%	262,547	111.7%	322,366	111.1%
	10	29	41,902	118.1%	148,721	109.4%	256,280	105.3%	297,661	112.1%	328,778	114.3%
	11	30	15,232	109.1%	104,115	111.6%	253,103	106.2%	297,953	109.3%	330,043	113.9%
	12	31	7,642	73.7%	64,776	108.3%	228,707	105.1%	291,105	105.1%	327,323	111.0%
2010	1	32	5,015	73.9%	27,888	89.6%	176,609	105.7%	284,169	103.5%	325,550	109.8%
	2	33	5,378	36.0%	18,034	56.2%	122,149	97.4%	271,137	100.2%	315,987	103.7%
	3	34	7,332	50.6%	17,724	48.9%	82,500	85.9%	246,431	97.1%	308,829	98.6%
	4	35	9,540	79.8%	22,250	53.8%	50,138	69.2%	198,859	95.4%	306,418	97.0%
	5	36	17,338	94.2%	34,211	76.3%	52,244	67.9%	156,360	91.9%	305,347	96.8%

The claimant's calculation of lost revenue in the amount of $52,479 appears to be excessive, as there is no annual upward trend discernible for gross receipts or number of rooms rented if based only on a function of time. While gross receipts were trending upward in the past for the four months concerned, this is only due to a change in room rates over the past two years, a change that was not continued into the 2010 summer season. Therefore, the only factor that could increase revenues for the 2010 summer season over the 2009 summer season would be if the motel revenue in the Economic Summary Area increased over the year before and dragged the XYZ Motel along with it. We will explore this possibility in Case Study 4 in an attempt to determine the motel's estimated lost revenue.

In the next chapter we introduce you to regression analysis and in great detail show you how to apply it to the measurement of economic damages.

Note

1. The p-value for R shown in Figure 2.3 is not part of the built-in Excel display, but was calculated separately in the following two-step manner. First, we need to develop a test statistic, which for R is: $t = R*SQRT(n - 2/1 - R^2)$, where n equals the 36 months at issue, and 2 equals the degrees of freedom we lose because there are two variables, receipts and time. Substituting, we have: $t = -.217*SQRT(36 - 2/1 - .0472) = -1.296$. The second step involves the TDIST formula to produce the p-value as follows: $p = TDIST(ABS(-1.296), 36-2,2) = .204$, where the last argument, 2, indicates we are specifying a two-tailed test. Unfortunately, the data analysis tool does not provide this formula. You must calculate it separately and then enter it by right clicking on the data label text box on the chart.

CHAPTER 3

Case Study 3—An Introduction to Regression Analysis and Its Application to the Measurement of Economic Damages

Not only are economic damages measured in terms of a stream of lost profits, but when a business is destroyed by the acts of the defendant the measure of damages becomes the value of the business immediately before the destructive act. Our purpose in this case study is twofold. First, we demonstrate how the value of a business's fixed and intangible assets can be estimated by applying regression analysis techniques to the direct market data method. Second, this case study serves as a primer on regression analysis as many of the statistical solutions to the measurement of damages for lost profits offered in the other case studies depend upon the use of this tool.

What Is Regression Analysis and Where Have I Seen It Before?

Technically speaking, curve fitting, or regression analysis, or simply regression is a generic term for all methods attempting to fit a model to observed data in order to quantify the relationship between two groups of variables. The fitted model may then be used either to describe the relationship between the two groups of variables, or to predict new values.

The two groups of variables involved in regression are usually denoted x and y, and the purpose of regression is to build a model where $y = f(x)$. Such a model tries to explain the variations in the y-variable, or dependent variable, based on the variations in the x-variable, or independent variable. The link between x and y is achieved through a common set of data for which both x- and y-values have been collected, as when an economist may seek to evaluate price increases based on either demand or changes in the money supply, or changes in inflation or interest rates.

For example, in business valuation, where it is commonly known that, ceteris paribus, value is a function of cash flow, various databases such as Bizcomps, Pratt's

Stats, Done Deals, and IBA have collected data sets from market transactions that include for each transaction, among other items of interest, selling price and seller's discretionary earnings (SDE). Regression is then used to relate selling price, the y-variable, to SDE, the x-variable. Once you have built a regression model, you can predict the selling price for your subject company, using the company's SDE as its predictor variable.

While regression is a technique that has not yet been accorded widespread use in business valuation, still there are some valuation applications that we are all familiar with. For instance, your personal residence was appraised for assessment purposes using a form of regression known as multiple regression, wherein the selling prices of all homes in the municipality over a given time period are regressed against such x-variables as square footage, age, number of bathrooms, lot size, and so on. Plugging the x-variables of your home into the model produces its assessed value.

In business valuation, the pioneering work of Jay Abrams relating equity value and the subject company's discount rate to Ibbotson's 10 deciles of stock market returns was accomplished using regression, as was a similar study carried out by Grabowski and King using 25 percentiles, instead of 10 deciles, to determine the equity risk premium based on various proxies for size. Grabowski and King went on to regress the equity risk premium against annual average operating margin, the coefficient of variation of annual operating margin, and the coefficient of variation of annual returns to shareholders' equity. Each of these examples provided practitioners with the models' output, that is, the x-variable coefficients, which when multiplied by the appropriate x-variable produced the subject company's value or discount rate or equity risk premium, with no additional knowledge or work required of the user. However, all of these business valuation regression applications are confined to the income approach.

In this case study we introduce you to and show you how to use regression analysis as it applies in general to the market approach, and more specifically to the direct market data method using the Bizcomps database. With this tool you can determine the amount of commercial damages when the measure is the value of the business's assets just prior to the defendant's actions. In addition, if the discount rate used to reduce future damages to a present value is the injured company's weighted average cost of capital (WACC), then the equity portion of the WACC formula can be computed by way of the direct market data method after making the necessary adjustments to move from asset value to equity value. We will demonstrate how to do this in a later case study.

A Brief Introduction to Simple Linear Regression

When you plot two variables against each other in a scatterplot, the values usually do not fall in a perfectly exact straight line. When you perform a linear regression analysis, you attempt to find the line that best estimates the relationship between the two variables (the y- or dependent variable and the x- or independent variable). The line you find is called the fitted regression line, and the equation that specifies the line is called the regression equation.

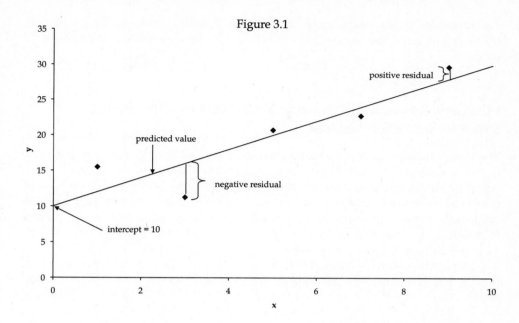

Figure 3.1

If the data in a scatterplot fall approximately in a straight line, you can use linear regression to find an equation for the regression line drawn over the data. Usually, you will not be able to fit the data perfectly, so some points will lie above and some below the fitted regression line.

The regression line that Excel fits has an equation of the form $y = a + bx$. Once again, y is the dependent variable, the one you are trying to predict, and x is the independent or predictor variable, the one that is doing the predicting. Finally, a and b are called coefficients. Figure 3.1 shows a line with $a = 10$ and $b = 2$. The short vertical line segments represent the errors, also called residuals, which are gaps between the line and the points. The residuals are the differences between the observed dependent values and the predicted values. Because a is where the line intercepts the vertical axis, a is sometimes called the intercept or constant term in the model. Because b tells how steep the line is, b is called the slope. It gives the ratio, known as rise over run, between the vertical change and the horizontal change along the line. In Figure 3.1, y increases from 10 to 30 when x increases from 0 to 10, so the slope is: b = vertical change/horizontal change = $(30 - 10)/(10 - 0) = 2$.

Suppose that x is years on the job and y is salary. Then the y-intercept ($x = 0$) is the salary for a person with zero years' experience, the starting salary. The slope is the change in salary per year of service. A person with a salary above the line would have a positive residual, and a person with a salary below the line would have a negative residual.

If the line trends downward so that y decreases when x increases, then the slope is negative. For example, if x is age of used cars and y is price for used cars, then the slope gives the drop in price per year of age. In this example, the intercept is the price when new, and the residuals represent the difference between the actual price and the predicted price. All other things being equal, if the straight line is the correct model, a positive residual means a car is selling for more than it should, and a negative residual means a car is selling for less than it should (that is, it's a bargain).

I Get Good Results with Average or Median Ratios—Why Should I Switch to Regression Analysis?

There are multiple reasons for using regression analysis, but, as they say, a picture is worth a thousand words. First, let us build some basic intuition. Figure 3.2 is a schedule showing a truncated set of market transactions, along with three sets of predicted values derived from the average price/SDE ratio, the median price/SDE ratio, and a linear regression equation. Included in the schedule are various metrics including means that were derived by using Excel's AVERAGE function, standard deviations (the average amount of dispersions around the mean) derived with STDEV, and the median, derived with MEDIAN. Also shown is the coefficient of variation (COV), which is obtained by dividing the standard deviation by the mean, and which places all the outputs on a standardized footing for comparative purposes. For Table 3.1, the COV for the ratio of selling price to SDE is 31.9 percent (.43/1.36). For the average ratio of selling price to SDE, it is 29.2 percent (15,886/54,444). For the linear regression model, the COV is 5.7 percent (2,801/49,000).

The coefficient of dispersion (COD) is the average of the absolute deviations (AAD) from the median divided by the median. For Table 3.1, the COD is 10 percent (5,000/50,000). This too is used for comparative purposes. We use the standard deviation function to measure the dispersion about the average of a single column

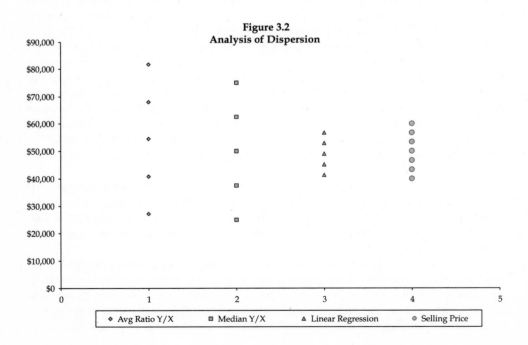

Figure 3.2
Analysis of Dispersion

A	B	C	D	E	F	G	H	I	J
1	Table 3.1								
2		Y	X			Selling Price as Determined By			
3		Selling Price	SDE	Ratio Y/X		Avg Ratio Y/X	Median Ratio Y/X	Linear Regression	
4		40,000	20,000	2.00		27,222	25,000	41,333	
5		43,333	20,000	2.17		27,222	25,000	41,333	
6		43,333	30,000	1.44		40,833	37,500	45,167	
7		46,667	30,000	1.56		40,833	37,500	45,167	
8		50,000	40,000	1.25		54,444	50,000	49,000	
9		50,000	40,000	1.25		54,444	50,000	49,000	
10		46,667	50,000	0.93		68,056	62,500	52,833	
11		53,333	50,000	1.07		68,056	62,500	52,833	
12		56,667	60,000	0.94		81,667	75,000	56,667	
13		60,000	60,000	1.00		81,667	75,000	56,667	
14									
15	Mean =	49,000		1.36		54,444		49,000	
16	Std Dev =	6,295		0.43				5,714	
17	COV (Std Dev) =			31.9%					
18	COV (RMSE) =					29.2%		5.7%	
19	Median =			1.25			50,000		
20	AAD =			0.32			5,000		
21	COD =			25.8%			10.0%		
22	RMSE =					15,886	13,229	2,801	
24		*Elements of the Linear Equation:*							
25		Intercept = a =						33,667	
26		Slope = b =						0.3833	
27		*Equation (y = a + bx):*							
28		Linear Regression = Predicted Selling Price = 33,667 + .3833(SDE)							
29									

of numbers. Other Excel functions are used to measure the size of the average deviation of the predicted values from the observed selling prices, known as the root mean squared error (RMSE) or the average deviation between two columns of numbers, in this case the observed and the predicted. One of the Excel formulas for RMSE for the average output found in cell G22 is:

$$=\text{SQRT(SUMXMY2(C4:C13,G4:G13)/(COUNT(C4:C13)}-1))$$

where C4:C13 are the observed values of *y* for this data set, G4:G13 are the predicted values of *y* for this data set, and 1 represents a loss of one degree of freedom. The formula for RMSE for the median output is found in cell H22 and substitutes H4:H13 for G4:G13 in the average formula above. For regression, the function is STEYX(C4:C13,D4:D13), with the *x*-variables used in conjunction with the observed *y*-variables, and is found in cell I22. The last two items to be addressed are the Excel functions for computing the intercept and the slope, which are, surprise, INTERCEPT(C4:C13,D4:D13) and SLOPE(C4:C13,D4:D13), and which are found in cells I25 and I26, respectively.

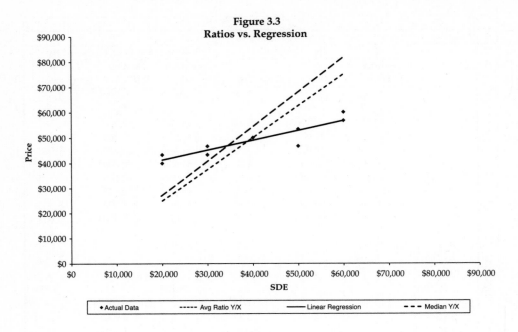

Figure 3.3
Ratios vs. Regression

Reduced dispersion is a meaningful goal as it increases our confidence in the central tendency, be it mean or median, and the regression trendline by narrowing the range of values that surrounds them. A narrower range of values implies a more accurate estimate of the population mean or a point estimate. It is obvious from the schedule and the demonstrated metrics—COV, COD, and RMSE—that when it comes to reducing dispersion and fitting the data, the average ratio is outperformed by the median ratio, which is outperformed by the regression equation. In fact, as shown in Figure 3.2, using the average and median ratios increases dispersion as those methods produce predicted values both greater and lesser than the actual selling prices. This is not true of the regression model, in which the predicted values are greater than the smallest selling price and less than the largest selling price, thereby reducing dispersion by 10 percent. If value truly is a range, then you want that range to be as narrow as possible. As we now know, regression analysis narrows that range considerably more than any average or median of ratios.

Now, for that picture! Figure 3.3 shows the original selling prices and the predicted selling prices derived from the three prediction methods. No comments are necessary, except to say that this is one example of how the use of average or median ratios can lead you far astray from a reasonable conclusion of value.

Other reasons for substituting regression analysis for average ratios are the following:

1. It is a fundamental axiom of finance and business valuation that cash flows, and by proxy, revenues, drive value. Don't we, as business valuators, want to establish a model that explores the relationship between selling price and cash flow or revenues? An average or median ratio cannot model that relationship, cannot determine the magnitude of the relationships between the two variables, and

cannot be used to make accurate predictions. We have yet to see a finance text that encourages the use of average ratios for valuing publicly traded companies in lieu of a regression model. Nor have we seen any articles in peer-reviewed research journals that explore areas of interest using average or median ratios. Regression analysis is the tool of choice for exploring relationships and making predictions among financial experts and scientists. So should it be for business valuators.

2. Most of the Standard Industrial Classification (SIC) code number data sets are not linear in the relationship between price and SDE or revenue. They are curvilinear, and as such, value predictions based on averages or medians always incorrectly value a company that has a value driver in the upper or lower ranges of the distribution. Regression can very easily be modified to deal with this problem.

3. Assume two companies, each with sales of $1.0 million, but one has SDE of $180.0 million, and the other has SDE of $260.0 million. Ceteris paribus, the company with the higher SDE should sell for more. Using just a multiple of sales, however, does not accomplish this, and in fact, overvalues one company and undervalues the other. Regression analysis allows one to predict an entity's value based on revenue while also controlling for (accounting for or taking into consideration) operating margin.

4. The distributions of both selling prices and SDE or revenue are rarely normal, or near-bell shaped, or even symmetrical (they are skewed to the right). This makes the predictions derived from averages and median ratios unreliable because the variation in predicted prices is not due to unbiased measurement error. That is, since the data are not symmetrical and normal, one cannot explain the variation in the data as just residual noise—it can also be something else. Therefore, one needs to transform the data, both the *x*-variable and/or the *y*-variable, into normal and symmetrical distributions. Regression analysis more easily handles this task than does a univariate transformation process.

5. And finally, regression analysis provides for stronger courtroom testimony because it allows the valuation analyst to speak to the relationship between the value drivers, SDE or revenue, and the item at issue, value, in more definitive terms than average or median ratios allow.

How Does One Perform a Regression Analysis Using Microsoft Excel?

Like all Microsoft Office products, there are at least two ways to do anything in Excel, including regression analysis (RA). Rather than develop a tutorial that demonstrates all the possible ways Excel's RA features can be put to use, let's focus on instructing you in the use of those functions that we use daily in our business valuation (BV) and commercial damages practices.

As shown above, a picture is worth a thousand words, so let's start there. Table 3.2 represents a sample of 15 sales transactions drawn from the Bizcomps database, without correcting for the fact that some of the transactions include seller financing with below-market rates of interest, an infirmity we will address later in this case study. For ease of instruction we are only showing those columns of information provided by Bizcomps that are pertinent to the task at hand.

Table 3.2
BIZCOMPS DATA

	Data No.	SIC CODE #	Business Type	Annual Revenue	SDE	Sales Date	Selling Price	Percent Down	Terms	Area	Days on Market
1											
2											
3	1	2396	Silk Screen Printing	205	50	8/31/1993	82	70	2 Yrs @ 8%	Baton Rouge, LA	
4	2	2396	Silk Screen Printing	248	33	8/13/1999	42	100	N/A	Midwest	120
5	3	2396	Silk Screen Printing	283	58	9/23/1998	112	28	4 Yrs @ 8%	Ohio	201
6	4	2396	Silk Screen Printing	299	89	9/30/1998	185	21	6 Mos @ 10%	Tampa, FL	110
7	5	2396	Silk Screen Printing	346	83	6/30/1994	126	39	5 Yrs @ 9%	Central Florida	
8	6	2396	Silk Screen Printing	350	122	12/7/2001	220	45	4 Yrs @ 10%	Florida	118
9	7	2396	Silk Screen Printing	376	88	6/12/2001	179	100	N/A	Spokane, WA	120
10	8	2396	Silk Screen Printing	379	78	10/22/2002	160	100	N/A	San Diego, CA	87
11	9	2396	Silk Screen Printing	401	84	10/1/1998	145	33	10 Yrs @ 8%	Spokane, WA	350
12	10	2396	Silk Screen Printing	403	53	5/31/2002	106	76	10 Yrs @ 7	Tulsa, OK	90
13	11	2396	Silk Screen Printing	406	84	4/26/2002	138	50	3 Yrs	Colorado	166
14	12	2396	Silk Screen Printing	412	88	4/16/2002	230	100	N/A	San Francisco	236
15	13	2396	Silk Screen Printing	416	65	9/12/2002	93	100	N/A	Florida	54
16	14	2396	Silk Screen Printing	436	102	11/30/2000	450	100	N/A	Denver, CO	
17	15	2396	Silk Screen Printing	448	138	1/20/2000	233	20	10 Yrs @ Pr+2.3	Stockton, CA	170

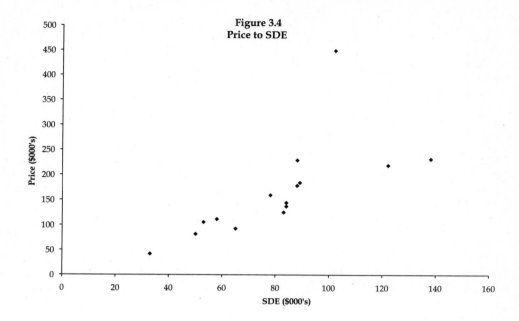

To create Figure 3.4 from the data presented in Table 3.2, from Table 3.2 select the range F4:F18, then hold down the control key and select the range H4:H18. Click on Insert, click Scatter, and select "Scatter with only Markers." Remove the legend by right-clicking and selecting Delete. After adding chart and axis titles from Layout, click on Design, and move the chart to its own worksheet. Your chart should look like Figure 3.4. Now, right click on any one of the data points, choose "add trendline," select Linear type, and select "Display equation on chart" and "Display R-squared value on chart." Click OK and save the workbook. Your chart should now look like Figure 3.5.

You now have a visual presentation of the relationship between the x-variable, SDE and the y-variable, selling price, along with the equation for predicting selling prices, as well as a measure of goodness of fit, the equation's r-squared value. The chart is dynamic, not static, which means that if we change any of the data in Table 3.2, the chart automatically updates. Don't mind the low R^2 and the outlying data points—we'll deal with those later on in the case study. For now, let's focus on learning about Excel's RA functions.

A static presentation of RA, useful for reports, can be found in Excel's Analysis ToolPak. If you don't already have the ToolPak loaded into Excel, click on the Office button, click on Excel Options, click on Add-ins and select Analysis ToolPak and Analysis ToolPak-VBA, and click OK. This loads the ToolPak for you. To use the ToolPak, go to Data, click on Data Analysis, scroll down and select Regression, and click OK. This brings up the regression analysis tool. From Table 3.2, the Input Y range is H4:H18, and the Input X range is F4:F18. Select "Labels" and for output select "New Worksheet Ply," and then click OK, and save the workbook. Your output will look like Table 3.3 after you have deleted columns H and I, selected the whole output section A3:G20, clicked on Home, Format, and chosen AutoFit Column Width. Notice that R square is the same number as R^2 in Figure 3.5, and that

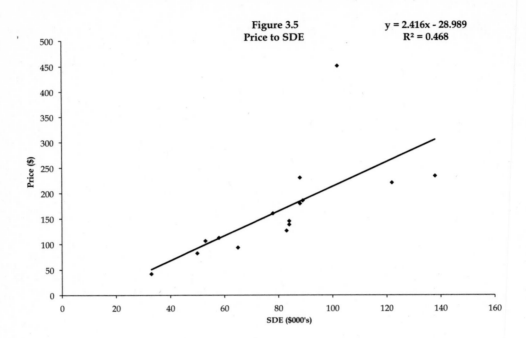

Figure 3.5
Price to SDE

$y = 2.416x - 28.989$
$R^2 = 0.468$

the coefficients for the Intercept and SDE are the same numbers as in the equation in Figure 3.5. We will explain the purpose of the additional information contained in the Summary Output later in this case study.

Another way to create an RA summary output that contains almost as much information as the static regression analysis tool output is to use an Excel array formula in conjunction with one of its statistical functions. Beneath the columns for SDE and Selling Price in Table 3.2 that you previously created, select and highlight with the cursor an area 2 columns wide and 5 rows deep, say, the range H23:I27. Then click on Formulas, More Functions, Statistical, select "LINEST," and click OK. For "Known Y's" select H4:H18, for "Known X's" select F4:F18, then enter "TRUE" for both "Const" and "Stats.". Do NOT click OK. Instead, hold down Control and Shift at the same time and simultaneously press Enter. Save the workbook. Your output should look like Table 3.4. We have added a title and explanatory phrases to describe the output. This output, with some additional minor calculations, provides the same information as the regression analysis tool with the added benefit of being dynamic, that is, if we add or delete rows to or from the data set, the output in cells H23:I27 changes accordingly.

In addition to the three ways described above of simultaneously creating all the elements of the regression equation, we also saw earlier in the case study that we can create the elements individually by use of the SLOPE and INTERCEPT functions. This is also true of many of the other elements in the Summary Output in Table 3.3, which we will demonstrate later on in the case study as we explain their development and function. Now that we know how to develop the simple linear RA equation, let's explore two of the options Excel gives us to put it to use.

Those options consist of TREND, a function that implements the equation in one step, and secondly, the creation of a formula that draws on the intercept and

	A	B	C	D	E	F	G
1	**Table 3.3**						
2							
3	SUMMARY OUTPUT						
4							
5	*Regression Statistics*						
6	Multiple R	0.684					
7	R Square	0.468					
8	Adjusted R Square	0.427					
9	Standard Error	72.910					
10	Observations	15					
11							
12	ANOVA						
13		*df*	*SS*	*MS*	*F*	*Significance F*	
14	Regression	1	60710.293	60710.293	11.421	0.005	
15	Residual	13	69106.640	5315.895			
16	Total	14	129816.933				
17							
18		*Coefficients*	*Standard Error*	*t Stat*	*p-value*	*Lower 95%*	*Upper 95%*
19	Intercept	-28.989	60.899	-0.476	0.642	-160.553	102.574
20	SDE	2.416	0.715	3.379	0.005	0.872	3.961
21							

F	G	H	I	J	K	L	N
1							
2			Table 3.4				
3			SUMMARY OUPUT				
23	Coefficient - SDE	2.416	-28.989	Coefficient - Intercept			
24	Standard Error - SDE	0.715	60.899	Standard Error - Intercept			
25	R Square	0.468	72.910	Standard Error			
26	F stat	11.421	13	Residual df			
27	Regression Sum of Squares	60,710.29	69,106.64	Residual Sum of Squares			
28							

SDE coefficients from the array formula summary output. Somewhere to the right of Table 3.2, say, starting at column O, please enter in row 3 the labels "Trend" and "Array Formula Output" in columns O and P. Select cell O4, click on Formulas, More Functions, Statistical, select "TREND," and then click OK. For "Known Y's" select H4:H18 and press the F4 function key to make the range reference absolute; for "Known X's" select F4:F18 and press the F4 key; for "X" select F4 and enter "TRUE" for Const. Then click OK. Cell O4 should present 91.83 as the predicted value.

Select P3 and enter the following formula: =+$I$23+$H$23*F4. This is the slope and intercept formula that we used earlier in the case study but with the difference that the coefficients have already been determined by the LINEST function, rather than using the SLOPE and INTERCEPT functions directly in the formula.

Cell P4 should also present 91.83 as the predicted value. Next, copy cells O4 and P4 down to row 18 and save the workbook. If each row does not contain the same numbers across the columns as shown in Table 3.5, you did not succeed in making the range references absolute in row 4, and you should try that step again. Let's perform two more calculations to set up the worksheet for use in the next section of this case study, and then we'll finish by predicting the value of a sample subject company.

These next two calculations are automatically performed for you in the regression analysis tool, and they can be part of the output if you select "residuals" and "standardized residuals" in the regression command. However, as the regression tool is static, its use is inappropriate for the type of exploratory analysis we will be doing. In cells Q3 and R3 of what was originally Table 3.2 but what is now Table 3.5, place the labels "Residuals" and "Standardized Residuals." In cell Q4 enter the formula =+P4-H4 and copy it down to row 18. This number is the difference between the value that the regression equation predicted for each individual selling price (the regression line) and the actual selling price. In cell R4 enter the formula =+Q4/'Table 3.2'!$I$25 and copy it down to row 18. This formula divides each residual by the standard error of the estimate (SEE), the standard deviation of the residuals. The result shows how many standard deviations each residual is from the average, which makes it easy to identify outliers, a topic we will explore shortly. We can't use Excel's STANDARDIZE function for this purpose as it uses $n - 1$ in its denominator, whereas the SEE is computed using $n - 2$ in its denominator.

From the values shown in the Residual column of Table 3.5, you can see that there is one residual that seems larger than the others. It is data no. 14, found in row 17, which has a standardized residual value of 3.189. You'll want to keep an eye on this observation as we continue to explore this regression model. As we'll show you

Table 3.5
BIZCOMPS DATA

Data No.	SIC CODE #	Business Type	Annual Revenue	SDE	Sales Date	Selling Price	Percent Down	Terms	Area	Days on Market	Trend	Array Formula Output	Residual	Standardized Residual
1	2396	Silk Screen Printing	205	50	8/31/1993	82	70	2 Yrs @ 8%	Baton Rouge, LA		91.83	91.83	9.83	0.135
2	2396	Silk Screen Printing	248	33	8/13/1999	42	100	N/A	Midwest	120	50.75	50.75	8.75	0.120
3	2396	Silk Screen Printing	283	58	9/23/1998	112	28	4 Yrs @ 8%	Ohio	201	111.16	111.16	-0.84	-0.012
4	2396	Silk Screen Printing	299	89	9/30/1998	185	21	6 Mos @ 10%	Tampa, FL	110	186.06	186.06	1.06	0.015
5	2396	Silk Screen Printing	346	83	6/30/1994	126	39	5 Yrs @ 9%	Central Florida		171.57	171.57	45.57	0.625
6	2396	Silk Screen Printing	350	122	12/7/2001	220	45	4 Yrs @ 10%	Florida	118	265.80	265.80	45.80	0.628
7	2396	Silk Screen Printing	376	88	6/12/2001	179	100	N/A	Spokane, WA	120	183.65	183.65	4.65	0.064
8	2396	Silk Screen Printing	379	78	10/22/2002	160	100	N/A	San Diego, CA	87	159.48	159.48	-0.52	-0.007
9	2396	Silk Screen Printing	401	84	10/1/1998	145	33	10 Yrs @ 8%	Spokane, WA	350	173.98	173.98	28.98	0.398
10	2396	Silk Screen Printing	403	53	5/31/2002	106	76	10 Yrs @ 7	Tulsa, OK	90	99.08	99.08	-6.92	-0.095
11	2396	Silk Screen Printing	406	84	4/26/2002	138	50	3 Yrs	Colorado	166	173.98	173.98	35.98	0.494
12	2396	Silk Screen Printing	412	88	4/16/2002	230	100	N/A	San Francisco	236	183.65	183.65	-46.35	-0.636
13	2396	Silk Screen Printing	416	65	9/12/2002	93	100	N/A	Florida	54	128.07	128.07	35.07	0.481
14	2396	Silk Screen Printing	436	102	11/30/2000	450	100	N/A	Denver, CO		217.48	217.48	-232.52	-3.189
15	2396	Silk Screen Printing	448	138	1/20/2000	233	20	10 Yrs @ Pr+2.3	Stockton, CA	170	304.46	304.46	71.46	0.980
Subject Company				81							166.73	166.73		

49

later on, the residuals play an important role in determining the appropriateness of any regression model. Now let's predict the value of our sample subject company.

In cell F21 of Table 3.5, we compute the number 81, the average SDE of our sample, which represents the SDE of our subject company. We wish to predict the selling price, or value, of certain of its assets using the direct market data method. That is, based on the relationship between value and SDE of other silk screen printing companies that have been sold, what is the predicted value of our sample subject company's assets? Copy cells O18:P18 down to O21:P21, skipping over rows 19 and 20. Save the workbook. Your answer should be 166.73, and it should appear in both cells. Since this number represents the combined value of the sample subject company's intangible and fixed assets, if we wished to arrive at the value of the destroyed intangible assets, it is necessary to subtract the fair market value of the company's fixed assets. Fixed asset value cannot be computed from the information contained in the transaction databases, and therefore it needs to be obtained from management or through an appraisal process.

As promised, we'd like to return to a topic we referred to at the beginning of this case, the topic of seller financing. We all know that seller financing almost always carries a below-market rate of interest that results in the selling price being over-stated. To prove this point, divide your data set into two segments, one that consists of all cash transactions and the other of seller-financed transactions. You will find that the one that consists of all cash transactions (9 count) has a price/SDE average ratio of 1.78, and the other, those that had some seller financing involved (6 count), has an average ratio of 2.30. This overstatement, which typically runs between 9 per-cent and 13 percent of the selling price, can be relieved by following Toby Tatum's procedure as outlined in his seminal text, *Transaction Patterns*. You can convert the six transactions that were supported by seller financing into all-cash equivalent selling prices by use of present value techniques, which should be done so that there is comparability among all the data, both all-cash and seller-financed transactions.

The discount rate used to present the value of the seller-financed sales is derived from a formula developed by Toby Tatum (see his third chapter). Essentially, it starts with 14 percent and adds 1 percent for each 1/10th of the selling price that is seller-financed. So, if a transaction is 70 percent seller-financed, the discount rate is 21 percent. This makes sense for two reasons:

1. It's the formula that reduces the average price/SDE multiple for seller-financed transactions down to the average price/SDE multiple for all-cash transactions in the Bizcomps database.
2. Because seller paper is usually behind the bank, is not collateralized, will not be recovered upon a default, and so on, it is essentially a very low-grade junk bond, and not a publicly traded junk bond, either. Once revised, the selling prices would then be substituted back into the Bizcomps worksheet for further analysis.

We haven't demonstrated this technique for two reasons:

1. We already have enough topics to show you.
2. We think Tatum's book is something you should have in your library if you are going to apply RA to the Bizcomps database.

Why Does Simple Linear Regression Rarely Give Us the Right Answer, and What Can We Do about It?

The data sets that Bizcomps makes available to us by way of SIC code numbers and North American Industry Classification System (NAICS) code numbers are rarely distributed in such a manner that the application of simple linear regression gives us a relevant and reliable answer. This is because the individual databases are:

1. Hardly ever linear.
2. Infrequently homogeneous as to variance (the larger the x variable, the greater the dispersion about the regression line).
3. Not often normal, or near-bell shaped, or even symmetrical.

If the data are linear, then we can proceed to use simple linear regression without having to resort to more complex models, that is, we can stick with the basic tools that Excel provides us. The reasons that homogeneity and normality, or at least symmetry are good things will be discussed later on in this case study, but at this point, suffice it to say that, without these qualities, standard statistical tests and confidence intervals will not be reliable, nor will you be able to explain away the variation in your data as noise, or ordinary and expected random error—simple tests will make it apparent that your model is deficient.

Fortunately, to fix these three problems we only need one procedure, and that is transformation of either or both the x and y variables. This is so because data that is not normally, or near-bell shaped, distributed is also often neither linear nor homogeneous. Thus, transformation provides a simple way both to fix statistical problems (nonsymmetrical and heterogeneous distributions) and to fit curves to data (curvilinear regression). For example, using 143 transactions from SIC code no. 2752, Figure 3.6 shows the distribution of the raw-data form of the x variable, SDE, being

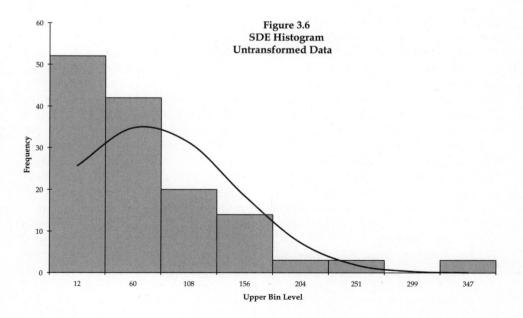

Figure 3.6
SDE Histogram
Untransformed Data

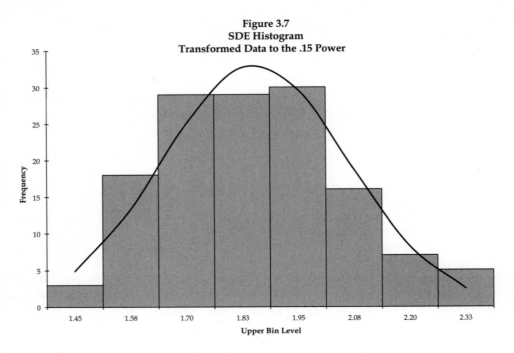

Figure 3.7
SDE Histogram
Transformed Data to the .15 Power

skewed positively to the right and therefore non-normal in its shape. A superimposed normal distribution curve points out the discrepancy in shape between the two distributions. Since powers less than 1 can pull in the upper tail of a distribution and help make a skewed distribution more symmetrical, we applied this technique, with the results shown in Figure 3.7, where the transformed data's histogram's outline is now near-bell shaped and better resembles that of the normal curve.

Transformation of variables is not new to business valuation, as both Jay Abrams and Roger Grabowski, in their work with the Ibbotson and Duff & Phelps databases respectively, have shown. In both instances, the x variable, market size, was transformed logarithmically to straighten out the curved distribution that is generated when discount rates are plotted against market size. However, transformation by logarithms does not work as well with the Bizcomps data sets as transformation by exponents, as we can select the exponent that works best in the situation, while the logarithm of any number is fixed. Therefore, because of the flexibility afforded our transformation process by exponents, that will be the transforming process we demonstrate in this case study. So, let's set up our worksheet so that we can transform our data and at the same time efficiently identify and remove outliers from the data set. We'll explain later in the case study why removing outliers is not only permitted, but in the circumstances, often required.

Returning to the last worksheet you created, our Table 3.5, the last column of figures you have should be titled "Standardized Residual" in column R. Starting in cell T2 and continuing to cell Y2, enter the labels: "Transformed X," "Transformed Y," "Predicted Y," "Residual," "Standardized Residual," and "Delete if X" as shown in Table 3.6. As placeholder amounts, in cell T1 enter 1, in cell U1 enter 1, and in cell Y1 enter 2.5 as the standard deviation cutoff point. Further on, we transform the x and y variables using the placeholder amounts in cells T1 and U1.

TABLE 3.6

Table 3.6
BIZCOMPS DATA

Data No.	SIC CODE #	Business Type	Annual Revenue	SDE	Sales Date	Selling Price	Percent Down	Terms	Area	Days on Market	Trend	Array Formula Output	Residual	Standardized Residual	Transformed X	Transformed Y	Predicted Y	Residual	Standardized Residual	Delete if X
															1	1	1			2.5
1	2396	Silk Screen Printing	205	50	08/31/1993	82	70	2 Yrs @ 8%	Baton Rouge, LA	120	91.83	91.83	9.83	0.135	50	82	91.83	9.83	0.13	
2	2396	Silk Screen Printing	248	33	08/13/1999	42	100	N/A	Midwest	201	50.75	50.75	8.75	0.120	33	42	50.75	8.75	0.12	
3	2396	Silk Screen Printing	283	58	09/23/1998	112	28	4 Yrs @ 8%	Ohio	110	111.16	111.16	-0.84	-0.012	58	112	111.16	-0.84	-0.01	
4	2396	Silk Screen Printing	299	89	09/30/1998	185	21	6 Mos @ 10%	Tampa, FL	118	186.06	186.06	1.06	0.015	89	185	186.06	1.06	0.01	
5	2396	Silk Screen Printing	346	83	06/30/1994	126	39	5 Yrs @ 9%	Central Florida	120	171.57	171.57	45.57	0.625	83	126	171.57	45.57	0.62	
6	2396	Silk Screen Printing	350	122	12/07/2001	220	45	4 Yrs @ 10%	Florida	87	265.80	265.80	45.80	0.628	122	220	265.80	45.80	0.63	
7	2396	Silk Screen Printing	376	88	06/12/2001	179	100	N/A	Spokane, WA	350	183.65	183.65	4.65	0.064	88	179	183.65	4.65	0.06	
8	2396	Silk Screen Printing	379	78	10/22/2002	160	100	N/A	San Diego, CA	90	159.48	159.48	-0.52	-0.007	78	160	159.48	-0.52	-0.01	
9	2396	Silk Screen Printing	401	84	10/01/1998	145	33	10 Yrs @ 8%	Spokane, WA	166	173.98	173.98	28.98	0.398	84	145	173.98	28.98	0.40	
10	2396	Silk Screen Printing	403	53	05/31/2002	106	76	10 Yrs @ 7	Tulsa, OK	236	99.08	99.08	-6.92	-0.095	53	106	99.08	-6.92	-0.09	
11	2396	Silk Screen Printing	406	84	04/26/2002	138	50	3 Yrs	Colorado	54	173.98	173.98	35.98	0.494	84	138	173.98	35.98	0.49	
12	2396	Silk Screen Printing	412	88	04/16/2002	230	100	N/A	San Francisco		183.65	183.65	-46.35	-0.636	88	230	183.65	-46.35	-0.64	
13	2396	Silk Screen Printing	416	65	09/12/2002	93	100	N/A	Florida		128.07	128.07	35.07	0.481	65	93	128.07	35.07	0.48	
14	2396	Silk Screen Printing	436	102	11/30/2000	450	100	N/A	Denver, CO		217.48	217.48	-232.52	-3.189	102	450	217.48	-232.52	-3.19	
15	2396	Silk Screen Printing	448	138	01/20/2000	233	20	10 Yrs @ P+2.3	Stockton, CA	170	304.46	304.46	71.46	0.980	138	233	304.46	71.46	0.98	X
		Subject Company		81							166.73	166.733			81.000		166.733			

SUMMARY OUTPUT

Coefficient - SDE	2.416	-28.989	Coefficient - Intercept
Standard Error - SDE	0.715	60.899	Standard Error - Intercept
R Square	0.468	72.910	Standard Error
F stat	11.421	13	Residual df
Regression Sum of Squares	60,710.29	69,106.64	Residual Sum of Squares

Mean	0.00
Std Dev	70.258
SEE	72.910
R^2	0.468
COV	43.73%

In cell T4, enter the formula =F4^$T$2, and in cell U4 enter =H4^$U$2. This transforms the variables by raising each to the power of 1. Copy cells T4 and U4 down to cells T18 and U18. Next, let's compute the predicted value for y using the transformed x and y variables and then back-transform the result right in the formula itself using the reciprocal of the y transforming exponent.

In cell V4 enter =TREND($U$4:$U$18,$T$4:$T$18,T4,TRUE)^(1/$U$2). Raising the predicted value of y to the power of the reciprocal of the transforming exponent translates that value back into the original state in which y was expressed. Just as the square root of 9 can be expressed in Excel as $9^.5 = 3$, back-transforming makes $3^{(1/.5)} = 9$. Rather than doing this in two steps, that is, predict y in its transformed state, and then in another cell back-transform it into its original language, we have elected to do it one step. In cell W4 enter +V4-H4, which creates the residual. Copy cells V4 and W4 down to cells V18 and W18. In cell W23 enter =AVERAGE(W4:W18); in cell W24 enter =STDEV(W4:W18) and in cell W25 enter =SQRT(SUMXMY2(V4:V18,H4:H18)/(COUNT(H4:H18)-2)), which last formula gives us the standard error of the estimate (SEE), that is, the standard deviation about the regression line. Shortly, we will use the SEE to select the best exponents for the x and y variables in cells T2 and U2. Also, place the labels "Mean," "Std Dev," "SEE" and "R^2" in cells V23 through V26.

In cell X4 enter +W4/$W$25, which standardizes the residual; and finally in cell Y4 enter =IF (OR (X4>$Y$2,X4<-$Y$2),"X",""). This marks those residuals that are greater than 2.5 or less than −2.5 standard deviations. Copy cells X4 and Y4 down to cells X18 and Y18. As we previously mentioned, data no. 14 exceeds 2.5 standard deviations from the mean, as indicated by the X in cell Y17. Given the small size of the data set and the large size of the outlier, whose residual has no chance of being reduced by the transformation, it should be removed from the data set at this time by deleting row 17. With larger data sets, outliers discovered at this stage can be left in until Solver is set up and run at least once before they are removed. Notice, though, when we remove data no. 14 that data no. 12 in cell R15 in Table 3.7 now has a standardized residual greater than 2.5. Rather than delete this data point, let's see if transformation by exponents reduces dispersion enough to make its residual less than 2.5 standard deviations.

At this point we set up Excel's powerful optimization feature called Solver Add-In, which can calculate solutions to what-if scenarios based on adjustable cells and constraint cells. This allows us to minimize SEE and simultaneously uncover any other outliers that may exist in the data set.

After deleting row 17, our worksheet is now shown in Table 3.7. Click on cell W23, select Data, Solver (if you don't have Solver loaded, go to the Office Button, click on Excel Options, Add-ins, scroll down, find and select Solver Add-in, and click OK), set Target Cell to W24, set Equal To: Min., By Changing Cells: T2:U2, then add the following constraint: W22=0. Click on Options, set Precision and Convergence to .000001, set Tolerance to 20 percent, choose Use Automatic Scaling, click OK, and click Solve. If cell W22 doesn't show zero for a result, run Solver a second time. The results are shown in Table 3.8. Checking to see if there are any more outliers to be removed, we note that there are none and that the back-transformed standardized residual of data no. 12 has been reduced to 2.39 in cell X15. If there were any outliers, denoted by an X in column Y, then we would delete that row(s) and run Solver again, this time by just clicking on Solver, Solve (Solver remembers

TABLE 3.7

Table 3.7
BIZCOMPS DATA

Data No.	SIC CODE #	Business Type	Annual Revenue	SDE	Sales Date	Selling Price	Percent Down	Terms	Area	Days on Market	Trend	Array Formula Output	Residual	Standardized Residual	Transformed X (1)	Transformed Y (1)	Predicted Y (1)	Residual	Standardized Residual	Delete if X (2.5)
1	2396	Silk Screen Printing	205	50	08/31/1993	82	70	2 Yrs @ 8%	Baton Rouge, LA	120	90.77	90.77	8.77	0.331	50.000	82.000	90.77	8.77	0.33	
2	2396	Silk Screen Printing	248	33	08/13/1999	42	100	N/A	Midwest	120	58.65	58.65	16.65	0.629	33.000	42.000	58.65	16.65	0.63	
3	2396	Silk Screen Printing	283	58	09/23/1998	112	28	4 Yrs @ 8%	Ohio	201	105.88	105.88	-6.12	-0.231	58.000	112.000	105.88	-6.12	-0.23	
4	2396	Silk Screen Printing	299	89	09/30/1998	185	21	6 Mos @ 10%	Tampa, FL	110	164.45	164.45	-20.55	-0.776	89.000	185.000	164.45	-20.55	-0.78	
5	2396	Silk Screen Printing	346	83	06/30/1994	126	39	5 Yrs @ 9%	Central Florida		153.11	153.11	27.11	1.024	83.000	126.000	153.11	27.11	1.02	
6	2396	Silk Screen Printing	350	122	12/07/2001	220	45	4 Yrs @ 10%	Florida	118	226.79	226.79	6.79	0.256	122.000	220.000	226.79	6.79	0.26	
7	2396	Silk Screen Printing	376	88	06/12/2001	179	100	N/A	Spokane, WA	120	162.56	162.56	-16.44	-0.621	88.000	179.000	162.56	-16.44	-0.62	
8	2396	Silk Screen Printing	379	78	10/22/2002	160	100	N/A	San Diego, CA	87	143.67	143.67	-16.33	-0.617	78.000	160.000	143.67	-16.33	-0.62	
9	2396	Silk Screen Printing	401	84	10/01/1998	145	33	10 Yrs @ 8%	Spokane, WA	350	155.00	155.00	10.00	0.378	84.000	145.000	155.00	10.00	0.38	
10	2396	Silk Screen Printing	403	53	05/31/2002	106	76	10 Yrs @ 7	Tulsa, OK	90	96.44	96.44	-9.56	-0.361	53.000	106.000	96.44	-9.56	-0.36	
11	2396	Silk Screen Printing	406	84	04/26/2002	138	50	3 Yrs	Colorado	166	155.00	155.00	17.00	0.642	84.000	138.000	155.00	17.00	0.64	
12	2396	Silk Screen Printing	412	88	04/16/2002	230	100	N/A	San Francisco	236	162.56	162.56	-67.44	-2.546	88.000	230.000	162.56	-67.44	-2.55	X
13	2396	Silk Screen Printing	416	65	09/12/2002	93	100	N/A	Florida	54	119.11	119.11	26.11	0.986	65.000	93.000	119.11	26.11	0.99	
15	2396	Silk Screen Printing	448	138	01/20/2000	233	20	10 Yrs @ Pr+2.3	Stockton, CA	170	257.02	257.02	24.02	0.907	138.000	233.000	257.02	24.02	0.91	
		Subject Company		81							149.33	149.334			81		149.334			

	Mean	0.00
	Std Dev	25.449
	SEE	26.489
	R²	0.8080
	COV	18.08%

SUMMARY OUPUT

Coefficient - SDE	1.889		Coefficient - Intercept	-3.693
Standard Error - SDE	0.266		Standard Error - Intercept	22.291
R Square	0.808		Standard Error	26.489
F stat	50.490		Residual df	12
Regression Sum of Squares	35,425.80		Residual Sum of Squares	8,419.70

55

TABLE 3.8

Table 3.8 — BIZCOMPS DATA

Data No.	SIC CODE #	Business Type	Annual Revenue	SDE	Sales Date	Selling Price	Percent Down	Terms	Area	Days on Market
1	2396	Silk Screen Printing	205	50	08/31/1993	82	70	2 Yrs @ 8%	Baton Rouge, LA	
2	2396	Silk Screen Printing	248	33	08/13/1999	42	100	N/A	Midwest	120
3	2396	Silk Screen Printing	283	58	09/23/1998	112	28	4 Yrs @ 8%	Ohio	201
4	2396	Silk Screen Printing	299	89	09/30/1998	185	21	6 Mos @ 10%	Tampa, FL	110
5	2396	Silk Screen Printing	346	83	06/30/1994	126	39	5 Yrs @ 9%	Central Florida	118
6	2396	Silk Screen Printing	350	122	12/07/2001	220	45	4 Yrs @ 10%	Florida	118
7	2396	Silk Screen Printing	376	88	06/12/2001	179	100	N/A	Spokane, WA	120
8	2396	Silk Screen Printing	379	78	10/22/2002	160	100	N/A	San Diego, CA	87
9	2396	Silk Screen Printing	401	84	10/01/1998	145	33	10 Yrs @ 8%	Spokane, WA	350
10	2396	Silk Screen Printing	403	53	05/31/2002	106	76	10 Yrs @ 7	Tulsa, OK	90
11	2396	Silk Screen Printing	406	84	04/26/2002	138	50	3 Yrs	Colorado	166
12	2396	Silk Screen Printing	412	88	04/16/2002	230	100	N/A	San Francisco	236
13	2396	Silk Screen Printing	416	65	09/12/2002	93	100	N/A	Florida	54
14	2396	Silk Screen Printing	448	138	01/20/2000	233	20	10 Yrs @ Pr+2.3	Stockton, CA	170

Subject Company — SDE 81

SUMMARY OUPUT

Coefficient - SDE	1.889	Coefficient - Intercept	-3.693
Standard Error - SDE	0.266	Standard Error - Intercept	22.291
R Square	0.808	Standard Error	26.489
F stat	50.490	Residual df	12
Regression Sum of Squares	35,425.80	Residual Sum of Squares	8,419.70

Top values: Delete if X = 2.5 ; -4.045094586 ; -2.565066698

	Trend	Array Formula Output	Residual	Standardized Residual	Trans-formed X	Trans-formed Y	Predicted Y	Residual	Standar-dized Residual	Delete if X
	90.77	90.77	-8.77	-0.331	0.0000001341	0.0000123293	80.05	1.95	0.08	
	58.65	58.65	-16.65	-0.629	0.0000007202	0.0000065894	42.15	-0.15	-0.01	
	105.88	105.88	6.12	0.231	0.0000000736	0.0000055414	99.79	12.21	0.50	
	164.45	164.45	20.55	0.776	0.0000000130	0.0000015295	174.24	10.76	0.44	
	153.11	153.11	-27.11	-1.024	0.0000000173	0.0000040965	161.10	-35.10	-1.45	
	226.79	226.79	-6.79	-0.256	0.0000000036	0.0000009807	226.94	-6.94	-0.29	
	162.56	162.56	16.44	0.621	0.0000000136	0.0000016645	172.12	6.88	0.28	
	143.67	143.67	16.33	0.617	0.0000000222	0.0000022197	149.49	10.51	0.43	
	155.00	155.00	-10.00	-0.378	0.0000000164	0.0000028572	163.36	-18.36	-0.76	
	96.44	96.44	9.56	0.361	0.0000001060	0.0000063820	87.36	18.64	0.77	
	155.00	155.00	-17.00	-0.642	0.0000000164	0.0000032439	163.36	-25.36	-1.05	
	162.56	162.56	67.44	2.546	0.0000000136	0.0000008750	172.12	57.88	2.39	
	119.11	119.11	-26.11	-0.986	0.0000000464	0.0000089271	117.43	-24.43	-1.01	
	257.02	257.02	-24.02	-0.907	0.0000000022	0.0000008464	241.49	-8.49	-0.35	
	149.334	149.334			1.905455E-08		156.521			

	Mean	0.00
Std Dev	23.292	
SEE	24.244	
R²	0.8408	
COV	16.55%	

Mean 156.521

your previous settings). We would continue to repeat this process until no more Xs showed up in column Y.

We have just accomplished a number of things, including having changed the values in cells T2 and U2 just enough so that the transformed variables used in the regression equation produce the lowest possible SEE, while at the same time producing the necessary outcome of a mean value of zero for the resulting residuals (by definition, if the trendline minimizes the squared deviations, then deviations above the trendline equal deviations below the trendline, and the average of the deviations is therefore zero). In cell W25, enter the formula =RSQ(V4:V17,H4:H17) so that we can compute R^2 for the transformed model. Checking the output metrics of SEE and R^2 for both the transformed model and the untransformed, or original, model, we see that the original model shown in Table 3.6 has an SEE and R^2 of 72.910 and .468, as shown in cells I26 and H26, respectively, while the transformed model's metrics in Table 3.8 are 23.292 and .8408 for SEE and R^2, as shown in cells W24 and W25, respectively. Granted, the SEE of 26.489 and R^2 of .808 shown in cells I25 and H25 of the untransformed model in Table 3.8 are also improvements over the original model. These improvements, obtained just by removing data no. 14, are still not as good as those obtained by transforming the x and y variables. In fact, when we compare coefficients of variation, that of the transformed model, 16.55 percent, is 8.48 percent better than that of the untransformed model's 18.08 percent derived by the formula (I25/AVERAGE(H4:H17)). Therefore, the transformed model gives us a higher R^2, a lower SEE, and at the same time allows us to minimize the data numbers that must be removed as outliers by allowing us to keep data no. 12 in the model. Graphical presentations of these outcomes are presented in Figures 3.8 and 3.9.

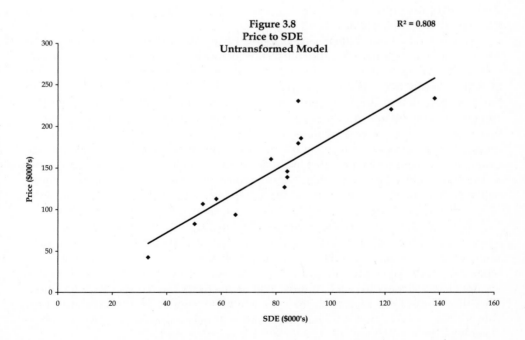

Figure 3.8
Price to SDE
Untransformed Model

$R^2 = 0.808$

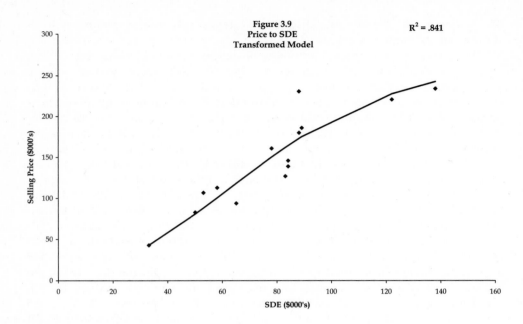

We can see from the scatterplot of Figure 3.9 that the data set is in fact curvilinear, but that by transforming the data, we were able to fit a line to the data by using Excel's simple linear regression functions without having to resort to more complex nonlinear models. Also, by curving the regression line we were able to keep data no. 12 in the model by making its standardized residual less than the 2.55 standard deviations of the untransformed model, and thus preventing it from being an outlier that would have to be removed.

As we have seen, outliers are extreme observations that for one reason or another do not belong with the other observations in our data sets. There are two ways that outliers can be introduced into the Bizcomps databases, the first of which results from incorrect recording, or especially data entry errors that can put wild values into the data sets. The second cause of outliers is that data sets are not homogeneous to which a single regression model applies, but rather a heterogeneous mix of two or more types of transactions, one of which is more frequent. The infrequent observations of the other types appear as outliers. For example, if those transactions that are seller-financed have not been converted into a cash equivalent selling price, then a scatter graph of price to SDE or annual revenue will include outliers caused by the less frequent observations, which might be either of the two types of selling prices, depending on the makeup of the data set.

What one does when outliers are identified in the data set is not without controversy. If the outlier is a result of a data entry error or is otherwise suspect in terms of its reliability or accuracy, then it should be clearly removed from the data set or repaired before any further analysis. But what should be done about outliers that are not clearly erroneous, such as those that lie between 2 and 4 standard deviations from the mean of the regression line? Somehow, leaving those observations in the data set has come to be viewed as the "honest" thing to do, and removing them is viewed as "cherry-picking" or "cheating" or "making it work."

The issue of outlier removal is greatly influenced by what one is trying to accomplish. If you are performing basic science and trying to establish a relationship between, say, the number of cigarettes smoked and the onset of lung cancer, then outliers are important to your research as they will be counterintuitive to what was expected and therefore spark new research.

For our purposes, the relationship between SDE and selling price is a fundamental axiom of business valuation—it doesn't need to be established or proven. Therefore, outliers are not helpful sources of new research, but are anomalies. Outliers typically represent one of the following:

1. Input errors.
2. Fools for buyers who have overpaid.
3. Fools for sellers who have accepted less than fair market value.
4. Distressed sellers.
5. Synergistic buyers.

Items 2 to 5 violate the fair market value standard of value, and therefore do not belong in the data set. For that reason, it is necessary to delete them along with the obvious data input errors. If your data set contains 75 data points, and 65 of them are within 2.5 standard deviations of the mean, why do you need the other 10, and what helpful information do they contain?

If a data set is heterogeneous and contains all types of transactions, why wouldn't you want to exclude those that do not fit the fair market value standard of value? By definition, it is true that any transaction outside the mainstream does not conform to that standard, whatever the reason. For example, how can a sale that is 4.5 standard deviations from the mean be at fair market value? Mustn't it be at investment value—value to a particular buyer? Even if you make the heroic assumption that a sale at 4.5 standard deviations is truly a fair market value transaction, this question remains: Why did it sell for such a high multiple? Perhaps it has the best location, the best management, superior service, loyal customers, and so on. All these things tend to make its SDE far in excess of the average enterprise in its SIC code number. Therefore, it sold at a premium; that is, not only was its SDE multiplied by the average multiple, but the buyer paid a premium for its superior performance and the fact that its recipe for success has been systematized by management such that it will survive the closing.

Now, ask yourself: Does your subject company enjoy such profits, have such systems in place, and so forth? If not, then how can the outlier company be similar and relevant to your valuation assignment? It can't be, and therefore, it should be removed from the data set. So, remove the outliers because they either don't represent fair market value transactions, or even if, in the extreme, they do. Do not fear that you are "making it work." The cutoff metric is set before you start to eliminate outliers, and it robotically makes the selections. Hence, you are not "cherry picking" the transactions that you keep in the data set—an algorithm decides what transactions fall outside the test metric you have set to determine fair market value.

Finally, in Table 3.8, copy cells O17, P17, T17, and V17 to Row 20. The resulting predicted value for our subject's company's fixed and intangible assets shown in cell V20 is 156.521 based on its SDE of 81. This is a reduction in value of 7.187 from the original untransformed data set shown in Table 3.7, indicating that asset values derived from SDE amounts that are near the average SDE value will not be affected nearly as much by outlier removal and transformations as those SDE values near the upper or lower limits of the data set. We get the most bang for our buck with these procedures the further our SDE amount is from the average.

Should We Treat the Value Driver Annual Revenue in the Same Manner as We Have Seller's Discretionary Earnings?

For as long as transaction databases have been available, it has been received wisdom that annual revenue (AR) is as least as good, if not a better, predictor of value than seller's discretionary earnings (SDE). In this section of the case study we will examine this assertion, and if the valuation analyst truly needs to include AR as part of the valuation equation, we suggest a more appropriate model than merely regressing selling price against AR.

There are a number of reasons, some practical and some logical, for not using AR as the sole predictor of value. In the practice arena, if we use the remaining 14 data points as shown in Table 3.9 and simply regress selling price against AR, we get the graphic results shown in Figure 3.10. Notice how dispersed the data points are around the trendline. Many of the data points look as if they might be outliers, but the degree of dispersion is so great that they are all within 2 standard errors of the trendline. This ocular conclusion is ratified by the very low R^2 of .29, indicating that the variation in AR only explains 29 percent of the variation in selling price. Not shown is the standard error of the estimate (SEE) of 50.38, an amount almost double that derived from using SDE as the x variable. This is a fairly typical result, and the authors have found that after performing the outlier removing process previously demonstrated on scores of SIC code no. databases, AR rarely has better metrics than the SDE of the same data set, and in most instances isn't even close.

A maxim of financial valuation is that investors buy cash flow. Therefore, when AR is the value driver, it is only serving as a proxy for cash flow, the underlying assumption being that the buyer can repair or reconstruct the company's cost structure so as to produce the necessary cash flow to justify the purchase price. The fact that some buyers pay a seller a premium for the right to make the company (more) profitable might account for some of the outliers in the databases.

Another reason for choosing SDE over AR is that all of the qualitative factors that drive value are captured in SDE, and not necessarily in sales. These qualitative factors might be an advantageous lease, superior management, efficient and effective employees, and so forth. While AR is a "cleaner" number, to be successful a business needs to manage its costs. How well management does this is not reflected in AR, but is so reflected in SDE.

An objection to using SDE is that it is an unadjusted and therefore unreliable number. But is it really unadjusted? The transactions in the databases come from business brokers, who have cleaned up the sellers' income statements by removing all personal expenses so as to enhance the cash flow of the business and ultimately its selling price. The end result of this clean-up process is adjusted SDE numbers that are more closely correlated with selling prices than AR.

The final and most compelling reason not to use AR as the value driver in a regression equation can best be demonstrated with the following question. Should the assets of two companies sell for the same price when they both have AR of

Table 3.9

BIZCOMPS DATA

Data No.	SIC CODE #	Business Type	Annual Revenue	SDE	Sales Date	Selling Price	Price/AR	SDE/AR	Trend	Array Formula Output	Residual	Standardized Residual	Trans-formed X	Trans-formed Y	Predicted Y	Residual	Standardized Residual	Delete if X
													-1.9972	-1.749847				2.5
1	2396	Silk Screen Printing	205	50	8/31/1993	82	0.40	0.24	92.07	92.07	10.07	0.377	16.74	4.970	91.28	9.28	0.26	
2	2396	Silk Screen Printing	248	33	8/13/1999	42	0.17	0.13	57.92	57.92	15.92	0.597	56.16	22.361	50.50	8.50	0.24	
3	2396	Silk Screen Printing	283	58	9/23/1998	112	0.40	0.20	105.66	105.66	-6.34	-0.238	23.70	5.063	99.29	-12.71	-0.36	
4	2396	Silk Screen Printing	299	89	9/30/1998	185	0.62	0.30	165.55	165.55	-19.45	-0.729	11.25	2.317	179.76	-5.24	-0.15	
5	2396	Silk Screen Printing	346	83	6/30/1994	126	0.36	0.24	152.69	152.69	26.69	1.000	17.31	5.857	150.49	24.49	0.70	
6	2396	Silk Screen Printing	350	122	12/7/2001	220	0.63	0.35	228.44	228.44	8.44	0.316	8.21	2.253	277.18	57.18	1.63	
7	2396	Silk Screen Printing	376	88	6/12/2001	179	0.48	0.23	161.66	161.66	-17.34	-0.650	18.18	3.665	157.98	-21.02	-0.60	
8	2396	Silk Screen Printing	379	78	10/22/2002	160	0.42	0.21	142.14	142.14	-17.86	-0.669	23.51	4.522	133.71	-26.29	-0.75	
9	2396	Silk Screen Printing	401	84	10/1/1998	145	0.36	0.21	153.25	153.25	8.25	0.309	22.69	5.930	144.84	-0.16	0.00	
10	2396	Silk Screen Printing	403	53	5/31/2002	106	0.26	0.13	92.91	92.91	-13.09	-0.491	57.49	10.349	80.91	-25.09	-0.71	
11	2396	Silk Screen Printing	406	84	4/26/2002	138	0.34	0.21	153.12	153.12	15.12	0.567	23.26	6.608	144.25	6.25	0.18	
12	2396	Silk Screen Printing	412	88	4/16/2002	230	0.56	0.21	160.75	160.75	-69.25	-2.595	21.82	2.773	152.75	-77.25	-2.20	
13	2396	Silk Screen Printing	416	65	9/12/2002	93	0.22	0.16	115.92	115.92	22.92	0.859	40.75	13.755	103.16	10.16	0.29	
15	2396	Silk Screen Printing	448	138	1/20/2000	233	0.52	0.31	257.09	257.09	24.09	0.903	10.50	3.139	284.89	51.89	1.48	

| | | Subject Company | 400 | 45 | | | | | | | | | | | | | | |

| | | | | | | Average | 0.4101 | 0.113 | 77.427 | 77.427 | | | 78.53 | | 66.582 | 0.162883 | | |
| | | | | | | | | 0.224 | | | | | | | | | | |

Residual statistics:

Mean	-0.84	
Std Dev	25.624	
SEE	26.686	
R^2	0.8054	
COV	18.22%	

Mean	0.00	
Std Dev	33.720	
SEE	35.097	
R^2	0.7468	
COV	23.96%	

SUMMARY OUPUT

Coefficient - SDE/AR	1.945	Coefficient - Intercept	-0.025
Standard Error - SDE/AR	0.310	Standard Error - Intercept	0.072
R Square	0.767	Standard Error of the Estimate	0.070
F stat	39.469	Residual df	12
Regression Sum of Squares	0.195	Residual Sum of Squares	0.059

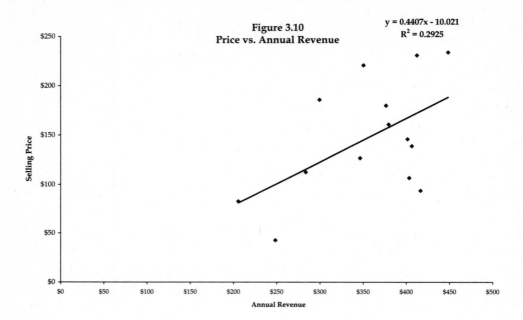

Figure 3.10
Price vs. Annual Revenue

$y = 0.4407x - 10.021$
$R^2 = 0.2925$

$1,000,000 each, but one of them has SDE of $350,000 and the other has SDE of $200,000? The answer is, of course not! Somehow, the selling price of each must reflect its own degree of profitability. In his textbook, *Investment Valuation*, Professor Aswath Damodaran says that "the key determinant of a revenue multiple is the profit margin—the net margin for price-to-sales ratios and operating margins for value-to-sales ratios." He goes on to say that other "key determinants of the revenue multiple of a firm are its expected risk, payout ratios and growth characteristics." Unfortunately, these last three determinants are not available to us through any of the transaction databases. But profit margin, the most important determinant, is available through the medium of SDE as found in Bizcomps.

All this, of course, raises the question: Why use AR in any case if it is inferior to SDE as a value driver? One answer would be that use of AR is appropriate if the subject company's return on sales, as measured by SDE/AR, was close to the industry average return on sales. Another answer is that there are some fact-specific situations where the correct use of AR combined with SDE gives one the best answer available. For example, consider the situation where the seller has expended great effort in developing sales, but for one reason or another, the company has a profit margin that is way below average. Valuing the company based on sales would certainly overvalue it, while valuing it based on SDE alone would undervalue it. There must be some way to value the company such that the seller is rewarded for building sales, but punished for not doing it profitably enough. There is, and the remainder of this chapter will be devoted to showing you how to account for low profitability coupled with AR by use of a formula that adjusts the price-to-sales ratio upward or downward based on the degree of profitability, measured as SDE/AR, of the subject company relative to its peers in the data set.

Once more, let's use the same data set that we left off with earlier, the one with 14 data points as shown in Table 3.9, data nos. 1 to 13 and 15, having eliminated data no.

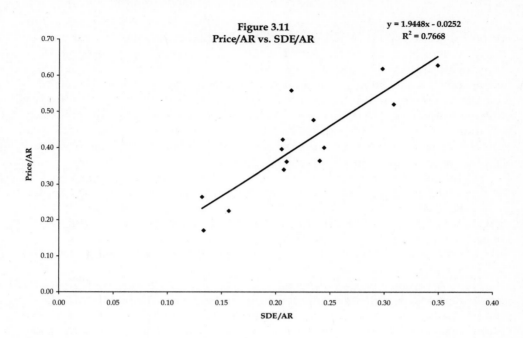

Figure 3.11
Price/AR vs. SDE/AR

$y = 1.9448x - 0.0252$
$R^2 = 0.7668$

14 as an outlier. First we'll do this as a linear regression, and then we'll do it a second time using the transformation techniques we learned earlier. Still working with the worksheet shown in Table 3.9, since we are adding new columns to the worksheet, we removed enough columns to the right of the label "Selling Price" such that the label "Trend" winds up in column I. Put the cursor in column I and insert 2 columns to the left. Label column I "Price/AR" and label column J "SDE/AR." In cell I4, enter the formula + H4/E4, and in cell J4 enter the formula + F4/E4, and then copy cells I4 and J4 down to row 17. Figure 3.11, based on columns I and J of Table 3.9, indicates that there is a definite linear relationship between the two variables.

Make the references to column H absolute in cells S24, S25, and S26, and then copy the block of cells R22:S26 to L22:M26. In cell K4, change the formula to read: =TREND($I$4:$I$17,$J$4:$J$17,I4, TRUE)*E4, and then copy cell K4 down to row 17. Change the array formula in cells E23:F27 to read: =LINEST(I4:I17,J4:J17,TRUE,TRUE)—remember to highlight all 10 cells, make your changes to the formula, and then press Control, Shift, and Enter simultaneously to alter the array. In cell L4, change the formula to read: =(+$F$23+$E$23*J4)*E4; make sure that cell M4 contains the formula = L4–H4, and that cell N4 contains the formula =M4/$M$24. Then copy cells L4, M4, and N4 down to row 17. Now let's create some variables for our subject company by entering 400 for AR in cell E20 and 45 for SDE in cell F20. Then copy cells J17, K17, and L17 down to row 20 (skip rows 18 and 19). In cells I21 and J21 compute the averages of rows I4:I17 and J4:J17, respectively. In the previous examples we were using an SDE of 81, which is the average SDE of our sample. For the instant case, we are substituting an SDE of 45, an amount that is substantially less than the average SDE, in order to simulate the typical situation that calls for this methodology—average or above-average revenue coupled with an SDE that produces a below-average return on sales.

This valuation model produces a value of 77.427 as shown in cells K20 and L20. If our subject company was deemed to have average profitability as measured by SDE/AR, then its value would have been 164.035, obtained by multiplying AR of $400 by the average price/AR ratio of .4101 shown in cell I21. But since our subject company's profitability is about 50 percent of the average of those companies in the data set (compare cell J20 with cell J21), its price/AR ratio has been reduced by the regression model to .1936 (77.427/400) to reflect this low degree of profitability relative to sales. Also notice that with the use of a linear model, data no. 12 is an outlier. Rather than immediately removing this data number, let's try a transformation procedure as we did earlier with the price to SDE model.

Continuing to work with Table 3.9, reset both cells P2 and Q2 to .1. In cell P4 change the formula to read: =J4^$P$2. In cell Q4 change the formula to read: =I4^$Q$2. In cell R4 change the formula to read: =TREND ($Q$4:$Q$17,$P$4:$P$17,P4,TRUE)^(1/$Q$2)*E4. Check to be sure that cell S4 contains the formula R4-H4 and that cell T4 contains the formula =S4/$S$24. Now copy cells P4:T4 down to Row 17, and then copy cells P17 and S17 down to cells P20 and S20 (skipping rows 18 and 19). Next, click on Data, Solver, and click on Solve (again, Solver remembers your previous settings). Since Solver always searches for the perfect answer, it frequently destabilizes the model attempting to provide a solution. As this is probably what you have just experienced, we need to place some constraints on the model so that the best does not become the enemy of the good, and we get a meaningful solution. Click on Data, Solver, Add; in "Cell reference" put P2:Q2; in the next box choose <=; and in "constraint" place 1. Repeat this process with the same cell references, choose >=, and make the constraint –5. This limits how far Solver can roam in its search for a solution. Why did we choose these constraints? Trial and error—by substituting various values in cells P2 and Q2, we can estimate the points at which the model destabilizes and then place these estimates in the Solver function. While each data set will have its own set of constraints, the authors never set theirs higher than 5 or lower than –5, and very often, as in this case, one or the other constraint will be considerably closer to zero than either of these arbitrary maximums. Now click on Solver and Solve, and repeat the process. Very often, especially in a complicated model such as this one, Solver needs two or more tries to optimize the model and produce usable results.

Let's compare the results of the two models, transformed and untransformed, to see which has the better metrics. While the predicted value for selling price is lower with the transformed model, and there is no standardized residual greater than 2.5, as there is in the untransformed model, the metrics for the transformed model are worse than those of the untransformed model. This just goes to show that in this area of damages analysis, as in all others, often there are unexpected surprises, blind alleys, dead-ends, and cul-de-sacs. What course of action do the authors recommend at this point? As always, reasonableness, informed judgment, and common sense come into play.

Save your file, and then make a copy of Table 3.9, move it to the right of Figure 3.11, and name it Table 3.10. One possible solution to this conundrum is to remove data no. 12, as it is more than 2.5 standardized residuals from the mean in the untransformed model, and at 2.20 standardized residuals in the transformed model, it is greater than 2.0 standardized residuals and close to the cutoff point of 2.5. Place your cursor in Row 14 and delete that row. Next, let's effect one more change and

Table 3.10

BIZCOMPS DATA

Data No.	SIC CODE #	Business Type	Annual Revenue	SDE	Sales Date	Selling Price	Price/AR	SDE/AR	Trend	Array Formula Output	Residual	Standardized Residual	Trans-formed X	Trans-formed Y	Predicted Y	Residual	Standardized Residual	Delete if X
													0.970979	1.1137661				2.5
1	2396	Silk Screen Printing	205	50	8/31/1993	82	0.40	0.24	89.56	89.56	-7.56	-0.424	0.25	0.360	90.14	-8.14	-0.46	
2	2396	Silk Screen Printing	248	33	8/13/1999	42	0.17	0.13	53.90	53.90	-11.90	-0.666	0.14	0.138	52.93	-10.93	-0.61	
3	2396	Silk Screen Printing	283	58	9/23/1998	112	0.40	0.20	101.80	101.80	10.20	0.571	0.21	0.356	102.61	9.39	0.53	
4	2396	Silk Screen Printing	299	89	9/30/1998	185	0.62	0.30	162.47	162.47	22.53	1.262	0.31	0.586	162.39	22.61	1.27	
5	2396	Silk Screen Printing	346	83	6/30/1994	126	0.36	0.24	148.41	148.41	-22.41	-1.255	0.25	0.325	149.41	-23.41	-1.32	
6	2396	Silk Screen Printing	350	122	12/7/2001	220	0.63	0.35	225.48	225.48	-5.48	-0.307	0.36	0.596	223.48	-3.48	-0.20	
7	2396	Silk Screen Printing	376	88	6/12/2001	179	0.48	0.23	156.93	156.93	22.07	1.237	0.24	0.438	158.06	20.94	1.18	
8	2396	Silk Screen Printing	379	78	10/22/2002	160	0.42	0.21	136.98	136.98	23.02	1.290	0.22	0.383	138.07	21.93	1.23	
9	2396	Silk Screen Printing	401	84	10/1/1998	145	0.36	0.21	147.85	147.85	-2.85	-0.159	0.22	0.322	149.03	-4.03	-0.23	
10	2396	Silk Screen Printing	403	53	5/31/2002	106	0.26	0.13	86.35	86.35	19.65	1.101	0.14	0.226	84.66	21.34	1.20	
11	2396	Silk Screen Printing	406	84	4/26/2002	138	0.34	0.21	147.61	147.61	-9.61	-0.539	0.22	0.301	148.80	-10.80	-0.61	
13	2396	Silk Screen Printing	416	65	9/12/2002	93	0.22	0.16	109.52	109.52	-16.52	-0.925	0.16	0.189	109.31	-16.31	-0.92	
15	2396	Silk Screen Printing	448	138	1/20/2000	233	0.52	0.31	252.64	252.64	-19.64	-1.100	0.32	0.483	252.10	-19.10	-1.07	
			400	45		Average	0.3987	0.113	70.637	70.637			0.120		67.343			
								0.225										

Statistics (Array Formula Output / Residual columns):

Mean	0.12
Std Dev	17.091
SEE	17.851
R^2	0.9057
COV	12.74%

Statistics (Predicted Y / Residual columns):

Mean	0.00
Std Dev	17.039
SEE	17.797
R^2	0.9061
COV	12.70%

SUMMARY OUPUT

Coefficient - SDE	1.981	-0.046	Coefficient - Intercept
Standard Error - SDE	0.225	0.053	Standard Error - Intercept
R Square	0.875	0.051	Standard Error
F stat	77.236	11	Residual df
Regression Sum of Squares	0.202	0.029	Residual Sum of Squares

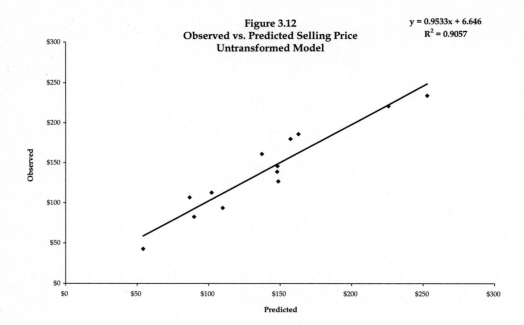

alter the constraint for cells P2:Q2 from <=1 to <=5, and run Solver twice more. Once again let's compare the results as shown in Table 3.10.

This time, the output metrics show the transformed model just barely outper-forming the untransformed model. Comparing Figures 3.12 and 3.13, it is hard to tell which has the better goodness-of-fit, though in Figure 3.13 the trendline passes

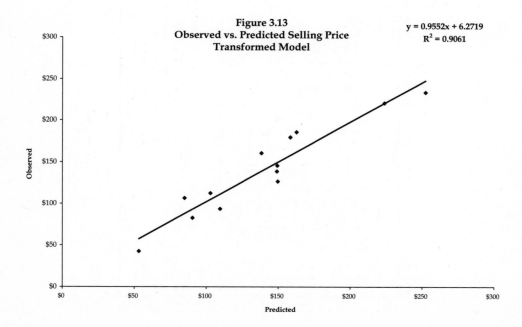

TABLE 3.11

Label	X Variable	Predicted Selling Price
AR—using the raw price to AR data from Table 3.10	$ 400	$158.958
SDE—using the transformed model from Table 3.8	$ 45	$ 68.194
Untransformed SDE/AR	.113	$ 70.637
Transformed SDE/AR	.120	$ 67.343

through the data point 223.48, 220, while in Figure 3.12 it just skims it. Typically transformations and outlier removal present greater differences in the output between transformed and untransformed models. The small difference in this case may be just because of the truncated nature and narrow range of variables of this particular data set that was created for ease of demonstration. Please do not rely on this example as a reason to not transform your data sets. In the authors' experience, 9 times out of 10, transforming the data set produces far superior results than what we see here.

In conclusion, we can see that using price/AR as a function of SDE/AR produces a more realistic value when sales are relatively high and profits are relatively low, as opposed to the use of either AR or SDE alone as the sole value driver. With this particular data set, after removing two data numbers as outliers, the value results are as shown in Table 3.11.

Table 3.11 indicates that the use of AR alone overvalues the subject company's assets by a considerable amount, and that the use of either SDE alone or in combination with AR as demonstrated in this case study produces a more realistic value.

Figure 3.14 presents a line chart comparing predicted selling prices estimated using the transformed price/revenue to SDE/revenue model with the observed

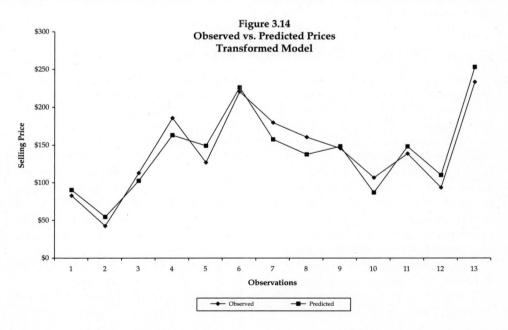

Figure 3.14
Observed vs. Predicted Prices
Transformed Model

TABLE 3.12

Residual Cutoff	Lowest COV	Number of Observations
2.0 Standard deviations	16.11%	90
2.5 Standard deviations	22.31%	118
3.0 Standard deviations	27.80%	128

selling prices. With an R^2 of .9061 and an SEE of 17.797 we should expect this close a fit between the two data sets.

One more relevant topic is the question: How small should one make the outlier cutoff? The authors consistently use 2.5 standard deviations, as experience has shown them that as we drop the cutoff to 2 standard deviations, thereby obtaining both lower SEEs and corresponding COVs, too many data points are given up to achieve this desired result.

The cutoff of 2.5 standardized residuals was chosen as a compromise between the textbook-recommended 3 and the Toby Tatum-suggested 2. One of the authors, starting with a data set of 137 observations, and using lowest COV and observation count as his metrics, ran a transforming model with three different cutoff figures and came up with the results shown in Table 3.12.

The decrease from 3 to 2.5 standard deviations results in a decrease in the COV of 24.6 percent, at a cost of an 8.4 percent decrease in the number of observations, for a ratio of 2.93 (24.6/8.4) to 1. On the other hand, a decrease from 3 to 2 standard deviations results in a decrease in the COV of 72 percent, at a cost of a 42 percent decrease in the number of observations, for a ratio of 1.71 (72/42) to 1. More than a third of the observations are given up to get that highly desirable low COV of 16.11 percent. We think that this is too high a price to pay and recommend a cutoff of 2.5 standard deviations.

What Are the Meaning and Function of the Regression Tool's Summary Output?

We now have the results of various regression models and have put them to use developing estimates of asset values for situations where the value of a business has been destroyed. There remain two items that need to be discussed. The first is the meaning and function of the RA summary output, and the second is what is known as "tests of residuals." Both of these items deal with the question of how well the model fits the data. While a poor-fitting model can convey useful information, such models will usually fail a Daubert test. Therefore, in the arena of lost profits we will want to present to the trier of fact RA models that can demonstrate goodness of fit. To this end, there are specific metrics included in the summary output that will further explicate the results of the model. For this explication we will be using as our demonstration model the summary output available through Excel's regression tool found in its Analysis ToolPak.

The summary output is discussed in three sections: regression statistics, ANOVA (ANalysis Of VAriance), and information concerning the intercept and slope coefficients. The regression statistics section illustrates the summary statistics of the regression equation that includes multiple R, R square, adjusted R square, standard error, and observations. The analysis of variance (ANOVA) section includes the analysis of variance considerations, including sum-of-squares, mean squares, the F-statistic, and F significance. The section concerning the regression coefficients deals with the statistical significance of and confidence intervals about those coefficients. Each part of the summary output is discussed and its applicability to the model's goodness-of-fit assignment duly articulated. Please note that the summary output that follows was derived from Table 3.8 by regressing selling price against SDE for the 14 remaining data points (nos. 1 to 13 and no. 15) and is now shown in Table 3.13. To aid your understanding, we display the summary output twice—once with numbers and a second time showing the formula or function that produces the output of a specific cell. Recognizing that there can be more than one formula for the output of any particular cell, we have chosen the simplest and easiest to understand.

Regression Statistics

Multiple R, or the coefficient of correlation, is equal to the correlation between the observed values of the dependent variable y (selling price) and the values of the independent variable x (SDE). It measures the strength of the linear relationship between the two variables. The value of multiple R lies between −1 and +1, and the closer your result is to −1 or +1, the stronger the relationship, be it negative or positive. As a result, large values of multiple R represent a greater correlation between SDE and selling price. For example, a multiple R value of 1 represents a model that is perfectly linear where all the points in a scatterplot lie on the trendline. In our example, shown in Table 3.13, multiple R is .899, which is very close to 1. This indicates that SDE and selling price are highly correlated. As a rule of thumb, coefficients of correlation that are below .70 are not useful in a valuation or lost profits setting. The Excel function for multiple R is CORREL(y,x). Multiple R can also be derived by taking the square root of R square.

R square, or the coefficient of determination, is a goodness-of-fit measure for a regression model that ranges between 0 and 1. R square is the proportion of variation in the y (dependent) variable) (selling price) that is explained by changes in the variation of the x (independent) variable (SDE). The value of .808 suggests that 80.8 percent of the selling price of a business's fixed and intangible assets can be explained by the variation in the independent variable SDE, or seller's discretionary earnings. The remaining 19.2 percent is presumed to be a combination of random variation in the data and the effect of independent variables that are missing from the model. As a rule of thumb, coefficients of determination that are less than .50 are not useful in a valuation or lost profits setting. The Excel function for R square is RSQ(y,x). It can also be derived by squaring multiple R.

Since the addition of extra x variables into the regression equation has the result of making R square larger, adjusted R square has been introduced to penalize those models that have extra x variables that have no additional explanatory value. In a model with only one x variable, it conveys no useful information. However, in multiple regression analysis, if the addition of a new x variable does not increase adjusted R square, then that variable should not be included in the model unless its t statistic is greater than 1.0. There is no Excel function for adjusted R square.

Table 3.13
BIZCOMPS DATA

		X	Y				
				Predicted	Example - Row 6 82 - 90.768 = -8.768	Example - Row 6 50² = 2,500	Example - Row 6 (50 - 79.50)² = 870.25
	Data No.	SDE	Observed Selling Price	Selling Price	Residuals	Sum-of-Squares X	Deviations Squared X
6	1	50	82	90.768	-8.768	2,500.00	870.25
7	2	33	42	58.651	-16.651	1,089.00	2,162.25
8	3	58	112	105.882	6.118	3,364.00	462.25
9	4	89	185	164.448	20.552	7,921.00	90.25
10	5	83	126	153.112	-27.112	6,889.00	12.25
11	6	122	220	226.792	-6.792	14,884.00	1,806.25
12	7	88	179	162.558	16.442	7,744.00	72.25
13	8	78	160	143.666	16.334	6,084.00	2.25
14	9	84	145	155.002	-10.002	7,056.00	20.25
15	10	53	106	96.436	9.564	2,809.00	702.25
16	11	84	138	155.002	-17.002	7,056.00	20.25
17	12	88	230	162.558	67.442	7,744.00	72.25
18	13	65	93	119.106	-26.106	4,225.00	210.25
19	15	138	233	257.020	-24.020	19,044.00	3,422.25
20							
21	Average	79.50	146.50				
22	Standard Deviation	27.63	58.08				
23	SUMSQ	98,409.00				98,409.00	
24	DEVSQ	9,925.50					9,925.50

SUMMARY OUTPUT

	Regression Statistics
Multiple R	0.899
R Square	0.808
Adjusted R Square	0.792
Standard Error	26.489
Observations	14

70

35	ANOVA					
36		df	SS	MS	F	Significance F
37	Regression	1	35425.797	35425.797	50.490	0.000
38	Residual	12	8419.703	701.642		
39	Total	13	43845.500			
40						

41		Coefficients	Standard Error	t Stat	P-value	Lower 95%	Upper 95%
42	Intercept	-3.693	22.291	-0.166	0.871	-52.262	44.875
43	SDE	1.889	0.266	7.106	0.000	1.310	2.469
44							

SUMMARY OUTPUT WITH FUNCTIONS OR FORMULAS FOR SIMPLE LINEAR REGRESSION

45		
46		
47	Regression Statistics	
48	Multiple R	=CORREL(D6:D19,C6:C19)
49	R Square	=RSQ(D6:D19,C6:C19)
50	Adjusted R Square	=1-(E38/(D39/C39))
51	Standard Error	=STEYX(D6:D19,C6:C19)
52	Observations	=COUNT(C6:C19)
53		

54	ANOVA					
55		df	SS	MS	F	Significance F
56	Regression	=COUNT(C43)	=DEVSQ(E6:E19)	=D37/C37	=E37/E38	=FDIST(F37,C37,C38)
57	Residual	=COUNT(D6:D19)-COUNT(C42:C43)	=SUMSQ(F6:F19)	=D38/C38		
58	Total	=SUM(C37:C38)	=DEVSQ(D6:D19)			
59						

60		Coefficients	Standard Error	t Stat	P-value	Lower 95%	Upper 95%
61	Intercept	=INTERCEPT(D6:D19,C6:C19)	=SQRT((C23)/(C33*C24))*C32	=C42/D42	=TDIST(ABS(E42),C38,2)	=C42-(TINV(0.05,C38)*D42)	=C42+(TINV(0.05,C38)*D42)
62	SDE	=SLOPE(D6:D19,C6:C19)	=C32/SQRT(C24)	=C43/D43	=TDIST(ABS(E43),C38,2)	=C43-(TINV(0.05,C38)*D43)	=C43+(TINV(0.05,C38)*D43)
63							

The standard error (of the estimate), also known as root mean square error, provides an estimate of the distribution of the prediction errors when predicting y values from x values in the regression model. In other words, the standard error of the estimate (SEE) measures the size of a typical deviation of an observed value from the regression line. Think of the standard error as a way of averaging the size of the deviations from the regression line. The larger the value, the less well the regression model fits the data, and therefore the model will not be as good at predicting the outcome as a lower standard error model. It has been said that for a successful regression model, the SEE should be considerably smaller than the standard deviation of the dependent variable. In other words, the observations should vary less about the regression line than about the mean. The standard deviation of the dependent variable, selling price, is 58.08 as shown in cell D22 in Table 3.13. Since the standard error for our regression model is 26.49, as shown in cell C32, it is fair to state that the regression model is much better at predicting selling prices based on SDE than is the average of y. The standard error can also be used to calculate the coefficient of variation (COV), which is the standard error divided by the average of y (the dependent variable). In this case the average selling price is 146.50 (cell D21, Table 3.13) making the COV 18.08 percent, an excellent outcome when using the Bizcomps database as COVs as high as 25 to 30 percent are very common. The SEE can also be used like any other standard error to create confidence intervals about the predicted value. For example, as seen in Table 3.8, with an SDE of 81 we can say that 95 times out of 100 the model produces normally distributed asset selling prices between 149.334 − (2*26.489), or 43.37 and 149.334 + (2*26.489), or 255.29. That is, while the average or expected selling price is 149.334, there is a 2.5 percent probability that the selling price would be less than 43.37 or greater than 255.29. This is just an approximate range as there are more precise formulas to calculate confidence and prediction intervals based on the value of the x variable and the number of observations in the data set.

The observation value is the size of the sample used in the regression. In this case, the regression is based on the values from 14 market transactions.

The ANOVA table tells us if the overall regression model results in a significantly acceptable level of predictability for the outcome (dependent) variable by analyzing the variability of the selling prices. Total variability, the sum of the squared deviations between each observed selling price and the average of all selling prices, is divided into two parts: The first is the variability due to the regression line, and the second is the difference between the observed and predicted selling prices. This is shown in the summary table by use of the various sums of squares (SS). Let's go through each of them.

First, let's begin with df, the degrees of freedom column. Basically, degrees of freedom represents the number of observations that are not constrained by having to calculate a parameter. There are 13 in total in cell C39, as one degree of freedom is used to calculate the average of the y variable. There are only 12 degrees of freedom for residual SS as 2 are needed to calculate the slope and the intercept. Regression SS has only 1 degree of freedom that represents the number of x variables present in the model.

As a strategy for predicting an outcome, for lack of a better estimate, one may choose to use the mean as a fairly good guess. Substituting the mean as a model, we can calculate the difference between the observed values and those values predicted by the mean.

The Regression row of the SS column refers to differences between the mean value of the outcome (dependent) variable y and the regression line. If this value is large relative to residual SS, then the regression model is different from the mean, which is our best guess as to the outcome. On the other hand, if this number is small relative to residual SS, than using the regression model is not much better than using the mean as an estimate. Excel's DEVSQ() function applied to the predicted y values produces regression SS.

The Residual row of the SS column accounts for the differences between the observed data and the regression line, or predicted selling prices. Since most observed values will not sit on the trendline, this value represents the degree of error when the regression model is fitted to the data. A low number here relative to regression SS indicates a model that fits the data well. Excel's SUMSQ() function applied to the residuals produces residual SS.

The Total row represents the sum of squared differences of all the observed data points about the mean. It imparts no information by itself, but serves as a preliminary value that gets broken down into its constituent parts—regression SS and residual SS, from which additional information can be obtained. Excel's DEVSQ() function applied to the observed Y values produces total SS.

The first use of the SS numbers is to calculate R square by dividing regression SS by total SS ($35,425.797/43,845.500 = .808$). As we already know, R square is the proportion of variation in the y (dependent) variable that is explained by the variation in the x (independent) variable. Regression SS/total SS suggests that if the model was a perfect predictor of y, then regression SS would equal total SS and therefore R square would be 1. Put another way, if the degree of variability in observed y and predicted y were the same, then there would be no residual SS, all the data points would lie on the trendline, and multiple R and R squared would be 1.

The next column over is denoted as MS, which stands for the mean sum of squares for regression and residual, which are easily calculated by dividing the SS numbers by the degrees of freedom (df) column. The practical use for these numbers is to calculate the F-ratio. In the ANOVA table there is a column for the F-statistic, which is a measure of how much the model has improved our ability to predict the outcome compared to just using the mean of the dependent variable as a predictor. The calculation is regression MS/residual MS. If the model provides a good overall fit, we would expect the improvement in the prediction due to the model to be large. That is, the regression MS would be large and the difference between the model and observed data would be small (residual MS). As a result, a good model should have a large F-ratio (greater than 1). In addition, the significance of the F-ratio is assessed using critical values (p-values). The p-value, or significance F, tells us the probability of finding an F statistic as large as 50.490 if there was no linear relationship between x and y. With a probability of zero, we have to conclude that the outcome of the model and the relationship between x and y is not due to mere chance. In our model, the F-ratio is statistically significant, that is, not a chance outcome, as the significance F number in cell G37 is much less than .05. However, in a model with a single x coefficient (SDE in this case), F and significance F are redundant just like adjusted R square, as the t-statistic is the square root of F (or, in reverse, $7.106^2 = 50.490$). The p-value for the F-statistic is computed using Excel's FDIST function, where x is the F-statistic, and degrees of freedom are 1 for regression and 12 for residual.

Just as R square can be derived from the ANOVA table, so can the standard error be computed by simply taking the square root of residual MS (or, in reverse, $26.489^2 = 701.642$).

The next section of the Summary Output is that dealing with the intercept and slope coefficients. These two numbers represent the point of interception on the Y-axis and the slope of the least squares regression line, respectively. With these coefficients our regression equation becomes:

$$y = 1.889x - 3.693$$

The balance of the coefficient section informs us if the intercept and the slope of the regression line are different from zero, and therefore whether or not we have a statistically significant regression model. To do this we need a standard error for each coefficient in order to calculate a test statistic for each. The formula for the intercept's standard error is:

$$SQRT((SUMSQ(x)/(COUNT(x)*DEVSQ(x))*STEYX(y,x))$$

The formula for the slope's standard error is:

$$STEYX(y,x)/SQRT(DEVSQ(x))$$

Now let's assess the individual predictor (independent) variable, SDE. The t-statistic measures the number of standard deviations from zero that the SDE coefficient is, computed by dividing the coefficient by its standard error. The t-statistic tests the null hypothesis that the value of this variable is zero. If the variable has a significant t-Stat and p-value (greater than 2 and less than .05, respectively) we would accept that the value is significantly different from zero, and therefore the independent variable contributes significantly to our ability to predict the selling price for any particular business. In our case, SDE is statistically significant, as its p-value is less than .05 and its t-statistic is greater than 2. So, it is safe to say that SDE contributes significantly to our model, that is, it is significantly greater than zero, and therefore the model is a better predictor of value than the average selling price of the 14 businesses in our database. Excel's function for computing p-values is TDIST, where x is the absolute value of the t-statistic, deg_freedom is residual degrees of freedom, and tails equals 2 in the appropriate input sections of the function dialogue box.

Just a quick note on the intercept. A t-statistic of −.166 (less than 2.0) and a p-value greater than .05 (p = .871) indicate that the intercept does not differ from zero, and therefore the regression line goes through the origin (the point where the X and Y axes meet). The interpretation of the intercept is less important than that of the x variable. It is literally the predicted selling price when there is no SDE. However, none of the observations in our 14-market transaction sample had an SDE of zero. Therefore, in a situation like this, where the range of independent variables does not include zero, it is best to think of the intercept term as an "anchor" for the regression line such that it bisects the point on the scatterplot where the average of the independent variable intersects the average of the dependent variable. This regression line allows us to predict selling prices for the range of observed SDE values.

The standard error computed above is a measure of how precise an estimator the sample average is of the population average—the smaller the standard error is relative to the coefficient value, the narrower the prediction interval will be. We can use this concept to explain the lower 95 percent and upper 95 percent limits, which are the remaining items in the summary output. These lower and upper limits allow us to report with 95 percent confidence that for each $1 increase in SDE, the selling price of any particular business increases between $1.310 and $2.469. As can be deduced from the slope's standard error formula, this interval can be narrowed by increasing the number of observations and/or extending the range of the x variable. However, while this might be possible in an academic research setting, in the valuation and lost profits venues the sample size and the range of the x variable are usually fixed by the given situation.

Tests and Analysis of Residuals

Quantitative models always rest on assumptions about the way the world works, and regression models are no exception. There are five principal assumptions that justify the use of linear regression models for purposes of prediction:

1. The relationship between the independent (x) variable and the dependent (y) variable is linear; that is, the straight-line model is correct.
2. The residuals (error terms) are normally distributed with zero mean.
3. The residuals have a constant variance; that is, they are homoscedastic.
4. The successive residuals are independent of each other; that is, there is no auto- or serial correlation.
5. The x values are fixed and are not correlated with the error terms.

If the regression equation includes more than one independent variable, then an additional assumption is made:

6. The x variables are not linearly correlated; that is, there is no multicollinearity.

If any of these assumptions are violated (i.e., if there is nonlinearity, serial correlation, heteroscedasticity, and/or non-normality), then the forecasts, confidence intervals, and economic insights yielded by a regression model may be (at best) inefficient or (at worst) seriously biased or misleading. Therefore, whenever regression is used to fit a line to data, these assumptions should be tested. Fortunately, these assumptions do not need to be perfectly satisfied as regression is robust to minor violations.

One thing to keep in mind, though, is that a regression model with significant t-statistics, a low SEE, and a high R^2 is not proof that these assumptions have not been violated. Therefore, you need to go through a series of diagnostic tests to verify that your data is in accord with these assumptions. To demonstrate some of the diagnostic tests that are available to the analyst, let's use the 13 sales transactions shown in Table 3.14. Each of the six assumptions has more than one, and for some of the assumptions, many more tests than we will be discussing and demonstrating here. To explore those additional tests either consult a statistical textbook or perform an Internet search for each of the assumptions.

Table 3.14
Setup Worksheet for Testing Regression Assumptions

Observation	Annual Revenue	SDE	Observed Selling Price	LINEST Array Output		Predicted Selling Price	Residuals	Standardized Residuals	Sorted Residuals	Normal Probability	Absolute Standardized Residuals
1	205	50	82	1.827	-3.938	87.388	5.388	0.303	-26.377	-29.768	0.303
2	248	33	42	0.179	14.974	56.337	14.337	0.806	-22.203	-20.674	0.806
3	283	58	112	0.904	17.794	102.001	-9.999	-0.562	-21.469	-15.096	0.562
4	299	89	185	103.767	11	158.623	-26.377	-1.482	-13.132	-10.712	1.482
5	346	83	126	32854.16455	3482.759	147.664	21.664	1.218	-9.999	-6.902	1.218
6	350	122	220			218.899	-1.101	-0.062	-1.101	-3.387	0.062
7	376	88	179			156.797	-22.203	-1.248	4.491	0.000	1.248
8	379	78	160			138.531	-21.469	-1.207	5.388	3.387	1.207
9	401	84	145			149.491	4.491	0.252	11.491	6.902	0.252
10	403	53	106			92.868	-13.132	-0.738	14.337	10.712	0.738
11	406	84	138			149.491	11.491	0.646	15.123	15.096	0.646
12	416	65	93			114.786	21.786	1.224	21.664	20.674	1.224
13	448	138	233			248.123	15.123	0.850	21.786	29.768	0.850

76

Testing the Linearity Assumption

To test the linearity assumption we have created two scatterplots in Figure 3.15. The top charts plots the observed selling prices on the Y axis and the associated SDE on the X axis. The relationship between x and y appears to be linear, except for the two data points in the upper right-hand corner. There appears to be some curvature to the plot at that point, indicating that a linear model might not be appropriate for

Figure 3.15
Testing the Linearity Assumption

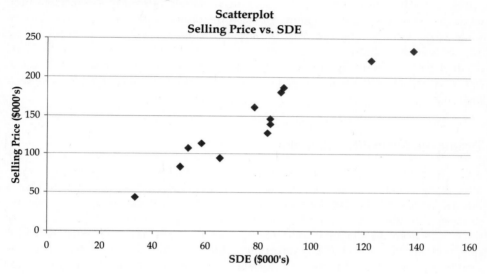

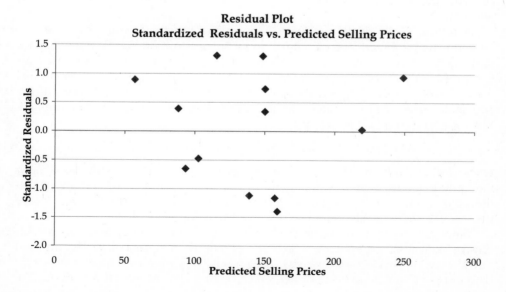

the data. Further testing using Excel's chart trendline function reveals that a second-degree polynomial model fits the data only slightly better than the linear model (R^2 of .9162 vs. .9042), so it is probably safe to assume that the linearity assumption has not been severely violated. In addition, the separately calculated (not shown) P-value of the second-degree term, SDE^2, is .257, indicating its nonstatistical significance and giving further support to the notion that the model conforms to the linearity assumption.

A second test of the linearity assumption is to plot the standardized residuals against the predicted selling prices. The advantage of using standardized residuals over residuals is that we can quickly see if there are any outliers present, for example, residuals greater than, say, 3 standard deviations. If the relationship between selling prices and SDE is linear, then a random pattern should appear in the residual plot, which is the bottom chart in Figure 3.15. On the other hand, if we see curvature or some other systematic pattern, then we should change our model to incorporate the nonlinear relationship. We believe that it is valid to conclude that the standardized residual plot is essentially random, so no additional modeling is required. Because our sample size is so small (13 observations), it can be difficult to detect nonlinear patterns.

Testing the Normality Assumption

A simple test for normally distributed errors is a normal probability plot of the residuals. As we demonstrated in Case Study1, this is a plot of the residuals against a normal distribution having the same mean and variance. If the residuals are normal, the points on this plot should fall close to the trendline. A bow-shaped pattern of deviations from the diagonal indicates that the residuals have excessive skewness (i.e., they are not symmetrically distributed, with too many large errors in the same direction). An S-shaped pattern of deviations indicates that the residuals have excessive kurtosis—that is, there are either too many or two few large errors in both directions.

A normal p-plot of the residuals is shown in Figure 3.16, and they appear to be normally distributed, even if there is some bowing. A more formal test, Filliben's Probability Plot Correlation Test for Normality, is also shown in Figure 3.16. This test measures the correlation coefficient between the residuals and their normal correspondents against a predetermined metric with 95 percent confidence. If the correlation coefficient is greater than the test statistic, then normality is presumed. The formula in cell D47 is as follows:

$$=1.0063-0.1288/SQRT(B47)-0.6118/B47+1.3505/B47^2$$

where B47 is the number of observations. Cells D49 and D51 are calculated using the CORREL function and by taking the square root of the R^2 (.9435) displayed on the normal p-plot shown in Figure 3.16, respectively. In this circumstance, where case = .971 and is greater than r = .932, we can assume normality.

Since our p-plot indicates some bowing and S-shape, we should test for excessive skewness and kurtosis, which would indicate non-normality. The function SKEW in cell G29 is SKEW(residuals). The formula for a rough estimate of SES (standard errors of skewness) (after Brown) in cell G30 is = SQRT(6/COUNT(residuals)).

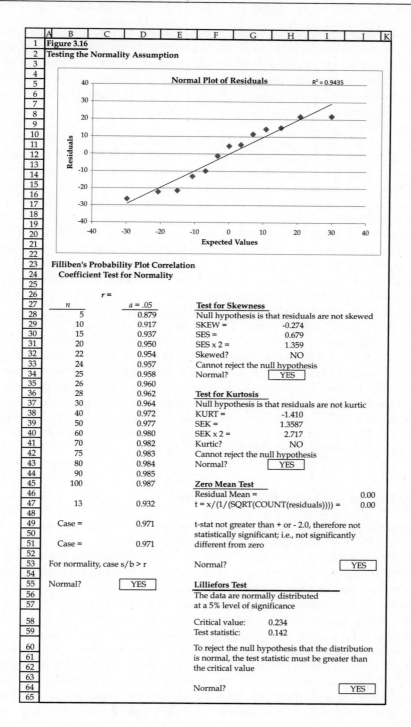

	A	B	C	D	E	F	G	H	I	J	K
1		Figure 3.16									
2		Testing the Normality Assumption									
3											

Normal Plot of Residuals $R^2 = 0.9435$

Residuals / Expected Values

Filliben's Probability Plot Correlation Coefficient Test for Normality

$r =$

n	$a = .05$	
5	0.879	**Test for Skewness**
10	0.917	Null hypothesis is that residuals are not skewed
15	0.937	SKEW = −0.274
20	0.950	SES = 0.679
22	0.954	SES x 2 = 1.359
24	0.957	Skewed? NO
25	0.958	Cannot reject the null hypothesis
26	0.960	Normal? YES
28	0.962	
30	0.964	**Test for Kurtosis**
40	0.972	Null hypothesis is that residuals are not kurtic
50	0.977	KURT = −1.410
60	0.980	SEK = 1.3587
70	0.982	SEK x 2 = 2.717
75	0.983	Kurtic? NO
80	0.984	Cannot reject the null hypothesis
90	0.985	Normal? YES
100	0.987	
		Zero Mean Test
		Residual Mean = 0.00
13	0.932	t = x/(1/(SQRT(COUNT(residuals)))) = 0.00

Case =   0.971   t-stat not greater than + or − 2.0, therefore not
statistically significant; i.e., not significantly
Case =   0.971   different from zero

For normality, case s/b > r   Normal?   YES

Normal?   YES   **Lilliefors Test**
The data are normally distributed
at a 5% level of significance

Critical value: 0.234
Test statistic: 0.142

To reject the null hypothesis that the distribution
is normal, the test statistic must be greater than
the critical value

Normal?   YES

In this case, since the absolute value of SKEW is less than SES × 2, our residuals are not skewed. Another way to state the results of this test is to say, with approximately 95 percent confidence, that the skewness statistic might fall between −1.359 and + 1.359. In this instant case, as the skewness statistic is −.274, we can assume that the skewness is within the expected range of random fluctuations in that statistic and therefore it indicates that the distribution of residuals has no significant skewness problem.

The function KURT in cell G38 is KURT(residuals). The formula for a rough estimate of SEK (standard errors of kurtosis) (after Brown) in cell G39 is SQRT(24/COUNT(residuals)). In this case, since the absolute value of KURT is less than SEK × 2, our residuals are not kurtic. Another way to state the results of this test is to say, with approximately 95 percent confidence, that the kurtosis statistic might fall between −2.717 and + 2.717. In this instant case, as the kurtosis statistic is −1.410, we can assume that the kurtosis is within the expected range of random fluctuations in that statistic and therefore it indicates that the distribution of residuals has no significant kurtosis problem.

Another test for normality can be found in Gerry's Stats Tools. This is a Lilliefors test, and its output, shown in Figure 3.16, indicates that the residuals are normally distributed, as the test statistic is less than the critical value of t.

The final clause of the normality assumption is that the residuals have a mean or average that equals zero. We can investigate the mean of the residuals by taking a simple average of the 13 residuals (AVERAGE(Residuals)) = .000000. While this number appears to be zero, it is not exactly zero. This raises the question: Is it statistically significantly different from zero? To answer this question we need to create a t-statistic. Following Rogalski and Vinso, we develop the following: $t = X/(1/SQRT(COUNT(residuals)))$ where t is the t-statistic and X is the mean of the residuals. In Figure 3.16 we solve for t and find that it is less 2.0, demonstrating that the mean is not statistically significantly different from zero.

Testing the Constant Variance Assumption

This assumption concerns variation about the population regression line. Specifically, it states that the variation of the y's about the regression line is the same, regardless of the values of the x's. A technical term for this property is homoscedasticity, or constant error variance, and the lack of this property is called heteroscedasticity, or nonconstant error variance. In our instant case, constant error variance implies that variation in selling price is the same regardless of the value of SDE.

The easiest way to detect nonconstant error variance is through a visual inspection of a scatterplot of the absolute standardized residuals versus selling price to see if the residuals exhibit a funnel shape, indicating that the variance gets larger as selling price increases. The scatterplot in Figure 3.17 shows random scatter, and it lacks a funnel shape. Since we are using absolute values of the residuals, we can draw a trendline on the scatterplot and look for an upward slope that would designate an ever-increasing variance, or heteroscedasticity. Here the trendline appears to be almost flat, denoting homoscedasticity.

If the informal visual test provided by the scatterplot is inconclusive, we can perform a more formal test by regressing the absolute standardized residual against

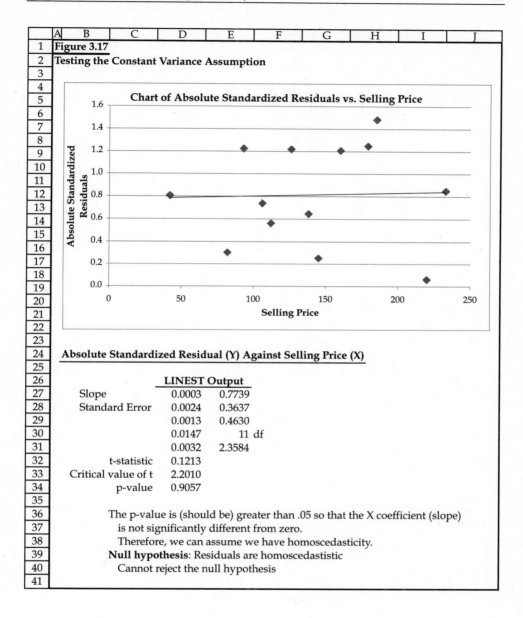

Figure 3.17
Testing the Constant Variance Assumption

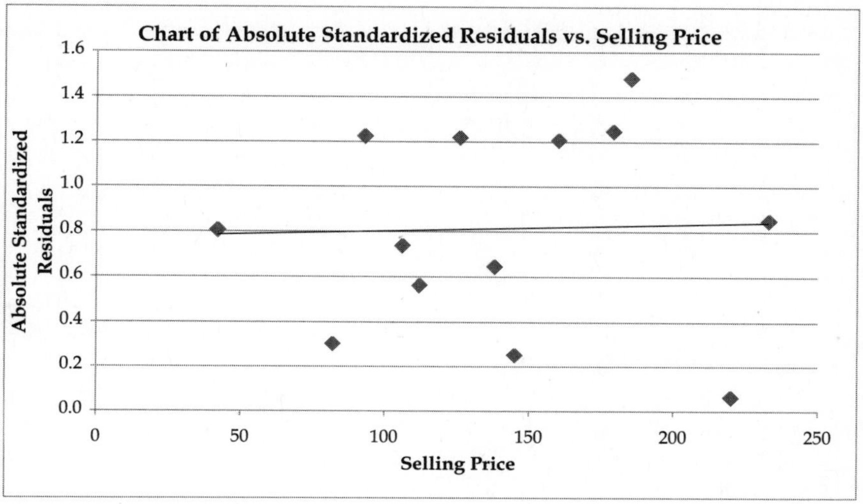

Absolute Standardized Residual (Y) Against Selling Price (X)

	LINEST Output	
Slope	0.0003	0.7739
Standard Error	0.0024	0.3637
	0.0013	0.4630
	0.0147	11 df
	0.0032	2.3584
t-statistic	0.1213	
Critical value of t	2.2010	
p-value	0.9057	

The p-value is (should be) greater than .05 so that the X coefficient (slope) is not significantly different from zero.
Therefore, we can assume we have homoscedasticity.
Null hypothesis: Residuals are homoscedastistic
Cannot reject the null hypothesis

selling price (after Glejser)[1]. If the slope coefficient is not statistically different from zero, then we have constant error variance. If, however, the slope coefficient is statistically different from zero, then we have nonconstant error variance. Therefore, we need to test for the significance of the slope coefficient.

In the bottom half of Figure 3.18 we show the output of Excel's LINEST array function. For the slope coefficient we specify the t-statistic in cell D32 as .1213 (.0003/.0024), the critical value of t at 95 percent confidence in cell D33 as 2.2010 (TINV(.05,11)) and the p-value of the t-statistic in cell D34 as .9057 (TDIST(.1213,11,2)). Since the critical value of t (2.2010) is greater than the t-statistic

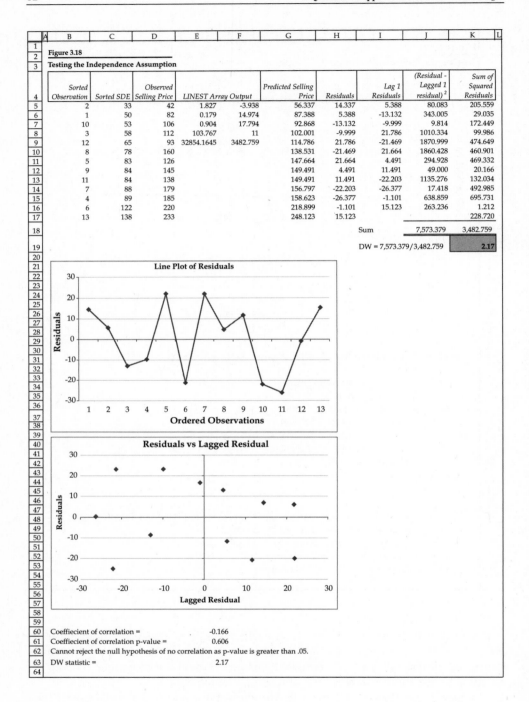

Figure 3.18

Testing the Independence Assumption

Sorted Observation	Sorted SDE	Observed Selling Price	LINEST Array Output		Predicted Selling Price	Residuals	Lag 1 Residuals	(Residual - Lagged 1 residual)^2	Sum of Squared Residuals
2	33	42	1.827	-3.938	56.337	14.337	5.388	80.083	205.559
1	50	82	0.179	14.974	87.388	5.388	-13.132	343.005	29.035
10	53	106	0.904	17.794	92.868	-13.132	-9.999	9.814	172.449
3	58	112	103.767	11	102.001	-9.999	21.786	1010.334	99.986
12	65	93	32854.1645	3482.759	114.786	21.786	-21.469	1870.999	474.649
8	78	160			138.531	-21.469	21.664	1860.428	460.901
5	83	126			147.664	21.664	4.491	294.928	469.332
9	84	145			149.491	4.491	11.491	49.000	20.166
11	84	138			149.491	11.491	-22.203	1135.276	132.034
7	88	179			156.797	-22.203	-26.377	17.418	492.985
4	89	185			158.623	-26.377	-1.101	638.859	695.731
6	122	220			218.899	-1.101	15.123	263.236	1.212
13	138	233			248.123	15.123			228.720
							Sum	7,573.379	3,482.759
							DW = 7,573.379 / 3,482.759		2.17

Coeffiecient of correlation =   -0.166
Coeffiecient of correlation p-value =   0.606
Cannot reject the null hypothesis of no correlation as p-value is greater than .05.
DW statistic =   2.17

(.1213) and the p-value is greater than .05, then the slope coefficient is not statistically significantly different from zero. Therefore, we can assume that we have constant error variance.

Testing the Independence Assumption

This assumption requires that the residuals be independent of each other. What this means is that information about some of the residuals provides no information about other residuals. For example, if we know that selling prices for the first four transactions are all above the regression line (positive residuals), we cannot infer anything about the residual for transaction 5 if the independence assumption holds.

For cross-sectional data such as selling prices and SDE, there is little reason to doubt the validity of the independence assumption unless the observations are ordered in some particular way, such as from smallest SDE to largest SDE. For cross-sectional data we take the independence assumption for granted. However, for time-series data, the independence assumption is often violated. This is because of a property called serial or autocorrelation. We present a number of ways to detect this property.

Since selling price and SDE are cross-sectional data and not likely to produce residuals that are autocorrelated, in Figure 3.18 we attempt to force the issue and induce autocorrelation by ordering SDE from smallest to largest value and then running the LINEST array function. We then calculate predicted selling prices and the accompanying residuals.

Our first test of the independence assumption involves a simple line chart of the residuals. If there is autocorrelation we would expect to see a large value followed by a small value, or large and small values could be grouped together rather than being randomly dispersed. An examination of the line chart in Figure 3.18 indicates that neither of these qualities is present.

The second test of the independence assumption is to plot one residual against its succeeding residual. If there is a trend in the data indicating that the previous residual has an effect on the succeeding residual, the plot slopes either upward to the right or downward. As with the line plot, there is no discernable pattern in the second plot in Figure 3.18.

A more formal test of the independence assumption is to correlate the residuals with the lag 1 residual and challenge the null hypothesis that the data are not correlated. In cell F60, we enter the formula =CORREL(H5:H16,I5:I16), which produces a value of −.166. While on a scale of −1 to +1 this is a small value, we need to test that it is not statistically significant at the 5 percent level. For this test we use the StatPlus function CORRELP(H5:H16, I5:I16), whose output in cell F61 is in the amount of .606. Since this is greater than .05, we cannot reject the null hypothesis of no correlation, and we can presume that the independence assumption is not violated.

Our final test of the assumption of independence is the Durbin-Watson (DW) test statistic. This formal test is the ratio between the sum of the squared differences between each residual and its lag 1, and the sum of the squared residuals. If the ratio is approximately close to either 0 or 4, we can assume that the residuals are not independent. A DW value near 2 implies independence, while values in between are inconclusive. This test statistic is also available in StatPlus, DW(H5:H17), and its output is shown in cell F63 in Figure 3.18 in the amount of 2.17, the same value shown in cell K19.

Two additional tests of the independence assumption are available in StatPlus. They are the ACF plot with its attendant statistics and the runs test. We encourage those readers that have StatPlus to employ these tests on their own. In any case, we will explore their use in a later case study.

Testing the No Errors-in-Variables Assumption

This assumption means that the x variable is nonstochastic, that is, x is fixed, it is not correlated with the residuals, and therefore x is truly independent. Independent in this context means that x is measured without error—hence the term "no errors-in-variables." One way to test this assumption is to review the correlation coefficient for the two variables, the x's and the residuals. Cell G19 in Table 3.15 shows the correlation coefficient. Using the test statistic developed for the zero mean test, we find that t = 0, as shown in cell G20 in Table 3.15. Since this result is not greater than ± 2.0, we can assume that there is no correlation. We test this conclusion with the StatPlus function CORRELP(D5:D17,C5:C17) and obtain the result 1.0 in cell G24. Since this is greater than .05, we again conclude that there is no correlation.

Final confirmation of no correlation is acquired by regressing the residuals against SDE using Excel's LINEST array function. The output, shown in cells D26:E33 in Table 3.15, shows slope and intercept coefficients of zero with t-statistics of zero, considerably less than ± 2.0. Therefore, we can conclude that there is no relationship between the residuals and the independent variable.

Testing the No Multicollinearity Assumption

When constructing a regression model, we want to include independent variables that have a high correlation with the dependent variable. At the same time, we want to exclude independent variables that are highly correlated with each other. For example, suppose we used SDE to predict selling price. Since it is reasonable to expect that as SDE increases, selling price increases, we should expect these variables to be highly correlated. Suppose we add a second independent variable to the model, annual revenue. Since SDE and annual revenue are supposed to be independent, but aren't (typically, as one increases, so does the other), we run into a problem. This problem is called multicollinearity.

Multicollinearity wreaks havoc with the regression algebra. It can make variables that are positively correlated with the dependent variable look as if they are negatively correlated and vice versa, thereby causing the coefficients to change signs. It can foul up the individual P-values, thus making it impossible to determine which variables are significant and which ones aren't.

Consider the Bizcomps data we have used throughout this case study to determine the impact of annual revenue and SDE on selling price, the dependent variable. Before developing the estimated regression model, let's create two scatterplots, one

	A	B	C	D	E	F	G	H	I	J
1					Table 3.15					
2	Testing the No Errors-in-Variables Assumption									
3										
4			*SDE*	*Residuals*						
5			50	5.39						
6			33	14.34						
7			58	-10.00						
8			89	-26.38						
9			83	21.66						
10			122	-1.10						
11			88	-22.20						
12			78	-21.47						
13			84	4.49						
14			53	-13.13						
15			84	11.49						
16			65	21.79						
17			138	15.12						
18										
19			Coefficient of Correlation =				-2.718E-16			
20			t = x/(1/(SQRT(COUNT(residuals)))) =				-9.799E-16			
21			t-stat not greater than + or - 2.0, therefore not							
22			statistically significant; i.e., not significantly							
23			different from zero							
24			p-value =				1.000			
25			p-value greater than .05, therefore the realtionship							
26			between SDE and the residuals is not statistically different							
27			from zero.							
28										
29				(0.0000000)	0.0000000					
30				0.179307355	14.9742907					
31				0.00000	17.7936621					
32				0.00000	11					
33				0.00000	3482.75853					
34			t-stat	0.00000	0.00000					
35			Both the constant and slope coefficients are equal to zero, with t-stats less than 2.0,							
36			indicating no relationship between the residuals and the independent variable.							
37										

for each predictor variable against selling price. The two charts at the top of Figure 3.19 indicate that for this specific sample, both annual revenue and SDE are positively related to sales, which is consistent with logic and valuation theory.

However, the highly significant (R^2 and F are large and the coefficient of variation is low) regression model shown here and in Figure 3.19 defies both logic and the two scatterplots:

$$y = 4.912 - .037 \times \text{Annual revenue} + 1.879 \times \text{SDE}$$

where y is the predicted selling price.

This model tells us that as SDE increases by $1,000, selling price increases by $1,879. That is consistent with the SDE scatterplot in Figure 3.19. However, the model also tells us that for each $1,000 of annual revenue, selling price decreases

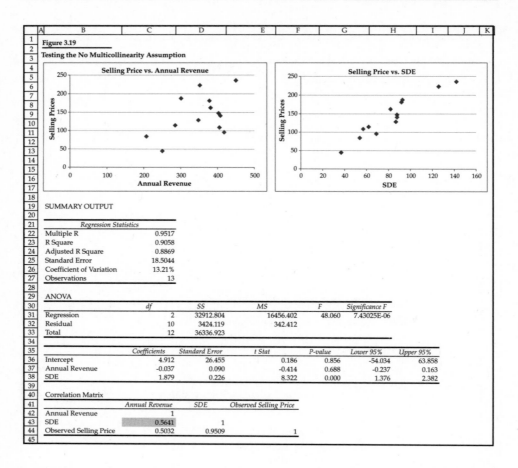

Figure 3.19

Testing the No Multicollinearity Assumption

SUMMARY OUTPUT

Regression Statistics	
Multiple R	0.9517
R Square	0.9058
Adjusted R Square	0.8869
Standard Error	18.5044
Coefficient of Variation	13.21%
Observations	13

ANOVA

	df	SS	MS	F	Significance F
Regression	2	32912.804	16456.402	48.060	7.43025E-06
Residual	10	3424.119	342.412		
Total	12	36336.923			

	Coefficients	Standard Error	t Stat	P-value	Lower 95%	Upper 95%
Intercept	4.912	26.455	0.186	0.856	-54.034	63.858
Annual Revenue	-0.037	0.090	-0.414	0.688	-0.237	0.163
SDE	1.879	0.226	8.322	0.000	1.376	2.382

Correlation Matrix

	Annual Revenue	SDE	Observed Selling Price
Annual Revenue	1		
SDE	0.5641	1	
Observed Selling Price	0.5032	0.9509	1

by about $37. That simply doesn't make any sense. The amount of annual revenue cannot be negatively related to selling price! It defies the annual revenue scatterplot in Figure 3.19 and logic. What is happening here is the effect of multicollinearity.

We can assess multicollinearity by computing a correlation matrix using Excel's Correlation tool in the Analysis Toolpak. Let's examine the correlation matrix shown in Figure 3.19. The bottom row indicates the correlation of each predictor variable with the dependent variable. The two correlation coefficients indicate that for this specific sample the SDE predictor variable is strongly and positively related to selling price, while the annual revenue predictor variable is more weakly related to selling price, but still positively so. This result agrees with the two scatterplots at the top of Figure 3.19. The correlation coefficient (shaded gray) measures the strength of the linear relationship between the two predictor variables. Note that its absolute value (.5641) is greater than the absolute value of the correlation coefficient of selling price and annual revenue (.5032). Since the absolute value of the correlation coefficient between the two predictor variables is not greater than *both* the correlation coefficients between the predictor variables and the dependent variable, then we have a less severe case of multicollinearity. This is further evidenced by the fact that only the p-value for annual revenue is greater than .05 (.688). A strong case of multicollinearity causes all the predictor variables to have large p-values. However, since there is a logic-defying sign change for annual revenue, we must conclude that multicollinearity is a serious problem for this model. The solution is to remove the predictor variable that has a p-value greater than .05 and rerun the model.

Conclusion

This case study is intended to introduce practitioners to the statistical method of regression analysis and to demonstrate how this procedure can improve their valuations, especially when used in combination with an income method. This technique has always been a popular tool of economists. Regression analysis has also found its way into the courts as evidence of damages in contractual actions, torts, and antitrust cases. These developments should further emphasize the importance for valuation and damages practitioners to understand this technique.

In this case study, we focused on bivariate simple regression analysis, and while there are many other forms of RA available to you, the tools we have provided you in this case are all that you will ever need to competently apply RA in the use of the direct market data method and derive good valuation results to assist in measuring damages when a business has been destroyed.

In the next case study we return to the XYZ Motel and demonstrate the use of a cross-sectional or causal model to forecast "but for" sales.

Note

1. Glejser, H. "A new test for heteroscedasticity." *Journal of the American Statistical Association*, Vol. 64 (1969), 16–32.

CHAPTER 4

Case Study 4—Choosing a Sales Forecasting Model: A Trial and Error Process

Let's pick up where we left off at the end of Case Study 2 with the XYZ Motel. Having determined that there is no upward trend in the monthly data, we need to choose a forecasting model that produces a result that approximates last year's sales for the same four-month period. While a seasonally adjusted time series model probably does the job very nicely, in this case study we would like to demonstrate a cross-sectional or causal model. Since the period of interruption was closed, a search was made for an independent variable that would correlate closely with the motel's sales. The gross sales for lodging places for the Brunswick Economic Summary Area (ESA) was found and downloaded from the State Planning Office that coincided with the 36 months prior to the incident date and the four months of the period of interruption. Since the monthly sales of the XYZ Motel are included in the monthly ESA data, they were subtracted from the monthly ESA data so as not to distort comparability between the two sets of data.

An advantage of using data external to the plaintiff's records is that the sales forecast is based on independent, corroborating, third-party data, thereby heightening relevance and reliability.

Correlation with Industry Sales

Comparing the monthly percentage of total sales and the cumulative monthly percentage of sales for the motel versus the Brunswick ESA during the subject four months, as shown in columns M and N in Table 4.1, indicates a high degree of correlation that we thought might carry over into the whole year. The 36 months of comparative sales were graphed on a log scale so that the same visual weight would be given to comparable percentage changes in both sets of numbers. The result is Figure 4.1, which on a visual basis indicates a high degree of correlation.

Conversion to Quarterly Data

Typically, quarterly data are easier to forecast than monthly data, because aggregating the data into quarters usually eliminates a great deal of noise or randomness in

Table 4.1
XYZ MOTEL
HISTORICAL SALES

	2007-2008 $	%	CUM %	2008-2009 $	%	CUM %	2009-2010 $	%	CUM %	2010-2011 $	3 YEAR AVERAGE MONTH	CUM %
JUNE	27,241	9.5%	9.5%	31,249	9.9%	9.9%	32,038	10.5%	10.5%	25,346	9.96%	9.96%
JULY	55,473	19.3%	28.8%	57,299	18.2%	28.1%	57,112	18.7%	29.2%	43,217	18.73%	28.70%
AUGUST	58,073	20.2%	49.0%	56,579	17.9%	46.0%	59,838	19.6%	48.8%	55,136	19.26%	47.95%
SEPTEMBER	45,159	15.7%	64.8%	43,827	13.9%	59.9%	46,981	15.4%	64.2%	41,151	15.01%	62.96%
OCTOBER	37,917	13.2%		35,490	11.3%		41,902	13.7%		164,850	-15.88%	
NOVEMBER	11,902	4.1%		13,967	4.4%		15,232	5.0%			CHANGE FROM PRIOR YEAR	
DECEMBER	5,268	1.8%		10,362	3.3%		7,642	2.5%				
JANUARY	4,995	1.7%		6,788	2.2%		5,015	1.6%				
FEBRUARY	6,816	2.4%		14,940	4.7%		5,378	1.8%			SALES DURING PERIOD OF INTERRUPTION	
MARCH	6,073	2.1%		14,490	4.6%		7,332	2.4%				
APRIL	9,152	3.2%		11,951	3.8%		9,540	3.1%				
MAY	18,966	6.6%		18,409	5.8%		17,338	5.7%				
	287,035	100.0%		315,352	100.0%		305,347	100.0%				

% CHANGE FROM PRIOR YEAR		9.9%	-3.2%
OCT-NOV %	53.4% 52.5%	53.0%	54.9%
TOTAL, JUNE TO SEPT	185,945	188,954	195,968
% CHANGE FROM PRIOR YEAR		1.6%	3.7%
THREE YEAR AVERAGE			190,289
TOTAL, OCT TO MAY	101,090	126,398	109,379
% CHANGE FROM PRIOR YEAR		25.0%	-13.5%
TOTAL, DEC TO MAY	51,271	76,941	52,244
% CHANGE FROM PRIOR YEAR		50.1%	-32.1%

BRUNSWICK ECONOMIC SUMMARY AREA
HISTORICAL SALES

	2007-2008 $	%	CUM %	2008-2009 $	%	CUM %	2009-2010 $	%	CUM %	2010-2011 $	3 YEAR AVERAGE MONTH	CUM %
JUNE	1,073,000	9.3%	9.3%	1,147,000	10.4%	10.4%	1,302,000	11.4%	11.4%	1,428,000	10.37%	10.37%
JULY	2,278,000	19.8%	29.1%	1,844,000	16.7%	27.1%	2,426,000	21.2%	32.6%	2,601,000	19.24%	29.61%
AUGUST	2,959,000	25.7%	54.8%	2,381,000	21.6%	48.6%	2,306,000	20.2%	52.8%	2,424,000	22.49%	52.10%
SEPTEMBER	1,354,000	11.8%	66.6%	1,374,000	12.4%	61.1%	1,253,000	11.0%	63.8%	1,191,000	11.73%	63.83%
OCTOBER	811,000	7.0%		916,000	8.3%		941,000	8.2%		7,644,000	4.90%	
NOVEMBER	488,000	4.2%		542,000	4.9%		578,000	5.1%			CHANGE FROM PRIOR YEAR	
DECEMBER	380,000	3.3%		352,000	3.2%		433,000	3.8%				
JANUARY	289,000	2.5%		368,000	3.3%		244,000	2.1%				
FEBRUARY	242,000	2.1%		537,000	4.9%		432,000	3.8%			AREA SALES DURING PERIOD OF INTERRUPTION	
MARCH	364,000	3.2%		489,000	4.4%		289,000	2.5%				
APRIL	662,000	5.8%		489,000	4.4%		600,000	5.3%				
MAY	608,000	5.3%		605,000	5.5%		618,000	5.4%				
	11,508,000	100.0%		11,044,000	100.0%		11,422,000	100.0%				

% CHANGE FROM PRIOR YEAR		-4.0%	3.4%
TOTAL, JUNE TO SEPT	7,664,000	6,746,000	7,287,000
% CHANGE FROM PRIOR YEAR		-12.0%	8.0%
TOTAL, OCT TO MAY	3,844,000	4,298,000	4,135,000
% CHANGE FROM PRIOR YEAR		11.8%	-3.8%
TOTAL, DEC TO MAY	2,545,000	2,840,000	2,616,000
% CHANGE FROM PRIOR YEAR		11.6%	-7.9%

the data. To test this assumption, we computed the coefficient of variation for motel sales for both months and quarters by dividing the standard deviation of each by the average of each. We do not show this calculation, but encourage you to replicate it. The results, 76.5 percent for months and 67.8 percent for quarters, confirm the assumption. Therefore, months were converted to quarters and presented on the log scale graph shown in Figure 4.2. Visually, the two lines are almost identical, further indicating a very high degree of correlation between the quarterly XYZ Motel sales and the Brunswick ESA sales. The scatter plot shown in Figure 4.3 indicates a curvilinear relationship between the XYZ Motel and ESA sales (as ESA sales increase,

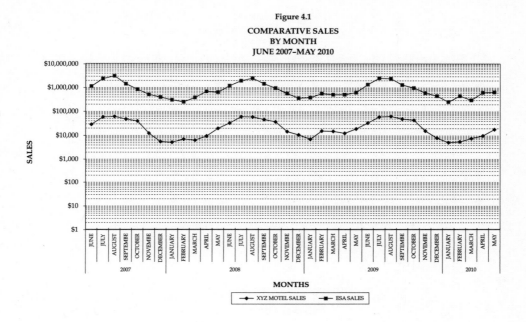

Figure 4.1

COMPARATIVE SALES
BY MONTH
JUNE 2007–MAY 2010

the rate of change in XYZ Motel sales slows down, forming a curved trendline). Using the trendline feature offered in Excel charts, we applied the various models available and determined that the best fit to the data was that of a quadratic (second-degree polynomial) trendline, another visual tool that demonstrates the correlative and nonlinear nature of the relationship.

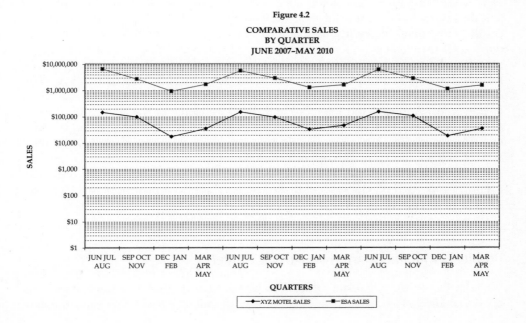

Figure 4.2

COMPARATIVE SALES
BY QUARTER
JUNE 2007–MAY 2010

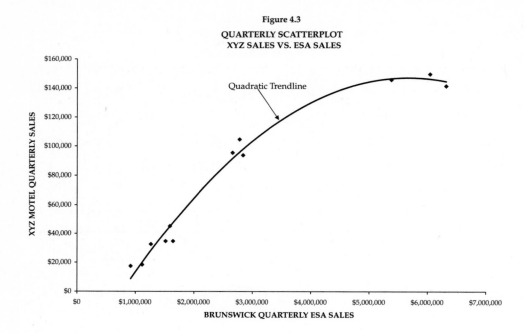

Figure 4.3

QUARTERLY SCATTERPLOT
XYZ SALES VS. ESA SALES

Quadratic Regression Model

To prove this mathematically, the next step is to model the curvilinear relationship between the data by running a regression analysis of the quarterly data. This required creating a second independent variable by raising ESA quarterly sales to the power of 2. This second variable causes the trendline to curve downward as the value of ESA sales increases. The setup sheet for this regression is shown in Table 4.2, and the regression output results are shown in Table 4.3. All three coefficients have p-values less than .05, indicating that they are statistically significant and belong in the model. A coefficient of correlation of .992 and a coefficient of determination of .985 indicates an extremely high level of strength in the curved but still linear relationship between ESA sales and motel sales, as well as implying that 98.5 percent of the variation in XYZ Motel sales are accounted for, or explained by, the variation in ESA sales. Applying the intercept and the coefficients of the regression output to ESA sales and ESA sales^2 for the quarters June, July, August, and September, October, November 2010 produces a predicted sales volume for those four months of $186,163, as shown on the upper half of Table 4.3[1].

October and November 2010 sales were removed by subtracting the historical average proportion of 53.4 percent that those two months represent of that quarter's sales from the predicted value for that quarter.

Problems with the Quarterly Quadratic Model

While at first blush this result appears to be satisfactory, there are three issues we need to address. First, we can smell the smoke of multicollinearity, as ESA sales and

			XYZ		
			Motel	ESA	ESA
	Year	Quarter	Sales	Sales	Sales^2
8	2007	JUN, JUL, AUG	140,787	6,310,000	39,816,100,000,000
9	2007	SEP, OCT, NOV	94,978	2,653,000	7,038,409,000,000
10	2007–2008	DEC, JAN, FEB	17,080	911,000	829,921,000,000
11	2008	MAR, APR, MAY	34,191	1,634,000	2,669,956,000,000
12	2008	JUN, JUL, AUG	145,127	5,372,000	28,858,384,000,000
13	2008	SEP, OCT, NOV	93,284	2,832,000	8,020,224,000,000
14	2008–2009	DEC, JAN, FEB	32,090	1,257,000	1,580,049,000,000
15	2009	MAR, APR, MAY	44,850	1,583,000	2,505,889,000,000
16	2009	JUN, JUL, AUG	148,988	6,034,000	36,409,156,000,000
17	2009	SEP, OCT, NOV	104,115	2,772,000	7,683,984,000,000
18	2009–2010	DEC, JAN, FEB	18,034	1,109,000	1,229,881,000,000
19	2010	MAR, APR, MAY	34,211	1,507,000	2,271,049,000,000

(Table 4.2 — XYZ MOTEL — SETUP SHEET FOR QUADRATIC REGRESSION MODEL; spreadsheet columns A–G, rows 1–20)

ESA sales^2 are highly correlated with one another. The question of multicollinearity is one of severity and ultimate impact on the model. In a predictive model, such as the one at hand, multicollinearity can be ignored as it has no effect on the estimated value of y and the SEE. If we felt that multicollinearity was an issue, we would look to see if the signs of the x coefficients made sense, and in this case they do. Then we would look to see if the standard errors of the x coefficients were too large and the related t-statistics were close to zero. In this case, our model's t-statistics at 10.8 and −7.0 as shown in Table 4.3 are significantly different from zero. And lastly, we must default to the variable inclusion principle, which states that whenever higher order terms are included in a model, the implied lower order terms will also be included. For example, if you include x^2 in the model, then you will also include x. But x and x^2 are highly correlated. Nevertheless, both x and x^2 are needed in the model, despite the fact that they are highly correlated. Such is the case with the quadratic model presented in Figure 4.3, Table 4.2, and Table 4.3.

Second, the predicted amount of $186,163 is about $10,000 less than the same period the year before. This doesn't seem reasonable, as ESA sales for the 2010 season are 4.9 percent higher than for the 2009 season.

Third, we have an extrapolation problem—ESA sales for the quarter consisting of June, July, and August in the amount of $6,453,000 are outside the relevant range for the independent variable, which range is bracketed by the lowest and highest values of ESA sales in the 12 quarters leading up to the date of the incident. Extrapolating beyond the relevant range takes us into unchartered territory, as we do not know how sales actually behave outside the range, and consequently our estimate of forecasted sales will be unreliable. In fact, since we have a quadratic,

	B	C	D	E	F	G	H	
1				Table 4.3				
2				XYZ MOTEL				
3			QUADRATIC REGRESSION OF QUARTERLY SALES AGAINST QUARTERLY ESA SALES					
4								
5			(X)	(X^2)	(Y)			
6					XYZ			
7			ESA	ESA	MOTEL	FORECASTED	PREDICTED	
8	YEAR	QUARTER	SALES	SALES^2	SALES	SALES	SALES	
9	2007	JUN, JUL, AUG	6,310,000	39,816,100,000,000	140,787	143,899		
10		SEP, OCT, NOV	2,653,000	7,038,409,000,000	94,978	91,049		
11	2008	DEC, JAN, FEB	911,000	829,921,000,000	17,080	8,373		
12		MAR, APR, MAY	1,634,000	2,669,956,000,000	34,191	47,191		
13		JUN, JUL, AUG	5,372,000	28,858,384,000,000	145,127	145,937		
14		SEP, OCT, NOV	2,832,000	8,020,224,000,000	93,284	97,443		
15	2009	DEC, JAN, FEB	1,257,000	1,580,049,000,000	32,090	27,747		
16		MAR, APR, MAY	1,583,000	2,505,889,000,000	44,850	44,662		
17		JUN, JUL, AUG	6,034,000	36,409,156,000,000	148,988	145,616		
18		SEP, OCT, NOV	2,772,000	7,683,984,000,000	104,115	95,343		
19	2010	DEC, JAN, FEB	1,109,000	1,229,881,000,000	18,034	19,639		
20		MAR, APR, MAY	1,507,000	2,271,049,000,000	34,211	40,835		
21		JUN, JUL, AUG	6,453,000	41,641,209,000,000			142,644	
22		SEP, OCT, NOV	2,720,000	7,398,400,000,000			93,488	
23		LESS: OCT & NOV @ 53.4% OF THAT QUARTER'S SALES					(49,969)	
24								
25					SUMMARY:			
26					JUNE, JULY, AUGUST		142,644	
27					SEPTEMBER		43,520	
28					TOTAL		186,163	
29	SUMMARY OUTPUT - QUARTERLY DATA							
30								
31		*Regression Statistics*						
32	Multiple R		0.992					
33	R Square		0.985					
34	Adjusted R Square		0.981					
35	Standard Error		7,005					
36	Coefficient of Variation		9.3%					
37	Observations		12					
38								
39	ANOVA							
40			*df*	*SS*	*MS*	*F*	*Significance F*	
41	Regression		2	28,533,702,428	14,266,851,214	290.8	0.000	
42	Residual		9	441,568,858	49,063,206			
43	Total		11	28,975,271,285				
44								
45			*Coefficients*	*Standard Error*	*t Stat*	*p-value*	*Lower 95%*	*Upper 95%*
46	Intercept		(49,641.041)	8664.630	-5.729	0.000	-69241.812	-30040.271
47	ESA Sales		0.069	0.006	10.788	0.000	0.055	0.084
48	ESA Sales^2		-6.114E-09	0.000	-7.036	0.000	0.000	0.000
49								

curvilinear relationship that will eventually become a parabola (an inverted U), if we extend the forecast upper range any further, forecasted sales get smaller and smaller. This explains why the predicted sales amount of $186,163 is less than we would have expected—we are predicting outside the relevant range with a quadratic model that diminishes predicted sales even as the independent variable gets larger.

Substituting a Monthly Quadratic Model

This outcome is a disappointment, as we had very high goodness of fit metrics with the quarterly model, especially a low coefficient of variation of 9.3 percent. This measure of accuracy is calculated by dividing the standard error of the estimate by the average of the dependent variable, and it gives the average percentage deviation about the trend line. But discard it we must and so a new model is

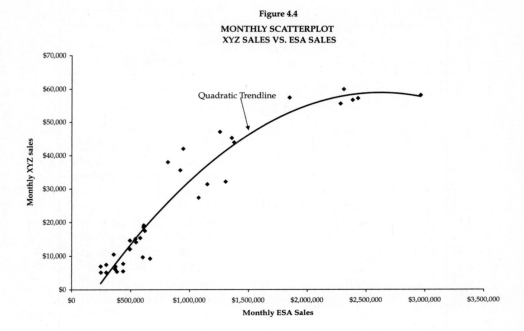

Figure 4.4

MONTHLY SCATTERPLOT
XYZ SALES VS. ESA SALES

called for. Since the relationship between XYZ sales and ESA sales remains curvilinear, let's return to the monthly quadratic model. A preliminary look at Figure 4.4 indicates that this model ought to work very well, even though there is more variation, or dispersion, about the trendline than in the quarterly scatterplot. The setup sheet for this regression is shown in Table 4.4, the regression output results are shown in Table 4.5, and the forecasted and predicted sales are shown in Table 4.6. Figure 4.5 is a line chart comparing historical motel sales with those forecasted by the model, as well as presenting predicted sales for the four-month period of interruption.

The results of this model are quite good, with all three coefficients being statistically significant, and all four months of ESA sales in the prediction period are within the relevant range, so our predicted sales are made by interpolating and not by extrapolating. However, the regression statistics are not as good as those of the quarterly data. Multiple R and R square are lower, and while the standard error is lower, as a percentage of average monthly sales it is more than double the quarterly model at 20.5 percent.

Conclusion

At $200,000, predicted sales during the period of interruption are higher than last year's for the same period. However, this could happen because, since the room rate for the period of interruption is given, it would only require this year's occupancy rate to equal last year's. This seems feasible, as comparative period ESA sales are 4.9 percent higher this year.

	Year	Month	XYZ Motel Sales	ESA Sales	ESA Sales^2
					Table 4.4
					XYZ MOTEL
					SETUP SHEET FOR QUADRATIC REGRESSION MODEL
8	2007	JUNE	27,241	1,073,000	1,151,329,000,000
9		JULY	55,473	2,278,000	5,189,284,000,000
10		AUGUST	58,073	2,959,000	8,755,681,000,000
11		SEPTEMBER	45,159	1,354,000	1,833,316,000,000
12		OCTOBER	37,917	811,000	657,721,000,000
13		NOVEMBER	11,902	488,000	238,144,000,000
14		DECEMBER	5,268	380,000	144,400,000,000
15	2008	JANUARY	4,995	289,000	83,521,000,000
16		FEBRUARY	6,816	242,000	58,564,000,000
17		MARCH	6,073	364,000	132,496,000,000
18		APRIL	9,152	662,000	438,244,000,000
19		MAY	18,966	608,000	369,664,000,000
20		JUNE	31,249	1,147,000	1,315,609,000,000
21		JULY	57,299	1,844,000	3,400,336,000,000
22		AUGUST	56,579	2,381,000	5,669,161,000,000
23		SEPTEMBER	43,827	1,374,000	1,887,876,000,000
24		OCTOBER	35,490	916,000	839,056,000,000
25		NOVEMBER	13,967	542,000	293,764,000,000
26		DECEMBER	10,362	352,000	123,904,000,000
27	2009	JANUARY	6,788	368,000	135,424,000,000
28		FEBRUARY	14,940	537,000	288,369,000,000
29		MARCH	14,490	489,000	239,121,000,000
30		APRIL	11,951	489,000	239,121,000,000
31		MAY	18,409	605,000	366,025,000,000
32		JUNE	32,038	1,302,000	1,695,204,000,000
33		JULY	57,112	2,426,000	5,885,476,000,000
34		AUGUST	59,838	2,306,000	5,317,636,000,000
35		SEPTEMBER	46,981	1,253,000	1,570,009,000,000
36		OCTOBER	41,902	941,000	885,481,000,000
37		NOVEMBER	15,232	578,000	334,084,000,000
38		DECEMBER	7,642	433,000	187,489,000,000
39	2010	JANUARY	5,015	244,000	59,536,000,000
40		FEBRUARY	5,378	432,000	186,624,000,000
41		MARCH	7,332	289,000	83,521,000,000
42		APRIL	9,540	600,000	360,000,000,000
43		MAY	17,338	618,000	381,924,000,000

Table 4.5
XYZ MOTEL
QUADRATIC REGRESSION OF MONTHLY SALES AGAINST MONTHLY ESA SALES

SUMMARY OUTPUT - MONTHLY DATA

Regression Statistics	
Multiple R	0.9656
R Square	0.9323
Adjusted R Square	0.9282
Standard Error	5,168
Coefficient of Variation	20.50%
Observations	36

ANOVA

	df	*SS*	*MS*	*F*	*Significance F*
Regression	2	12,146,437,216.26	6,073,218,608.13	227.39	5.01066E-20
Residual	33	881,391,163.83	26,708,823.15		
Total	35	13,027,828,380.09			

	Coefficients	*Standard Error*	*t Stat*	*p-value*	*Lower 95%*	*Upper 95%*
Intercept	-10507.850	2587.859	-4.060	0.00028332	-15772.894	-5242.807
ESA Sales	0.053	0.005	10.520	0.00000000	0.043	0.063
ESA Sales^2	-0.000000010	0.0000000017	-5.824	0.00000162	-0.000000014	-0.000000007

		(X)	(X²)	(Y)		
				XYZ		
		ESA	ESA	MOTEL	FORECASTED	PREDICTED
YEAR	MONTH	SALES	SALES²	SALES	SALES	SALES
2007	JUNE	1,073,000	1,151,329,000,000	27,241	34,699	
	JULY	2,278,000	5,189,284,000,000	55,473	57,651	
	AUGUST	2,959,000	8,755,681,000,000	58,073	57,608	
	SEPTEMBER	1,354,000	1,833,316,000,000	45,159	42,682	
	OCTOBER	811,000	657,721,000,000	37,917	25,813	
	NOVEMBER	488,000	238,144,000,000	11,902	12,945	
	DECEMBER	380,000	144,400,000,000	5,268	8,170	
2008	JANUARY	289,000	83,521,000,000	4,995	3,964	
	FEBRUARY	242,000	58,564,000,000	6,816	1,726	
	MARCH	364,000	132,496,000,000	6,073	7,443	
	APRIL	662,000	438,244,000,000	9,152	20,140	
	MAY	608,000	369,664,000,000	18,966	17,973	
	JUNE	1,147,000	1,315,609,000,000	31,249	36,956	
	JULY	1,844,000	3,400,336,000,000	57,299	52,775	
	AUGUST	2,381,000	5,669,161,000,000	56,579	58,248	
	SEPTEMBER	1,374,000	1,887,876,000,000	43,827	43,189	
	OCTOBER	916,000	839,056,000,000	35,490	29,541	
	NOVEMBER	542,000	293,764,000,000	13,967	15,243	
	DECEMBER	352,000	123,904,000,000	10,362	6,894	
2009	JANUARY	368,000	135,424,000,000	6,788	7,625	
	FEBRUARY	537,000	288,369,000,000	14,940	15,033	
	MARCH	489,000	239,121,000,000	14,490	12,988	
	APRIL	489,000	239,121,000,000	11,951	12,988	
	MAY	605,000	366,025,000,000	18,409	17,850	
	JUNE	1,302,000	1,695,204,000,000	32,038	41,325	
	JULY	2,426,000	5,885,476,000,000	57,112	58,441	
	AUGUST	2,306,000	5,317,636,000,000	59,838	57,835	
	SEPTEMBER	1,253,000	1,570,009,000,000	46,981	39,997	
	OCTOBER	941,000	885,481,000,000	41,902	30,396	
	NOVEMBER	578,000	334,084,000,000	15,232	16,743	
	DECEMBER	433,000	187,489,000,000	7,642	10,543	
2010	JANUARY	244,000	59,536,000,000	5,015	1,822	
	FEBRUARY	432,000	186,624,000,000	5,378	10,499	
	MARCH	289,000	83,521,000,000	7,332	3,964	
	APRIL	600,000	360,000,000,000	9,540	17,647	
	MAY	618,000	381,924,000,000	17,338	18,378	
	JUNE	1,428,000	2,039,184,000,000			44,518
	JULY	2,601,000	6,765,201,000,000			58,802
	AUGUST	2,424,000	5,875,776,000,000			58,433
	SEPTEMBER	1,191,000	1,418,481,000,000			38,246
	Total Predicted Value					200,000

Table 4.6
XYZ MOTEL
FORECASTED AND PREDICTED SALES FROM MONTHLY QUADRATIC REGRESSION

While neither the independent nor the dependent variable in our sample was normally distributed, tests of the residuals (not shown), that is, the difference between the forecasted values and the actual monthly sales amounts, indicated that they were normally distributed, had equal variances along the trendline (homoscedasticity), and were without serial correlation (one residual's value did not depend on the preceding residual's value)—all good things that validate the regression results. Through trial and error, we found we had to trade off a less accurate result (more

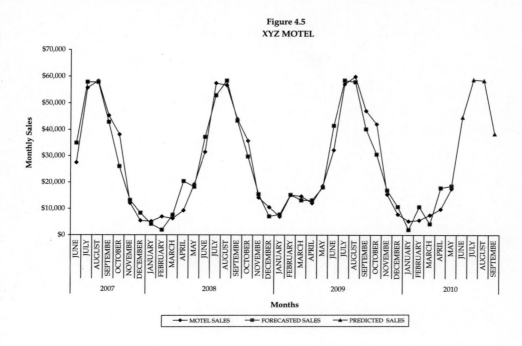

Figure 4.5
XYZ MOTEL

variance about the trendline) for a more precise point estimate of loss ($200,000 better reflects expected sales than $186,163).

In the next chapter we stay with the XYZ Motel and apply a different regression model to the sales forecasting problem.

Note

1. For example, the forecasted sales for the quarter consisting of June, July, and August 2010 are computed as follows:

   $-49,641 + .069 \times 6,453,000 - 6.114E-.09 \times 41,614,209,000,000 = 142,644.$

CHAPTER 5

Case Study 5—Time Series Analysis with Seasonal Adjustment

When the XYZ Motel was last seen in Case Study 4, it had been determined that lost sales during the period of interruption were $200,000 using a cross-sectional model in which we regressed monthly XYZ Motel sales against ESA sales. In Case Study 5 we try another approach to modeling lost sales, that of time series analysis with a seasonal adjustment. Again, the 12 quarters of motel sales are presented in Table 5.1 and on the accompanying line chart in Figure 5.1, as better results are expected using less variable quarterly data than more variable monthly data, as we explained in Case Study 4. We will not experience the extrapolation or out-of-sample problem that occurred in Case Study 4 with the quarterly data, as our x variables are time and a seasonal index, and no longer ESA quarterly sales.

Exploratory Data Analysis

Exploratory data analysis is expanded with Figures 5.2 and 5.3, which show, respectively, sales by quarter by year, and sales by year by quarter. The lack of uniformity on these charts can be explained by the facts that for the four months at issue (June, July, August, and September), room rates decreased by 2.2 percent from the summer of 2007 to the summer of 2008, while occupancy rates increased 3.9 percent during the same period, and from the summer of 2008 to the summer of 2009 room rates increased 8 percent while occupancy rates decreased 4 percent. All in all, these ups and downs account for the slight increase in room sales over time as shown by the top two lines in Figure 5.2. However, the story is very different for the bottom two lines in Figure 5.2. Here there was an 81.9 percent increase in the number of rooms from the period December 2008 to May 2009 over the same period for the year before, but a decrease of 44.0 percent from the 2008 to 2009 period to the 2009 to 2010 period. This same information is presented in a different form in Figure 5.3, where room sales for the period June to November 2009 are the highest of the three periods, but then fall off considerably for the period December 2009 to May 2010. The question becomes: Which trend has more influence on room sales in the summer of 2010—sales of a year before, or sales in the immediate prior six months?

	A	B	C	D	E	F
1			**Table 5.1**			
2			**XYZ MOTEL**			
3			**QUARTERLY SALES, JUNE 2007–MAY 2010**			
4						
5		**Quarter**	**2007–2008**	**2008–2009**	**2009–2010**	
6		JUN, JUL, AUG	140,787	145,127	148,988	
7		SEP, OCT, NOV	94,978	93,284	104,115	
8		DEC, JAN, FEB	17,080	32,090	18,034	
9		MAR, APR, MAY	34,191	44,850	34,211	
10						
11		FY Total	287,035	315,352	305,347	
12						

Seasonal Indexes versus Dummy Variables

To begin to answer that question, a time-series regression model needs to be selected to account for the large amount of seasonality present in the data, as well as to control for the very small amount of trend that we see in Figure 5.4. The calculations behind this display of maximal seasonality and little trend for the XYZ Motel's sales was explained and demonstrated in Case Study 2. To include seasonality in the model, four seasonal indexes were created, one for each quarter, rather than using dummy variables. The benefit of this choice is that only 1 degree of freedom is used instead of the 3 degrees of freedom that dummy variables would consume. We take this approach, as minimizing the number of lost degrees of freedom also minimizes the standard error of the estimate, which in turn keeps our range of forecasted sales as

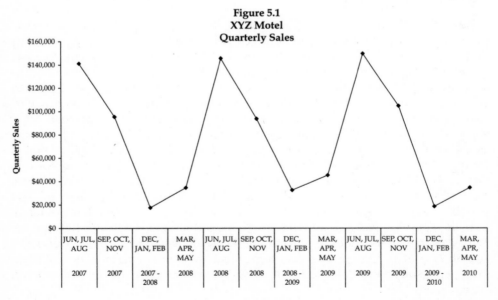

Figure 5.1
XYZ Motel
Quarterly Sales

Quarter

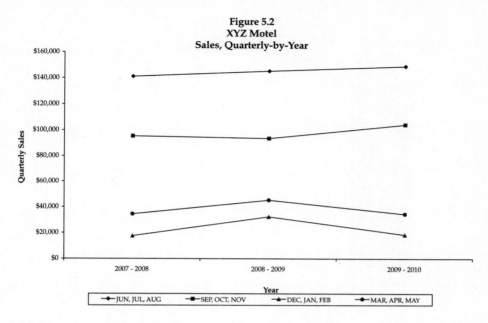

narrow as possible. The process of creating the seasonal indexes and then optimizing them is shown in Figure 5.5.

Creation of the Optimized Seasonal Indexes

The idea of seasonal indexes can be deduced from the seasonal sales patterns of a retailer, whose sales are dramatically different in January than December. If annual sales by month are known, it can be determined by how much December's sales

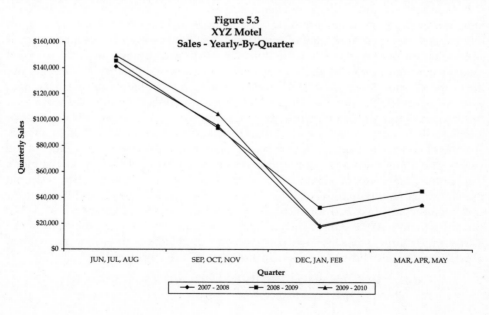

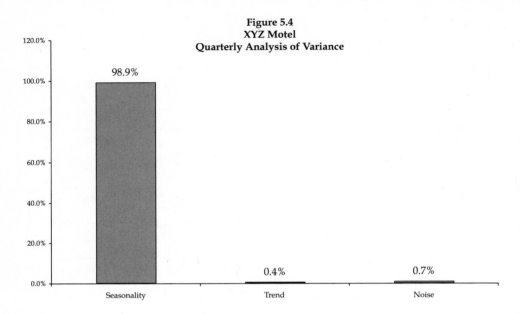

Figure 5.4
XYZ Motel
Quarterly Analysis of Variance

are above the average and how much January's sales are below the average. If these monthly or, as in this case study, quarterly ratios are collected over time, they can then be averaged to get the average ratio by which any particular month or quarter is above or below average annual sales. To compensate for any trend, no matter how small, in the historical sales data, instead of using average annual sales as the baseline, a linear trend is computed to serve that purpose.

The development of seasonal indexes can be optimized by minimizing root mean squared error (RMSE), which is the average distance or deviation between actual sales and the seasonal forecast. This minimization is accomplished by using Excel's Solver[1] optimizer add-in to change the slope and intercept of the linear trend-line, and at the same time, adjusting the four seasonal indexes while constraining them to still average 100 percent of quarterly sales. Solver works by iterating the possible solutions until it arrives at a combination of slope, intercept, and four seasonal indexes that minimizes RMSE. The seasonal forecast is obtained by multiplying the linear trend amount for any quarter by its optimized seasonal index. For example, for time period 1, the trend amount of $72,688 is multiplied by the seasonal index for this case study's quarter 1 (June, July, and August) of 192.94 percent to produce a seasonally forecasted amount of $140,241, which is shown in cell G7 in Figure 5.5.

We obtain the seasonal index[2] for each quarter by computing the average of the values in column F on a quarter-by-quarter basis. For example, the seasonal index for quarter 1 equals the average of the values in cells F7, F11, and F15. The seasonal index for quarter 2 equals the average of the values in cells F8, F12, and F16. Similar computations are required to calculate seasonal indexes for quarters 3 and 4. We can use separate AVERAGE() functions for each quarter to compute these averages. However, for large data sets, such an approach would be tedious and prone to error. Thus, the averages shown in cells C24 through C27 are calculated as:

=SUMIF($B$7:$B$18,B24,$F$7:$F$18)/COUNTIF($B$7:$B$18,B24)

Figure 5.5
XYZ MOTEL
SCHEDULE OF QUARTERLY OPTIMIZED SEASONAL INDEXES

Qtr	Time Period	Actual Sales	Linear Trend	Actual as a % of Trend	Seasonal Forecast
1	1	140,787	72,688	193.7%	140,241
2	2	94,978	73,299	129.6%	94,345
3	3	17,080	73,909	23.1%	21,680
4	4	34,191	74,520	45.9%	36,528
1	5	145,127	75,131	193.2%	144,954
2	6	93,284	75,741	123.2%	97,490
3	7	32,090	76,352	42.0%	22,396
4	8	44,850	76,963	58.3%	37,725
1	9	148,988	77,573	192.1%	149,667
2	10	104,115	78,184	133.2%	100,634
3	11	18,034	78,795	22.9%	23,113
4	12	34,211	79,406	43.1%	38,923

Quarter	Unadjusted Seasonal Index	Normalizing Factor	Adjusted Seasonal Index	Optimized Seasonal Index
1	193.0%	0.999931083	192.96%	192.94%
2	128.6%	0.999931083	128.63%	128.71%
3	29.3%	0.999931083	29.34%	29.33%
4	49.1%	0.999931083	49.08%	49.02%
	400.028%		100.0%	100.0%

Original
Slope	Intercept
-3649.04	99,363.28

Optimized
Slope	Intercept
610.69	72,077.30

RMSE = 5,004
RSQ = 0.991
CoV = 6.61%

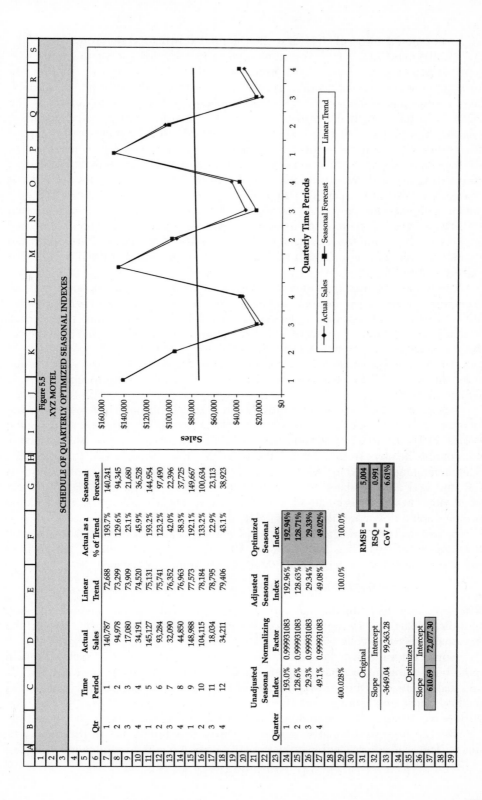

Quarterly Time Periods

Sales

♦ Actual Sales ■ Seasonal Forecast — Linear Trend

which is entered into cell C24 and then copied down to and through cell C27. The SUMIF() and COUNTIF() functions perform conditional sums and counts. The SUMIF() function in the previous formula sums the values in cells F7 through F18 for which the corresponding value in cells B7 to B18 equals the value in cell B24. This corresponds to the sum of the values in column F that occur in quarter 1. The COUNTIF() function in the previous equation counts the number of elements in cells B7 through B18 that equals the value in cell B24—or the number of quarter 1 observations. Since the sum of the 4 seasonal indexes in cell C29 is greater than 400.0 percent, we need to normalize each quarter's index by multiplying it by a normalizing factor derived from the ratio 4/C29, where 4 is the number of periods in a year—in this case, quarters. The product for quarter 1 is shown in cell E24, with similar computations performed on the other three quarters in cells E25 through E27. The average of the four quarters, which now is exactly 100.0 percent, is shown in cell E29. The optimized seasonal indexes in cells F24 though F27 are populated for now by referencing cells E24 through E27. The function AVERAGE(F24:F27) is placed in cell F29.

The optimized seasonal index for quarter 1 shown in cell F24 indicates that, on average, the actual sales value in the first quarter of any given year is 192.94 percent of (or 92.94 percent larger than) the estimated trend value for the same time period. Similarly, the optimized seasonal index for quarter 3 shown in cell F26 indicates that, on average, the actual sales value in the third quarter of any given year is 29.33 percent of (or approximately 71 percent less than) the estimated trend value for the same time period. The seasonal indexes for the second and fourth quarters have similar interpretations.

To calculate the linear trend values shown in cells E7 through E18, we first create an intercept and a slope for the trendline in cells D33 and C33, respectively, using the INTERCEPT(D7:D18,C7:C18) and SLOPE(D7:D18,C7:C18) functions. We then copy the column headers from cells C31 through D32 down to cells C35 through D36, while changing the title in cell C35 from Original to Optimized. The values in cells C37 and D37 are populated for now by referencing cells C33 and D33. The linear trend value in cell E7 is created by the formula =+$D$37+$C$37*C7. This formula is then copied down and through cell E18.

Before we perform the final step in creating optimized seasonal indexes by invoking Solver, which is found on the far right of the data ribbon, we need to create a formula for our target cell, RMSE. That formula, in cell G31, is:

$$=SQRT(SUMXMY2(D7:D18,G7:G18)/(COUNT(D7:D18)-2))$$

where we are calculating the standard error of the estimate, or the standard deviation of the residuals, that is, the difference between actual sales in cells D7:D18 and the seasonal forecast in cells G7:G18.

Now, click on Solver to open it, set objective as RMSE, cell G31, select the Min radio button, for the By Changing Variable Cells option select cells F24:F27,C37:D37, and make Subject to the Constraints: F29 = 1. Choose GRG Nonlinear as the solving method, click on Options, and check Use Automatic Scaling. Click OK and then click Solve. If necessary, open Solver and click Solve again.

We can use the calculated seasonal indexes to refine or adjust the trend estimates. This is accomplished in column G of Figure 5.6 with the following formula:

$$=E7*VLOOKUP(B7,\$B\$24:\$F\$27,5)$$

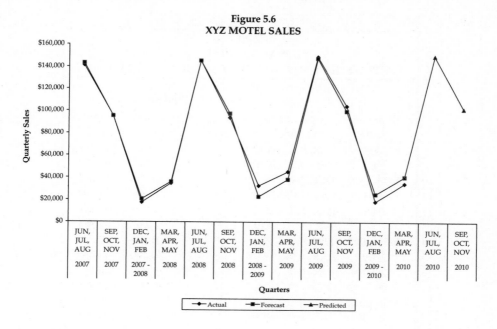

Figure 5.6
XYZ MOTEL SALES

which is entered into cell G7 and then copied down to and through cell G18. This formula takes the estimated trend value for each time period and multiplies it by the appropriate seasonal index for the quarter in which the time period occurs. The trend estimates for quarter 1 observations are multiplied by 192.94 percent, the trend estimates for quarter 2 observations are multiplied by 128.71 percent, and so on for quarters 3 and 4 observations.

Figure 5.5 has a chart that shows the actual sales versus the seasonal forecast calculated in column G. As this chart illustrates, the use of seasonal indexes is very effective on this particular data set.

Once the seasonal indexes have been created, the regression input worksheet can be set up as shown in Table 5.2. This is an example of multiple linear regression, as more than one predictor variable is being used. In this case, the two variables are trend and the seasonal indexes that were just created. Using Excel's regression tool, found in the Analysis Toolpak add-in, the upper portion of Table 5.3 was created. We note that the t-Stat for the Trend predictor variable is less than 2.0, and its P-value is greater than .05. This result is expected, as the great majority of variation in quarterly sales is explained by seasonality. However, since the t-Stat is greater than 1, let's leave this variable in the model as by doing so we reduce the SEE and increase adjusted R^2.

From the intercept, trend, and seasonal index coefficients found in the summary output, sales were predicted for the four-month period of interruption as shown in the lower portion of Table 5.3, and the chart in Figure 5.6 was created to show actual, forecasted, and predicted sales. The excellent correspondence of forecasted sales to actual sales can be seen, which observed goodness-of-fit gives confidence that the predicted sales are accurate.

The predicted sales produced by the quarterly time series model for the four–month period are $197,100 as found in Table 5.3. This amount differs from the

	A	B	C	D	E	F	G
1			Table 5.2				
2			XYZ MOTEL				
3			SETUP SHEET FOR MULTIPLE REGRESSION MODEL				
4							
5					Optimized	XYZ	
6					Seasonal	Motel	
7		Year	Quarter	Trend	Index	Sales	
8		2007	JUN, JUL, AUG	1	1.929	140,787	
9		2007	SEP, OCT, NOV	2	1.287	94,978	
10		2007–2008	DEC, JAN, FEB	3	0.293	17,080	
11		2008	MAR, APR, MAY	4	0.490	34,191	
12		2008	JUN, JUL, AUG	5	1.929	145,127	
13		2008	SEP, OCT, NOV	6	1.287	93,284	
14		2008–2009	DEC, JAN, FEB	7	0.293	32,090	
15		2009	MAR, APR, MAY	8	0.490	44,850	
16		2009	JUN, JUL, AUG	9	1.929	148,988	
17		2009	SEP, OCT, NOV	10	1.287	104,115	
18		2009–2010	DEC, JAN, FEB	11	0.293	18,034	
19		2010	MAR, APR, MAY	12	0.490	34,211	
20							

$200,000 predicted by the monthly cross-sectional model we used in Case Study 4. Assuming that this difference is significant, as it well may be in other matters you come across in your litigation support practice, a way is needed to choose the more appropriate outcome. That way is to develop a composite model, one that combines two or more prediction models and produces a better result than any of its constituent models. To accomplish this, the monthly data need to be revisited, as the cross-sectional quarterly model cannot be used because of its extrapolation defect; that is, forecasting outside the range of the x variable, and a monthly time series model needs to be created.

Creation of the Monthly Time Series Model

Just as in the quarterly time series model, optimized seasonal indexes need to be created, which is accomplished in Figure 5.7 by following the steps used for Figure 5.5, except for the necessary changes being made to account for 12 periods in a year rather than four. The regression setup worksheet and summary output are shown in Table 5.4 and Table 5.5, respectively. Note that the predicted sales for the four-month period of interruption are $196,304, an amount closer to the quarterly time series model prediction of $197,100 than it is to the cross-sectional model prediction of $200,000.

Creation of the Composite Model

Now that there are two monthly models that predict room sales, time series, and cross-sectional, the composite regression model can be set up in Table 5.6. From the summary output shown in Table 5.7, room sales can be predicted by multiplying

Table 5.3
XYZ MOTEL
Quarterly Regression Model for Prediction
Summary Output

Regression Statistics

Multiple R	0.9952
R Square	0.9904
Adjusted R Square	0.9883
Standard Error	5,549
Coefficient of Variation	7.3%
Observations	12

ANOVA

	df	SS	MS	F	Significance F
Regression	2	28,698,191,208	14,349,095,604	466.08	8.17711E-10
Residual	9	277,080,077	30,786,675		
Total	11	28,975,271,285			

	Coefficients	Standard Error	t Stat	p-value	Lower 95%	Upper 95%
Intercept	(3,785.99)	4,887.42	-0.775	0.458	(14,842)	7,270
Trend	569.92	485.53	1.174	0.271	(528)	1,668
Seasonal Index	75,726.07	2,566.89	29.501	0.000	69,919	81,533

PREDICTION

Regression Equation:

Predicted Quarterly Sales = -3,785.99 + Trend x 569.92 + Seasonal Factor x 75,726.07

Quarter	Intercept	Trend	Seasonal Factor	Prediction
Jun, Jul, Aug	(3,786)	13	1.929	149,725
Sep, Oct, Nov	(3,786)	14	1.287	101,663
Less: Oct & Nov @ 53.4% of that Quarter's Sales				(54,288)
Total Predicted Sales				197,100

109

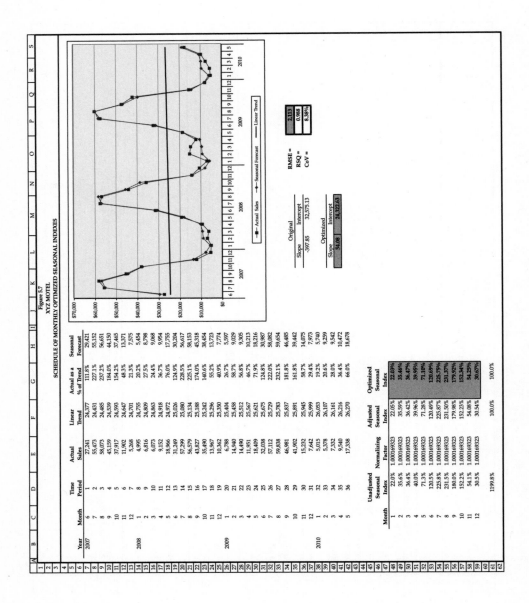

Figure 5.7
XYZ MOTEL
SCHEDULE OF MONTHLY OPTIMIZED SEASONAL INDEXES

Year	Month	Time Period	Actual Sales	Linear Trend	Actual as a % of Trend	Seasonal Forecast
2007	6	1	27,241	24,377	111.8%	29,421
	7	2	55,473	24,431	227.1%	55,152
	8	3	58,073	24,485	237.2%	56,651
	9	4	45,159	24,539	184.0%	44,150
	10	5	37,917	24,593	154.2%	37,465
	11	6	11,902	24,647	48.3%	13,371
	12	7	5,268	24,701	21.3%	7,575
2008	1	8	4,995	24,755	20.2%	5,454
	2	9	6,816	24,809	27.5%	8,798
	3	10	6,073	24,863	24.4%	9,068
	4	11	9,152	24,918	36.7%	9,954
	5	12	18,966	24,972	76.0%	17,755
	6	13	31,249	25,026	124.9%	30,204
	7	14	57,299	25,080	228.5%	56,617
	8	15	56,579	25,134	225.1%	58,153
	9	16	43,827	25,188	174.0%	45,318
	10	17	35,490	25,242	140.6%	38,454
	11	18	13,967	25,296	55.2%	13,723
	12	19	10,362	25,350	40.9%	7,774
2009	1	20	6,788	25,404	26.7%	5,597
	2	21	14,940	25,458	58.7%	9,029
	3	22	14,490	25,512	56.8%	9,305
	4	23	11,951	25,567	46.7%	10,213
	5	24	18,409	25,621	71.9%	18,216
	6	25	32,038	25,675	124.8%	30,987
	7	26	57,112	25,729	222.0%	58,082
	8	27	59,838	25,783	232.1%	59,654
	9	28	46,981	25,837	181.8%	46,485
	10	29	41,902	25,891	161.8%	39,442
	11	30	15,232	25,945	58.7%	14,075
	12	31	7,642	25,999	29.4%	7,973
2010	1	32	5,015	26,053	19.2%	5,740
	2	33	5,378	26,107	20.6%	9,259
	3	34	7,332	26,161	28.0%	9,542
	4	35	9,540	26,216	36.4%	10,472
	5	36	17,338	26,270	66.0%	18,678

Month	Unadjusted Seasonal Index	Normalizing Factor	Adjusted Seasonal Index	Optimized Seasonal Index
1	22.0%	1.000169323	22.05%	22.03%
2	35.6%	1.000169323	35.59%	35.66%
3	36.4%	1.000169323	36.42%	36.47%
4	40.0%	1.000169323	39.96%	39.95%
5	71.3%	1.000169323	71.28%	71.16%
6	120.5%	1.000169323	120.49%	120.69%
7	225.8%	1.000169323	225.87%	225.79%
8	231.5%	1.000169323	231.50%	231.37%
9	180.0%	1.000169323	179.98%	179.92%
10	152.2%	1.000169323	152.23%	152.34%
11	54.1%	1.000169323	54.08%	54.25%
12	30.5%	1.000169323	30.54%	30.67%
	1199.8%		100.0%	100.0%

RMSE = 2,113
RSQ = 0.988
CoV = 8.38%

Original
Slope -397.85 Intercept 32,575.13

Optimized
Slope 54.08 Intercept 24,322.63

110

	A	B	C	D	E	F	G
1					Table 5.4		
2					XYZ MOTEL		
3			SETUP SHEET FOR MULTIPLE REGRESSION MODEL				
4							
5					Optimized	XYZ	
6					Seasonal	Motel	
7		Year	Month	Trend	Index	Sales	
8		2007	JUNE	1	120.69%	27,241	
9			JULY	2	225.75%	55,473	
10			AUGUST	3	231.37%	58,073	
11			SEPTEMBER	4	179.92%	45,159	
12			OCTOBER	5	152.34%	37,917	
13			NOVEMBER	6	54.25%	11,902	
14			DECEMBER	7	30.67%	5,268	
15		2008	JANUARY	8	22.03%	4,995	
16			FEBRUARY	9	35.46%	6,816	
17			MARCH	10	36.47%	6,073	
18			APRIL	11	39.95%	9,152	
19			MAY	12	71.10%	18,966	
20			JUNE	13	120.69%	31,249	
21			JULY	14	225.75%	57,299	
22			AUGUST	15	231.37%	56,579	
23			SEPTEMBER	16	179.92%	43,827	
24			OCTOBER	17	152.34%	35,490	
25			NOVEMBER	18	54.25%	13,967	
26			DECEMBER	19	30.67%	10,362	
27		2009	JANUARY	20	22.03%	6,788	
28			FEBRUARY	21	35.46%	14,940	
29			MARCH	22	36.47%	14,490	
30			APRIL	23	39.95%	11,951	
31			MAY	24	71.10%	18,409	
32			JUNE	25	120.69%	32,038	
33			JULY	26	225.75%	57,112	
34			AUGUST	27	231.37%	59,838	
35			SEPTEMBER	28	179.92%	46,981	
36			OCTOBER	29	152.34%	41,902	
37			NOVEMBER	30	54.25%	15,232	
38			DECEMBER	31	30.67%	7,642	
39		2010	JANUARY	32	22.03%	5,015	
40			FEBRUARY	33	35.46%	5,378	
41			MARCH	34	36.47%	7,332	
42			APRIL	35	39.95%	9,540	
43			MAY	36	71.10%	17,338	
44							

A	B	C	D	E	F	G	H	I
1								
2				Table 5.5				
3				XYZ MOTEL				
4				Monthly Time Series Regression Model for Prediction				
5				Summary Output				
6								
7		*Regression Statistics*						
8	Multiple R	0.9941						
9	R Square	0.9882						
10	Adjusted R Square	0.9875						
11	Standard Error	2,159						
12	Coefficient of Variation	8.6%						
13	Observations	36						
14								
15	ANOVA							
16		*df*		*SS*	*MS*	*F*	*Significance F*	
17	Regression		2	12,873,965,085.00	6,436,982,542.50	1,380.58	1.55718E-32	
18	Residual		33	153,863,295.09	4,662,524.09			
19	Total		35	13,027,828,380.09				
20								
21		*Coefficients*		*Standard Error*	*t Stat*	*p-value*	*Lower 95%*	*Upper 95%*
22	Intercept	(1,223.84)		987.29	(1.240)	0.2239	(3,232)	785
23	Trend	62.70		35.79	1.752	0.0891	(10)	136
24	Index	25,278.68		492.99	51.276	0.0000	24,276	26,282
25								
26	**PREDICTION**							
27	**Regression Equation:**							
28	Predicted Monthly Sales = -1,223.84 + Trend x 62.70 + Seasonal Factor x 25,278.68							
29								
30	*Month*	*Intercept*		*Trend*	*Seasonal Factor*	*Prediction*		
31	Jun	(1,223.839)		37	1.207	31,606		
32	Jul	(1,223.839)		38	2.257	58,225		
33	Aug	(1,223.839)		39	2.314	59,709		
34	Sep	(1,223.839)		40	1.799	46,765		
35								
36	Total Predicted Sales					196,304		
37								

A	B	C	D	E	F	G
1			Table 5.6			
2			XYZ MOTEL			
3		SETUP SHEET FOR COMPOSITE REGRESSION MODEL				
4						
5			Cross-	Time	XYZ	
6			Sectional	Series	Motel	
7	Year	Month	Model	Model	Sales	
8	2007	JUNE	34,699	29,348	27,241	
9		JULY	57,651	55,967	55,473	
10		AUGUST	57,608	57,452	58,073	
11		SEPTEMBER	42,682	44,508	45,159	
12		OCTOBER	25,813	37,599	37,917	
13		NOVEMBER	12,945	12,866	11,902	
14		DECEMBER	8,170	6,967	5,268	
15	2008	JANUARY	3,964	4,847	4,995	
16		FEBRUARY	1,726	8,305	6,816	
17		MARCH	7,443	8,623	6,073	
18		APRIL	20,140	9,564	9,152	
19		MAY	17,973	17,502	18,966	
20		JUNE	36,956	30,101	31,249	
21		JULY	52,775	56,720	57,299	
22		AUGUST	58,248	58,204	56,579	
23		SEPTEMBER	43,189	45,260	43,827	
24		OCTOBER	29,541	38,352	35,490	
25		NOVEMBER	15,243	13,618	13,967	
26		DECEMBER	6,894	7,720	10,362	
27	2009	JANUARY	7,625	5,600	6,788	
28		FEBRUARY	15,033	9,058	14,940	
29		MARCH	12,988	9,376	14,490	
30		APRIL	12,988	10,316	11,951	
31		MAY	17,850	18,254	18,409	
32		JUNE	41,325	30,853	32,038	
33		JULY	58,441	57,472	57,112	
34		AUGUST	57,835	58,957	59,838	
35		SEPTEMBER	39,997	46,013	46,981	
36		OCTOBER	30,396	39,104	41,902	
37		NOVEMBER	16,743	14,371	15,232	
38		DECEMBER	10,543	8,472	7,642	
39	2010	JANUARY	1,822	6,352	5,015	
40		FEBRUARY	10,499	9,810	5,378	
41		MARCH	3,964	10,128	7,332	
42		APRIL	17,647	11,069	9,540	
43		MAY	18,378	19,007	17,338	
44						

Table 5.7
XYZ MOTEL
Composite Regression Model for Prediction
Summary Output

Regression Statistics	
Multiple R	0.9943
R Square	0.9887
Adjusted R Square	0.9880
Standard Error	2,111
Coefficient of Variation	8.4%
Observations	36

ANOVA

	df	SS	MS	F	Significance F
Regression	2	12,880,729,214.19	6,440,364,607.10	1,444.82	7.41618E-33
Residual	33	147,099,165.89	4,457,550.48		
Total	35	13,027,828,380.09			

	Coefficients	Standard Error	t Stat	p-value	Lower 95%	Upper 95%
Intercept	-142.107	597.719	-0.238	0.814	-1358.1762	1073.9618
Cross-Sectional Model	0.090	0.073	1.232	0.227	-0.0589	0.2398
Time Series Model	0.915	0.071	12.835	0.000	0.7701	1.0603

PREDICTION

Regression Equation:

Predicted Monthly Sales = -142.107 + Cross-Sectional Prediction x .090 + Time Series Prediction x .915

Month	Intercept	Cross-Sectional Variable	Time Series Variable	Composite Prediction
Jun	(142.107)	4,026	28,925	32,809
Jul	(142.107)	5,318	53,287	58,463
Aug	(142.107)	5,284	54,646	59,788
Sep	(142.107)	3,459	42,800	46,116
Total Composite Predicted Sales				197,177

TABLE 5.8

	Quarterly Time Series	Monthly Cross-Sectional	Monthly Time Series	Composite
Prediction	$197,100	$200,000	$196,304	$197,177
R-Square	.9904	.9323	.9882	.9887
Adjusted R-Square	.9883	.9282	.9875	.9880
Standard Error	$5,549	$5,168	$2,159	$2,111
Coefficient of Variation	7.3%	20.5%	8.6%	8.4%

each independent variable's coefficient by that model's monthly room sales prediction and then adding that product to the intercept. Doing so produces a four-month room sales prediction in the amount of $197,177, an amount that differs from the quarterly time series model prediction by only $77.

Note that the cross-sectional variable has a t-statistic of less than 2 and a p-value greater than .05. This means that this variable is not statistically significant at the 5 percent level, and this would usually mandate its removal from the model, certainly if it were the only variable in a simple regression model. However, this is a multiple regression model with a slightly different set of rules that allows the retention in the model of a variable even if its absolute t-statistic is less than 2, as long as it is greater than 1.[3]

So, which is the best model? Perhaps Table 5.8 can help you make your decision.

Conclusion

As previously suggested, since quarterly models typically have less variability than monthly models, it should come as no surprise that the quarterly time series model has the best metrics, and therefore it ought to be the model of choice. It can also be concluded that, other than the cross-sectional model, the other three models balanced off the historical upward trend in tourist season room sales with the historical downward trend in off-season room sales to come up with a prediction that is only slightly more than the $195,968 from the previous year.

In the next chapter we leave the XYZ Motel sales forecasting problem and turn to the lost profits case of Precision Machine Works, where we introduce the idea of interrupted time series to measure the significance of an intervention in the company's sales stream.

Notes

1. Solver comes with Excel and can be found in the Add-Ins drop-down menu. Scroll down to Solver and simply check the box, and then click OK.
2. Additional information can be found in J. M. Wooldridge, *Econometric Analysis of Cross Section and Panel Data*, 2nd ed. (Cambridge, MA: Massachusetts Institute of Technology, 2010), chap. 6. See also Cliff T. Ragsdale, *Spreadsheet Modeling and Decision Analysis*, Chapter 11, 3rd ed. (Cincinnati, OH: South-Western College Publishing, 2001).

3. If one examines any of the regression tool summary outputs and locates the cell in the ANOVA section where the column headed SS intersects with the row labeled Residual, one finds what is called residual sum of squares (RSS). RSS measures the impact of all potential independent or predictor variables not yet in the model—it represents the squared, un-explained, or unaccounted for difference between the actual sales data and the predicted sales values. So, if a predictor variable is removed from the model, RSS must increase, thereby increasing the numerator of the standard error formula. Since the standard error formula is the square root of RSS divided by the degrees of freedom, removing a predictor variable also increases the number of degrees of freedom by 1, thereby increasing the denominator of the formula.

   If a predictor variable with an absolute t-statistic value of less than 1 is eliminated, the increase in RSS is smaller than the relative increase in the degrees of freedom. As a consequence, the standard error decreases. The reverse is also true—leaving in the model a predictor variable whose absolute t-statistic is greater than 1 produces a smaller standard error and thereby increases the accuracy of the model.

CHAPTER 6

Case Study 6—Cross-Sectional Regression Combined with Seasonal Indexes to Determine Lost Profits

This case study concerns the calculation of lost profits that the plaintiff alleges were caused by the tortious acts of the company's general manager. After soliciting its customers and employees, the general manager left the employ of Precision Machine Works, L.P. at the end of March 2007, which the plaintiff alleges resulted in it suffering operating losses for a two-year period.

Outline of the Case

An issue we had to deal with early on was that forecasting incremental sales was made problematical by the company's completed contract accounting method that produced monthly sales figures that showed no trend or pattern. We were able to deal with this in two ways. First, monthly sales were converted to quarterly sales, which removed much of the randomness from the data; and second, we discovered that the company's machine shop sales in the oil patch section of Houston, TX are highly correlated with the spot price of crude oil. Because of this, we were able to use a multiple regression model that included the predictor variables seasonal indexes and the spot price of oil to calculate incremental sales. Incremental cost of sales and operating expenses were developed for the interruption and recovery periods by regressing these variables against sales.

A schedule of monthly sales of the Precision Machine Works, L.P. for the period beginning April 2004 and ending June 2008 is shown in Table 6.1. Declining sales after that date are not included as they are the result of a hurricane and not the actions of the general manager, who is the defendant in this case.

Figure 6.1 shows the same information as Table 6.1, but conveyed in a line chart, with the diamonds representing monthly sales up through March 2007 and the squares representing monthly sales from April 2007 through June 2008, the latter period representing the period of interruption.

		2004–2005	2005–2006	2006–2007	2007–2008	2008–2009
7	April	$ 71,197	$ 120,757	$ 139,704	$ 118,178	$ 80,919
8	May	58,892	82,623	121,757	136,007	36,748
9	June	67,254	90,629	196,778	55,745	78,568
10	July	57,586	95,148	135,051	91,181	-
11	August	69,197	129,761	144,167	92,110	-
12	September	57,161	108,665	137,610	46,899	-
13	October	85,495	129,369	230,183	44,499	-
14	November	38,026	51,575	92,239	49,206	-
15	December	60,660	103,064	64,970	43,843	-
16	January	101,357	56,449	97,704	19,590	-
17	February	68,553	270,210	138,570	40,921	-
18	March	99,360	132,125	83,488	36,858	-
20	Total	$ 834,737	$ 1,370,375	$ 1,582,221	$ 309,930	$ 196,235

Table 6.1 — PRECISION MACHINE WORKS, L.P. SALES HISTORY April 2004–June 2008

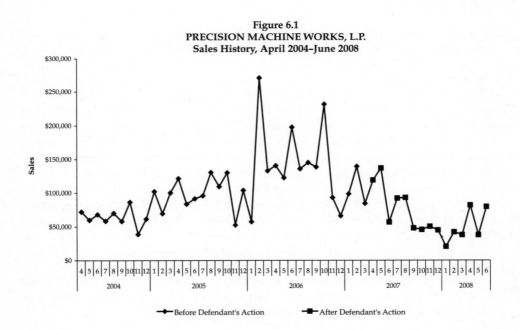

Figure 6.1
PRECISION MACHINE WORKS, L.P.
Sales History, April 2004–June 2008

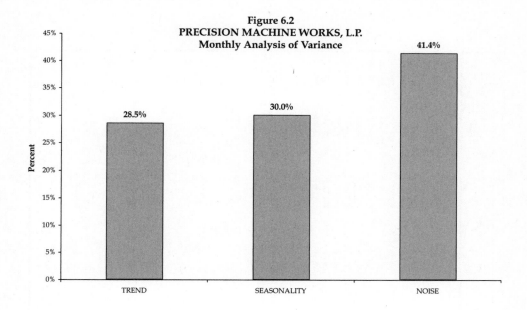

Figure 6.2
PRECISION MACHINE WORKS, L.P.
Monthly Analysis of Variance

Testing for Noise in the Data

Since the monthly data appears to contain a considerable amount of noise, an analysis of variance (ANOVA) was performed, the results of which are shown in Figure 6.2, with supporting calculations in Table 6.2 and Table 6.3 (an explanation of Table 6.2 can be found in Case Study 2). As suspected, the data is very noisy, which makes it difficult to discern trends and patterns. The cause of the noise is the method the company uses to account for its sales. It uses the completed contract method, which necessarily produces an excessive degree of spikiness, or noise, in the historical sales data. Converting monthly sales into quarterly sales can reduce noise as this process smoothes out the high and low months in any quarter, as can be seen in Figure 6.3.

Converting to Quarterly Data

The quarterly analysis of variance chart in Figure 6.4 indicates the higher degree of trend, the lower amount of seasonality, and the lower amount of noise, by 37 percent (26.1 percent noise versus 41.4 percent noise), in the quarterly sales history of the company when compared with the monthly sales figures.

Optimizing Seasonal Indexes

Figure 6.5 displays a schedule of optimized seasonal indexes, computed by calculating the average difference of each quarter of the year from the trendline. A quadratic or second-degree polynomial trend function is used to account for the slight curvature in actual sales, indicating that the rate of growth in sales slows down over time.

Table 6.2
PRECISION MACHINE WORKS, L.P.
MONTHLY ANALYSIS OF VARIANCE

Year	Month	Period	Actual Sales
2004	4	1	71,197
	5	2	58,892
	6	3	67,254
	7	4	57,586
	8	5	69,197
	9	6	57,161
	10	7	85,495
	11	8	38,026
	12	9	60,660
2005	1	10	101,357
	2	11	68,553
	3	12	99,360
	4	13	120,757
	5	14	82,623
	6	15	90,629
	7	16	95,148
	8	17	129,761
	9	18	108,665
	10	19	129,369
	11	20	51,575
	12	21	103,064
2006	1	22	56,449
	2	23	270,210
	3	24	132,125
	4	25	139,704
	5	26	121,757
	6	27	196,778
	7	28	135,051
	8	29	144,167
	9	30	137,610
	10	31	230,183
	11	32	92,239
	12	33	64,970
2007	1	34	97,704
	2	35	138,570
	3	36	83,488

SOURCE OF VARIANCE	PERCENT
TREND	28.5%
SEASONALITY	30.0%
NOISE	41.4%
TOTAL	100.0%

		Year		(A)
Month	2004–2005	2005–2006	2006–2007	AVG
4	71,197	120,757	139,704	110,553
5	58,892	82,623	121,757	87,757
6	67,254	90,629	196,778	118,220
7	57,586	95,148	135,051	95,928
8	69,197	129,761	144,167	114,375
9	57,161	108,665	137,610	101,145
10	85,495	129,369	230,183	148,349
11	38,026	51,575	92,239	60,613
12	60,660	103,064	64,970	76,231
1	101,357	56,449	97,704	85,170
2	68,553	270,210	138,570	159,111
3	99,360	132,125	83,488	104,991
(B) AVG	69,562	114,198	131,852	

SEASONAL VARIANCE OF THE MONTHLY AVERAGES - (A)   8,685,642,520

TREND VARIANCE OF THE YEARLY AVERAGES - (B)   2,061,380,923

TOTAL VARIANCE OF THE 36 MONTHS - (C)   86,721,972,161

Table 6.3

PRECISION MACHINE WORKS, LP

MONTHLY ANALYSIS OF VARIANCE OUTPUT

ANOVA: Two-Factor Without Replication

SUMMARY	Count	Sum	Average	Variance
April	3	331,658	110,553	1,251,399,305
May	3	263,272	87,757	1,007,777,985
June	3	354,661	118,220	4,765,088,471
July	3	287,785	95,928	1,500,678,078
August	3	343,125	114,375	1,582,679,887
September	3	303,436	101,145	1,660,410,915
October	3	445,047	148,349	5,503,852,416
November	3	181,840	60,613	796,030,944
December	3	228,694	76,231	544,638,025
January	3	255,510	85,170	622,007,983
February	3	477,333	159,111	10,482,835,923
March	3	314,973	104,991	615,170,563
2004 - 2005	12	834,737	69,561	331,516,179
2005 - 2006	12	1,370,375	114,198	3,136,641,475
2006 - 2007	12	1,582,221	131,852	2,166,878,816

ANOVA

Source of Variation	SS	df	MS	F	p-value	F crit
Rows	26,056,905,859	11	2,368,809,624	1.45	2.20E-01	2.26
Columns	24,736,645,683	2	12,368,322,841	7.57	0.00	3.44
Error	35,928,495,312	22	1,633,113,423			
Total	86,722,046,853	35				

Source of Variation	Percent
Seasonality	30.05%
Trend	28.52%
Noise	41.43%
Total	100.0%

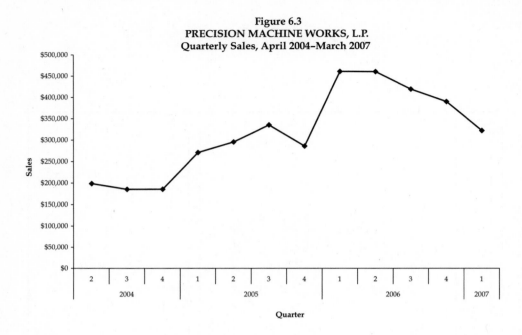

Figure 6.3
PRECISION MACHINE WORKS, L.P.
Quarterly Sales, April 2004–March 2007

This can easily be determined by regressing sales against time using Excel's trendline feature in its chart module and comparing the results of the various model options. The model that best fits the data, and thereby accounts best for the curvature in the trendline, is a second-degree polynomial model. The indexes thus calculated in Figure 6.5 allow seasonality to be accounted for in the prediction model, to the extent it exists. The step-by-step process for creating optimized seasonal indexes was demonstrated in Case Study 5 and therefore is not repeated here, except to note that

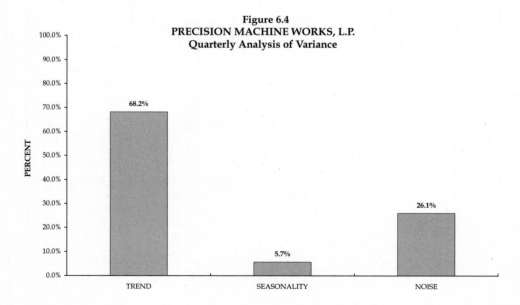

Figure 6.4
PRECISION MACHINE WORKS, L.P.
Quarterly Analysis of Variance

Year	Qtr	Time Period	Time Period Squared	Actual Sales	Quadratic Trend	Actual as a % of Trend	Seasonal Forecast
2004	2	1	1	$ 197,343	$ 168,752	116.9%	$ 183,010
	3	2	4	183,944	197,193	93.3%	189,543
	4	3	9	184,181	226,373	81.4%	181,711
2005	1	4	16	269,270	256,293	105.1%	295,147
	2	5	25	294,009	286,952	102.5%	311,196
	3	6	36	333,574	318,351	104.8%	306,001
	4	7	49	284,008	350,489	81.0%	281,339
2006	1	8	64	458,784	383,366	119.7%	441,484
	2	9	81	458,239	416,983	109.9%	452,212
	3	10	100	416,828	451,339	92.4%	433,830
	4	11	121	387,392	486,435	79.6%	390,464

Original Regression Coefficients

Time Period Squared	Time Period	Intercept
(1,367.12)	44,341.66	112,071.20

	Optimized
Intercept	141,051.10
Time Period	27,331.64
Time Period Squared	369.71
RMSE =	18,060.35
RSQ =	0.9760

Quarter	Unadjusted Seasonal Indexes	Normalizing Factor	Optimized Seasonal Indexes
1	112.4%	1.000960667	115.16%
2	109.8%	1.000960667	108.45%
3	96.8%	1.000960667	96.12%
4	80.7%	1.000960667	80.27%
	399.6%		100.0%

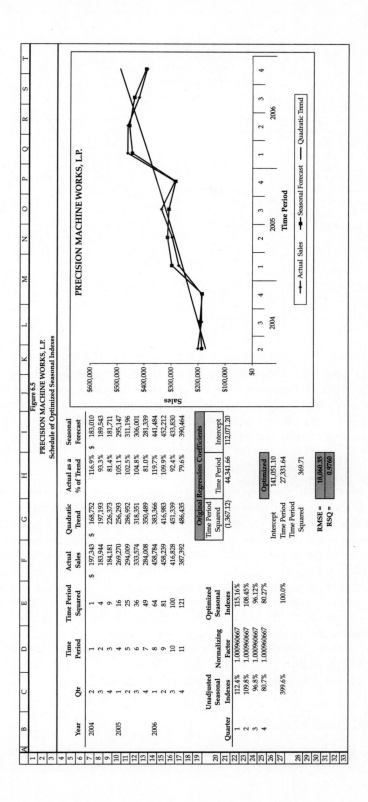

PRECISION MACHINE WORKS, L.P.

Sales

Time Period

2004   2005   2006

— Actual Sales   — Seasonal Forecast   — Quadratic Trend

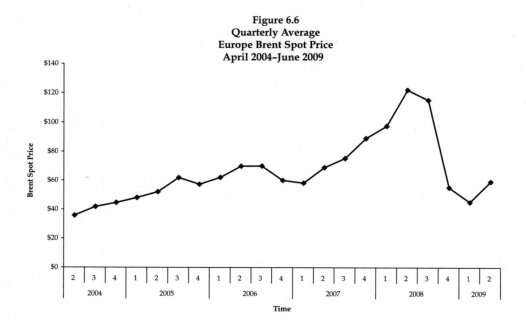

Figure 6.6
Quarterly Average
Europe Brent Spot Price
April 2004–June 2009

the original regression coefficients found in cells G21:I21 in Figure 6.5 are calculated using Excel's LINEST array function, but this time selecting only those three cells rather than a 2x5 array and leaving the Stats argument blank in the dialogue box. In addition, Solver's "By Changing Variable Cells" reference should include the three coefficients found in cells H26:H28.

Exogenous Predictor Variable

Once the seasonal indexes were developed, it was necessary to find an exogenous variable, that is, a predictor variable other than time that did not come from within the company itself. A conversation with the owner elicited the notion that company sales were tied to the price of oil—the higher the price, the more willing wildcatters were to explore for oil, and the more they explored, the more their machinery broke down; hence their greater need for machine parts for repairs. The chart in Figure 6.6 shows the quarterly average Europe Brent spot price for a barrel of oil for the period April 2004 to June 2009. Daily spot prices were converted to quarterly averages to allow for comparison with Precision's quarterly sales.

A chart showing the very high degree of correlation between Precision's quarterly sales and the quarterly average Europe Brent spot price for a barrel of oil for the period April 2004 to March 2007 is shown in Figure 6.7.

Interrupted Time Series Analysis

A setup worksheet for the interrupted time series regression analysis is presented in Table 6.4. Interrupted time series analysis tests to see if there was a statistically and

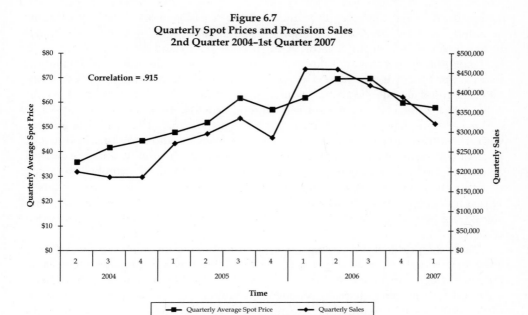

Figure 6.7
Quarterly Spot Prices and Precision Sales
2nd Quarter 2004–1st Quarter 2007

Correlation = .915

		A	B	C	D	E	F	G	H
	1				Table 6.4				
	2				PRECISION MACHINE WORKS, L.P.				
	3				Setup Sheet to Account for Trend Change				
	4								
	5		Year	Quarter	Revenue	Spot Price	Trend Change	Seasonal Index	
	6		2004	2	$ 197,343	$35.45	0	108.45%	
	7			3	183,944	41.39	0	96.12%	
	8			4	184,181	44.16	0	80.27%	
	9		2005	1	269,270	47.63	0	115.16%	
	10			2	294,009	51.63	0	108.45%	
	11			3	333,574	61.47	0	96.12%	
	12			4	284,008	56.87	0	80.27%	
	13		2006	1	458,784	61.68	0	115.16%	
	14			2	458,239	69.50	0	108.45%	
	15			3	416,828	69.62	0	96.12%	
	16			4	387,392	59.66	0	80.27%	
	17		2007	1	319,762	57.76	0	115.16%	
	18			2	309,930	68.58	1	108.45%	
	19			3	230,190	74.88	2	96.12%	
	20			4	137,548	88.56	3	80.27%	
	21		2008	1	97,369	96.93	4	115.16%	
	22			2	196,235	121.40	5	108.45%	
	23								

substantively significant change in the Precision Machine Works, L.P.'s sales trend beginning in April 2007 and continuing through June 2008. If that trend change is significant, it will occur regardless of spot oil prices and seasonal factors; that is, something else is driving sales downward. To capture this potential change in trend, a third predictor variable is included in the model to account for a potentially different trend in sales from that which is embedded in the spot price of oil. In column F of Table 6.4 we enter zeros beginning with the second quarter of 2004 and ending with the first quarter of 2007. Since we suspect that sales fell off beginning with the second quarter of 2007, in spite of seasonality and increases in the spot price of oil, we enter a sequence of numbers from 1 to 5 beginning with the second quarter of 2007 and ending with the second quarter of 2008. This number sequence of 1 to 5, which could have been any five-number sequence that grew by a factor of one for each period, indicates that we are hypothesizing a new trend in sales that should not be taking place if the only influence on the sales trend is the spot price of oil.

Table 6.5 presents the summary output of the regression analysis referred to in Table 6.4. Attention should be given to the highlighted cells in the t-Stat and p-value columns, where absolute t-Stats greater than 2 and p-values less than .05 have been obtained for the trend change coefficient, indicating that the decrease in the sales of Precision Machine Works, L.P. was not due to mere chance, but was the result of some external, intervening phenomenon. And the amount of the coefficient for trend change, −$142,830, is substantial; that is, it has a large effect size and is therefore practically significant.

A line chart in Figure 6.8 compares actual to predicted sales for the 17-quarter period beginning April 2004 and ending June 2008 after controlling for the downward trend in sales post-March 2007, that is, the only way to match up actual sales with predicted sales is to include the trend change variable in the model. The goodness-of-fit metrics evident in Table 6.5 are graphically demonstrated here. Put another way, without the effect of the −$142,830 trend change coefficient, forecasted sales would have continued climbing as the spot price of oil was increasing throughout this period.

"But For" Sales Forecast

Having shown that a damaging event took place after March 31, 2007, sales for the period of April 2007 to September 2011 need to be forecasted but for the intervening actions of the defendant. Figure 6.9 is a setup worksheet for the cross-sectional regression analysis that also shows seasonally adjusted predicted or incremental sales. Note that the variable for trend change included in Table 6.4 has not been used here, as it was only put in the previous model to demonstrate a relationship and not for predicting what sales would have been but for the defendant's intervening actions.

To forecast what would have been but for the actions of the defendant, we set up Figure 6.9 by filling in the optimized seasonal indexes in cells E7 through E36 for each quarter beginning with the second quarter of 2004 and ending with the third quarter of 2011. In cells F7 through F27 we enter the spot price of oil for each quarter. In cells F28 through F36 we enter the average historical quarterly spot

A	B	C	D	E	F	G	H	I

Table 6.5

PRECISION MACHINE WORKS, L.P.

Regression Model for Structural Change

Summary Output - Quarterly Index Model

Regression Statistics

Multiple R	0.9592
R Square	0.9200
Adjusted R Square	0.9015
Standard Error	34.018
Coefficient of Variation	12.15%
Observations	17

ANOVA

	df	SS	MS	F	Significance F
Regression	3	1.73003E+11	5766787292	49.83334032	2.17385E-07
Residual	13	15043742401	1157210954		
Total	16	1.88047E+11			

	Coefficients	Standard Error	t Stat	p-value	Lower 95%	Upper 95%
Intercept	(293,349)	80,034	(3.67)	0.00285	(466,252.80)	(120,445.79)
Spot Price	8,502	912	9.33	0.00000	6,532.94	10,471.72
Trend Change	(142,830)	12,150	(11.76)	0.00000003	(169,079.57)	(116,580.91)
Seasonal Index	144,828	63,676	2.27	0.04053	7,264.74	282,392.12

127

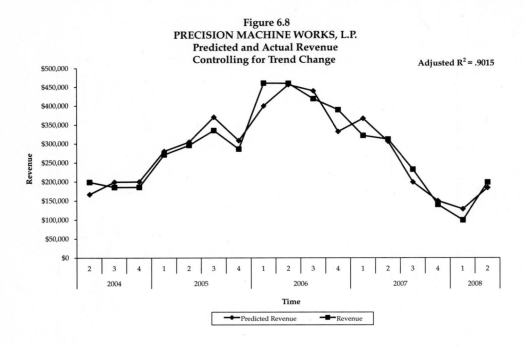

Figure 6.8
PRECISION MACHINE WORKS, L.P.
Predicted and Actual Revenue
Controlling for Trend Change

Adjusted R^2 = .9015

price computed by AVERAGE($F$7:$F$27). By doing so, we have assumed that the average quarterly spot price of oil over the past 21 quarters is a good proxy for the future spot price of oil. To date, the spot price has not dropped below the calculated average of $65.68, and as we shall see, there is an upside limit to potential sales activity. In column R, actual quarterly sales have been transformed by being raised to the power of .68571923 in order to make the sales data more bell-shaped, linear, and homoscedastic, that is, more amenable to regression analysis. To initiate this process, we enter the number 1 as a placeholder in cell R5, and then transform actual sales in cell R7 with the formula =+G7$^{\wedge}$$S$5. We then copy cell R7 down to and through cell R18. In column S we show the seasonally adjusted predicted sales computed with the following formula entered in cell S7:

$$=TREND(\$R\$7:\$R\$18,\$E\$7:\$F\$18,E7:F7)^{\wedge}(1/\$R\$5)$$

which is then copied down to and through cell S27. Beginning with the third quarter of 2009, when the spot price of oil goes from a historical value with a built-in trend to a proxy calculated as the 21-quarter historical average that is trendless, we need to introduce a trend factor back into the model. We do this by modifying the previous equation to include time period in column D. The formula in cell S28 now becomes:

$$=TREND(\$R\$7:\$R\$18,\$D\$7:\$F\$18,D28:F28)^{\wedge}(1/\$R\$5)$$

and is then copied down to and through cell S36.

The last thing we need to do before we run Solver is to create the formula for RMSE in cell Y31, which is:

$$=SQRT(SUMXMY2(S7:S18,G7:G18)/(COUNT(S7:S18)-3))$$

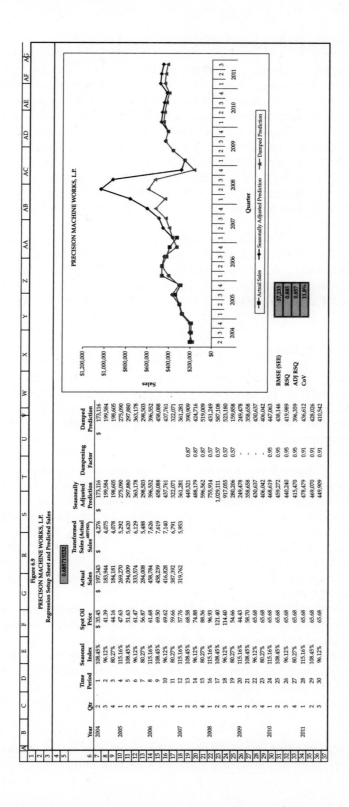

Figure 6.9

PRECISON MACHINE WORKS, L.P.
Regression Setup Sheet and Predicted Sales

Transformed Sales exponent: 0.68719232

Year	Qtr	Time Period	Seasonal Index	Spot Oil Price	Actual Sales	Transformed Sales (Actual Sales^.68719232)	Seasonally Adjusted Prediction	Dampening Factor	Damped Prediction
2004	2	1	108.45%	$ 35.45	$ 197,343	$ 4,276	$ 173,116		$ 173,116
	3	2	96.12%	41.39	183,944	4,075	199,584		199,584
	4	3	80.27%	44.16	184,181	4,078	198,605		198,605
2005	1	4	115.16%	47.63	269,270	5,292	275,090		275,090
	2	5	108.45%	51.63	294,009	5,620	297,880		297,880
	3	6	96.12%	61.47	333,574	6,129	363,178		363,178
	4	7	80.27%	56.87	284,008	5,488	298,503		298,503
2006	1	8	115.16%	61.68	458,784	7,626	396,552		396,552
	2	9	108.45%	69.50	458,239	7,619	458,088		458,088
	3	10	96.12%	69.62	416,828	7,140	437,761		437,761
	4	11	80.27%	59.66	387,392	6,791	322,071		322,071
2007	1	12	115.16%	57.76	319,762	5,953	361,281		361,281
	2	13	108.45%	68.58			449,321	0.87	390,909
	3	14	96.12%	74.88			488,179	0.87	424,716
	4	15	80.27%	88.56			596,562	0.87	519,009
2008	1	16	115.16%	96.93			755,914	0.57	431,249
	2	17	108.45%	121.40			1,029,111	0.57	587,108
	3	18	96.12%	114.40			917,055	0.57	523,180
	4	19	80.27%	54.66			280,206	0.57	159,858
2009	1	20	115.16%	44.43			249,478	-	249,478
	2	21	108.45%	58.70			358,658	-	358,658
	3	22	96.12%				430,637	-	430,637
	4	23	80.27%	65.68			406,042	-	406,042
2010	1	24	115.16%	65.68			468,619	0.95	447,063
	2	25	108.45%	65.68			459,272	0.95	438,146
	3	26	96.12%	65.68			440,240	0.95	419,989
	4	27	80.27%	65.68			415,470	0.95	396,359
2011	1	28	115.16%	65.68			478,479	0.91	436,612
	2	29	108.45%	65.68			469,070	0.91	428,026
	3	30	96.12%	65.68			449,909	0.91	410,542

RMSE (SEE)	37,233
RSQ	0.885
ADJ RSQ	0.857
CoV	11.8%

PRECISION MACHINE WORKS, L.P.

Legend: —■— Actual Sales —◆— Seasonally Adjusted Prediction —▲— Damped Prediction

X axis: Quarter (2004–2011)
Y axis: Sales ($0 to $1,200,000)

Transforming the Dependent Variable

Now we are ready to optimize the dependent variable exponent in cell R5 by use of Solver. Open Solver and enter Y31 in the Set Object argument, click the Min radio button, and enter R5 in the By Changing Variable Cells argument. Select GRG Nonlinear as the solving method, click Options, and select Use Automatic Scaling. Click OK and click Solve. Open Solver and repeat the click on Solve if necessary.

Predicted quarterly sales in column U have been damped down to limit annual sales to about $1.7 million, using the dampening factors in column T. The amount of sales recorded in 2006, the year prior to that of the injury, is $1.7 million. The company's owner indicated that no matter the amount of potential sales, he intended to limit his annual sales to about $1.7 million, as that was what he felt was within his span of control.

Table 6.6 contains the summary output of the time series regression analysis referred to in Figure 6.9. Attention is called to all of the goodness-of-fit metrics in the back-transformed column. As previously noted in another case study, although the predictor variable seasonal index has an absolute t-statistic of less than 2, it is left in the model as it contributes to a lower standard error of the estimate (SEE).

Dealing with Mitigation

The lost sales of the company are not expected to continue in perpetuity, but instead are expected to be made up or mitigated sometime in the future. In order to predict the length of the period of interruption, we need to know if and when historical sales have bottomed out and are starting to climb to pre-interruption levels. Once we have established that point in time, we can begin to count off our mitigation period.

The chart in Figure 6.10 indicates, by comparing the ratio of consecutive nine months of sales compared to the same totals from a year ago, that the fall-off in sales that began in mid-2007 had bottomed out and a turn-around in sales had started by June 2008. For example, sales for the nine months ending March 31, 2007 equaled those for the nine months ending March 31, 2006. This ratio remained constant for the first month that the defendants left, April 2007, but after that no period has equaled or done better than the same period the year before. After accounting for the drop-off in sales in the fourth quarter of 2008, mitigation picks up strongly in the first quarter of 2009.

A schedule showing the cumulative amount of sales lost during the period April 2007 to September 2011 is shown in Table 6.7. These amounts assume that, starting with the third quarter of 2008, the company would begin to recover and begin to mitigate its damages, eventually, by the end of the third quarter in 2011, restoring sales to where they would have been but for the actions of the defendant. Using Excel's Goal Seek, we established a growth rate in sales such that by the end of the third quarter of 2011, mitigating sales would equal predicted sales. The formula in cell G9 is:

$$=RATE(11,,-G16,I27)$$

where 11 is the number of periods from the fourth quarter of 2008 to the third quarter of 2011, -G16 is the starting value of $125,000, and I27 is the ending value

Table 6.6

PRECISION MACHINE WORKS, L.P.
CROSS-SECTIONAL ANALYSIS
SUMMARY OUTPUT

Regression Statistics		*Transformed*	*Back-Transformed*
Multiple R		0.9456	0.9409
R Square		0.8941	0.8853
Adjusted R Square		0.8706	0.8567
Standard Error		463	37.233
Coefficient of Variation		7.9%	11.8%
Observations		12	12

ANOVA

	df	*SS*	*MS*	*F*	*Significance F*
Regression	2	16,258,046	8,129,023	37.999	4.09039E-05
Residual	9	1,925,360	213,929		
Total	11	18,183,406			

	Coefficients	*Standard Error*	*t Stat*	*p-value*	*Lower 95%*	*Upper 95%*
Intercept	(2,119.66)	1,229.01	-1.725	0.1187	(4,900)	661
Seasonal Index	1,998.78	1,005.41	1.988	0.0780	(276)	4,273
Spot Oil Price	108.91	12.86	8.468	0.0000	80	138

Regression Equation:

Forecasted Quarterly Sales = $(-2{,}119.66 + \text{Spot Oil Price} \times 1{,}998.78 + \text{Seasonal Factor} \times 108.91)^{(1/.6857192 3)}$

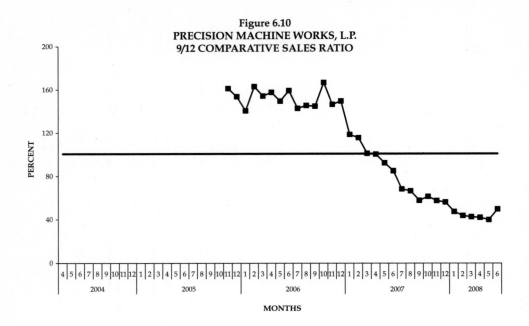

Figure 6.10
PRECISION MACHINE WORKS, L.P.
9/12 COMPARATIVE SALES RATIO

	A	B	C	D	E	F	G	H	I	J	K	L
1							Table 6.7					
2							PRECISION MACHINE WORKS, L.P.					
3							SCHEDULE OF LOST SALES					
4							APRIL 2007–SEPTEMBER 2011					
5												
6							PROJECTED					
7							SALES					
8						ACTUAL	GROWTH @		PREDICTED		LOST	
9		YEAR	QTR			SALES	11.42%		SALES		SALES	
10		2007	2		$	309,930			$ 390,909		$ 80,979	
11			3			230,190			424,716		194,526	
12			4			137,548			519,009		381,461	
13		2008	1			97,369			431,249		333,880	
14			2			196,235		$ 196,235	587,108		390,873	
15			3					150,000	523,180		373,180	
16			4					125,000	159,858		34,858	
17		2009	1					139,271	249,478		110,207	
18			2					155,171	358,658		203,487	
19			3					172,886	430,637		257,752	
20			4					192,623	406,042		213,419	
21		2010	1					214,614	447,063		232,448	
22			2					239,116	438,146		199,030	
23			3					266,415	419,989		153,574	
24			4					296,830	396,359		99,528	
25		2011	1					330,718	436,612		105,893	
26			2					368,475	428,026		59,551	
27			3					410,542	410,542		-	
28												
29							Cumulative Lost Sales			$	3,424,645	
30												

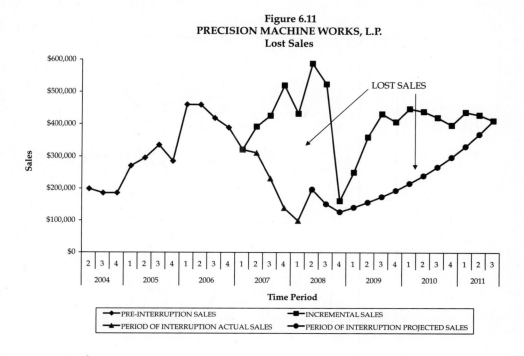

Figure 6.11
PRECISION MACHINE WORKS, L.P.
Lost Sales

of $410,542. We started using the formula with the first quarter of 2009 rather than the third quarter of 2008 as we needed to separately account for the decrease in sales in the third and fourth quarters of 2008 by subjectively choosing sales figures for those quarters to keep mitigating sales less than incremental sales. The difference between the two estimates, what sales would have been but for the actions of the defendants and make up or mitigating sales that the company is expected to enjoy between the third quarter of 2008 and the third quarter of 2011, are the company's lost sales shown in column K.

Figure 6.11 presents a line chart showing actual sales prior to April 2007, actual sales after 2007 through June 2008, incremental sales for the period April 2007 to September 2011, and mitigating sales expected during the recovery period of July 2008 to September 2011. The open space between the lines represents sales lost during the period of interruption due to the actions of the defendant.

Computing Saved Costs and Expenses

The next step is to compute saved or avoided expenses associated with the lost sales. That process begins by examining the company's Statements of Operations derived from tax returns for the years ended December 31, 2003 to 2008 as shown in Table 6.8. Discussions with the company's owner regarding the nature and function of certain expenses caused them to be recategorized from operating expenses to cost of sales, which produced a narrow range of cost of sales for the four-year period.

Table 6.8

PRECISION MACHINE WORKS, L.P.
STATEMENT OF OPERATIONS
FOR THE PERIODS ENDED DECEMBER 31,

	DOLLARS							PERCENT						
	2003	2004	2005	2006	2007	2008	AVERAGE	2003	2004	2005	2006	2007	2008	AVERAGE
GROSS SALES	$ 783,845	$ 749,096	$1,180,861	$ 1,721,243	$ 997,430	$ 577,617	$ 1,001,682	100.0%	100.0%	100.0%	100.0%	100.0%	100.0%	100.0%
COST OF GOODS SOLD														
Materials	167,968	165,436	209,889	151,314	117,642	57,423	144,945	21.4%	22.1%	17.8%	8.8%	11.8%	9.9%	14.5%
Cost of Labor	233,464	220,780	294,307	382,962	270,724	237,664	273,317	29.8%	29.5%	24.9%	22.2%	27.1%	41.1%	27.3%
Employee Benefits - Direct Labor	1,020	8,900	20,427	-	-	7,212	6,260	0.1%	1.2%	1.7%			1.2%	0.6%
Payroll Taxes - Direct Labor	18,453	17,460	20,396	35,231	36,862	28,833	26,206	2.4%	2.3%	1.7%	2.0%	3.7%	5.0%	2.6%
Shop Supplies	7,337	-	28,609	55,023	41,814	39,619	28,734	0.9%		2.4%	3.2%	4.2%	6.9%	2.9%
Outside Service	11,168	-	70,103	262,572	25,525	-	61,561	1.4%		5.9%	15.3%	2.6%		6.1%
Contract Labor	-	-	1,070	650	20,870	29,429	8,670			0.1%	0.0%	2.1%	5.1%	0.9%
Insurance - Direct Labor	-	-	-	39,414	39,300	5,784	14,083				2.3%	3.9%	1.0%	1.4%
Repair and Maintenance	10,607	7,266	9,276	28,006	32,872	-	14,671	1.4%	1.0%	0.8%	1.6%	3.3%		1.5%
Warehouse Expense	1,345	-	-	-	-	-	224	0.2%						0.0%
Utilities	8,434	8,480	11,241	15,306	20,232	17,265	13,493	1.1%	1.1%	1.0%	0.9%	2.0%	3.0%	1.3%
Freight	-	1,303	1,080	1,778	503	2,620	1,214		0.2%	0.1%	0.1%	0.1%	0.5%	0.1%
Equipment Rental	-	-	-	-	-	28,914	4,819						5.0%	0.5%
Equipment Repairs	-	-	-	-	-	38,016	6,336						6.6%	0.6%
Total	459,796	429,625	666,398	972,256	606,344	492,779	604,533	58.7%	57.4%	56.4%	56.5%	60.8%	85.3%	60.4%
GROSS PROFIT	324,049	319,471	514,463	748,987	391,086	84,838	397,149	41.3%	42.6%	43.6%	43.5%	39.2%	14.7%	39.6%

134

	1 $	1 %	2 $	2 %	3 $	3 %	4 $	4 %	5 $	5 %	6 $	6 %	Total $	Total %
OPERATING EXPENSES														
Amortization	7,967	1.0%	7,967	1.1%	7,967	0.7%	7,967	0.5%	7,966	0.8%	7,967	0.8%	7,967	0.8%
Auto Expense	6,630	0.8%	7,187	1.0%	9,272	0.8%	8,729	0.5%	8,995	0.9%	4,739	0.8%	7,592	0.8%
Bank Charges	143	0.0%	169	0.0%					15	0.0%			55	0.0%
Commissions	1,986	0.3%											331	0.0%
Dues	400	0.1%	335	0.0%	227	0.0%	455	0.0%	897	0.1%			386	0.0%
Depreciation	96,048	12.3%	68,944	9.2%	49,066	4.2%	34,920	2.0%	34,531	3.5%	34,010	5.9%	52,920	5.3%
Depreciation - Section 179							44,000	2.6%					7,333	0.7%
Equipment Rental									385	0.0%			64	0.0%
Freight	1,219	0.2%	87	0.0%									218	0.0%
Interest	26,518	3.4%	23,755	3.2%	18,708	1.6%	9,926	0.6%	3,976	0.4%			13,814	1.4%
Insurance	24,649	3.1%	12,170	1.6%	2,057	0.2%	1,507	0.1%	1,278	0.1%	885	0.2%	7,091	0.7%
Legal									10,299	1.0%	7,018	1.2%	2,886	0.3%
Marketing	97	0.0%	70	0.0%	285	0.0%	2,162	0.1%	691	0.1%			551	0.1%
Meals and Entertainment	407	0.1%	729	0.1%	1,115	0.1%	392	0.0%	346	0.0%			498	0.0%
Meals and Entertainment (M-1)	407	0.1%	729	0.1%	1,114	0.1%	391	0.0%	346	0.0%			498	0.0%
Office Expense	3,798	0.5%	10,630	1.4%	5,628	0.5%	4,979	0.3%	3,906	0.4%	2,367	0.4%	5,218	0.5%
Professional						0.1%							167	0.0%
Postage	111	0.0%		0.0%	1,000		238	0.0%	82	0.0%	65	0.0%	83	0.0%
Rent	19,500	2.5%	19,800	2.6%	92,400	7.8%	158,900	9.2%	67,115	6.7%	35,456	6.1%	65,529	6.5%
Salaries and Wages	53,250	6.8%	58,930	7.9%	108,798	9.2%	264,538	15.4%	257,793	25.8%	218,058	37.8%	160,228	16.0%
Taxes and Licenses	12,720	1.6%	12,741	1.7%	18,599	1.6%	17,419	1.0%	9,636	1.0%			11,853	1.2%
Telephone	3,539	0.5%	3,424	0.5%	5,126	0.4%	4,196	0.2%	7,312	0.7%	3,936	0.7%	4,589	0.5%
Uniforms and Laundry	2,514	0.3%	2,748	0.4%	3,482	0.3%	3,510	0.2%	3,349	0.3%	974	0.2%	2,763	0.3%
Utilities	444	0.1%	446	0.1%	592	0.1%	806	0.0%	1,065	0.1%	909	0.2%	710	0.1%
TOTAL	262,347	33.5%	230,861	30.8%	325,436	27.6%	565,035	32.8%	419,983	42.1%	316,384	54.8%	353,341	35.3%
OPERATING INCOME	61,702	7.9%	88,610	11.8%	189,027	16.0%	183,952	10.7%	(28,897)	-2.9%	(231,546)	-40.1%	43,808	4.4%
PROFIT DISTRIBUTION	62,400	8.0%	90,000	12.0%	183,680	15.6%	174,000	10.1%					85,013	8.5%
ADDITION TO PARTNERS' EQUITY	$ (698)	-0.1%	$ (1,390)	-0.2%	$ 5,347	0.5%	$ 9,952	0.6%	$ (28,897)	-2.9%	$ (231,546)	-40.1%	$ (41,205)	-4.1%

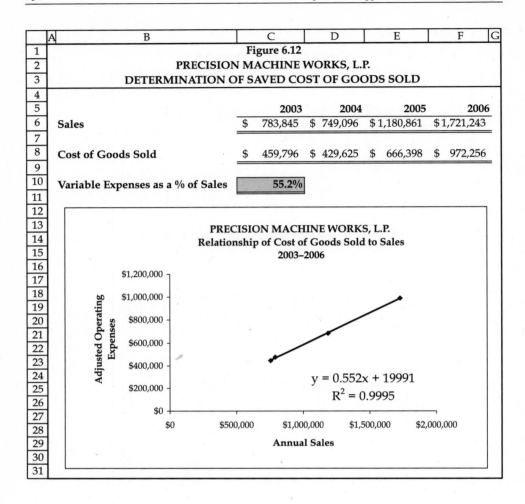

		2003	2004	2005	2006
Sales		$ 783,845	$ 749,096	$ 1,180,861	$ 1,721,243
Cost of Goods Sold		$ 459,796	$ 429,625	$ 666,398	$ 972,256
Variable Expenses as a % of Sales		55.2%			

Figure 6.12
PRECISION MACHINE WORKS, L.P.
DETERMINATION OF SAVED COST OF GOODS SOLD

PRECISION MACHINE WORKS, L.P.
Relationship of Cost of Goods Sold to Sales
2003–2006

$$y = 0.552x + 19991$$
$$R^2 = 0.9995$$

Because of that narrow range, the well-fitted regression model depicted in Figure 6.12 would be expected. This shows how the variable or saved portion of cost of goods sold of 55.2 percent of sales was determined by regressing cost of goods sold against sales.

Figure 6.13 exhibits how the variable or saved portion of operating expenses was determined by regressing operating expenses against sales. The intercept value of $111,279 can be loosely interpreted to represent the fixed portion of operating expenses,[1] and the x coefficient of .1362 represents the variable portion of operating expenses. The one time effect of Section 179 depreciation, produced by an asset purchased in late December, was removed as was rent expense since changes in rent, normally a fixed expense, occurred due to numerous moves during the period, and not in response to changes in sales volume.

The total economic loss as measured by lost profits is shown in Table 6.9 prior to any discounting to present value.

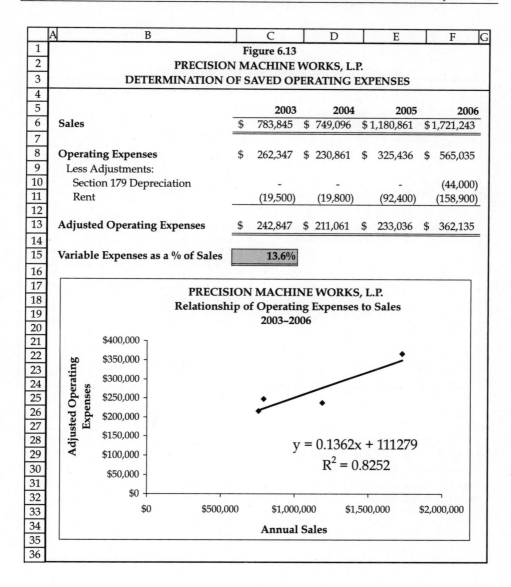

A	B	C	D	E	F	G
1	Figure 6.13					
2	PRECISION MACHINE WORKS, L.P.					
3	DETERMINATION OF SAVED OPERATING EXPENSES					
4						
5		2003	2004	2005	2006	
6	Sales	$ 783,845	$ 749,096	$ 1,180,861	$ 1,721,243	
7						
8	Operating Expenses	$ 262,347	$ 230,861	$ 325,436	$ 565,035	
9	Less Adjustments:					
10	Section 179 Depreciation	-	-	-	(44,000)	
11	Rent	(19,500)	(19,800)	(92,400)	(158,900)	
12						
13	Adjusted Operating Expenses	$ 242,847	$ 211,061	$ 233,036	$ 362,135	
14						
15	Variable Expenses as a % of Sales	13.6%				
16						

PRECISION MACHINE WORKS, L.P.
Relationship of Operating Expenses to Sales
2003–2006

$$y = 0.1362x + 111279$$
$$R^2 = 0.8252$$

Conclusion

In this case study we dealt with almost a complete set of issues that might arise in a lost profits case, including testing the significance of an intervening act, forecasting sales using a causal model, developing mitigating sales, and determining saved expenses.

In the next chapter we explore another facet of commercial damages: how to determine if the plaintiff's alleged fall-off in sales due to the defendant's actions is significant or not.

	B	C	D	E	F	G	H	I	J
1					Table 6.9				
2					PRESICION MACHINE WORKS, L.P.				
3					TOTAL ECONOMIC LOSS SUSTAINED				
4									
5						SAVED		SAVED		
6						COST OF	LOST	OPERATING		LOST
7				LOST	SALES @	GROSS	EXPENSES @		NET
8	YEAR	QTR	PERIOD	SALES	55.20%	PROFIT	13.62%		PROFITS
9	2007	2	1	$ 80,979	$ (44,700)	$ 36,279	$ (11,028)	$	25,251
10		3	2	194,526	(107,377)	87,149	(26,491)		60,659
11		4	3	381,461	(210,563)	170,897	(51,947)		118,950
12	2008	1	4	333,880	(184,299)	149,581	(45,468)		104,113
13		2	5	390,873	(215,759)	175,114	(53,229)		121,885
14		3	6	373,180	(205,993)	167,187	(50,820)		116,368
15		4	7	34,858	(19,241)	15,617	(4,747)		10,870
16	2009	1	8	110,207	(60,833)	49,374	(15,008)		34,366
17		2	9	203,487	(112,323)	91,164	(27,711)		63,453
18		3	10	257,752	(142,277)	115,475	(35,101)		80,374
19		4	11	213,419	(117,805)	95,613	(29,063)		66,550
20	2010	1	12	232,448	(128,310)	104,139	(31,655)		72,484
21		2	13	199,030	(109,863)	89,167	(27,104)		62,063
22		3	14	153,574	(84,772)	68,802	(20,914)		47,889
23		4	15	99,528	(54,939)	44,589	(13,554)		31,036
24	2011	1	16	105,893	(58,452)	47,441	(14,421)		33,020
25		2	17	59,551	(32,872)	26,679	(8,110)		18,570
26									
27									
28		Total		$ 3,424,645	$ (1,890,379)	$ 1,534,266	$ (466,368)	$	1,067,898
29									

Note

1. Since no value of the independent variable is near zero, we would be committing the error of extrapolation by insisting that the intercept value is truly the fixed cost element. However, the model output is still relevant, as we are only using the variable cost coefficient in our damages claim.

CHAPTER 7

Case Study 7—Measuring Differences in Pre- and Postincident Sales Using Two Sample t-Tests versus Regression Models

A typical lost profits case begins with the plaintiff complaining that sales, and ergo profits, have declined from a base period due to the alleged actions of the defendant. For the damages expert, whether he or she works for the plaintiff or the defendant, the first item on the to-do list is to test that assertion. This case study presents two tools that can be used to test the assertion of declining sales over time. Both tools will be demonstrated and the results obtained from each will be compared and contrasted.

Preliminary Tests of the Data

ABC Retailer is a convenience store that also sells gasoline. Its sales fell off dramatically after a customer's truck backed into the pump island and rendered the pumps unable to dispense gasoline. Subsequent issues with the Department of Environmental Protection prevented a quick replacement of the pumps, and so the losses dragged on. Figure 7.1 shows seven months of sales before the incident and eight months of sales after the incident. We want to compare the averages of the two periods to determine whether a significant difference exists between them. In order to test for this difference, we use the two-sample t-statistic. This test requires that the data be near–bell shaped, and the skewness and kurtosis amounts indicate that this is approximately so. But before we apply the t-test, we need to determine if the variances of both data sets, pre- and postincident sales, have equal variances or not, as the t-test formula is modified accordingly for one or the other determination.

To make this test we employ Excel's F-Test Two-Sample for Variances found in the Analysis Toolpak.[1]

This test is conducted by calculating the ratio of the variances of the two data sets. If the variances are equal, then the null hypothesis is that the ratio should be approximately 1. If the alternative hypothesis is simply that the variances are

Figure 7.1
ABC Retailer, Inc.
t-Test of Different Means

t-Test Model

Month	Sales Before	Sales After	Month
Feb-2009	1,014	997	Sep-2009
Mar-2009	1,041	947	Oct-2009
Apr-2009	1,056	937	Nov-2009
May-2009	1,099	958	Dec-2009
Jun-2009	1,151	960	Jan-2010
Jul-2009	1,201	921	Feb-2010
Aug-2009	1,230	948	Mar-2010
		997	Apr-2010

	Sales Before	Sales After
Skewness =	0.315	0.529
Kurtosis =	-1.639	-0.524
Variance =	6,870	728

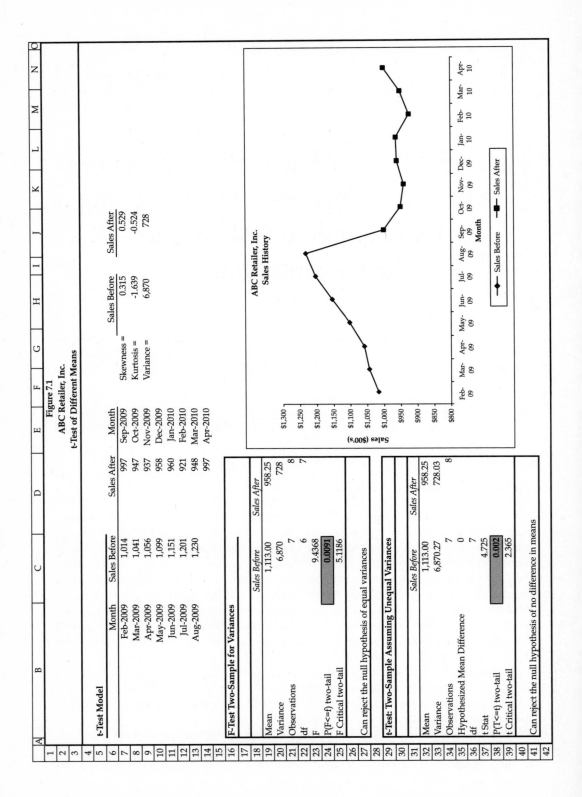

ABC Retailer, Inc.
Sales History

F-Test Two-Sample for Variances

	Sales Before	Sales After
Mean	1,113.00	958.25
Variance	6,870	728
Observations	7	8
df	6	7
F	9.4368	
P(F<=f) two-tail	0.0091	
F Critical two-tail	5.1186	

Can reject the null hypothesis of equal variances

t-Test: Two-Sample Assuming Unequal Variances

	Sales Before	Sales After
Mean	1,113.00	958.25
Variance	6,870.27	728.03
Observations	7	8
Hypothesized Mean Difference	0	
df	7	
t Stat	4.725	
P(T<=t) two-tail	0.002	
t Critical two-tail	2.365	

Can reject the null hypothesis of no difference in means

unequal, then a two-tail test is appropriate, as we are testing for both greater and lesser than qualities. If the resulting ratio is far away from 1, either too small (close to 0) or too large, we can reject the null hypothesis.

After calling up the F-Test Two Sample for Variance dialogue box, we enter the range C6:C13 in the Variable 1 Range argument as that is the variable with the larger variance, and we enter the range D6:D14 in the Variable 2 Range argument.

Then check the labels check box. For a 5 percent level of significance two-tail test, we need to enter .025 in the alpha edit box, select an output range, and then click OK. The resulting output is shown in Figure 7.1 in the range B16 through D25. The p-value in the summary output, .004574, is for a one-tail test. Because we are performing a two-tail test, we multiply the p-value from the Excel-generated table by 2. For ABC Retailer, the p-value of the two-tail test is .0091, which is less than .05, meaning that we can reject the null hypothesis of equality and accept the alternative hypothesis that the variances are unequal. This then necessitates the use of the t-test Two Sample Assuming Unequal Variances analysis tool.

Using the t-Test Two Sample Assuming Unequal Variances Tool

After calling up the t-Test Two Sample Assuming Unequal Variances dialogue box from the Analysis ToolPak, we enter the range C6:C13 in the Variable 1 Range argument, and we enter the range D6:D14 in the Variable 2 Range argument. We then enter a zero in the Hypothesized Mean Difference edit box and check the labels check box. For a 5 percent level of significance two-tail test, we need to enter .05 in the alpha edit box, select an output range, and then click OK.

The resulting output is shown in Figure 7.1 in the range B29 through D39. With a p-value of .002, there is only a .2 percent chance of obtaining the observed difference in randomly selected sample means, or a difference more extreme, in either direction, assuming the null hypothesis is true. That is, even if there isn't any difference in the means of the populations of all retail sales pre- and postincident, there is only a .2 percent chance of getting random samples whose means differ by $154.75 (1,113.00 − 958.25) or more in either direction.

Another way of interpreting the results of this test is to compare the t-stat of 4.725 with the 2.365 critical value of t. As the former is larger than the latter, and therefore in the rejection region, we can reject the null hypothesis of equal means and conclude with 95 percent confidence that the two data sets are not drawn from the same population. We must conclude that the differences were not caused by chance. That is, some wrongful action may have caused the decrease in revenue. A graphical presentation of this conclusion is also presented in Figure 7.1, where we can see a drop-off in sales that continues without any significant upward trend.

Regression Approach to the Problem

We can also account for this downward shift in sales by using an interrupted time series regression model with a dummy variable of 0 to account for sales before the incident and a dummy variable of 1 to account for sales after the incident. This new variable attempts to control for an abrupt change in the direction of sales, that is, a direction different from that accounted for by the trend variable. If the fall-off in sales is statistically significant, the absolute t-Stat for the shift coefficient will be greater than 2 and its p-value will be less than .05. Table 7.1 presents those metrics

Table 7.1
ABC Retailer, Inc.
Regression Test for Differences in Means

	A	B	C	D	E	F	G
					Shift		
5		Month	Sales	Trend	Dummy		
6		Feb-2009	1,014	1	0	Sales Before	
7		Mar-2009	1,041	2	0	Sales Before	
8		Apr-2009	1,056	3	0	Sales Before	
9		May-2009	1,099	4	0	Sales Before	
10		Jun-2009	1,151	5	0	Sales Before	
11		Jul-2009	1,201	6	0	Sales Before	
12		Aug-2009	1,230	7	0	Sales Before	
13		Sep-2009	997	8	0	Sales Before	
14		Oct-2009	947	9	1	Sales After	
15		Nov-2009	937	10	1	Sales After	
16		Dec-2009	958	11	1	Sales After	
17		Jan-2010	960	12	1	Sales After	
18		Feb-2010	921	13	1	Sales After	
19		Mar-2010	948	14	1	Sales After	
20		Apr-2010	997	15	1	Sales After	

SUMMARY OUTPUT

Regression Statistics

Multiple R	0.807
R Square	0.651
Adjusted R Square	0.593
Standard Error	62.793
Observations	15

ANOVA

	df	SS	MS	F	Significance F
Regression	2	88,407.165	44,203.582	11.211	0.002
Residual	12	47,314.869	3,942.906		
Total	14	135,722.033			

	Coefficients	Standard Error	t Stat	p-value	Lower 95%	Upper 95%
Intercept	1,047.588	40.416	25.920	0.000	959.528	1,135.648
Trend	11.322	7.505	1.509	0.157	(5.030)	27.674
Shift	(230.782)	64.996	(3.551)	0.004	(372.397)	(89.167)

with values of 3.551 and .004, respectively, demonstrating that the shift in sales was not caused by chance, the same result we got with the t-Test analysis tool.

A New Data Set—Different Results

Figure 7.2 presents another set of pre- and postincident data that we will subject to the same two procedures: a t-test of equal means and an interrupted time series regression analysis. We go through the same procedure; first, testing for a near–bell shape in the data; second, testing for equal variances; and after finding so, conducting the t-Test Two Sample Assuming Equal Variances. The t-test results in Figure 7.2 indicate, with a p-value of .340, that we cannot reject the null hypothesis of equal means, and that therefore the decrease in sales is not statistically significant. But this result doesn't square with the graph in Figure 7.2, which presents a definite downward trend in sales after August 2009. However, the regression results for the interrupted time series shown in Table 7.2 confirm that there is a definite change in the trend of sales, from upward to downward. How is it that the t-Test Two Sample Assuming Equal Variances analysis tool was unable to detect this change?

To answer that question, we examine the output in Figure 7.2. We can see that the average monthly sales figure while trending upward almost equals the average monthly sales figure while trending downward. The t-Test Two Sample Assuming Equal Variances only compares averages—it doesn't care if those averages were produced from data while it is trending up or trending down. The t-test analysis tool worked with the data in Figure 7.1, as the downward trend produced a monthly average postincident that was significantly different from the monthly average of preincident sales, as can be discerned in the chart in Figure 7.1. Therefore, a cautionary attitude should prevail when applying the t-Test Two Sample Assuming Equal Variances analysis tool to time series data, and a good deal of exploratory data analysis should first be undertaken.

Selecting the Appropriate Regression Model

Another situation that permits the use of the t-Test Two Sample Assuming Equal Variances analysis tool and interrupted time series analysis is the case of the retail cigarette store company that suffered a fire loss at location X on February 19, 2010. We explored the possibility that customers migrated from location X to one of its other two locations, Y and Z, thereby minimizing the company's loss by mitigating the amount of lost sales suffered by Location X.

We began with location Y by obtaining 64 months of pre-incident sales and four months of postincident sales, as shown in Table 7.3. Once again, we conducted the same tests, finding that the pre- and post-fire loss variances were equal, allowing us to use the t-Test Two Sample Assuming Equal Variances analysis tool. The test result indicates that the two means are equal as the t-statistic is less than 2 and the two-tail p-value is greater than .05. This means that we cannot reject the null hypothesis of no difference in mean values, and we can conclude that post-fire loss sales are, on average, no greater than pre-fire loss sales.

	A	B	C	D	E	F	G	H	I	J	K	L	M

Figure 7.2
DEF Restaurant, Inc.
t-Test of Different Means

t-Test Model

Month	Sales Before	Sales After		Month			Sales Before		Sales After
Nov-2008	914	1,081		Sep-2009		Skewness =	0.282		-0.683
Dec-2008	957	1,121		Oct-2009		Kurtosis =	-0.964		-1.019
Jan-2009	978	1,103		Nov-2009		Variance =	7,092		1,687
Feb-2009	998	1,094		Dec-2009					
Mar-2009	1,008	1,038		Jan-2010					
Apr-2009	1,028	1,014		Feb-2010					
May-2009	1,082								
Jun-2009	1,102								
Jul-2009	1,144								
Aug-2009	1,174								

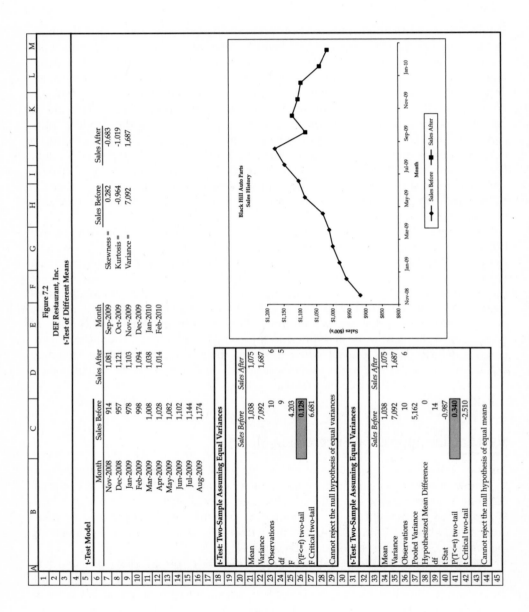

t-Test: Two-Sample Assuming Equal Variances

	Sales Before	Sales After
Mean	1,038	1,075
Variance	7,092	1,687
Observations	10	6
df	9	5
F	4.203	
P(F<=f) two-tail	0.128	
F Critical two-tail	6.681	

Cannot reject the null hypothesis of equal variances

t-Test: Two-Sample Assuming Equal Variances

	Sales Before	Sales After
Mean	1,038	1,075
Variance	7,092	1,687
Observations	10	6
Pooled Variance	5,162	
Hypothesized Mean Difference	0	
df	14	
t Stat	-0.987	
P(T<=t) two-tail	0.340	
t Critical two-tail	-2.510	

Cannot reject the null hypothesis of equal means

Table 7.2
DEF Restaurant, Inc.
Regression Test for Differences in Means

Month	Sales	Trend	Trend Change Dummy	
Nov-2008	914.3	1	0	Sales Before
Dec-2008	956.6	2	0	Sales Before
Jan-2009	977.7	3	0	Sales Before
Feb-2009	997.9	4	0	Sales Before
Mar-2009	1008.4	5	0	Sales Before
Apr-2009	1027.6	6	0	Sales Before
May-2009	1082.3	7	0	Sales Before
Jun-2009	1101.5	8	0	Sales Before
Jul-2009	1144.4	9	0	Sales Before
Aug-2009	1173.5	10	0	Sales Before
Sep-2009	1080.5	11	1	Sales After
Oct-2009	1120.7	12	2	Sales After
Nov-2009	1103.4	13	3	Sales After
Dec-2009	1094.1	14	4	Sales After
Jan-2010	1037.9	15	5	Sales After
Feb-2010	1013.6	16	6	Sales After

SUMMARY OUTPUT

Regression Statistics

Multiple R	0.964
R Square	0.929
Adjusted R Square	0.918
Standard Error	20.522
Observations	16

ANOVA

	df	SS	MS	F	Significance F
Regression	2	71,818.813	35,909.406	85.265	0.000
Residual	13	5,474.927	421.148		
Total	15	77,293.740			

	Coefficients	Standard Error	t Stat	p-value	Lower 95%	Upper 95%
Intercept	891.739	13.514	65.985	0.00000000	862.543	920.935
Trend	26.250	2.018	13.010	0.00000001	21.891	30.609
Trend Change Dummy	(47.782)	4.671	(10.229)	0.00000014	(57.874)	(37.691)

A	B	C	D	E	F	G	H	I	J
1				Table 7.3					
2				Cigarette Stores, LLC					
3				Location Y					
4				t-Test for Two Means					
5									
6					Year				
7	Month	2004–2005	2005–2006	2006–2007	2007–2008	2008–2009	2009–2010		
8	Oct	49,733	49,460	55,918	55,039	59,447	59,127		
9	Nov	48,929	58,881	51,428	56,803	56,763	58,072		
10	Dec	61,941	46,762	52,278	64,063	60,514	72,504		
11	Jan	46,366	43,893	58,715	77,307	70,907	53,069		
12	Feb	49,642	47,167	50,424	59,221	60,984	53,739	Post-incident	
13	Mar	63,452	57,779	50,283	58,876	60,808	67,128	Post-incident	
14	Apr	53,464	46,313	50,214	60,795	77,402	52,256	Post-incident	
15	May	58,782	47,479	66,752	75,968	59,847	52,174	Post-incident	
16	Jun	69,900	58,662	57,304	57,991	60,049			
17	Jul	55,889	46,112	57,604	75,042	77,242			
18	Aug	41,826	59,365	71,577	58,316	63,693			
19	Sep	50,939	61,855	73,458	79,945	76,354			
20									
21	F-Test Two-Sample for Variances								
22									
23		Pre	Post						
24	Mean	59,011	56,324						
25	Variance	88,461,241	52,393,464						
26	Observations	64	4						
27	df	63	3						
28	F	1.688							
29	P(F<=f) two-tail	0.755							
30	F Critical two-tail	13.988							
31									
32	Cannot reject the null hypothesis of equal variances								
33									
34									
35	t-Test: Two-Sample Assuming Equal Variances								
36									
37		Pre	Post						
38	Mean	59,011	56,324						
39	Variance	88,461,241	52,393,464						
40	Observations	64	4						
41	Pooled Variance	86,821,796							
42	Hypothesized Mean Difference	0							
43	df	66							
44	t Stat	0.559							
45	P(T<=t) one-tail	0.289							
46	t Critical one-tail	1.668							
47	P(T<=t) two-tail	0.578							
48	t Critical two-tail	1.997							
49									
50	Cannot reject the null hypothesis of equal means								
51									

Next, we turn to interrupted time series analysis and run a regression model that assigns a dummy variable of 1 to the four post-fire loss months and a dummy variable of 0 to the 64 pre-fire loss months. The setup sheet is shown in Table 7.4 and the summary regression output along with a line chart of the 68 months of sales and a prediction trendline imposed thereon is shown in Figure 7.3. The shift variable p-value is less than .05, indicating that the post-fire loss sales are statistically significantly different from the pre-fire loss sales, a conclusion diametrically opposed to that of the t-Test Two Sample Assuming Equal Variances analysis tool. A closer examination of the chart in Figure 7.3 gives us the answer to this conundrum.

We used a linear regression model to produce the results in Figure 7.3, but the close examination indicates that the relationship between sales and time is not linear, but curvilinear. Sales rise at the beginning, fall, rise once more, and then fall again. Fitting a trendline to this data set requires a third-degree polynomial,[2] which setup sheet we present in Table 7.5, as a third-degree polynomial causes a trendline to undulate, while a second-degree polynomial only causes a trendline to

	B	C	D	E
1		Table 7.4		
2		Cigarette Shopper		
3		Location Y		
4		Setup Sheet		
5		Linear Interrupted Time Series Analysis		
6				
7	Trend	Shift	Sales	
8	1	0	49,733	
9	2	0	48,929	
10	3	0	61,941	
11	4	0	46,366	
12	5	0	49,642	
13	6	0	63,452	
14	7	0	53,464	
15	8	0	58,782	
16	9	0	69,900	
17	10	0	55,889	
18	11	0	41,826	
19	12	0	50,939	
20	13	0	49,460	
21	14	0	58,881	
22	15	0	46,762	
23	16	0	43,893	
24	17	0	47,167	
25	18	0	57,779	
26	19	0	46,313	
27	20	0	47,479	
28	21	0	58,662	
29	22	0	46,112	
30	23	0	59,365	
31	24	0	61,855	
32	25	0	55,918	
33	26	0	51,428	
34	27	0	52,278	
35	28	0	58,715	
36	29	0	50,424	
37	30	0	50,283	
38	31	0	50,214	
39	32	0	66,752	
40	33	0	57,304	
41	34	0	57,604	
42	35	0	71,577	
43	36	0	73,458	
44	37	0	55,039	
45	38	0	56,803	
46	39	0	64,063	

(Continued)

(*continued*)

47	40	0	77,307
48	41	0	59,221
49	42	0	58,876
50	43	0	60,795
51	44	0	75,968
52	45	0	57,991
53	46	0	75,042
54	47	0	58,316
55	48	0	79,945
56	49	0	59,447
57	50	0	56,763
58	51	0	60,514
59	52	0	70,907
60	53	0	60,984
61	54	0	60,808
62	55	0	77,402
63	56	0	59,847
64	57	0	60,049
65	58	0	77,242
66	59	0	63,693
67	60	0	76,354
68	61	0	59,127
69	62	0	58,072
70	63	0	72,504
71	64	0	53,069
72	65	1	53,739
73	66	1	67,128
74	67	1	52,256
75	68	1	52,174
76			

convert into a parabola. We also show in Figure 7.4 the summary output for the third-degree polynomial regression model that also includes a dummy variable for the four months of post-fire loss sales. We can see that the shift variable p-value is greater than .05, indicating that the post-fire loss sales are no longer statistically significantly different from the pre-fire loss sales, a conclusion that now conforms to that of the t-Test Two Sample Assuming Equal Variances analysis tool. We have solved our problem by properly fitting a regression model to the data, one that takes into consideration the undulating course of the sales data over time. Thus, we are able to conclude that, based on the results of both approaches to the question, post-fire sales did not increase at location Y.

Finding the Facts Behind the Figures

We now turn our attention to location Z, for which we gathered sales data for four months before and after February 2010. (See Table 7.6.)

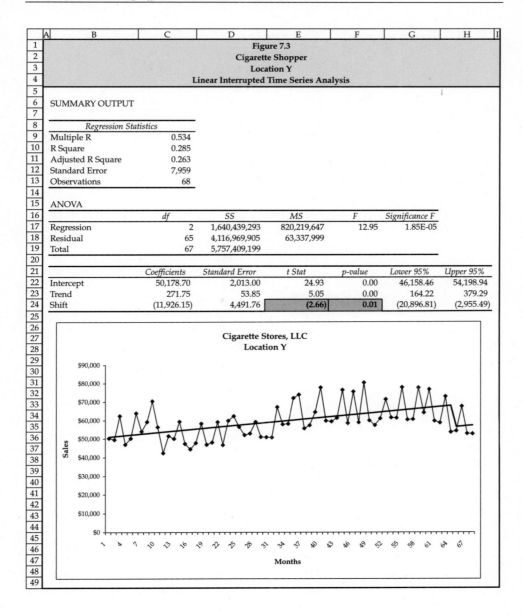

Figure 7.3
Cigarette Shopper
Location Y
Linear Interrupted Time Series Analysis

SUMMARY OUTPUT

Regression Statistics	
Multiple R	0.534
R Square	0.285
Adjusted R Square	0.263
Standard Error	7,959
Observations	68

ANOVA

	df	SS	MS	F	Significance F
Regression	2	1,640,439,293	820,219,647	12.95	1.85E-05
Residual	65	4,116,969,905	63,337,999		
Total	67	5,757,409,199			

	Coefficients	Standard Error	t Stat	p-value	Lower 95%	Upper 95%
Intercept	50,178.70	2,013.00	24.93	0.00	46,158.46	54,198.94
Trend	271.75	53.85	5.05	0.00	164.22	379.29
Shift	(11,926.15)	4,491.76	(2.66)	0.01	(20,896.81)	(2,955.49)

Once again, after testing for a near-bell shape in the data, the F-test for equal variances shows that they are statistically equal. Selecting all four pre-incident months and running the t-Test Two Sample Assuming Equal Variances analysis tool, we find that we can reject the null hypothesis of equal means and conclude that post-incident sales are statistically greater than pre-incident sales. However, we noticed that the two earliest months seemed abnormally low when compared to the other six months, so we inquired of management as to the cause of this difference. We were informed that location Z had opened in October 2009, only four months prior to the fire loss at location X. Therefore, we dropped the months of October and

Table 7.5
Cigarette Shopper
Location Y
Set-Up Sheet
Third-Degree Polynomial Interrupted Time Series Analysis

Trend	Trend^2	Trend^3	Shift	Sales
1	1	1	0	49,733
2	4	8	0	48,929
3	9	27	0	61,941
4	16	64	0	46,366
5	25	125	0	49,642
6	36	216	0	63,452
7	49	343	0	53,464
8	64	512	0	58,782
9	81	729	0	69,900
10	100	1,000	0	55,889
11	121	1,331	0	41,826
12	144	1,728	0	50,939
13	169	2,197	0	49,460
14	196	2,744	0	58,881
15	225	3,375	0	46,762
16	256	4,096	0	43,893
17	289	4,913	0	47,167
18	324	5,832	0	57,779
19	361	6,859	0	46,313
20	400	8,000	0	47,479
21	441	9,261	0	58,662
22	484	10,648	0	46,112
23	529	12,167	0	59,365
24	576	13,824	0	61,855
25	625	15,625	0	55,918
26	676	17,576	0	51,428
27	729	19,683	0	52,278
28	784	21,952	0	58,715
29	841	24,389	0	50,424
30	900	27,000	0	50,283
31	961	29,791	0	50,214
32	1,024	32,768	0	66,752
33	1,089	35,937	0	57,304
34	1,156	39,304	0	57,604
35	1,225	42,875	0	71,577
36	1,296	46,656	0	73,458
37	1,369	50,653	0	55,039
38	1,444	54,872	0	56,803
39	1,521	59,319	0	64,063
40	1,600	64,000	0	77,307

41	1,681	68,921	0	59,221
42	1,764	74,088	0	58,876
43	1,849	79,507	0	60,795
44	1,936	85,184	0	75,968
45	2,025	91,125	0	57,991
46	2,116	97,336	0	75,042
47	2,209	103,823	0	58,316
48	2,304	110,592	0	79,945
49	2,401	117,649	0	59,447
50	2,500	125,000	0	56,763
51	2,601	132,651	0	60,514
52	2,704	140,608	0	70,907
53	2,809	148,877	0	60,984
54	2,916	157,464	0	60,808
55	3,025	166,375	0	77,402
56	3,136	175,616	0	59,847
57	3,249	185,193	0	60,049
58	3,364	195,112	0	77,242
59	3,481	205,379	0	63,693
60	3,600	216,000	0	76,354
61	3,721	226,981	0	59,127
62	3,844	238,328	0	58,072
63	3,969	250,047	0	72,504
64	4,096	262,144	0	53,069
65	4,225	274,625	1	53,739
66	4,356	287,496	1	67,128
67	4,489	300,763	1	52,256
68	4,624	314,432	1	52,174

November 2009 from the t-Test as their low sales did not represent true operating performance. Running the t-Test Two Sample Assuming Equal Variances analysis tool again with only two pre-incident months produced a p-value of .061, a figure greater than .05, indicating that we cannot reject the null hypothesis of equality of means, and therefore conclude that sales at Location Z did not increase due to the fire loss at location X.

Conclusion

While the ostensible purpose of this case study was to compare and contrast two different tools to test differences between pre- and postincident sales, another purpose has presented itself. That second purpose is the presentation of the idea of exploratory data analysis, which can be facilely summed up with the phrase "graph your data." Whether your graph of choice is a box plot, histogram, scatterplot, line chart, stem-and-leaf plot, or any other kind of chart, you should condition yourself to begin every lost profits assignment by applying one or more of those tools to the data set(s) you are working with.

Table 7.6
Cigarette Shopper
Location Z
t-Test for Two Means

Month	Sales	
Oct-09	2,249	Pre-incident
Nov-09	7,223	Pre-incident
Dec-09	11,613	Pre-incident
Jan-10	8,486	Pre-incident
Feb-10	12,717	Post-incident
Mar-10	21,984	Post-incident
Apr-10	18,372	Post-incident
May-10	18,448	Post-incident

	Pre-incident	Post-incident
Skewness =	-0.67	-0.81
Kurtosis =	1.27	1.87

t-Test: Two-Sample Assuming Equal Variances
4-Month Pre-Incident period

	Pre-incident	Post-incident
Mean	7,393	17,880
Variance	15,164,522	14,689,270
Observations	4	4
Pooled Variance	14,926,896	
Hypothesized Mean Difference	0	
df	6	
t Stat	-3.839	
P(T<=t) one-tail	0.004	
t Critical one-tail	1.943	
P(T<=t) two-tail	0.009	
t Critical two-tail	2.447	

Can reject the null hypothesis of no difference in means

F-Test Two-Sample for Variances

	Pre-incident	Post-incident
Mean	7,393	17,880
Variance	15,164,522	14,689,270
Observations	4	4
df	3	3
F	1.032	
P(F<=f) two-tail	0.980	
F Critical two-tail	15.439	

Cannot reject the null hypothesis of equal variances

t-Test: Two-Sample Assuming Equal Variances
2-Month Pre-Incident period

	Pre-incident	Post-incident
Mean	10,049	17,880
Variance	4,890,941	14,689,270
Observations	2	4
Pooled Variance	12,239,688	
Hypothesized Mean Difference	0	
df	4	
t Stat	-2.585	
P(T<=t) one-tail	0.031	
t Critical one-tail	2.132	
P(T<=t) two-tail	0.061	
t Critical two-tail	2.776	

Cannot reject the null hypothesis of no difference in means

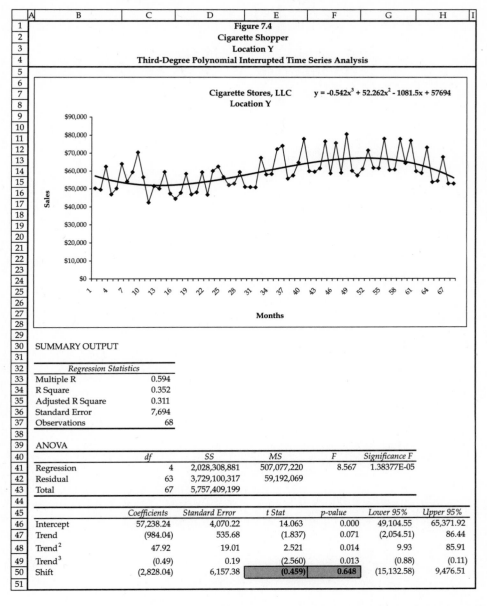

	Coefficients	Standard Error	t Stat	p-value	Lower 95%	Upper 95%
Intercept	57,238.24	4,070.22	14.063	0.000	49,104.55	65,371.92
Trend	(984.04)	535.68	(1.837)	0.071	(2,054.51)	86.44
Trend^2	47.92	19.01	2.521	0.014	9.93	85.91
Trend^3	(0.49)	0.19	(2.560)	0.013	(0.88)	(0.11)
Shift	(2,828.04)	6,157.38	(0.459)	0.648	(15,132.58)	9,476.51

In the next chapter we demonstrate how to establish that a damaging event actually has a statistically significant impact on monthly revenues.

Notes

1. Due to a quirk in Excel, when you fill in the dialogue box, the variance of variable 1 must be greater than the variance of variable 2.
2. First-degree polynomial = x; second-degree polynomial = x^2; third-degree polynomial = x^3.

CHAPTER 8

Case Study 8—Interrupted Time Series Analysis, Holdback Forecasting, and Variable Transformation

In a breach of contract matter, we were contacted by the buyer's attorney to measure damages in a lost profits case allegedly caused by the seller's failure to disclose that six months after the closing a competitor would be opening a new market, the Bayside Supermarket, on March 1, 2007, just 10 miles down the road on State Highway 1. In these types of cases, the first task is to establish that the damaging event actually had a statistically significant impact on the buyer's monthly revenues, and that the decrease in revenue was not the result of mere chance.

Graph Your Data

We begin the process by scheduling actual monthly sales for the Ali-Baba Supermarket, LLC dba American Supermarket for the four-year period 2004 to 2007 in Table 8.1, and the accompanying line chart in Figure 8.1.

Industry Comparisons

We investigated the possibility that the fall-off in sales that took place in 2007 also might have been suffered by the supermarket industry in the company's county and Economic Summary Area (ESA). A look at Table 8.2 refutes this idea, as the increase in sales for the county and ESA from 2006 to 2007 contrasts sharply with the reduction experienced by the company.

For our next step, we decided to use a methodology known as interrupted time series analysis (ITSA), which is a specific application of multiple regression analysis. Figure 8.2 shows that seasonality is 97 percent of the total variance of sales for the 36-month period January 2004 to December 2006 (we didn't include 2007 as that year might be distorted by the incident). To create these proportions of variance we used the techniques explained and demonstrated in Case Study 2. Specifically, we invoked Excel's ANOVA: Two-Factor Without Replication tool found in Data Analysis and populated the input range in the dialogue box with cells B6 through

		2004	2005	2006	2007
		Table 8.1			
		ALI-BABA SUPERMART, LLC			
		dba American Supermarket			
		Schedule of Monthly Sales			
January	$	331,907	$ 329,125	$ 339,568	$ 348,258
February		328,219	315,520	324,803	328,217
March		336,306	333,046	374,563	* 314,016
April		330,282	333,256	338,934	304,149
May		379,373	376,551	388,314	332,120
June		383,177	398,637	413,383	362,224
July		479,873	472,006	472,006	441,669
August		526,116	533,199	533,199	487,030
September		390,017	387,184	387,184	405,740
October		371,480	385,097	385,097	364,339
November		357,040	353,212	332,903	366,213
December		295,235	312,431	355,482	369,308
Annual Totals	$	4,509,026	$ 4,529,264	$ 4,645,436	$ 4,423,281

* = Bayside Supermarket opened

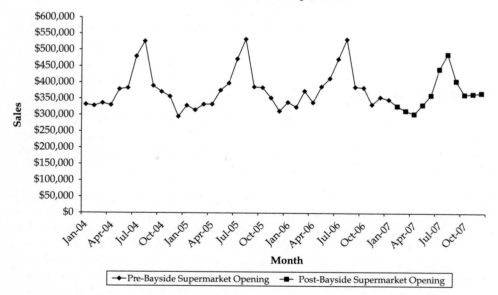

Figure 8.1

ALI-BABA SUPERMART, LLC
dba American Supermarket

A	B	C	D	E	F	G	H	I	J	K
1					Table 8.2					
2					ALI-BABA SUPERMART, LLC					
3					dba American Supermarket					
4					Schedule of Comparative Annual Sales					
6		Ali-Baba Supermarket			Bristol County			Fall River ESA		
7		$	% Change		$	% Change		$	% Change	
8	2004	$ 4,509,026			$32,315,300			$6,961,700		
9	2005	4,529,264	0.45%		33,462,600	3.55%		7,009,800	0.69%	
10	2006	4,645,436	2.56%		34,374,100	2.72%		7,160,000	2.14%	
11	2007	4,423,281	-4.78%		36,074,800	4.95%		7,424,900	3.70%	

E18 of Table 8.1. The output of this tool is shown in Table 8.3 after we added the explanatory words and percentages in cells B34 through C40.

Accounting for Seasonality

Therefore, the first element of our multiple regression ITSA model is seasonality, and that element is accounted for with a seasonal index or factor, rather than as a monthly dummy or indicator variable in order to preserve as many degrees of freedom as possible so that our standard error of the estimate is minimized.

Seasonal indexes reflect the average percentage by which observations in each "season" (month) differ from their projected trend values. For example, you can see

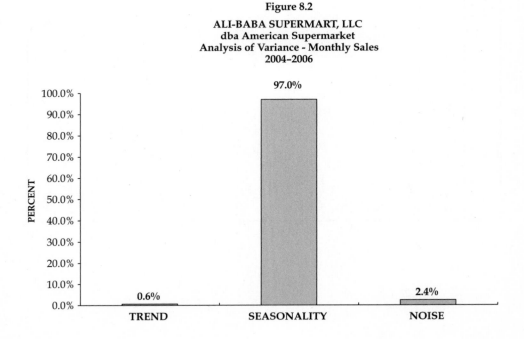

Figure 8.2
ALI-BABA SUPERMART, LLC
dba American Supermarket
Analysis of Variance - Monthly Sales
2004–2006

Table 8.3
ALI-BABA SUPERMART, LLC
ANALYSIS OF VARIANCE OUTPUT

Anova: Two-Factor Without Replication

SUMMARY	Count	Sum	Average	Variance
January	3	1,000,601	333,534	29,246,385
February	3	968,542	322,847	43,183,481
March	3	1,043,915	347,972	532,986,639
April	3	1,002,472	334,157	19,325,035
May	3	1,144,238	381,413	37,712,213
June	3	1,195,197	398,399	228,134,768
July	3	1,423,885	474,628	20,633,778
August	3	1,592,514	530,838	16,721,641
September	3	1,164,384	388,128	2,675,296
October	3	1,141,674	380,558	61,806,020
November	3	1,043,155	347,718	168,281,390
December	3	963,148	321,049	963,126,932
2004	12	4,509,026	375,752	4,398,088,011
2005	12	4,529,264	377,439	4,428,345,311
2006	12	4,645,436	387,120	3,800,403,332

ANOVA

Source of Variation	SS	df	MS	F	p-value	F crit
Rows	1.356E+11	11	12,322,789,133	81.0583	0.0000	2.2585
Columns	9.031E+08	2	451,572,211	2.9704	0.0721	3.4434
Error	3.345E+09	22	152,023,761			
Total	1.398E+11	35				

Source of Variation	Per Cent
Seasonality	96.96%
Trend	0.65%
Noise	2.39%
Total	100.0%

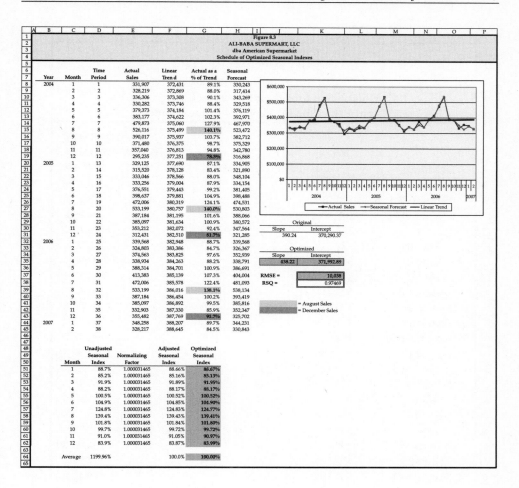

in Figure 8.3 that all the years involved American's sales in August are above the value predicted using a trend model, while December's sales fall below the value predicted using a trend model. Thus, if we determine seasonal indexes representing the average amount by which observations in a given month fall above or below the trendline, we can multiply our trend projections by these amounts and increase the accuracy of our forecasts. In so doing we followed the procedures set forth in Case Study 5. In developing the seasonal indexes for this case, we used only the 38 months through February 2007, as we felt that sales after that date were compromised by the defendant's actions and would detract from the model's predictive power if they were included. The complete process of developing the seasonal indexes is shown in Figure 8.3, where we used Solver to minimize RMSE in cell K37 by changing cells J35 and K35 as well as cells G51 though G62, with the constraint that cell G64 average 100.0 percent. While in this case the optimized seasonal indexes are only slightly different from the adjusted seasonal indexes, in other cases the differences can be and often are larger—but not by much, as we are only optimizing a process. We enter the 12 monthly seasonal indexes in column G of Table 8.4.

		Table 8.4					
		ALI-BABA SUPERMART, LLC					
		dba American Supermarket					
		Regression Model for Structural Change					
		Input Values for All Variables - Index Model					
	Month	Actual Sales	TREND	SHIFT	TREND CHANGE	MONTHLY SEASONAL INDEX	
8	January-04	$ 331,907	1	0	0	88.67%	
9	February-04	328,219	2	0	0	85.13%	
10	March-04	336,306	3	0	0	91.95%	
11	April-04	330,282	4	0	0	88.17%	
12	May-04	379,373	5	0	0	100.52%	
13	June-04	383,177	6	0	0	104.90%	
14	July-04	479,873	7	0	0	124.77%	
15	August-04	526,116	8	0	0	139.41%	
16	September-04	390,017	9	0	0	101.80%	
17	October-04	371,480	10	0	0	99.72%	
18	November-04	357,040	11	0	0	90.97%	
19	December-04	295,235	12	0	0	83.99%	
20	January-05	329,125	13	0	0	88.67%	
21	February-05	315,520	14	0	0	85.13%	
22	March-05	333,046	15	0	0	91.95%	
23	April-05	333,256	16	0	0	88.17%	
24	May-05	376,551	17	0	0	100.52%	
25	June-05	398,637	18	0	0	104.90%	
26	July-05	472,006	19	0	0	124.77%	
27	August-05	533,199	20	0	0	139.41%	
28	September-05	387,184	21	0	0	101.80%	
29	October-05	385,097	22	0	0	99.72%	
30	November-05	353,212	23	0	0	90.97%	
31	December-05	312,431	24	0	0	83.99%	
32	January-06	339,568	25	0	0	88.67%	
33	February-06	324,803	26	0	0	85.13%	
34	March-06	374,563	27	0	0	91.95%	
35	April-06	338,934	28	0	0	88.17%	
36	May-06	388,314	29	0	0	100.52%	
37	June-06	413,383	30	0	0	104.90%	
38	July-06	472,006	31	0	0	124.77%	
39	August-06	533,199	32	0	0	139.41%	
40	September-06	387,184	33	0	0	101.80%	
41	October-06	385,097	34	0	0	99.72%	
42	November-06	332,903	35	0	0	90.97%	
43	December-06	355,482	36	0	0	83.99%	
44	January-07	348,258	37	0	0	88.67%	

45	February-07	328,217	38	0	0	85.13%
46	March-07	314,016	39	1	0	91.95%
47	April-07	304,149	40	1	0	88.17%
48	May-07	332,120	41	1	0	100.52%
49	June-07	362,224	42	1	0	104.90%
50	July-07	441,669	43	1	0	124.77%
51	August-07	487,030	44	1	1	139.41%
52	September-07	405,740	45	1	2	101.80%
53	October-07	364,339	46	1	3	99.72%
54	November-07	366,213	47	1	4	90.97%
55	December-07	369,308	48	1	5	83.99%

Accounting for Trend

The second element to be accounted for in the model in Table 8.4 is the degree of trend, if any, over the 48-month period January 2004 to December 2007. Unlike the use of a time period of 38 months of sales, for the reasons given above, to develop the seasonal indexes, this element needs all 48 months to serve as an input variable for the period under examination. While seasonality is an overwhelming factor in Figure 8.2 and Table 8.3, there is still some small amount of trend that needs to be accounted for by assigning the number 1 to the first month in the time series, January 2004, the number 2 to February 2004, and so on, up to the number 48 for the month of December 2007. These values are placed in column D of Table 8.4 and labeled TREND.

Accounting for Interventions

The next element to be accounted for in the model is a possible intervention that occurred starting in March 2007. An intervention occurs when there is some outside influence at a particular time that affects the dependent or forecast variable. An intervention could have caused a shift in sales, either upward or downward, and can be accounted for by the use of a dummy variable consisting of zeros before March 2007 and ones after February 2007. The resulting regression coefficient measures the effect of the opening of the Bayside Supermarket if that effect occurred instantly. The dummy variables are placed in column E of Table 8.4 and labeled SHIFT.

The second possible intervention that could have caused a new trend in sales began in August 2007 and ran through December 2007, when American Supermarket lowered its prices in an attempt to entice its lost customers back to its premises. Starting with August 2007 we assign it number 1, to September of 2007 we assign the number 2, and so on up to the number 5 for December 2007, with zeros being assigned to all the other months prior to August 2007. We enter these values in column F of Table 8.4 and label the column TREND CHANGE. TREND CHANGE accounts for any gradual change in sales, if there is one. The completed regression input model for ITSA is shown in Table 8.4.

The regression output is shown in Table 8.5, where all the metrics indicate a very high degree of goodness of fit. In Figure 8.4 we create a column called

Table 8.5
ALI-BABA SUPERMART, LLC
dba American Supermarket
Regression Model for Structural Change
Summary Output - Index Model

Regression Statistics			
Multiple R	0.9841		
R Square	0.9684		
Adjusted R Square	0.9655		
Standard Error	11,250		
Coefficient of Variation	2.98%		
Observations	48		

ANOVA

	df	*SS*	*MS*	*F*	*Significance F*
Regression	4	1.66864E+11	41,715,914,115	330	1.19459E-31
Residual	43	5,441,985,705	126,557,807		
Total	47	1.72306E+11			

	Coefficients	*Standard Error*	*t Stat*	*p-value*	*Lower 95%*	*Upper 95%*
Intercept	(1,815)	10,887	(0.17)	86.8390351%	(23,772)	20,142
TREND	455	166	2.74	0.9011938%	119	790
SHIFT	(48,833)	6,214	(7.86)	0.0000001%	(61,365)	(36,302)
TREND CHANGE	14,896	2,021	7.37	0.0000004%	10,821	18,972
MONTHLY SEASONAL INDEX	373,424	10,329	36.15	0.0000000%	352,594	394,255

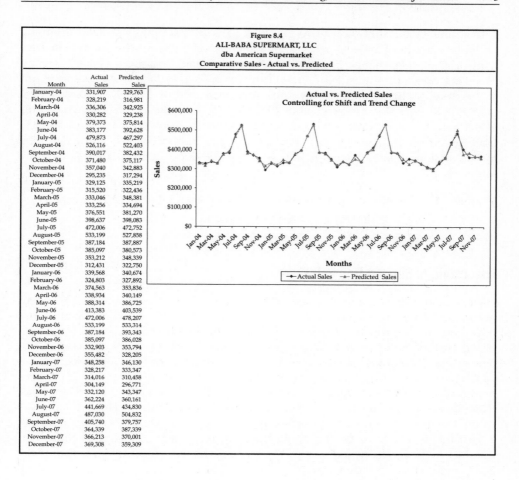

Figure 8.4
ALI-BABA SUPERMART, LLC
dba American Supermarket
Comparative Sales - Actual vs. Predicted

Month	Actual Sales	Predicted Sales
January-04	331,907	329,763
February-04	328,219	316,981
March-04	336,306	342,925
April-04	330,282	329,238
May-04	379,373	375,814
June-04	383,177	392,628
July-04	479,873	467,297
August-04	526,116	522,403
September-04	390,017	382,432
October-04	371,480	375,117
November-04	357,040	342,883
December-04	295,235	317,294
January-05	329,125	335,219
February-05	315,520	322,436
March-05	333,046	348,381
April-05	333,256	334,694
May-05	376,551	381,270
June-05	398,637	398,083
July-05	472,006	472,752
August-05	533,199	527,858
September-05	387,184	387,887
October-05	385,097	380,573
November-05	353,212	348,339
December-05	312,431	322,750
January-06	339,568	340,674
February-06	324,803	327,892
March-06	374,563	353,836
April-06	338,934	340,149
May-06	388,314	386,725
June-06	413,383	403,539
July-06	472,006	478,207
August-06	533,199	533,314
September-06	387,184	393,343
October-06	385,097	386,028
November-06	332,903	353,794
December-06	355,482	328,205
January-07	348,258	346,130
February-07	328,217	333,347
March-07	314,016	310,458
April-07	304,149	296,771
May-07	332,120	343,347
June-07	362,224	360,161
July-07	441,669	434,830
August-07	487,030	504,832
September-07	405,740	379,757
October-07	364,339	387,339
November-07	366,213	370,001
December-07	369,308	359,309

predicted sales using the coefficients from the regression output in Table 8.5. Also in Figure 8.4 is a line chart showing actual and predicted sales after accounting for SHIFT and TREND CHANGE. This line chart indicates the same conclusion as the regression output—that the model captures all the elements that drove sales during the entire period, including the downward shift and the succeeding upward trend. We also ran some ancillary tests on the residuals (not shown) for normality, homoscedasticity, and serial correlation, all of which the model passed. All of the t-stats for the independent variable coefficients shown in Table 8.5 are greater than two, and all of their p-values are significant at the 5 percent level, and TREND CHANGE, SHIFT, and MONTHLY SEASONAL INDEX are significant at the .000001 level (there is only one chance in a million that the sample overstates the case). This means that all of the independent variables are statistically significant and bring something to the model, including the two variables we are testing for, TREND CHANGE and SHIFT.

Interpretation of the regression results is straightforward. The TREND coefficient indicates that the trendline was almost flat up through the month of February 2007 (sales were increasing at the rate of only $455 per month). At the time that Bayside opened in March 2007, the flat trendline is interrupted, or becomes discontinuous with an immediate shift downward that took place at that time, with sales dropping off in the amount of $48,833 per month. Sometime after this downward shift in sales there was another change in direction of the trendline. Because it began lowering its selling prices in August 2007, American was able to induce customers to return to the store, such that the monthly sales trend increased by $14,896 in August 2007 ($14,896 \times 1$), by $29,792 in September 2007 ($14,896 \times 2$), and so on. These increases in the monthly trend only served to offset the monthly downward shift of $48,833 until November 2007 when sales returned to a pre-Bayside level of normality. The full regression equation is as follows, where y, the dependent variable, is monthly sales:

$$y = -1,815 + 455 \times \text{TREND} - 48,833 \times \text{SHIFT} + 14,896 \times \text{TREND CHANGE} + 373,424 \times \text{MONTHLY SEASONAL INDEX}$$

Forecasting "Should Be" Sales

Having demonstrated that the sales differentials that began in March 2007 were not caused by mere chance, we then moved on to predicting what sales should have been during the 10-month period beginning March 2007 absent the opening of the Bayside Supermarket. To do this we created another regression model, this time using 38 months of past data (January 2004 to February 2007) so that we can forecast the 10 months beginning March 2007 through December 2007. This model consists of two independent or predictor variables—TREND and SEASONAL INDEX, as we have no further need of the SHIFT and TREND CHANGE variables as the occurrences they were controlling for can be ignored in order to predict what sales would have been without them. In other words, including those two variables in the model would only produce what sales were from March to December 2007, and this we already know. We can also optimize this model by transforming by exponentiation of the dependent variable, sales, and the independent variable, TREND.

We do this because very often time series data are:

1. Rarely linear.
2. Infrequently homogeneous as to variance.
3. Not often distributed normally, or even symmetrically.

Fortunately, these three problems can be fixed with one procedure, and that is transformation of either or both the independent and dependent variables. Thus, transformation provides a simple way both to fix statistical problems (nonsymmetrical, non-normal, and heterogeneous distributions) and to better fit curves to data (linear regression). To accomplish this transformation, we used Excel's Solver function to create the two exponents that minimize the root mean squared error of the differences between actual sales and predicted sales. The worksheet that shows this process is in Figure 8.5, along with a chart showing forecasted sales from March 2007 through December 2007, and actual and predicted sales from January 2004 through February 2007. The instructions for Solver in Figure 8.5 are to minimize cell

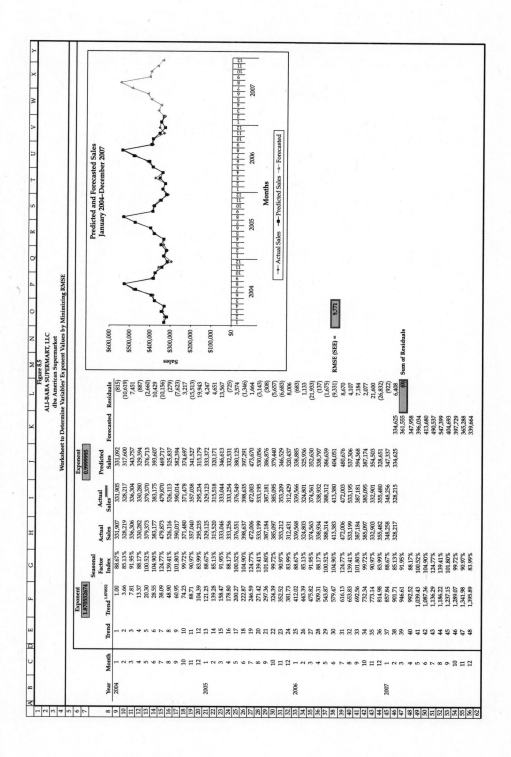

Figure 8.5
ALI-BABA SUPERMART, LLC
dba American Supermarket
Worksheet to Determine Variables' Exponent Values by Minimizing RMSE

Exponent 1.870852674
Exponent 0.9999995

Year	Month	Trend	Trend^1.870852674	Seasonal Factor Index	Actual Sales	Actual Sales^.999999	Predicted Sales	Forecasted	Residuals
2004	1	1	1.00	88.67%	331,907	331,905	331,092		(815)
	2	2	3.66	85.13%	328,219	328,217	317,600		(10,619)
	3	3	7.81	91.95%	336,306	336,304	343,757		7,451
	4	4	13.37	88.17%	330,282	330,280	329,394		(887)
	5	5	20.30	100.52%	379,373	379,370	376,713		(2,660)
	6	6	28.55	104.90%	383,177	383,175	393,607		10,429
	7	7	38.09	124.77%	479,873	479,870	469,717		(10,156)
	8	8	48.90	139.41%	526,116	526,113	525,837		(279)
	9	9	60.95	101.80%	390,017	390,014	382,394		(7,623)
	10	10	74.23	99.72%	371,480	371,478	374,697		3,217
	11	11	88.71	90.97%	357,040	357,038	341,527		(15,513)
	12	12	104.39	83.99%	295,235	295,234	315,179		19,943
2005	1	13	121.25	88.67%	329,125	329,123	333,372		4,247
	2	14	139.28	85.13%	315,520	315,518	320,171		4,651
	3	15	158.47	91.95%	333,046	333,044	346,613		13,567
	4	16	178.80	88.17%	333,256	333,254	332,531		(725)
	5	17	200.27	100.52%	376,551	376,549	380,125		3,574
	6	18	222.87	104.90%	398,637	398,635	397,291		(1,346)
	7	19	246.59	124.77%	472,006	472,003	473,670		1,664
	8	20	271.42	139.41%	533,199	533,195	530,056		(3,143)
	9	21	297.36	101.80%	387,184	387,181	386,876		(308)
	10	22	324.39	99.72%	385,097	385,095	379,440		(5,657)
	11	23	352.52	90.97%	353,212	353,209	346,529		(6,683)
	12	24	381.73	83.99%	312,431	312,429	320,437		8,006
2006	1	25	412.02	88.67%	339,568	339,566	338,885		(683)
	2	26	443.39	85.13%	324,803	324,801	325,936		1,133
	3	27	475.82	91.95%	374,563	374,561	352,630		(21,933)
	4	28	509.31	88.17%	338,934	338,932	338,797		(137)
	5	29	543.87	100.52%	388,314	388,312	386,639		(1,675)
	6	30	579.47	104.90%	413,383	413,380	404,051		(9,331)
	7	31	616.13	124.77%	472,006	472,003	480,676		8,670
	8	32	653.83	139.41%	533,199	533,195	537,306		4,107
	9	33	692.56	101.80%	387,184	387,181	394,368		7,184
	10	34	732.34	99.72%	385,097	385,095	387,174		2,077
	11	35	773.14	90.97%	332,903	332,901	354,503		21,600
	12	36	814.98	83.99%	355,482	355,480	328,651		(26,832)
2007	1	37	857.84	88.67%	348,258	348,256	347,337		(922)
	2	38	901.71	85.13%	328,217	328,215	334,625	334,625	6,408
	3	39	946.61	91.95%				361,555	
	4	40	992.52	88.17%				347,958	
	5	41	1,039.43	100.52%				413,680	
	6	42	1,087.36	104.90%				490,537	
	7	43	1,136.29	124.77%				547,399	
	8	44	1,186.22	139.41%				404,693	
	9	45	1,237.15	101.80%				397,729	
	10	46	1,289.07	99.72%				365,288	
	11	47	1,341.98	90.97%				339,664	
	12	48	1,395.89	83.99%					

RMSE (SEE) = 9,771

Sum of Residuals (0)

Predicted and Forecasted Sales
January 2004–December 2007

165

Table 8.6
dba American Supermarket
Ex Post (Holdback) Regression Model for Forecasting
Input Values for All Variables with Forecasted Values Shown

Exponent: **1.870553** Exponent: **0.999999**

Year	Month	TREND	TREND$^{1.870553}$	MONTHLY SEASONAL INDEX	Actual Sales	Actual Sales$^{.999999}$	Predicted Sales	Forecasted Sales
2004	1	1	1	88.67%	$ 331,907	$ 331,903	$ 330,899	
	2	2	3.6567	85.13%	328,219	328,215	317,351	
	3	3	7.8069	91.95%	336,306	336,301	343,618	
	4	4	13.3716	88.17%	330,282	330,278	329,197	
	5	5	20.2983	100.52%	379,373	379,368	376,713	
	6	6	28.5478	104.90%	383,177	383,173	393,679	
	7	7	38.0891	124.77%	479,873	479,867	470,107	
	8	8	48.8965	139.41%	526,116	526,109	526,462	
	9	9	60.9482	101.80%	390,017	390,012	382,426	
	10	10	74.2254	99.72%	371,480	371,475	374,700	
	11	11	88.7115	90.97%	357,040	357,036	341,396	
	12	12	104.3916	83.99%	295,235	295,232	314,941	
2005	1	13	121.2522	88.67%	329,125	329,121	333,213	
	2	14	139.2813	85.13%	315,520	315,516	319,961	
	3	15	158.4677	91.95%	333,046	333,042	346,517	
	4	16	178.8010	88.17%	333,256	333,251	332,381	
	5	17	200.2717	100.52%	376,551	376,546	380,177	
	6	18	222.8709	104.90%	398,637	398,632	397,419	
	7	19	246.5903	124.77%	472,006	471,999	474,120	
	8	20	271.4221	139.41%	533,199	533,192	530,745	
	9	21	297.3588	101.80%	387,184	387,179	386,976	
	10	22	324.3936	99.72%	385,097	385,092	379,515	
	11	23	352.5199	90.97%	353,212	353,207	346,473	
	12	24	381.7314	83.99%	312,431	312,427	320,279	
2006	1	25	412.0220	88.67%	339,568	339,564	338,809	
	2	26	443.3862	85.13%	324,803	324,799	325,814	
	3	27	475.8185	91.95%	374,563	374,558	352,625	
	4	28	509.3137	88.17%	338,934	338,930	338,741	
	5	29	543.8667	100.52%	388,314	388,309	386,790	
	6	30	579.4729	104.90%	413,383	413,378	404,282	
	7	31	616.1275	124.77%	472,006	471,999	481,232	
	8	32	653.8262	139.41%	533,199	533,192	538,105	
	9	33	692.5646	101.80%	387,184	387,179	394,582	394,582
	10	34	732.3387	99.72%	385,097			387,366
	11	35	773.1444	90.97%	332,903			354,568
	12	36	814.9778	83.99%	355,482			328,617
2007	1	37	857.8353	88.67%	348,258			347,389
	2	38	901.7132	85.13%	328,217			334,635

		Seasonal Index	Trend$^{1.870553}$		
	x coeff	383,637.71	19.25	(9,304.27)	Constant
	se x coeff	9,228.30	7.13	9,271.26	se constant
	r^2	0.9839	8,566.64	#N/A	se y est
	F stat	917.04	30	#N/A	deg freedom
	ss reg	1.34599E+11	2,201,617,347.54	#N/A	ss resid
	t stat x	41.57	2.70	(1.00)	t stat constant

Year	Month	Actual	Ex Post Forecast	Forecast Error	% Error
2006	10	385,097	387,366	(2,269)	-0.59%
	11	332,903	354,568	(21,665)	-6.51%
	12	355,482	328,617	26,865	7.56%
2007	1	348,258	347,389	869	0.25%
	2	328,217	334,635	(6,417)	-1.96%

MAPE =	3.372%	
MAD =	11,617	
WMAPE =	3.319%	

O38 (root mean square error) by changing cells F7 and J7, while constraining cell L47 (sum of the residuals) to sum to zero.

Testing the Model

But before we go on to finalize our lost sales calculations, perhaps we should test our model in a practical manner, in addition to the theoretical goodness-of-fit tests. One way to do this is to use an *ex post*, or holdback, time series forecast. For this process we separate the 38-month period of January 2004 through February 2007 into two parts—one of 33 months of data that we will use to construct a model, and the other five months that we will hold back and then compare to the five months forecasted by the model. We use the same exponents developed by Solver for trend and actual sales in Figure 8.5, and then, using Excel's TREND function, we produce predicted and forecasted sales in columns I and J, after back-transforming the TREND output by raising it to the power of 1/.999999. We use Excel's LINEST array function shown in cells D49 through F53 to obtain a summary regression output so we can examine the goodness-of-fit metrics of the model. The complete procedure is shown in Table 8.6, along with various measures of forecast error, which include MAPE (mean absolute percentage error), which is the average of the absolute percent errors; MAD (mean absolute deviation), which is the average of the absolute forecast errors; and WMAPE (weighted mean absolute percentage error), which is the sum of the absolute forecast errors divided by the sum of actual sales in cells D58 through D62. Based on these excellent metrics of less than 5 percent forecast error and the graphical presentation in Figure 8.6, it appears that

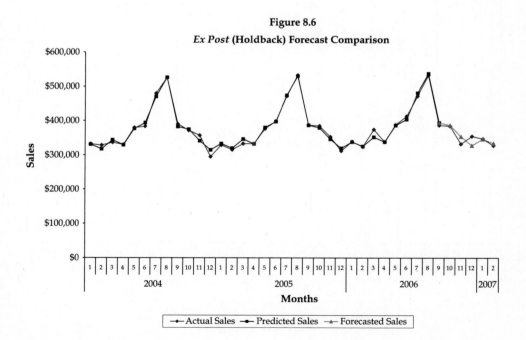

Figure 8.6

Ex Post **(Holdback) Forecast Comparison**

Table 8.7
ALL-BABA SUPERMART, LLC
dba American Supermarket
Regression Model for Prediction
Summary Output

Regression Statistics

	Transformed	Back-Transformed
Multiple R	0.9879	0.9879
R Square	0.9760	0.9760
Adjusted R Square	0.9746	0.9746
Standard Error	9,910	9,771
Coefficient of Variation	2.62%	2.59%
Observations	38	38

ANOVA

	df	SS	MS	F	Significance F
Regression	2	1.399E+11	6.994E+10	7.122E+02	4.446E-29
Residual	35	3.437E+09	9.820E+07		
Total	37	1.433E+11			

	Coefficients	Standard Error	t Stat	p-value	Lower 95%	Upper 95%
Intercept	(7,704.005)	10,451.532	(0.737)	0.466	(28,921.742)	13,513.732
Trend $^{1.870552}$	18.958	5.836	3.248	0.003	7.110	30.807
Seasonal Factor	382,053.701	10,130.550	37.713	0.000	361,487.590	402,619.812

PREDICTION

Regression Equation:

Forecasted Monthly Sales = $(-7{,}704.005 + \text{Trend}^{1.870552} \times 18.958 + \text{Seasonal Factor} \times 382{,}053.071)^{(1/.999999)}$

Month	Intercept	Trend	Trend $^{1.870552}$	Seasonal Factor	Transformed Prediction	Back-Transformed Prediction $^{(1/.999999)}$	Actual Sales	Lost Sales
Mar-07	(7,704)	39	946.61	91.95%	361,553	361,558	314,016	47,542
Apr-07	(7,704)	40	992.51	88.17%	347,955	347,960	304,149	43,811
May-07	(7,704)	41	1039.43	100.52%	396,032	396,037	332,120	63,917
Jun-07	(7,704)	42	1087.36	104.90%	413,678	413,683	362,224	51,459
Jul-07	(7,704)	43	1136.29	124.77%	490,534	490,541	441,669	48,872
Aug-07	(7,704)	44	1186.22	139.41%	547,395	547,403	487,030	60,373
Sep-07	(7,704)	45	1237.14	101.80%	404,690	404,695	405,740	(1,045)
Oct-07	(7,704)	46	1289.07	99.72%	397,726	397,731	364,339	33,393
Nov-07	(7,704)	47	1341.98	90.97%	365,285	365,290		
Dec-07	(7,704)	48	1395.88	83.99%	339,662	339,666		
Total Lost Sales								348,321

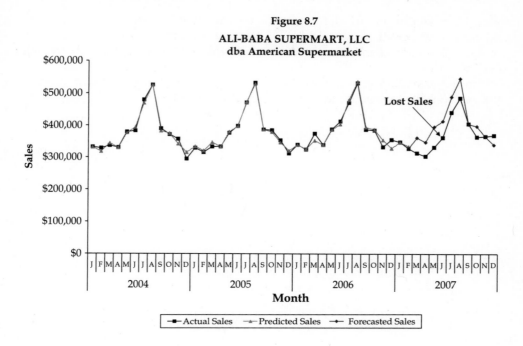

Figure 8.7

ALI-BABA SUPERMART, LLC
dba American Supermarket

our holdback model passes the performance test with flying colors, and we conclude that it is permissible to use the full 38-month model.

Final Sales Forecast

Table 8.7 presents the summary output of the time series regression analysis referred to in Figure 8.5. The column headed Back-Transformed Prediction lists the "should be" sales during the period March to December 2007.

Figure 8.7 is a line chart comparing actual sales (squares) first shown in Table 8.1, forecasted sales developed using the regression model shown in Table 8.7 (diamonds), and predicted sales (triangles) also developed using the regression model shown in Table 8.7. Lost sales are represented by the white space between the diamonds and the squares for the period March 2007 through October 2007 and amount to $348,321. Further determinations would consist of the amount of avoided costs, the length of the damages period, and the amount of any mitigation, or efforts made by the plaintiff to reduce its loss.

Conclusion

This case study has demonstrated how the use of binary dummy variables can be used in a regression model to account for a one-time effect that may take place in one month only or that may continue for a number of months. We also showed how a sequence of number, say 1 to 5, can represent a new five-month trend in sales, if we set the value at zero for all the other months in the series that are not included in the new trend period. The availability of these tools greatly enhances the flexibility of regression models and allows them to be adaptable to many unique forecasting circumstances.

In the next chapter, we show how an uncritical application of cost estimation theory can serve to produce an incorrect damages award.

CHAPTER 9

Case Study 9—An Exercise in Cost Estimation to Determine Saved Expenses

S o far all the previous case studies have concerned themselves mainly with fore-casting "but for" sales, that is, those sales that would have occurred but for the actions of the defendant or an insured peril. In this case study we demonstrate how an uncritical application of cost estimation theory can serve to produce an incorrect damages award.

Classifying Cost Behavior

We generally classify cost behavior into three major categories—those that vary directly with sales we call variable costs or expenses, those that do not vary with sales we call fixed costs or expenses, and those that vary somewhat with sales we call semivariable or semifixed costs or expenses. Examples of each are raw materials or purchased merchandise for variable costs, rent for a fixed cost, and telephone expense, where the base monthly charge is a fixed element of the cost and long-distance charges are the variable element.

If we think of these three cost categories in statistical terms, specifically in terms of the slope and intercept, or constant, of a regression line, we might say that a truly variable cost would exhibit a slope but no intercept, or an intercept of zero; that a truly fixed cost would exhibit an intercept but no slope; and that a semifixed cost would exhibit both an intercept and a slope.

In terms of a percentage of sales, true variable costs would maintain the same percentage of sales whether those sales were rising or falling. True fixed costs would show an ever-decreasing percentage of sales if those sales were rising, and the reverse if sales were falling. Semifixed expenses, as a percentage of sales, would fall somewhere in between the percentage shown by variable and fixed expenses, depending on the degree to which they were fixed or variable.

Without any statistical training, a damages analyst might attempt to determine the cost behavior of a cost or group of costs simply by making an informed decision based on an understanding of the nature of that cost or group of costs and how it relates to sales over time. For example, direct labor might be classified as a variable

					$			%	
					Auto	Meals and		Auto	Meals and
		Year	Cash Receipts		Expense	Travel		Expense	Travel
1		2000	50,763		22,920	11,557		45.2%	22.8%
2		2001	52,478		20,971	12,465		40.0%	23.8%
3		2002	55,679		20,504	11,771		36.8%	21.1%
4		2003	58,105		25,458	14,115		43.8%	24.3%
5		2004	62,072		22,747	13,336		36.6%	21.5%
6		2005	64,955		23,535	12,508		36.2%	19.3%
7		2006	68,039		26,205	14,147		38.5%	20.8%
8		2007	72,631		22,106	12,380		30.4%	17.0%
9		2008	78,078		25,671	14,585		32.9%	18.7%
10		2009	79,040		23,601	13,106		29.9%	16.6%
Average								37.0%	20.6%

Table 9.1
Insurance Salesman
Schedule of Receipts and Expenses

cost, and rent and liability insurance classified as fixed costs. Unfortunately, aside from being an arbitrary exercise, in this scheme of things there is no room for semifixed expenses, the category in which most costs lie.

An Arbitrary Classification

Table 9.1 is a schedule of cash receipts for an insurance salesman, along with two expenses, auto and meals and travel, for the 10 years prior to an incident in year 11 that reduced his gross income by some $25,000. Also shown is the corresponding annual percentage of receipts for each expense. Without the ability to use a statistical tool, the damages analyst might conclude that because of the nature of the expenses, they should be classified as 100 percent variable and thereby reduce lost receipts by 37.0 percent and 20.6 percent for auto and meals and travel expenses, respectively. That is, the idea that without the incurrence of these expenses sales would not be made is conflated with the idea that without sales these expenses would not exist. While this is true of pure variable costs, does it hold for this instant case?

Graph Your Data

As we know, the first thing you should do when confronted with the problem of determining the nature and strength of a relationship between two variables is to graph the data. Figure 9.1 graphs auto expenses against cash receipts and Figure 9.2 does the same for meals and travel. At first glance, because of the slope of the trendline, it appears that there are both fixed and variable elements to the relationship of both expenses to receipts, that is, these costs behave as if they were

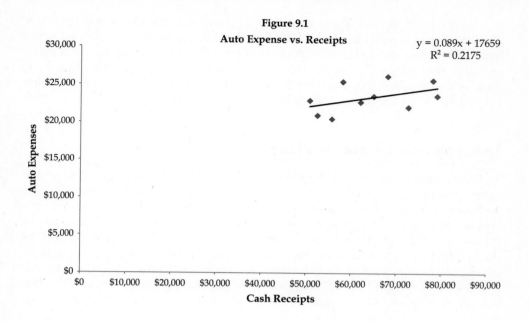

Figure 9.1

Auto Expense vs. Receipts

y = 0.089x + 17659
$R^2 = 0.2175$

semifixed. A glance at the regression equation in the upper right corner of each chart indicates that the fixed components are $17,659 and $9,483, and the variable components are $.089 and $.055 incurred for each dollar of receipts, respectively for auto expenses and meals and travel. Therefore, based on the regression equation and the correctness of the assumption of semifixed cost behavior, lost receipts would be reduced only by the variable component of each expense.

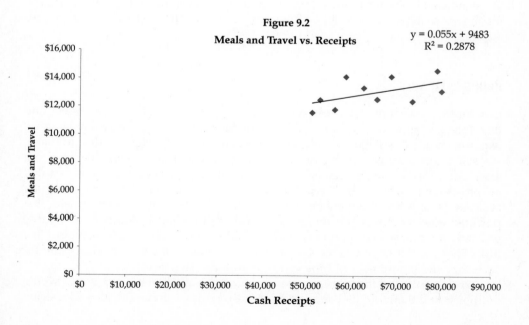

Figure 9.2

Meals and Travel vs. Receipts

y = 0.055x + 9483
$R^2 = 0.2878$

At this point we are comfortable rejecting the idea that the two expenses at issue are purely variable in nature. Based on the two graphs, we are leaning toward treating them as semifixed expenses, as the slope of the trendline appears to be steep enough to be statistically significantly different from zero, or a flat line. However, there is a way to test this assumption of a nonzero trendline, the results of which help us finally decide how to categorize these two expenses.

Testing the Assumption of Significance

To implement the test, we use Excel's regression tool, and we regress each expense against cash receipts. The summary output of the regression tool for auto expense is shown in Table 9.2 and for meals and travel in Table 9.3. For the cash receipts coefficient to be statistically significant its t-statistic should be greater than 2 and its P-value less than .05. In both cases, the cash receipts coefficient fails this test, as the highlighted cells in each summary output indicate. In fact, neither cash receipts coefficient is significant at the .10 level. Of course, a telling giveaway for both expenses is the low R^2 of .2175 and .2878, respectively, shown in Figures 9.1 and 9.2. Given a sample of 10 observations, R^2 would need to be at least .40 for cash receipts to be statistically significant at the .05 level.

We can conclude from this exercise that the nature of each of these two expenses is fixed relative to cash receipts, with a variable component that is neither statistically nor practically significant. This is borne out by a look at the t-statistics and p-values for the intercept for both expenses. Given the effect size of each intercept, we can say each is both practically and statistically significant, and both overshadow its respective cash receipts coefficient. Even if each intercept is statistically significant, that does not mean that the models are useful for predicting saved expenses. The significance test of the model as a whole is the F test, which both models fail, as the significance of F for both is greater than the .10 level, never mind the .05 level, forcing us to reject the model as a means of relating the two expenses to cash receipts.

Expense Drivers

Can we then conclude that these two expenses are essentially fixed in nature, and therefore no amount of either should be deducted from lost receipts as a saved expense? While this might be a valid conclusion for the damages analyst to make, we still haven't answered the question: What drives these two expenses if not sales? After discussing the plaintiff's business model with him, we discovered that he prospected for sales by driving a circuit around his home state on a regular basis, and that it was the number of annual trips, coupled with gasoline prices, that powered auto expenses and meals and travel. As to what powered sales, he told us it was the number of appointments he could secure for each of his circuit-riding trips. There was a great deal of variation in the number of appointments made for each trip, and the number of trips varied as well for each year.

To suggest that if the salesman were totally disabled, then both expenses would disappear and therefore they are variable in nature, is to ignore the idea of relevant

Table 9.2

Insurance Salesman

Regression of Auto Expenses vs. Cash Receipts

SUMMARY OUTPUT

Regression Statistics

Multiple R	0.466
R Square	0.217
Adjusted R Square	0.120
Standard Error	1821.696
Observations	10

ANOVA

	df	SS	MS	F	Significance F
Regression	1	7,379,074.74	7,379,074.74	2.224	0.174
Residual	8	26,548,614.88	3,318,576.86		
Total	9	33,927,689.62			

	Coefficients	Standard Error	t Stat	p-value	Lower 95%	Upper 95%
Intercept	17658.956	3874.172	4.558	0.002	8725.099	26592.813
Cash Receipts	0.089	0.060	1.491	0.174	-0.049	0.227

175

Table 9.3

Insurance Salesman

Regression of Meals and Tavel vs. Cash Receipts

SUMMARY OUTPUT

Regression Statistics

Multiple R	0.536
R Square	0.288
Adjusted R Squae	0.199
Standard Error	929.296
Observations	10

ANOVA

	df	SS	MS	F	Significance F
Regression	1	2,791,999.77	2,791,999.77	3.233	0.110
Residual	8	6,908,733.03	863,591.63		
Total	9	9,700,732.81			

	Coefficients	Standard Error	t Stat	p-value	Lower 95%	Upper 95%
Intercept	9482.943	1976.320	4.798	0.001	4925.542	14040.344
Cash Receipts	0.055	0.030	1.798	0.110	-0.015	0.125

range. What that means is that all costs are fixed in the short-term and variable in the long-term. The question in this case was not what would happen to the salesman's costs if he were totally disabled, or conversely, if he doubled his volume. Those two extreme cases are outside the relevant range of cash receipts exhibited over the last 10 years. The question before us is: Do we reduce a claim for lost cash receipts of, say, $25,000, by some amount of auto and meals and travel expense?

The answer depends on the nature of the business and the origin of the damages claim. Assume that the origin of the claim was a physical injury that allowed the salesman to make the same number of trips but prevented him from meeting with one-third of his usual appointments. Therefore his costs would not have decreased, but his gross revenue would have gone down. Of course, if his physical injury prevented him from making the usual number of trips, then the answer would be different. Or, if the origin of the claim was for defamation, then he would have made the usual number of trips, but since the defendant's action caused prospective customers to refuse to meet with him, then he would have no decrease in costs, but a decrease in revenue.

Assume that the business was not a sole proprietorship, but one with sales of $3,000,000 and 50 employees. If a defendant's action, say, poor quality merchandise, caused customers to stop placing orders, then the circuit-riding salespeople would see a drop in their commissions but with no concomitant decrease in auto and meals and travel expense.

So, what we have here are two costs that can be either fixed or variable, depending upon the facts and circumstances.

Conclusion

As a damages analyst, do not fall into the trap of classifying expenses based on how you think they ought to behave. Be aware of ambiguity. Always graph your data, run significance tests, understand the business model you are dealing with, and, although it applies strictly to business valuation, in the commendable words of Revenue Ruling 59-60, consider the elements of common sense, informed judgment, and reasonableness when weighing the facts involved in a lost profits case.

In the next chapter we continue to explore the nature of operating expenses and the procedures we need to apply in order to satisfy ourselves regarding the degree, if any, to which they can be deducted from lost revenue as saved expenses.

CHAPTER 10

Case Study 10—Saved Expenses, Bivariate Model Inadequacy, and Multiple Regression Models

C ase Study 9 concerned certain operating expenses that appeared to be candidates for treatment as saved expenses, but upon further analysis were found to be unrelated to revenue. In this chapter, we continue to explore the nature of operating expenses and the procedures we need to apply in order to satisfy ourselves regarding the degree, if any, to which they can be deducted from lost revenue as saved expenses.

The facts of the case involve an automobile dealership that was subject to an incident in August 2010 that closed its showroom for the remainder of the month. After determining lost revenue and subtracting cost of sales and other variable costs, the remaining issue was the handling of semifixed costs, as reported on the monthly reports that the dealer sent to the manufacturer. These costs consist mainly of salaries, floor plan interest, and advertising and promotion, which categories represent 41 percent, 19 percent, and 32 percent, respectively, of the semifixed monthly and annual totals. A summary by month of sales and semifixed expenses for the period January 2005 to July 2010 is presented in Table 10.1.

Graph Your Data

To begin to answer the question of how much, if any, of the semifixed expenses are a function of sales and therefore to be deducted from lost revenue, we start by graphing our data. Figure 10.1 is a scatterplot of semifixed expenses versus sales, with a trendline, the regression equation, and a value for R^2 added to the chart. There are three things about this chart that we notice. First, if we ignore the trendline, there doesn't seem too much of an upward trend to the unaided eye—all the data points seem to fill a square, rather than a cigar-shape that runs from the southwest corner to the northeast corner of the chart. Second, the sales coefficient of .0139 means that every increase of $1 in sales results in an increase in semifixed expense of 1.4¢. This is not practically significant, and we could decline to apply the regression equation to lost revenue as the results would hardly affect the claim. However, the sales coefficient is statistically significant, as we shall see in a moment. The third

	A	B	C	D	E	F	G	H	I
1					Table 10.1				
2					ABC AUTO DEALER				
3					SALES AND SEMIFIXED EXPENSE HISTORY				
4					JANUARY 2005–JULY 2010				
5									
6					Sales				
7			2005	2006	2007	2008	2009	2010	
8		January	542,031	1,059,492	1,066,415	858,302	1,098,714	1,398,941	
9		February	1,184,377	1,346,190	1,358,079	1,473,330	1,003,256	1,477,833	
10		March	994,851	1,223,169	1,246,516	942,492	1,170,697	1,677,812	
11		April	1,075,759	1,475,724	1,420,369	1,126,217	1,299,733	1,558,206	
12		May	1,298,158	1,148,249	1,409,451	1,484,850	1,049,551	1,483,778	
13		June	1,151,238	1,185,334	1,584,196	1,218,534	1,163,354	1,881,003	
14		July	847,832	1,279,766	1,158,455	1,199,198	1,209,272	2,212,787	
15		August	1,416,787	1,707,060	1,351,131	2,194,327	2,280,983		
16		September	1,367,035	1,084,419	1,304,312	1,438,776	2,110,847		
17		October	1,046,538	1,393,940	1,088,814	2,130,779	1,296,544		
18		November	1,163,405	1,154,945	1,012,541	1,293,185	1,646,731		
19		December	834,100	1,113,473	1,169,358	1,276,080	1,507,367		
20									
21					Semifixed Expenses				
22			2005	2006	2007	2008	2009	2010	
23		January	44,899	32,876	45,135	45,143	38,939	67,544	
24		February	54,290	24,311	64,433	44,391	30,037	60,556	
25		March	55,042	49,819	70,088	31,116	29,015	57,814	
26		April	52,320	34,274	87,341	41,662	35,045	61,569	
27		May	32,587	42,280	47,588	43,304	52,576	66,099	
28		June	35,149	54,129	81,393	39,910	32,808	59,295	
29		July	35,813	43,454	53,122	59,984	42,072	49,412	
30		August	38,227	44,864	46,442	72,034	56,982		
31		September	46,250	40,665	49,364	53,863	50,427		
32		October	32,031	38,946	42,141	50,104	64,663		
33		November	37,074	42,242	51,558	45,782	50,520		
34		December	49,227	54,227	45,470	21,015	63,563		
35									

item we notice is the very low value of .1302 for R^2. Perhaps another view of the data might show how the two variables match up.

Figure 10.2 is a line chart of the same data shown in Figure 10.1. We notice that while the two variables tend to move in the same general direction over longer periods of time, that is, when sales trend up or down semifixed expense tend to follow along, in very few individual months are they in sync with one another. In fact, for many of the months you can see the variables form a diamond shape, indicating that when one variable increases for the month, the other decreases. This is a confusing result, as there is no logical reason for increasing sales to lower semifixed expense, or vice-versa. For now, let's leave the confusion of Figure 10.2 and conclude that it is a pictorial presentation of a relationship between two variables that over a longer time period move in tandem but on a month-to-month basis seem to have no relationship, resulting in a low R^2 for the relationship as a whole.

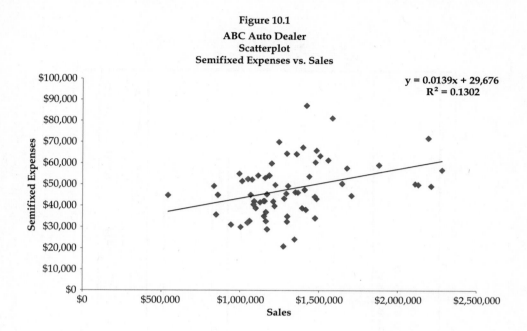

Figure 10.1
ABC Auto Dealer
Scatterplot
Semifixed Expenses vs. Sales

y = 0.0139x + 29,676
R² = 0.1302

Regression Summary Output of the First Model

Table 10.2 presents the summary output of the regression of semifixed expense against sales. We recognize R^2 and the intercept and sales coefficients from Figure 10.1. What is new and surprising information, given the data presentation in

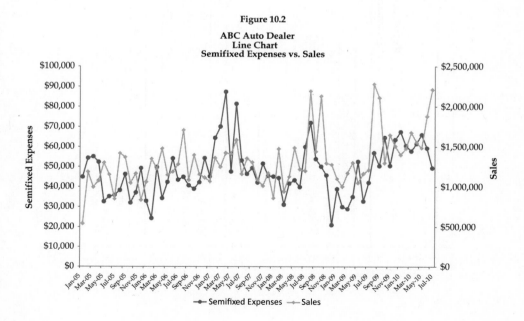

Figure 10.2
ABC Auto Dealer
Line Chart
Semifixed Expenses vs. Sales

Table 10.2

ABC AUTO DEALER

Regression of Semifixed Expenses vs. Sales

Summary Output – Simple Linear Model

Regression Statistics

Multiple R	0.361
R Square	0.130
Adjusted R Square	0.117
Standard Error	12,123.5
Observations	67

ANOVA

	df	SS	MS	F	Significance F
Regression	1	1,429,547,730.0	1,429,547,730.0	9.726	0.0027
Residual	65	9,553,683,676.1	146,979,748.9		
Total	66	10,983,231,406.0			

Term	Coefficients	Standard Error	t Stat	p-value	Lower 95%	Upper 95%
Intercept	29,675.8	6,060.9	4.896	0.00001	17,571.4	41,780.2
Sales	0.0139	0.0045	3.119	0.003	0.0050	0.0228

	A	B	C	D	E
1		**Table 10.3**			
2		**ABC AUTO DEALER**			
3		**Analysis of Independent Variable t-Statistic**			
4					
5		*Slope Computation:*			
6		Standard Deviation of Semifixed Expenses (Y)	A	12,900.1	
7		Standard Deviation of Sales (X)	B	335,120.5	
8					
9		Rise Over Run Ratio A ÷ B	C	0.0385	
10					
11		Coefficient of Correlation (R)	D	0.3608	
12					
13		Beta - Sales Coefficient - Trendline Slope C * D	E	0.0139	
14					
15		*Standard Error Computation*			
16		Standard Error of the Estimate (SEE)	F	12,123.5	
17					
18		Squared Deviations of X	G	7,412,179,143,135.1	
19					
20		Square Root of G	H	2,722,531.8	
21					
22		Standard Error of the Sales Coefficient F ÷ H	I	0.0045	
23					
24		*t Stat Computation*			
25		Slope ÷ Standard Error E ÷ I	J	3.12	
26					

the scatterplot and the line chart, is that the sales coefficient is statistically significant. What makes the sales coefficient statistically significant is an accident of the model. The standard deviation and the range of values for sales are each 26 times larger than the same values for semifixed expenses. With that much variance in the sales data, it's no wonder that the denominator of the standard error ratio is so large and the resulting standard error so small. We show this calculation in detail in Table 10.3.

Search for Other Independent Variables

At this point, while we wouldn't call the sales coefficient spuriously statistically significant, it is not a value one would rely on, both for the way it was calculated and because it is not practically significant at 1.4¢ to the $1. An implication for a model with a very low R^2 and a statistically significant x variable coefficient is that the model is misspecified, that is, there are other relevant independent variables that need to be included in the model. In addition, a way to test the viability of

Table 10.4
ABC AUTO DEALER
Potential Independent Variables for Multiple Regression Model

Month	No. of Employees	Total Assets	Units Sold	Current Assets	Inventory	Sales	Semifixed (Dependent Variable)
Jan-05	31	3,961,422	41	3,507,888	3,382,028	542,031	44,899
Feb-05	32	3,667,890	111	3,219,118	3,294,705	1,184,377	54,290
Mar-05	31	3,641,572	90	3,195,556	3,328,199	994,851	55,042
Apr-05	30	3,763,370	82	3,289,826	3,384,946	1,075,759	52,320
May-05	28	3,695,914	99	3,197,731	2,934,981	1,298,158	32,587
Jun-05	27	3,569,104	90	3,073,994	2,866,946	1,151,238	35,149
Jul-05	27	3,459,893	78	2,987,411	2,834,174	847,832	35,813
Aug-05	28	3,416,082	98	2,966,233	2,856,757	1,416,787	38,227
Sep-05	30	3,001,579	99	2,563,455	2,635,791	1,367,035	46,250
Oct-05	27	3,189,896	77	2,786,528	2,590,220	1,046,538	32,031
Nov-05	27	2,993,128	73	2,596,606	2,521,278	1,163,405	37,074
Dec-05	29	3,347,430	65	2,962,797	2,973,845	834,100	49,227
Jan-06	26	3,705,375	72	3,325,051	2,954,110	1,059,492	32,876
Feb-06	27	3,686,547	83	3,306,040	2,825,559	1,346,190	24,311
Mar-06	28	3,778,770	84	3,402,401	3,167,628	1,223,169	49,819
Apr-06	28	3,852,683	98	3,403,095	3,030,675	1,475,724	34,274
May-06	29	4,227,886	86	3,689,507	3,471,101	1,148,249	42,280
Jun-06	30	4,280,030	99	3,761,053	3,763,645	1,185,334	54,129
Jul-06	30	4,657,437	91	4,154,318	3,837,225	1,279,766	43,454
Aug-06	30	4,200,450	98	3,690,995	3,446,218	1,707,060	44,864
Sep-06	31	4,665,048	69	4,188,294	3,727,114	1,084,419	40,665
Oct-06	30	4,799,681	77	4,340,967	3,748,764	1,393,940	38,946
Nov-06	30	4,823,502	66	4,407,865	3,903,598	1,154,945	42,242
Dec-06	32	4,977,506	84	4,542,110	4,398,846	1,113,473	54,227
Jan-07	32	5,245,929	69	4,816,696	4,269,449	1,066,415	45,135
Feb-07	34	5,281,960	100	4,873,734	4,994,916	1,358,079	64,433
Mar-07	34	4,924,958	88	4,522,177	4,938,317	1,246,516	70,088
Apr-07	36	5,246,447	109	4,734,606	5,500,000	1,420,369	87,341
May-07	32	5,191,917	99	4,671,983	4,275,712	1,409,451	47,588
Jun-07	36	5,083,642	117	4,558,282	5,327,298	1,584,196	81,393
Jul-07	33	4,387,053	82	3,890,073	3,947,194	1,158,455	53,122
Aug-07	33	4,393,852	91	3,905,996	3,611,392	1,351,131	46,442
Sep-07	33	4,204,288	86	3,724,110	3,645,335	1,304,312	49,364

Month	No. of Employees	Total Assets	Units Sold	Current Assets	Inventory	Sales	Semifixed (Dependent Variable)
Oct-07	33	4,432,617	81	3,960,291	3,651,332	1,088,814	42,141
Nov-07	36	4,445,478	57	3,987,993	4,008,575	1,012,541	51,558
Dec-07	33	4,239,029	74	3,792,238	3,690,131	1,169,358	45,470
Jan-08	31	4,557,624	50	4,037,045	3,824,977	858,302	45,143
Feb-08	33	4,860,875	80	4,329,364	3,665,813	1,473,330	44,391
Mar-08	32	5,581,981	62	5,056,003	3,720,152	942,492	31,116
Apr-08	33	6,129,476	91	5,476,036	4,340,738	1,126,217	41,662
May-08	33	6,479,237	84	5,807,531	4,469,551	1,484,850	43,304
Jun-08	32	6,807,802	80	6,149,497	4,484,468	1,218,534	39,910
Jul-08	35	6,584,217	69	5,952,275	5,303,076	1,199,198	59,984
Aug-08	36	5,534,727	140	4,915,230	5,024,178	2,194,327	72,034
Sep-08	35	4,734,678	104	4,168,776	3,861,342	1,438,776	53,863
Oct-08	33	3,921,887	105	3,388,907	3,113,270	2,130,779	50,104
Nov-08	33	3,723,371	92	3,222,459	3,027,159	1,293,185	45,782
Dec-08	31	4,327,570	73	3,864,371	2,892,096	1,276,080	21,015
Jan-09	30	5,038,924	79	4,595,292	3,761,785	1,098,714	38,939
Feb-09	29	5,375,041	65	4,967,205	3,742,033	1,003,256	30,037
Mar-09	29	5,496,208	72	5,070,530	3,794,564	1,170,697	29,015
Apr-09	30	5,690,765	78	5,148,486	3,976,668	1,299,733	35,045
May-09	32	5,391,164	73	4,859,785	4,474,816	1,049,551	52,576
Jun-09	32	5,881,307	70	5,365,372	3,898,185	1,163,354	32,808
Jul-09	30	5,366,153	86	4,831,451	4,095,787	1,209,272	42,072
Aug-09	32	5,448,848	123	4,931,661	4,429,865	2,280,983	56,982
Sep-09	32	5,724,437	130	5,210,742	4,450,378	2,110,847	50,427
Oct-09	33	6,282,730	89	5,778,324	5,500,000	1,296,544	64,663
Nov-09	32	6,303,424	108	5,819,566	4,827,919	1,646,731	50,520
Dec-09	39	5,785,803	94	5,325,582	5,183,228	1,507,367	63,563
Jan-10	39	6,027,787	89	5,578,817	5,500,000	1,398,941	67,544
Feb-10	38	5,522,162	98	5,087,841	4,998,899	1,477,833	60,556
Mar-10	37	5,663,412	105	5,351,970	5,058,907	1,677,812	57,814
Apr-10	38	5,495,528	95	5,067,068	5,103,365	1,558,206	61,569
May-10	39	5,882,363	100	5,462,734	5,420,428	1,483,778	66,099
Jun-10	38	5,882,041	108	5,475,895	5,173,286	1,881,003	59,295
Jul-10	36	5,447,098	114	5,054,933	4,474,404	2,212,787	49,412

184

Table 10.5
ABC AUTO DEALER
Coefficients of Correlation Among Potential Independent Variables

Pearson Correlations	Independent Variables					Dependent Variable
	Current Assets	Inventory	Units Sold	No. of Employees	Sales	Semifixed
Current Assets	1.000	0.857	0.141	0.607	0.317	0.341
Inventory		1.000	0.322	0.816	0.375	0.750
Units Sold			1.000	0.340	0.834	0.488
No. of Employees				1.000	0.425	0.744
Sales					1.000	0.361
Semifixed						1.000

Pearson Probabilities	Independent Variables					Dependent Variable
	Current Assets	Inventory	Units Sold	No. of Employees	Sales	Semifixed
Current Assets	-	0.000	0.254	0.000	0.009	0.005
Inventory		-	0.008	0.000	0.002	0.000
Units Sold			-	0.005	0.000	0.000
No. of Employees				-	0.000	0.000
Sales					-	0.003
Semifixed						-

sales as an independent variable is to expand the model and bring in additional independent variables that have a logical relationship to the dependent variable, semifixed expenses. For that purpose, we scoured the monthly dealer financial statements and chose the accounts and data shown in Table 10.4 as independent variables in addition to sales. Before running our regression model, we set up a correlation matrix, which is shown in Table 10.5, to aid in selecting those independent variables to include in the regression model. From this matrix we can see that inventory and number of employees is correlated with semifixed expense to a much higher degree than any of the other independent variables. Therefore, we will include as independent variables in our model the sales term, the inventory term, and the number of employees term. The setup sheet for the model is shown in Table 10.6.

Regression Summary Output of the Second Model

The summary output of the regression is shown in Excel's format in Table 10.7. We notice that R^2 is .616, a considerable improvement over the sales model's .130. However, with 38.4 percent of the variation in semifixed expense unexplained, there might be room for improvement in the model if additional independent variables can be identified and logically justified for inclusion in the model. But it may be that given the asset size of the dealership, the range of its sales activity, and the size of its advertising and promotion budget, that semifixed expense is more fixed than semi,

Table 10.6
ABC AUTO DEALER
Setup Sheet for Multiple Regression Model

Month	Independent Variables			Dependent Variable
	No. of Employees	Inventory	Sales	Semifixed
Jan-05	31	3,382,028	542,031	44,899
Feb-05	32	3,294,705	1,184,377	54,290
Mar-05	31	3,328,199	994,851	55,042
Apr-05	30	3,384,946	1,075,759	52,320
May-05	28	2,934,981	1,298,158	32,587
Jun-05	27	2,866,946	1,151,238	35,149
Jul-05	27	2,834,174	847,832	35,813
Aug-05	28	2,856,757	1,416,787	38,227
Sep-05	30	2,635,791	1,367,035	46,250
Oct-05	27	2,590,220	1,046,538	32,031
Nov-05	27	2,521,278	1,163,405	37,074
Dec-05	29	2,973,845	834,100	49,227
Jan-06	26	2,954,110	1,059,492	32,876
Feb-06	27	2,825,559	1,346,190	24,311
Mar-06	28	3,167,628	1,223,169	49,819
Apr-06	28	3,030,675	1,475,724	34,274
May-06	29	3,471,101	1,148,249	42,280
Jun-06	30	3,763,645	1,185,334	54,129
Jul-06	30	3,837,225	1,279,766	43,454
Aug-06	30	3,446,218	1,707,060	44,864
Sep-06	31	3,727,114	1,084,419	40,665
Oct-06	30	3,748,764	1,393,940	38,946
Nov-06	30	3,903,598	1,154,945	42,242
Dec-06	32	4,398,846	1,113,473	54,227
Jan-07	32	4,269,449	1,066,415	45,135
Feb-07	34	4,994,916	1,358,079	64,433
Mar-07	34	4,938,317	1,246,516	70,088
Apr-07	36	5,500,000	1,420,369	87,341
May-07	32	4,275,712	1,409,451	47,588
Jun-07	36	5,327,298	1,584,196	81,393
Jul-07	33	3,947,194	1,158,455	53,122
Aug-07	32	3,611,392	1,351,131	46,442
Sep-07	33	3,645,335	1,304,312	49,364

Month	Independent Variables			Dependent Variable
	No. of Employees	Inventory	Sales	Semifixed
Oct-07	33	3,651,332	1,088,814	42,141
Nov-07	36	4,008,575	1,012,541	51,558
Dec-07	33	3,690,131	1,169,358	45,470
Jan-08	31	3,824,977	858,302	45,143
Feb-08	33	3,665,813	1,473,330	44,391
Mar-08	32	3,720,152	942,492	31,116
Apr-08	33	4,340,738	1,126,217	41,662
May-08	33	4,469,551	1,484,850	43,304
Jun-08	32	4,484,468	1,218,534	39,910
Jul-08	35	5,303,076	1,199,198	59,984
Aug-08	36	5,024,178	2,194,327	72,034
Sep-08	35	3,861,342	1,438,776	53,863
Oct-08	33	3,113,270	2,130,779	50,104
Nov-08	33	3,027,159	1,293,185	45,782
Dec-08	31	2,892,096	1,276,080	21,015
Jan-09	30	3,761,785	1,098,714	38,939
Feb-09	29	3,742,033	1,003,256	30,037
Mar-09	29	3,794,564	1,170,697	29,015
Apr-09	30	3,976,668	1,299,733	35,045
May-09	32	4,474,816	1,049,551	52,576
Jun-09	30	3,898,185	1,163,354	32,808
Jul-09	30	4,095,787	1,209,272	42,072
Aug-09	32	4,429,865	2,280,983	56,982
Sep-09	32	4,450,378	2,110,847	50,427
Oct-09	33	5,500,000	1,296,544	64,663
Nov-09	32	4,827,919	1,646,731	50,520
Dec-09	39	5,183,228	1,507,367	63,563
Jan-10	39	5,500,000	1,398,941	67,544
Feb-10	38	4,998,899	1,477,833	60,556
Mar-10	37	5,058,907	1,677,812	57,814
Apr-10	38	5,103,365	1,558,206	61,569
May-10	39	5,420,428	1,483,778	66,099
Jun-10	38	5,173,286	1,881,003	59,295
Jul-10	36	4,474,404	2,212,787	49,412

Table 10.7

ABC AUTO DEALER

Regression of Semifixed Expenses vs. Various Independent Variables

Summary Output - Multiple Regression Model

Regression Statistics

Multiple R	0.785
R Square	0.616
Adjusted R Square	0.598
Standard Error	8,181.608
Observations	67

ANOVA

	df	SS	MS	F	Significance F
Regression	3	6,766,092,763	2,255,364,254	33.693	4.080E-13
Residual	63	4,217,138,643	66,938,709		
Total	66	10,983,231,406			

	Coefficients	Standard Error	t Stat	p-value	Lower 95%	Upper 95%
Intercept	(27,980.617)	11,399.658	-2.4545	0.0169	(50,761.015)	(5,200.219)
Inventory	0.007	0.002	3.1317	0.0026	0.0024	0.0107
No. of Employees	1,504.552	546.489	2.7531	0.0077	412.480	2,596.624
Sales	0.002	0.003	0.4609	0.6465	-0.0051	0.0082

and a .616 R^2 is the best that can be done. Perhaps, we thought, because of the relationship shown in Figure 10.2, lagging some or all of the variables, including the dependent variable, would produce a better fitting model. However, lagged models did not produce any better results. But our assignment was not to determine what drives semifixed expense; it was to determine if sales, placed in the context of other predictor variables, was still a statistically significant factor in a prediction model for semifixed expense.

We note in Table 10.7 that sales is no longer statistically significant with a t-stat of .4609 and a p-value of .6765. Therefore, there would be no further reduction in the lost profits claim because of any saved semifixed expense. In other words, there is no material relationship between sales and semifixed expense when other predictor variables are included in the model. Of course, in this instant case, with a practically insignificant sales coefficient, we didn't have to demonstrate that sales becomes statistically insignificant when placed in context with other predictor variables—we could have just declined to use that term in the calculation of lost profits. But you may come across other lost profit claims where the facts and circumstances are such that the equivalent of the sales term is practically significant, say, .30¢ to $1, and the R^2 for that regression model is low enough to suggest that other independent variables might be missing. In that case, you need to test the sales coefficient in context with other predictor variables to be sure that it remains statistically significant if you are going to use it as part of your lost profits calculation.

Conclusion

To sum up this case study, we started out with the question of whether or not any amount of semifixed expense should be deducted from lost revenue. Regressing semifixed expenses against sales, we decided that the result was too practically insignificant to include in the calculation of lost profits. Observing that the sales coefficient was statistically significant, but the R^2 of the model was low, we wondered if bringing more independent variables into the model might diminish the significance of sales as an independent variable. We found this to be the case.

In the next chapter we offer you the opportunity to follow along as we review both the plaintiff's and defendant's experts' reports in a case involving a contract dispute.

CHAPTER 11

Case Study 11—Analysis of and Modification to Opposing Experts' Reports

I n a commercial damages case that has an expert on the other side, you will inevitably be asked to review that opposing expert's report and describe to counsel the errors in that report, including math mistakes, the use of unreliable and nonrelevant data, the use of improper methods and/or the misapplication of the proper methods, and any assumptions regarding the facts and data in the case that appear to be speculative. In this case study we offer you the opportunity to follow along as we review both the plaintiff's and defendant's experts' reports in a case involving a contract dispute between Vending Corporation of America (VCA) and the State C Department of Transportation (State C or State).

Background Information

The two parties entered into a seven-year contract on April 10, 2006, for VCA to install and service vending machines at highway rest stops in State C beginning on January 1, 2007. The State became dissatisfied with VCA's service and ultimately canceled the contract effective December 31, 2008, and VCA filed a breach of contract action and sued for the expected lost profits over the full five years remaining on the contract.

The contract called for VCA to install and operate vending machines at 12 rest stops in the first two years of the contract, and then build-out to a maximum of 70 stations over the last five years of the contract. The contract called for VCA to design and erect buildings to house the vending machines at each of the rest stops, as well as to install, operate, and service the vending machines. These expenses were to be the sole responsibility of VCA, with the State supplying the land rent-free and providing all necessary utilities.

VCA was to sell items in the vending machines at the prevailing prices for these items in the same locality. The State was to receive a royalty of 2 percent of gross sales in the first two years of the contract and then 3 percent of sales thereafter for the last five years of the contract.

VCA built the required 12 stations and installed the vending machines over a two-month period in late 2006 and began operating them on January 1, 2007. After a year and a half of operations, the State became unhappy with the performance of VCA, as royalties were below projections and maintenance of the vending machines and sanitary conditions at the stations were allegedly substandard. For these reasons the State notified VCA that it would not continue the vending machine program after December 31, 2008.

Over two years have passed, and trial is set to begin in mid-2011.

Stipulated Facts and Data

After this brief summary of the facts of the case, we are ready to begin examining each expert's report, which was prepared in early 2011. But first let's present the facts and data of the case, including those that were stipulated to by both parties. These facts and data fall into four categories: (1) those from the two years of operations by VCA in State C; (2) those from VCA operating 15 to 75 stations in State A over a seven-year period; (3) those from VCA operating 10 to 50 stations over a nine-year period in State B; and (4) industry statistics from the National Association of Vending Operators.

Table 11.1 presents the facts and data for category 1, the two-year operating history of VCA in State C. Table 11.2 presents the facts and data from the seven-year operating history of VCA in State A, and Table 11.3 presents the same information for the nine-year operating history of VCA in State B. Table 11.4 shows summary

A	B	C	D	E	F	G
1	Table 11.1					
2	VCA Operating History					
3	For the Years Ended December 31,					
4						
5				2007	2008	
6	Number of Stations			12	12	
7	Revenue per Station		$	42,551 $	59,707	
8	Vehicle Miles (millions)			232.10	243.70	
9	Revenue per Thousand Miles			2.20	2.94	
10						
11	Revenue			510,612	716,484	
12	Cost of Sales			342,110	480,044	
13	Gross Profit			168,502	236,440	
14	Gross Margin			33.0%	33.0%	
15	Variable Operating Expenses			185,820	254,196	
16	Expense Ratio			36.4%	35.5%	
17	G&A			94,704	96,204	
18	Net Operating Profit		$	(112,022) $	(113,960)	
19						
20	State C Data		2007	2010	% Change	
21	Average Vehicle Miles Driven per Day		736,035	896,041	5.0%	
22	Expected Growth Rate 2011–2013		4.0%			
23						

Table 11.2
State A
Facts and Data

Year	No. of Stations	Rev/Station	Total Revenue	Cost of Sales	Gross Margin	Vehicle Miles (millions)	Revenue/ Thousand Vehicle Miles	Year-to-Year % Change
2004	15	$ 74,098	$ 1,111,470	$ 722,460	35%	274.4	4.05	
2005	35	88,166	3,085,810	1,789,760	42%	277.5	11.12	174.53%
2006	55	88,474	4,866,070	2,822,325	42%	294.2	16.54	48.74%
2007	75	88,493	6,636,975	3,915,825	41%	319.7	20.76	25.51%
2008	75	96,742	7,255,650	4,280,850	41%	327.3	22.17	6.78%
2009	75	105,564	7,917,300	4,592,025	42%	342.0	23.15	4.43%
2010	75	109,366	8,202,450	4,675,425	43%	353.4	23.21	0.26%

Statement of Operations
Year Ended December 31, 2010

Revenue	$ 8,202,450
Cost of Sales	4,675,425
Gross Profit	3,527,025
Gross Margin	43.0%
Variable Operating Expenses	2,706,825
Expenses Ratio	33.0%
G&A	315,225
Net Operating Profit	$ 504,975
OP Ratio	6.2%

Table 11.3
State B
Facts and Data

Year	No. of Stations	Rev/Station	Total Revenue	Cost of Sales	Gross Margin	Vehicle Miles (millions)	Revenue/ Thousand Vehicle Miles	Year-to-Year % Change
2002	10	$ 45,958	$ 459,580	$ 307,920	33%	190.7	2.41	
2003	25	52,497	1,312,425	853,075	35%	195.3	6.72	178.84%
2004	40	52,607	2,104,280	1,325,680	37%	206.1	10.21	51.93%
2005	50	53,836	2,691,800	1,642,000	39%	211.1	12.75	24.89%
2006	50	59,406	2,970,300	1,841,600	38%	218.4	13.60	6.66%
2007	50	64,212	3,210,600	1,926,350	40%	225.9	14.21	4.50%
2008	50	66,615	3,330,750	1,965,150	41%	233.7	14.25	0.28%
2009	50	69,010	3,450,500	2,001,300	42%	241.8	14.27	0.12%
2010	50	71,927	3,596,350	2,121,800	41%	252.2	14.26	-0.07%

Statement of Operations
Year Ended December 31, 2010

Revenue	$ 3,596,350
Cost of Sales	2,121,800
Gross Profit	1,474,550
Gross Margin	41.0%
Variable Operating Expenses	1,150,800
Expenses Ratio	32.0%
G&A	118,250
Net Operating Profit	$ 205,500
OP Ratio	5.7%

	A	B	C	D	E
1		**Table 11.4**			
2		**Summary of Industry Statistics**			
3		**For the Year Ended December 31,**			
4					
5				**2009**	
6		Total Number of Companies		180	
7		Average Vending Sites per Company		145	
8		Total Vending Sites		26,100	
9		Average Revenue per Company		$ 11,382,500	
10		Average Revenue per Vending Site		$ 78,500	
11		Average Cost of Sales per Company		$ 6,374,200	
12		Average Cost of Sales Ratio per Company		56.0%	
13		Average Gross Margin per Company		44.0%	
14		Average Variable Operating Expenses			
15		per Company		$ 3,926,963	
16		Average Variable Expense Ratio		34.5%	
17		Average G&A Costs per Company		$ 353,147	
18		Average Profit Per Company		$ 728,190	
19		Average Profit Margin per Company		6.4%	
20		Average Profit per Vending Site		$ 5,022	
21		Average Real Growth in Revenue			
22		per Vehicle Mile - All Companies			
23		**Year of Operation**			
24		2	180%		
25		3	60%		
26		4	30%		
27		5	10%		
28		6	5%		
29		7+	0%		
30					

industry average statistics for 2009. All the facts and data contained in these four tables have been stipulated to by the parties.

As we go through the comparative analysis of these facts and data we need to keep in mind that very often, because the period of interruption for a commercial damages case can extend out to five years and sometimes beyond, small differences in assumptions can cause large changes in total damages.

The Flaw Common to Both Experts

To set the stage for that comparative analysis, we needed to find an element common to both experts' damages analysis. That common element and the fatal flaw in the damages model of both experts was to rely on operating data from States A and B to forecast revenue for State C. Whether the model was based on revenue per station, or revenue per thousand noncommuter vehicle miles driven, the use of averaged disparate data from State A and State B, rather than industry average data gleaned from 180 companies in all 50 states, caused both experts' analyses to be flawed.

Let's enumerate the reasons why State A and State B are not relevant and similar comparisons.

You wouldn't use comps from houses that are valued at >$2,000,000 and <$500,000 to value a house in the range of >$500,000 to <$1,000,000. Nor would you combine the two databases of comps and use some form of weighted average to determine the value of a house in the range of >$500,000 to <$1,000,000.

Matching up the seventh year of operations for both states, we find that State A is larger than State B by the factor for each category shown in the following table.

Category	Factor
Revenue	2.46
Noncommuter vehicle miles driven	1.51
Revenue per station	1.64
Number of stations	1.50
Revenue per thousand vehicle miles	1.56

Using the two sample t-test for means we are able to establish that the data for each category for each state is drawn from a different population, and therefore should not be used conjunctively to make inferences about State C. We show this for the revenue per station and noncommuter vehicle miles driven categories in Table 11.5. In both categories the t-statistic is greater than the critical value of 2.145, and the corresponding p-value is substantially less than .05, indicating that the means of both categories are statistically significantly different from each other.

Neither should either state be used by itself to make predictions concerning the revenues of State C, as the following table shows the lack of comparability among the three states for noncommuter vehicle miles driven in the first seven years of station operation.

State A (actual)	State B (actual)	State C (forecast)
274.4	190.7	232.1
277.5	195.3	243.7
294.2	206.1	255.9
319.7	211.1	268.7
327.3	218.4	279.4
342.0	225.9	290.6
353.4	233.7	302.0

A	B	C	D	E
1		**Table 11.5**		
2		**t-Test: Two-Sample Assuming Equal Variances**		
3		**Comparing State A to State B**		
4				
5	**Revenue per Station**			
6		*State A*	*State B*	
7	Mean	92,986	59,563	
8	Variance	143,521,400	78,712,591	
9	Observations	7	9	
10	Pooled Variance	106,487,795		
11	Hypothesized Mean Difference	0		
12	df	14		
13	t Stat	6.427		
14	P(T<=t) one-tail	0.000008		
15	t Critical one-tail	1.761		
16	P(T<=t) two-tail	0.000016		
17	t Critical two-tail	2.145		
18				
19				
20	**Non-Commuter Vehicle Miles Driven**			
21		*State A*	*State B*	
22	Mean	313	219	
23	Variance	971	434	
24	Observations	7	9	
25	Pooled Variance	664		
26	Hypothesized Mean Difference	0		
27	df	14		
28	t Stat	7.173		
29	P(T<=t) one-tail	0.000002		
30	t Critical one-tail	1.761		
31	P(T<=t) two-tail	0.000005		
32	t Critical two-tail	2.145		
33				

Because of the lack of relevant range (State A's minimum observation is greater than State C's, and State B's maximum observation is less than State C's), and in spite of the degree of correlation of the data between States A and B, using noncommuter vehicle miles driven along with other predictor variables in a regression model with the intent of predicting revenue for State C will tend to overstate revenue if State A data is used, and will tend to understate revenue if State B data is used. To demonstrate this point, the following table presents the results of the best-fitting multiple regression model for each state.

| | Revenue Prediction for State C Based on Data from | |
Year	State A	State B
2009	632,279	546,903
2010	632,279	724,387
2011	2,035,538	1,477,137
2012	4,194,399	2,539,646
2013	5,273,829	3,159,642
2014	5,813,544	3,558,382
2015	6,892,974	4,178,379

This is not a useful result because at this point in our analysis we don't know which of these two models best represents the expected revenue of State C, if either of them does. Given the high degree of disparity shown above, we will not continue this line of investigation any further.

While there is a very strong linear relationship between certain variables of State A and State B, for example, revenue, noncommuter miles, and revenue per station, as indicated by correlation coefficients that exceed .95 (not shown), these large correlation coefficients are driven by the lurking variable of rate of growth, and not by some direct cause and effect relationship between State A data and State B data. Therefore, we can't rely on the high degree of correlation between State A and State B variables to assume that a similar degree of correlation between either State A data or State B data with State C data will prove useful.

Defendant's Expert's Report

Having pointed out the reasons why one should not base revenue estimates for State C on activities in States A and/or B, we are now ready to present the experts' reports. We begin with the defendant's report as it has only one flaw, and that is its revenue forecast. Additionally, an explanation of how the defendant determined the costs and expenses associated with forecasted revenues serves as a basis for critiquing the plaintiff's expert's report. Table 11.6 presents the defendant's expert's calculation of undiscounted damages for the five-year loss period.

In their report, defendant's experts state that "the traffic and travel patterns in the three States are very different (note the disparity in revenue per station in State B versus State A)." Further on in their report they write that "State A and State B are not representative of State C." They abide by these statements when they estimate the costs and expenses for their detailed profit projection as they do not use State A or State B data to compute those costs and expenses.

Rather, for cost of sales they use VCA's own two-year experience in State C of 67 percent adjusted downward for volume discounts allowed by VCA's suppliers as shown in Table 11.6. For variable operating expenses, they begin with VCA's 35.9 percent actual average two-year experience. Adding 1 percent, as the royalty rate climbs from 2 percent to 3 percent beginning in Year 3 of the contract, would increase the variable cost rate to 36.9 percent, all other things held equal. Moreover,

Table 11.6
Defendant's Damages Model
Detailed Lost Profits Forecast

	Actual		Projected				
	2007	2008	2009	2010	2011	2012	2013
Stations	12	12	25	45	55	60	70
Vehicle Miles (millions)	232.10	243.70	255.90	268.70	279.41	290.60	302.00
Revenue per Thousand Miles	$ 2.20	$ 2.94	$ 8.13	$ 12.23	$ 15.31	$ 16.34	$ 17.07
Revenue	$ 510,612	$ 716,484	$ 2,081,651	$ 3,286,028	$ 4,278,163	$ 4,748,528	$ 5,155,156
Cost of sales	342,110	480,044	1,255,236	1,981,475	2,579,732	2,783,825	3,022,210
Gross Profit	168,502	236,440	826,416	1,304,553	1,698,431	1,964,703	2,132,946
Gross Margin	33.0%	33.0%	39.7%	39.7%	39.7%	41.4%	41.4%
Variable Operating Expenses	185,820	254,196	749,394	1,166,540	1,497,357	1,638,242	1,778,529
Expense Ratio	36.4%	35.5%	36.0%	35.5%	35.0%	34.5%	34.5%
G&A	94,704	96,204	100,000	150,000	200,000	250,000	300,000
Net Operating Profit	$ (112,022)	$ (113,960)	$ (22,979)	$ (11,987)	$ 1,074	$ 76,461	$ 54,417
Return on Revenue			-1.10%	-0.36%	0.03%	1.61%	1.06%
Total Undiscounted Lost Profits	$ 96,986		$ (22,979)	$ (11,987)	$ 1,074	$ 76,461	$ 54,417

Cost of Sales and Gross Margin Calculation							
Revenue	$ 510,612	$ 716,484	$ 2,081,651	$ 3,286,028	$ 4,278,163	$ 4,748,528	$ 5,155,156
Cost of Sales Without Volume Discount @ 67%	342,110	480,044	1,394,706	2,201,639	2,866,369	3,181,514	3,453,955
Volume Discount Factor	0	0	0.1	0.1	0.1	0.125	0.125
Cost of Sales With Volume Discount	342,110	480,044	1,255,236	1,981,475	2,579,732	2,783,825	3,022,210
Cost of Sales %	67.0%	67.0%	60.3%	60.3%	60.3%	58.6%	58.6%
Gross Margin	33.0%	33.0%	39.7%	39.7%	39.7%	41.4%	41.4%

Volume Discount Factors			Forecast Year	Historical % Change in Revenue/Thousand Vehicle Miles *			Projected Revenue/ Thousand Vehicle Miles
Purchase Volume		Discount		State A	State B	Average	
-	500,000	0.0%	2008				$ 2.94 Actual
500,001	1,000,000	5.0%	2009	174.53%	178.84%	176.69%	8.13
1,000,001	3,000,000	10.0%	2010	48.74%	51.93%	50.34%	12.23
3,000,001	5,000,000	12.5%	2011	25.51%	24.89%	25.20%	15.31
5,000,001	10,000,000	15.0%	2012	6.78%	6.66%	6.72%	16.34
10,000,001	99,000,000	17.5%	2013	4.43%	4.50%	4.47%	17.07

* 2008 has been considered the 1st year of operations as the contract limited the number of stations to 12 for 2007 and 2008.

the industry average is 34.5 percent. Therefore, they assumed that VCA's experience would gradually improve until it achieved parity with the industry average in 2012, as shown in Table 11.6. As to general and administrative expenses (G&A), they rounded up VCA's two-year experience to $100,000, and added $50,000 per year to get close to the $350,000 per company industry average.

However, when it came to forecasting revenue for the five-year loss period, they ignored their own protestations and averaged State A's and State B's year-to-year change in revenue per thousand vehicle miles as shown in Table 11.6. Table 11.7 shows the effect on revenue if defendant's experts had opted to use the industry average, and Table 11.8 shows the defendant's modified damages model after accounting for the change in revenue caused by using an industry average rather than an average derived from VCA's experience in State A and State B. Total modified undiscounted lost profits now amount to $318,486 as opposed to the defendant's original amount of $96,986 (Table 11.6), an increase of $221,500.

Table 11.7

Schedule of Defendant's Modified Revenue Calculations

Year	Industry Average % Change in Revenue/ Thousand Vehicle Miles *	Modified Projected Revenue/ Thousand Vehicle Miles	Projected Revenue/ Thousand Vehicle Miles per Defendant's Expert's Report	Forecasted Vehicle Miles (millions)	Modified Forecasted Revenue	Revenue per Defendant's Expert's Report	Delta
2008		$ 2.94	$ 2.94				
2009	180%	8.23	8.13	255.90	$ 2,106,569	$ 2,081,651	$ 24,917
2010	60%	13.17	12.23	268.70	3,539,101	3,286,028	253,074
2011	30%	17.12	15.31	279.41	4,784,214	4,278,163	506,052
2012	10%	18.83	16.34	290.60	5,473,398	4,748,528	724,870
2013	5%	19.78	17.07	302.00	5,972,520	5,155,156	817,364

* 2008 has been considered the 1st year of operations as the contract limited the number of

stations to 12 for 2007 and 2008.

Table 11.8
Defendant's Modified Damages Model
Detailed Lost Profits Forecast

	Actual		Projected				
	2007	2008	2009	2010	2011	2012	2013
Stations	12	12	25	45	55	60	70
Vehicle Miles (millions)	232.10	243.70	255.90	268.70	279.41	290.60	302.00
Revenue per Thousand Miles	2.20	2.94	8.23	13.17	17.12	18.83	19.78
Revenue	$ 510,612	$ 716,484	$ 2,106,569	$ 3,539,101	$ 4,784,214	$ 5,473,398	$ 5,972,520
Cost of sales	342,110	480,044	1,270,261	2,134,078	2,804,746	3,208,779	3,501,390
Gross Profit	168,502	236,440	836,308	1,405,023	1,979,469	2,264,618	2,471,130
Gross Margin	33.0%	33.0%	39.7%	39.7%	41.4%	41.4%	41.4%
Variable Operating Expenses	185,820	254,196	758,365	1,256,381	1,674,475	1,888,322	2,060,519
Expense Ratio	36.4%	35.5%	36.0%	35.5%	35.0%	34.5%	34.5%
G&A	94,704	96,204	100,000	150,000	200,000	250,000	300,000
Net Operating Profit	$ (112,022)	$ (113,960)	$ (22,057)	$ (1,358)	$ 104,994	$ 126,296	$ 110,611
Return on Revenue			-1.05%	-0.04%	2.19%	2.31%	1.85%
Total Undiscounted Lost Profits $ 318,486			$ (22,057)	$ (1,358)	$ 104,994	$ 126,296	$ 110,611

Cost of Sales and Gross Margin Calculation

	2007	2008	2009	2010	2011	2012	2013
Revenue	$ 510,612	$ 716,484	$ 2,106,569	$ 3,539,101	$ 4,784,214	$ 5,473,398	$ 5,972,520
Cost of Sales Without Volume							
Discount @ 67%	342,110	480,044	1,411,401	2,371,198	3,205,424	3,667,176	4,001,589
Volume Discount Factor	0	0	0.1	0.1	0.125	0.125	0.125
Cost of Sales With Volume							
Discount	342,110	480,044	1,270,261	2,134,078	2,804,746	3,208,779	3,501,390
Cost of Sales %	67.0%	67.0%	60.3%	60.3%	58.6%	58.6%	58.6%
Gross Margin	33.0%	33.0%	39.7%	39.7%	41.4%	41.4%	41.4%

Volume Discount Factors				Forecast Year	Industry Average % Change in Revenue/ Thousand Vehicle Miles *	Projected Revenue/ Thousand Vehicle Miles
Purchase Volume		Discount				
-	500,000	0.0%		2008		$ 2.94 Actual
500,001	1,000,000	5.0%		2009	180.00%	8.23
1,000,001	3,000,000	10.0%		2010	60.00%	13.17
3,000,001	5,000,000	12.5%		2011	30.00%	17.12
5,000,001	10,000,000	15.0%		2012	10.00%	18.83
10,000,001	99,000,000	17.5%		2013	5.00%	19.78

* 2008 has been considered the 1st year of operations as the contract limited the number of stations to 12 for 2007 and 2008.

Plaintiff's Expert's Report

Turning now to the plaintiff's calculation of lost profits, their expert's report is shown in Table 11.9. Notice that while the defendant's forecasted revenue is based on an expected rate of growth in revenue per thousand vehicle miles driven, the plaintiff forecasts revenue based on growth in revenue per rest station. The base amount of revenue per rest station for 2009 was calculated by weighting and then averaging the average State A and State B revenue per station for that year by the number of noncommuter vehicle miles driven in each state as adjusted for the number of noncommuter vehicle miles driven in State C. For example, for State A, the formula is 268.7(State C miles driven) × $105,564(average revenue per station for State A) = 353.4(State A miles driven) × X. Solving for X = $80,263. For State B, the formula is 268.7(State C miles driven) × $69,010(average revenue per station for State B) = 252.2(State B miles driven) × X. Solving for X = $73,525. Averaging $80,263 and $73,525 gives $76,894, rounded to $76,900, which amount was then grown at 6 percent per year for the remaining years of the contract.

Table 11.9
Plaintiff's Damages Model
Detailed Lost Profits Forecast

| | Actual | | | Projected | | | | |
	2007	2008	2009	2010	2011	2012	2013
Number of Rest Stations	12	12	25	45	55	60	70
Revenue per Rest Station	$ 42,551	$ 59,707	$ 76,900	$ 81,514	$ 86,405	$ 91,589	$ 97,084
Revenue	$ 510,612	$ 716,484	$ 1,922,500	$ 3,668,130	$ 4,752,266	$ 5,495,348	$ 6,795,913
Cost of Sales	342,110	480,044	1,107,360	2,112,843	2,737,305	3,165,320	3,914,446
Gross Profit	168,502	236,440	815,140	1,555,287	2,014,961	2,330,027	2,881,467
Gross Margin	33.0%	33.0%	42.4%	42.4%	42.4%	42.4%	42.4%
Variable Operating Expenses	185,820	254,196	624,813	1,192,142	1,544,487	1,785,988	2,208,672
Expense Ratio	36.4%	35.5%	32.5%	32.5%	32.5%	32.5%	32.5%
G&A	94,704	96,204	100,000	150,000	200,000	250,000	300,000
Net Operating Profit	$ (112,022)	$ (113,960)	$ 90,328	$ 213,145	$ 270,474	$ 294,039	$ 372,795
Return on Revenue			4.70%	5.81%	5.69%	5.35%	5.49%
			$ 90,328	$ 213,145	$ 270,474	$ 294,039	$ 372,795

Total Undiscounted Lost Profits $ 1,240,782

In spite of the coincidence that $76,900 is close to the industry average revenue per station of $78,500, the plaintiff makes the same error that the defendant did by relying on weighted averages of State A and State B data to compute both forecasted revenue and the 6 percent growth rate. We know from the results of the t-test for two means shown in Table 11.5 that the average revenues per station for State A and State B are not drawn from the same population and therefore should not be used conjunctively to forecast revenue for State C. But more importantly, while the 6 percent growth rate is slightly less than the two states' average 6.37 percent, there are no facts in evidence to support this rate of growth for State C, especially when the stipulated rate of growth in vehicle miles driven is 4 percent. In fact, if we ignore the increase from year one to year two of those two contracts, and make their time span more comparable to the remaining five years on State C's contract, the average growth rate is only 4.6 percent, essentially the equivalent of the growth rate in vehicle miles driven. As we will see, through the magic of compounding, it is the 6 percent growth rate that makes the plaintiff's revenue forecast unreasonably high.

For costs and expenses, the plaintiff simply averaged VCA's State A and State B cost of sales percentage and applied it to State C revenues for the loss period, without considering either VCA's actual operating experience in the first two years of the contract or the direct effect of volume discounts. Variable operating expenses are also the average of VCA's State A and State B expense ratio without considering the company's operating history in State C or the industry average. The plaintiff calculated G&A expenses in the same way as the defendant—rounded up VCA's two-year experience to $100,000 and added $50,000 per year to get close to the $350,000 per company industry average.

The Modified-Exponential Growth Curve

Returning to the plaintiff's revenue forecast, we need to modify it to account for two phenomena—the stipulated 4 percent expected increase in vehicle miles driven in State C during the last four years of the loss period and the modified-exponential growth curve exhibited by the year-to-year change in revenue per thousand vehicle miles as shown in Figure 11.1. The modified-exponential growth model belongs to a family of long-range sales forecasting models that predict that eventually a market will become saturated, meaning that the growth of demand slows and then almost stops. But different models treat the early growth differently because many products and services initially have slow revenue growth, while others show meteoric growth in revenue as soon as they are introduced. A model based on the modified-exponential approach will show forecast revenue taking off in hurry and then eventually leveling off as it reaches the saturation point.

To create our modified-exponential revenue forecast we will be using a model suggested by Professor Everette S. Gardner, Jr. in the August 1991 issue of *Lotus* magazine. Professor Gardner refers to this spreadsheet template as "Forecasting with No Data." The template is implemented with just four basic facts and assumptions:

1. Revenue in the first year.
2. Revenue at some point in the future.
3. The length of time between 1 and 2.
4. A saturation level.

Figure 11.1
Projected Revenue/Thousand Vehicle Miles
Modified Exponential Growth Curve

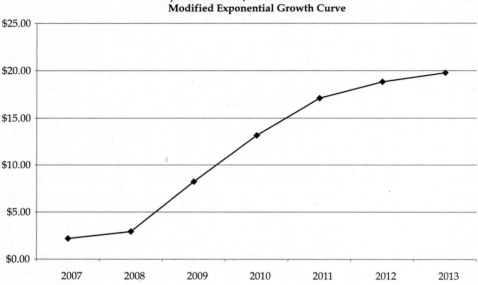

The "Forecasting with No Data" template presented in Professor Gardner's article offered four different growth curves: linear, logistic, simple exponential, and our choice for this case, modified exponential, which we present in Table 11.10.

The modified-exponential equation is:

$$\text{Forecast for period } n = A - B * R^n$$

In this equation A is the saturation level, and B and R are parameters that determine the shape of the growth curve. R is computed by subtracting A from the target level, dividing that difference by the difference between A and the first-period forecast, then raising that ratio to the power of 1 over the target period minus 1. For example, for this case $R = ((97,749 - 91,834)/(97,749 - 42,551))^{\wedge}(1/(7 - 1)) = .6892$. R is always less than 1. B is simply the difference between A and the first period forecast divided by R ((97,749 − 42,551)/.6892) = 80,091.

In Table 11.10, A is 97,749, B is 80,091 and R is .6892. For the first period, the forecast value is the same as the value entered in cell D6, because .6892 raised to the first power is .6892. Therefore, $B * R$ is 55,198, and $A - (B * R)$ is 42,551. In the second period, .6892 is raised to the second power (.4750), so $B * R$ is 38,042, and $A - (B * R)$ is 59,707. In subsequent periods, R is raised to larger powers and therefore decreases, so smaller and smaller amounts are subtracted from A as the forecast gets closer to the saturation level.

Let us explain the source of the four input elements. The first-period data is actual average revenue per rest station experienced by VCA in its first year of operations in State C. The target data of $91,834 was computed by taking the industry average revenue per rest station in 2009 of $78,500 and growing it by 4 percent per year for the next four years until the final contract year of 2013. The target period is the seventh and final year of the contract, the year that we expect to hit our

	A	B	C	D	E	F	G	H	I	J
1						Table 11.10				
2					Forecasting with No Data Template					
3					Modified-Exponential Model					
4										
5		INPUTS								
6		First-period data		$42,551		Target data		$91,834		
7		Saturation level		$97,749		Target period		7		
8										
9		Use Goal Seek to make D19 = 59,707 by changing cell D7.								
10										
11				Modified Exponential Model						
12				A =	97,749					
13				B =	80,091					
14				R =	0.6892					
15										
16										

Year	Period	Annual Revenue per Station Forecast	Gowth Amount	Growth Percent	Number of Rest Stations	Annual Revenue	
2007	1	$42,551			12	$510,612	Actual
2008	2	59,707	$17,156	40.32%	12	716,484	Actual
2009	3	71,531	11,824	19.80%	25	1,788,269	Forecast
2010	4	79,680	8,149	11.39%	45	3,585,583	Forecast
2011	5	85,296	5,616	7.05%	55	4,691,266	Forecast
2012	6	89,166	3,871	4.54%	60	5,349,979	Forecast
2013	7	91,834	2,668	2.99%	70	6,428,373	Forecast
2014	8	93,672	1,838	2.00%			
2015	9	94,939	1,267	1.35%			
2016	10	95,813	873	0.92%			
2017	11	96,415	602	0.63%			
2018	12	96,829	415	0.43%			
2019	13	97,115	286	0.30%			
2020	14	97,312	197	0.20%			
2021	15	97,448	136	0.14%			
2022	16	97,542	94	0.10%			
2023	17	97,606	64	0.07%			
2024	18	97,650	44	0.05%			
2025	19	97,681	31	0.03%			
2026	20	97,702	21	0.02%			
2027	21	97,717	15	0.01%			
2028	22	97,727	10	0.01%			
2029	23	97,734	7	0.01%			
2030	24	97,738	5	0.00%			
2031	25	97,742	3	0.00%			
2032	26	97,744	2	0.00%			
2033	27	97,746	2	0.00%			
2034	28	97,747	1	0.00%			
2035	29	97,747	1	0.00%			
2036	30	97,748	1	0.00%			
2037	31	97,748	0	0.00%			
2038	32	97,748	0	0.00%			
2039	33	97,749	0	0.00%			

target amount of $91,834. Since we have two years of actual operations, we need to make cell D19 equal that year's actual average revenue per rest station, that is, $59,707. We accomplish this by using Excel's Goal Seek function and instruct it to make cell D19 = $59,707 by changing cell D7, the saturation level. Rather than cut off the presentation at year 2013, we have run out the model until 2033 when the hypothetical saturation level is reached so you can see how the template works if $97,749 were a real saturation level. In fact, we don't know what will happen after 2013, but we suspect that revenue will continue to grow if vehicle miles driven also increases from year-to-year.

In column G we place the number of actual and expected rest stations for each year, and column H presents the product of columns D and G, that is, the expected annual revenue per rest station times the number of stations for each year.

We can now compare the results of the modified-exponential growth model for revenue per station with that of revenue per thousand vehicle miles driven. We show this comparison in Figure 11.2, which is a line chart with revenue per station growth on the left axis and growth in revenue per thousand vehicle miles driven on the right axis. Note the similar shape of both lines, indicating our model of choice closely reflects the growth exhibited by an industry average growth function.

We now transfer the forecasted revenues from column H of Table 11.10 to row 10 of Table 11.11, and we further modify the plaintiff's damages model by substituting the logic for costs and expenses as exhibited by the defendant's damages model. The end result in Table 11.11 is the modified plaintiff's damages model computed using a revenue per rest station approach, which was the plaintiff's original approach, but with a cost and expense structure that better reflects reality as it is built on VCA's experience in State C along with industry average data, rather than on the plaintiff's experience in States A and B. Total modified undiscounted lost profits now amount to $325,590 as opposed to the original plaintiff's claim in the amount of $1,240,782 (Table 11.9), a decrease of $915,192.

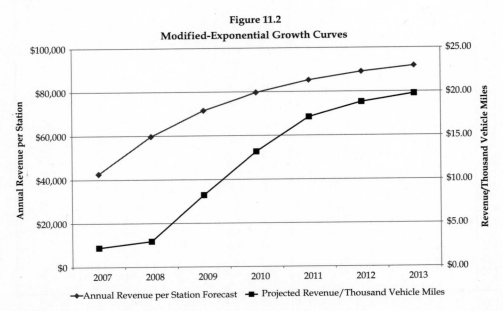

Figure 11.2
Modified-Exponential Growth Curves

Table 11.11

Plaintiff's Modified Damages Model

Detailed Lost Profits Forecast

		Actual			Projected			
		2007	2008	2009	2010	2011	2012	2013
Number of Rest Stations		12	12	25	45	55	60	70
Revenue per Rest Station		$42,551	$59,707	$71,531	$79,680	$85,296	$89,166	$91,834
Revenue	$	510,612	716,484	1,788,269	3,585,583	4,691,266	5,349,979	6,428,373
Cost of sales		342,110	480,044	1,078,326	2,162,107	2,750,255	3,136,425	3,768,634
Gross Profit		168,502	236,440	709,943	1,423,476	1,941,011	2,213,554	2,659,739
Gross Margin		33.0%	33.0%	39.7%	39.7%	41.4%	41.4%	41.4%
Variable Operating Expenses		185,820	254,196	643,777	1,272,882	1,641,943	1,845,743	2,217,789
Expense Ratio		36.4%	35.5%	36.0%	35.5%	35.0%	34.5%	34.5%
G&A		94,704	96,204	100,000	150,000	200,000	250,000	300,000
Net Operating Profit	$	(112,022)	(113,960)	(33,834)	594	99,068	117,811	141,951
Return on Revenue				-1.89%	0.02%	2.11%	2.20%	2.21%
Total Undiscounted Lost Profits	$ 325,590			(33,834)	594	99,068	117,811	141,951

Cost of Sales and Gross Margin Calculation

Revenue	$	510,612	716,484	1,788,269	3,585,583	4,691,266	5,349,979	6,428,373
Cost of Sales Without Volume Discount @ 67%		342,110	480,044	1,198,140	2,402,341	3,143,148	3,584,486	4,307,010
Volume Discount Factor		0	0	0.1	0.1	0.125	0.125	0.125
Cost of Sales With Volume Discount		342,110	480,044	1,078,326	2,162,107	2,750,255	3,136,425	3,768,634
Cost of Sales %		67.0%	67.0%	60.3%	60.3%	58.6%	58.6%	58.6%
Gross Margin		33.0%	33.0%	39.7%	39.7%	41.4%	41.4%	41.4%

Volume Discount Factors

Purchase Volume		Discount
-	500,000	0.0%
500,001	1,000,000	5.0%
1,000,001	3,000,000	10.0%
3,000,001	5,000,000	12.5%
5,000,001	10,000,000	15.0%
10,000,001	99,000,000	17.5%

Table 11.12
Summary Schedule of Operating Statistics

	Actual		Projected				
	2007	2008	2009	2010	2011	2012	2013
Stations							
Plaintiff	12	12	25	45	55	60	70
Plaintiff - Corrected	12	12	25	45	55	60	70
Defendant	12	12	25	45	55	60	70
Defendant - corrected	12	12	25	45	55	60	70
Vehicle Miles (millions)							
Plaintiff	232.10	243.70	255.90	268.70	279.41	290.60	302.00
Plaintiff - Modified	232.10	243.70	255.90	268.70	279.41	290.60	302.00
Defendant	232.10	243.70	255.90	268.70	279.41	290.60	302.00
Defendant - Modified	232.10	243.70	255.90	268.70	279.41	290.60	302.00
Revenue per Thousand Miles							
Plaintiff	2.20	2.94	7.51	13.65	17.01	18.91	22.50
Plaintiff - Modified	2.20	2.94	6.99	13.34	16.79	18.41	21.29
Defendant	2.20	2.94	8.13	12.23	15.31	16.34	17.07
Defendant - Modified	2.20	2.94	8.23	13.17	17.12	18.83	19.78
Revenue per Station							
Plaintiff	42,551	59,707	76,900	81,514	86,405	91,589	97,084
Plaintiff - Modified	42,551	59,707	71,531	79,680	85,296	89,166	91,834
Defendant	42,551	59,707	83,266	73,023	77,785	79,142	73,645
Defendant - Modified	42,551	59,707	84,263	78,647	86,986	91,223	85,322
Revenue							
Plaintiff	510,612	716,484	1,922,500	3,668,130	4,752,266	5,495,348	6,795,913
Plaintiff - Modified	510,612	716,484	1,788,269	3,585,583	4,691,266	5,349,979	6,428,373
Defendant	510,612	716,484	2,081,651	3,286,028	4,278,163	4,748,528	5,155,156
Defendant - Modified	510,612	716,484	2,106,569	3,539,101	4,784,214	5,473,398	5,972,520
Cost of sales							
Plaintiff	342,110	480,044	1,107,360	2,112,843	2,737,305	3,165,320	3,914,446
Plaintiff - Modified	342,110	480,044	1,078,326	2,162,107	2,750,255	3,136,425	3,768,634
Defendant	342,110	480,044	1,255,236	1,981,475	2,579,732	2,783,825	3,022,210
Defendant - Modified	342,110	480,044	1,270,261	2,134,078	2,804,746	3,208,779	3,501,390
Gross Profit							
Plaintiff	168,502	236,440	815,140	1,555,287	2,014,961	2,330,027	2,881,467
Plaintiff - Modified	168,502	236,440	709,943	1,423,476	1,941,011	2,213,554	2,659,739
Defendant	168,502	236,440	826,416	1,304,553	1,698,431	1,964,703	2,132,946
Defendant - Modified	168,502	236,440	836,308	1,405,023	1,979,469	2,264,618	2,471,130
Cumulative Revenue							
Plaintiff	510,612	1,227,096	3,149,596	6,817,726	11,569,992	17,065,340	23,861,253
Plaintiff - Modified	510,612	1,227,096	3,015,365	6,600,948	11,292,214	16,642,194	23,070,566
Defendant	510,612	1,227,096	3,308,747	6,594,775	10,872,938	15,621,466	20,776,623
Defendant - Modified	510,612	1,227,096	3,333,665	6,872,766	11,656,981	17,130,378	23,102,898

	Actual		Projected				
	2007	2008	2009	2010	2011	2012	2013
Gross Margin							
Plaintiff	33.0%	33.0%	42.4%	42.4%	42.4%	42.4%	42.4%
Plaintiff - Modified	33.0%	33.0%	39.7%	39.7%	41.4%	41.4%	41.4%
Defendant	33.0%	33.0%	39.7%	39.7%	39.7%	41.4%	41.4%
Defendant - Modified	33.0%	33.0%	39.7%	39.7%	41.4%	41.4%	41.4%
Variable Operating Expenses							
Plaintiff	185,820	254,196	624,813	1,192,142	1,544,487	1,785,988	2,208,672
Plaintiff - Modified	185,820	254,196	643,777	1,272,882	1,641,943	1,845,743	2,217,789
Defendant	185,820	254,196	749,394	1,166,540	1,497,357	1,638,242	1,778,529
Defendant - Modified	185,820	254,196	758,365	1,256,381	1,674,475	1,888,322	2,060,519
Expense Ratio							
Plaintiff	36.4%	35.5%	32.5%	32.5%	32.5%	32.5%	32.5%
Plaintiff - Modified	36.4%	35.5%	36.0%	35.5%	35.0%	34.5%	34.5%
Defendant	36.4%	35.5%	36.0%	35.5%	35.0%	34.5%	34.5%
Defendant - Modified	36.4%	35.5%	36.0%	35.5%	35.0%	34.5%	34.5%
G&A							
Plaintiff	94,704	96,204	100,000	150,000	200,000	250,000	300,000
Plaintiff - Modified	94,704	96,204	100,000	150,000	200,000	250,000	300,000
Defendant	94,704	96,204	100,000	150,000	200,000	250,000	300,000
Defendant - Modified	94,704	96,204	100,000	150,000	200,000	250,000	300,000
Net Operating Profit							
Plaintiff	(112,022)	(113,960)	90,328	213,145	270,474	294,039	372,795
Plaintiff - Modified	(112,022)	(113,960)	(33,834)	594	99,068	117,811	141,951
Defendant	(112,022)	(113,960)	(22,979)	(11,987)	1,074	76,461	54,417
Defendant - Modified	(112,022)	(113,960)	(22,057)	(1,358)	104,994	126,296	110,611
Return on Sales							
Plaintiff	-21.9%	-15.9%	4.7%	5.8%	5.7%	5.4%	5.5%
Plaintiff - Modified	-21.9%	-15.9%	-1.9%	0.0%	2.1%	2.2%	2.2%
Defendant	-21.9%	-15.9%	-1.1%	-0.4%	0.0%	1.6%	1.1%
Defendant - Modified	-21.9%	-15.9%	-1.0%	0.0%	2.2%	2.3%	1.9%
Total Lost Profits							
Undiscounted	1,240,782						
Plaintiff - Modified	325,590	2.18%					
Defendant	96,986		2.21%				
Defendant - Modified	318,486	2.23%					

Figure 11.3

Comparative Annual Revenue Line Chart

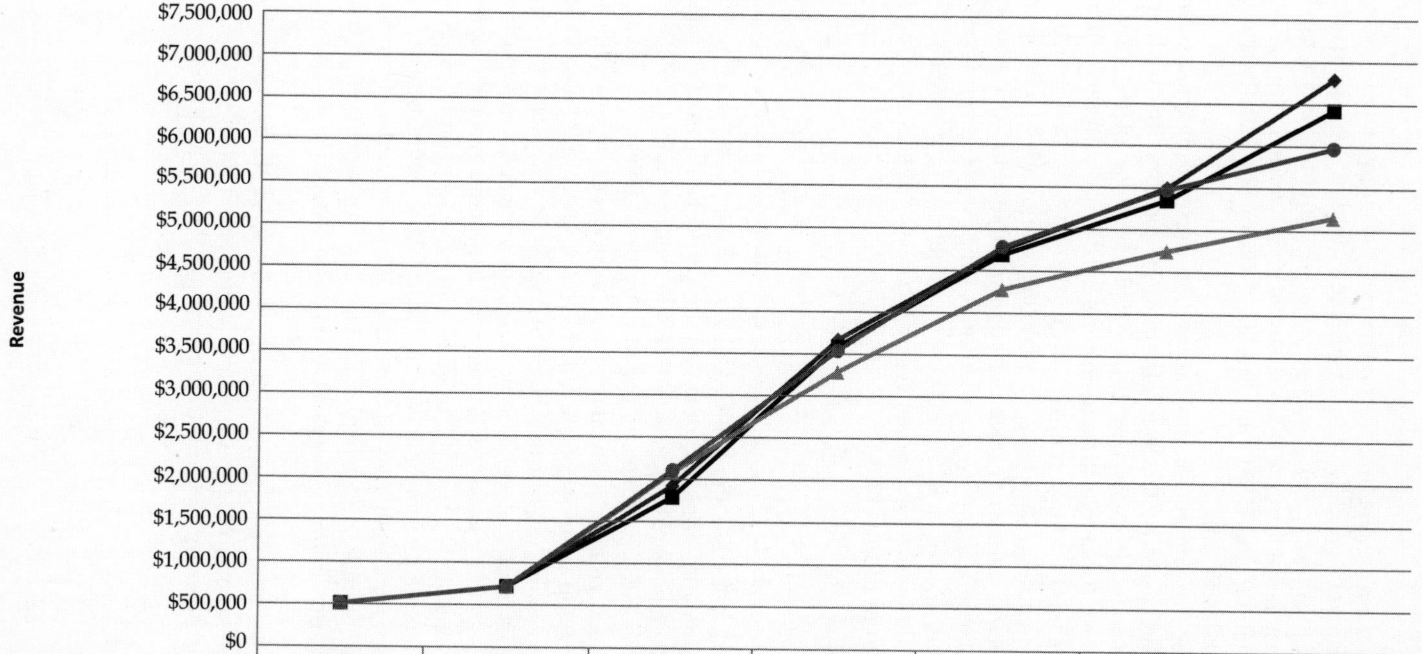

	2007	2008	2009	2010	2011	2012	2013
Plaintiff	510,612	716,484	1,922,500	3,668,130	4,752,266	5,495,348	6,795,913
Plaintiff - Modified	510,612	716,484	1,788,269	3,585,583	4,691,266	5,349,979	6,428,373
Defendant	510,612	716,484	2,081,651	3,286,028	4,278,163	4,748,528	5,155,156
Defendant - Modified	510,612	716,484	2,106,569	3,539,101	4,784,214	5,473,398	5,972,520

207

Four Damages Models

Table 11.12 is a summary schedule that compares the four models—the original plaintiff's and defendant's models along with their modified counterparts. While there are year-to-year differences in revenue because of the different annual growth rates embedded in each model, note that the cumulative seven-year revenue amount for the modified plaintiff and defendant models as found in cells J50 and J52 are within .14 percent of each other.

Figure 11.3, our final figure for this case study, presents revenue over the life of the contract as forecasted by the four different models. Note that in the plaintiff's original model, revenue skyrockets in 2013 mainly because of the exponentially applied growth rate of 6 percent kicking into high gear in that year. The modified plaintiff model also shows a large jump in 2013, but that is because of the opening of 10 new stations that year. In effect, the plaintiff's use of a 6 percent growth rate rather than a 4 percent rate accelerates the amount of revenue per station by one year, which by 2013 translates into an additional $367,500 of revenue over that of the modified plaintiff model, and $790,000 over the life of the contract. While it is hard to see major differences in earlier years, those differences can be spotted in the table at the bottom of the chart.

Conclusion

We conclude by indicating that the two modified models are only 2.21 percent apart, down from the $1,143,796 difference between the parties at the start of our analysis. We suggest that damages analysts need to refrain from mining the data they have available to them just because they can run the numbers. That is, the analyst should not blindly look for correlations or patterns among dozens of available variables, but instead first develop a theory of relationships, and then build a model to prove it. In this case, servicing vending machines at highway rest stops is not a value-added endeavor, but rather a commodity business subject to the traffic patterns, population densities, and tourism economics of a particular state. Therefore, the plaintiff's business activity in two other states did not necessarily prove useful to predicting the results of its foray into a third state. That could be better done by using the plaintiff's operating history in State C, or if available, data from other states that is relevant and similar to State C's data, along with industry-wide data, which allows for the disparity among individual states to be smoothed away by averaging 50 states' data.

The next chapter addresses the use of the elements of the fraud triangle, along with professional skepticism in the context of a business interruption loss to ensure that the claimant is properly restored to the position they would have been but for the peril.

CHAPTER 12

Case Study 12—Further Considerations in the Determination of Lost Profits

In addition to considering what standard methodologies to apply in the calculation of lost profits, a concurrent concern is how to include other qualitative variables that could be important to avoid overstating the loss. The combination of elements of the fraud triangle along with professional skepticism can make a difference in the effort to properly restore a claimant to the position they would have otherwise been in.

It is well known in fraud and forensic accounting that the fraud triangle embodies three components: pressure, opportunity, and rationalization. Pressure is derived from a financial issue that generally cannot be resolved by the fraudster in a lawful manner. Frequently, to a fraudster this problem must be fixed by concealment. When it relates to matters of business, an array of items can be viewed as causing pressure: eroding sales, excess debt, and/or fierce competition are some examples that could point an individual's behavior in this direction.

Opportunity surfaces when a fraudster recognizes a way to use their position to commit fraud. In occupational fraud, opportunity is usually created by weak internal controls. However, from a broad perspective, fraud opportunity can also arise within the framework of preparing a business interruption insurance claim for lost profits. The possibility of "cooking the books" in order to profit from a loss is an aspect of the process that should require further reflection. Owners of privately held companies have the inherent capacity to overstate a loss recovery by having control over the books and records.

Rationalization is the process whereby fraudsters justify the crime to themselves in a way that makes it acceptable. The natural intuition of a forensic accountant involved in such an environment is to be cognizant of the elements of the fraud triangle while balancing a degree of professional skepticism. Professional skepticism may be defined as an attitude that includes a questioning frame of mind and critical assessment of evidence.

Professional skepticism and fraud, from an accounting perspective, has a lengthy history of debate. From an external auditing perspective, Lawrence Dicksee's 1892 textbook, *Auditing: A Practical Manual for Auditors* (the authorized American edition was published in 1905), lists the objective of an audit as "threefold":

1. The detection of fraud.
2. The detection of technical errors.
3. The detection of errors in principle.

Dicksee goes on to emphasize that fraud detection is the most important component of the auditor's job, and the search for fraud should be "unwavering and constant." In addition, the author proclaims that the auditor who is able to find fraud is a better man than the auditor who does not find fraud. Audit standards have always required that auditors exercise some level of professional skepticism. Recent standards go further and now require auditors to increase that level of skepticism. It is implicit in these requirements that if an auditor is more cognizant of the possibility of fraud existing within a firm, then fraud detection will improve.

The intersection of auditing and forensic accounting lies at the crossroads of professional skepticism. We can incrementally extend the application of professional skepticism by using the fraud theory approach with its four chronological steps:

1. Analyzing the available data.
2. Developing a fraud theory.
3. Testing the theory.
4. Refining and/or amending the theory to systematically plan the course of further inquiry or to come to a conclusion.

A Review of Methods of Loss Calculation

The before-and-after method considers the notion of profits across a spectrum of time. The theoretical underpinning of this method is that the period of profits before the loss is compared to the period of profits after the loss. This method considers sales growth before the intervening act and compares it to sales growth after the intervening act. Under the before-and-after method, lost profits during the period of interruption, as measured by the sum of continuing expenses plus net income or net loss, are compared with either the predamage profits and/or the postdamage profits. The use of the before-and-after method does not usually require a voluminous amount of data. The method can be applied with only one or two years of monthly sales activity, making its simplicity an attractive choice for short-term losses.

When using the comparable method, a forensic accountant generally identifies relevant and similar companies or industries that are comparable to the loss-claiming company. The forensic accountant, using this information, projects the claimants' profits using the performance metrics of the comparable companies or industries. This method could be used when there is no historical information available for a subject company.

The "but for" method is generally based upon a financial model using assumptions about revenue and expenses. The theory behind this method is that the estimated loss of income is the difference between estimated profits and actual profits, and that "but for" the actions of the defendant this difference would be zero. Typical techniques used in the "but for" method of lost profits calculations are the time series or econometric forecasting methods that we have demonstrated elsewhere in this book.

Unlike those methods used in torts to determine lost profits, if a contract is infringed upon, the contract often contains explicit requirements for the calculation of liquidating and other damages in the event of a contractual violation. The analysis provided by the forensic accountant will follow the contract terms. For example, in a partnership agreement the damages for a buy-out of a partner could be limited to the net book value of the assets.

The mechanics of each method described above require a special set of skills just to carry out the calculations. However, additional skills are needed beyond the technical expertise that is required for the analysis of financial information. To avoid overcompensating a claimant for lost profits, a holistic view of the setting may be required. A questioning mind can begin by addressing qualitative issues surrounding the particular case such as the current operating status of the business, the age of the owner, and/or whether the claimant is represented by a third party who is compensated based upon the value of the claim, for example, a public adjuster or an attorney. The potential answers to these questions may lead to a distinctly different conclusion than one merely based on numbers.

For example, a damages analyst who considers the current operating status of the business might find that a business that is in disrepair could use a claim of loss situation as an opportunity to rescue the business. The age of the owner(s) could also be a relevant motivating factor; if a business is not sellable to a third party and the owners are approaching the age of retirement, a window of opportunity could present itself in the form of a lost profits claim. A claimant may also choose to be represented by a third party to present the loss to the insurance company. In such a case, these types of representatives are usually compensated by a percentage of the value of the claim. The obvious incentive is to obtain the largest recovery. This is not to state that these representatives will always submit an inflated claim of loss; the point is for the forensic accountant to be mindful of the actors' incentives within the case surroundings and consider their potential abuse in the determination of the loss. Regardless of the method of calculation applied, this cognizant process can be used across all of the approaches used to calculate lost profits.

A Case Study: Dunlap Drive-In Diner

Dunlap Drive-In Diner, Inc. (DDD), an S corporation, was an established restaurant operating in the same community for over three decades. The company was located in the center of town and had become a popular destination for local residents. Despite the fact that DDD had been in business at the same location for over three decades, neither the entity nor the individual shareholders owned the property that housed the restaurant. Rather, DDD had a long-term lease with the property owner. DDD had developed loyal customers over this long period that believed it was a tradition for family and friends to frequent the restaurant.

The company had been owned by the Dunlap family since inception. The current management consists of the two children of the founder, Reggie and Regina Dunlap (the Dunlaps). Both have worked in the business from childhood. As the

TABLE 12.1

Summary of Loss	
Lost Revenue (Notes):	$ 6,000,000
Multiplied by: Business Interruption Value	× 35.16%
Business Interruption Loss:	$ 2,109,600

Notes: Lost revenue for the 12-month loss period from the amended tax return.

years went by, the siblings decided to spend more time with their families and work fewer hours in the business. The Dunlaps hired a manager to attend to the daily operating necessities of DDD.

DDD was in a state of minor disrepair. In the past, the Dunlaps had always attended meticulously to the details of the restaurant's appearance but recently had overlooked the outdated décor and weathered tables. These factors could have contributed to the recent decline in revenue from previous years. However, due to the community goodwill that DDD had built up from their long-term residency in the area and their strategic location, the business still remained profitable. The restaurant location is not in a resort area and, as a result, has historically experienced a sluggish seasonal effect in the summer months of July and August. During the month of August, a generally slow period, the restaurant dining room was completely destroyed by a fire. The remainder of the building sustained substantial property damage, leaving it untenable. As such, the business had to discontinue operations.

Due to the significant damage and loss of business, the Dunlaps retained the services of an attorney to represent DDD before the insurance company. The attorney was compensated on a percentage of the claim paid by the insurance company.

Using the before-and-after method of calculation, the claim submitted by the claimant for a 12-month loss is illustrated in Table 12.1 and Table 12.2.

Skeptical Analysis Using the Fraud Theory Approach

Once we had the formal claim and any backup documentation in hand, we were able to begin analyzing the submission using the fraud theory approach. During this process, various issues and concerns surfaced. We deal with each of them in the subsequent sections of this chapter.

Revenue Adjustment

The records provided by the claimant consisted of the two preceding calendar years of corporate income tax returns. The company's business records were destroyed in the fire, and DDD had recently retained a new accounting firm to prepare the corporate income tax returns. The tax returns were the only records available.

TABLE 12.2

	Schedule of Business Interruption Value				
	Profit & Loss Statement according to *initial* filed tax return 12 months preceding loss	Adjustments included on amended corporate income tax return	Profit & Loss Statement according to *amended* tax return 12 months preceding loss	%	Net Income Plus Continuing Expenses as a % of Sales
Revenue	$ 4,800,000.00	1,200,000.00	$ 6,000,000.00	100.00%	
Cost of Goods Sold	2,880,000.00	720,000.00	3,600,000.00	60.00%	
Gross Profit	$ 1,920,000.00		$ 2,400,000.00	40.00%	
Expenses					
Officer's Compensation	-	300,000.00	300,000.00	5.00%	5.00%
Salaries and Wages	575,000.00		575,000.00	9.58%	9.58%
Depreciation/Amortization	55,000.00		55,000.00	0.92%	
Linens and Laundry	99,000.00		99,000.00	1.65%	
Delivery	59,000.00		59,000.00	0.98%	
Insurance	95,000.00		95,000.00	1.58%	1.58%
Rent	627,000.00		627,000.00	10.45%	10.45%
Telephone and Utilities	77,000.00		77,000.00	1.28%	
Employee Bonus	88,000.00		88,000.00	1.47%	1.47%
Total Expenses	$ 1,675,000.00		$ 1,975,000.00	32.92%	
Net Income	$ 245,000.00		$ 425,000.00	7.08%	7.08%

Business Interruption Value	
Net Income Plus Continuing Expenses	**35.16%**

Additionally, an amended corporate income tax return was submitted for the year immediately prior to the loss. The explanation on the amended tax return stated that in the initial filing an amount representing 25 percent of the gross revenue and its corresponding cost of sales was inadvertently omitted due to a lack of communication between the accounting firms during their transition. In addition, officers' compensation in the amount of $300,000 had been inadvertently left off the return. The amended return was dated in August of the loss year subsequent to the business interruption date.

FRAUD THEORY APPROACH   The damages analyst should always perform a search for issues that need to be addressed in the calculation of loss. Initial analysis of the amended corporate income tax return has revealed the following issues:

1. When removing the 25 percent omission, DDD had a flat year-over-year growth in their gross revenue.
2. When including the 25 percent omission, the net income increased as a percentage of sales, creating the potential for a larger recovery.
3. The filing date of the amended corporate income tax return was subsequent to the business interruption date.

Sample questions that should be asked to verify the authenticity of the amended corporate income returns are the following:

1. Has this amended return been filed with the proper federal and state taxing authorities?
2. Have the resultant taxes been paid?

DETERMINATION   In this case, the answers to these questions ranged from "My accountant takes care of that" to "The bookkeeper pays the bills—I'll ask." The only information subsequently provided was copies of checks for the increase in shareholder taxes as a result of the amended entity tax return that were not cashed by the taxing authorities. The next step in this process was to determine if the amended entity tax return was actually filed with the Internal Revenue Service (IRS). The claimant was asked to provide a transcript of the tax return from the IRS. This request was ignored. Accordingly, because of this lack of validation, the additional income reflected on the amended entity tax return should not be considered in the final calculation of loss.

Officer's Compensation Adjustment

Officer's compensation is generally an undeniable component of a lost profits claim. In theory, the officers' compensation is paid to the owners in either profits or compensation. Therefore, an increase in one results in a decrease in the other, and the effect is a wash.

FRAUD THEORY APPROACH   Upon further analysis it was established that the officers were not on the payroll prior to the loss date. This is most likely a product of the recent sales decline resulting in shrinking profitability and the concomitant inability to support the compensation that had been historically paid. Additionally, the owners had hired a manager to run the everyday operations of the restaurant, effectively reducing their operational responsibilities. Including officers' compensation in the business interruption claim was an attempt to provide continuity in the historical income and expense behavior of DDD. Although the officers/owners are entitled to the company's net income in the business interruption loss, without including officers' compensation the net profit percentage would seem inordinately high in the year immediately preceding the loss. An additional consequence of the amended corporate income tax return is that it creates the potential for a recovery greater than the actual loss sustained by fashioning the illusion of year-to-year comparability between net incomes. This could place DDD in a better position after the loss than prior to the loss.

Documents requested of the claimant:

- Payroll tax returns for the period preceding the loss.
- Related payroll tax payments.

DETERMINATION   Copies of the amended payroll tax returns were provided with a copy of the matching check to pay the additional payroll taxes. The check had not been cashed by the IRS. Naturally, doubts occurred about the validity of the claim due to the fact that the check had not cleared the bank. Again, a request was made for IRS transcripts of the payroll tax returns. This approach provides the confidence that the tax returns presented for the claim are the same tax returns on file with the taxing authorities.

Once again, the request was ignored by the claimant, and therefore the officers' compensation was not considered in the determination of loss.

Continuing Salaries and Wages (Payroll) Adjustment

Continuing payroll for DDD included the manager, chef, waitresses, busboys, and dishwashers. The employees had been employed by DDD for many years, and the claimant considered them key. The payroll tax returns provided by the claimant agreed with salaries and wages that allegedly continued during the loss period.

FRAUD THEORY APPROACH   To consider the issues with prior supporting documents, several steps were utilized.

1. Request to interview all of the employees considered to be continuing on the DDD payroll.
2. Theorize that the employees were collecting unemployment benefits during this period.
3. Verify the payroll tax returns and tax payments and compare them with unemployment records.

DETERMINATION   The request to interview the employees was denied, and the Dunlaps suggested that they themselves be interviewed as an alternative. During the interview it was discovered that the payroll tax returns were not filed with the proper taxing authorities. In addition, the related tax payments were also not paid. To verify the theory of the employees collecting unemployment benefits, a statement of account was requested from the state Department of Labor for the most recent period detailing unemployment benefits charged to DDD's account. The report from the Department of Labor provides the specific names, dates, and weekly unemployment benefits paid to employees of DDD. Upon receipt of the report from the Department of Labor, it was seen that every employee, except the manager and chef, listed as continuing on the DDD payroll was also collecting unemployment benefits. Therefore, the manager and chef were the only employees included in the claim of loss. Their salaries were approximately 30 percent of the annualized historical salaries and wages. This amount was continued and the remaining balance was removed from the loss calculation.

Rent Adjustment

Rent was included as a continuing expense in the claimant's presentation of loss. The fire made the entire building untenable. The restaurant did not have the option to partially operate due to the total devastation of the building. However, the claimant represented that rent was contractually obligated. A request for the entire lease was made.

FRAUD THEORY APPROACH   The lease should clearly indicate if rent is due regardless of tenability. Points of concern:

1. Is the entire lease provided?
2. Are there common area charges the tenant is responsible for?
3. Are operating expenses part of the tenant's lease?

DETERMINATION   The lease was provided, and a comprehensive review of the entire lease exposed a clause that indicated rents would not continue if the building were untenable. An additional clause pointed to an obligation of the lessee to continue paying a stated portion of operating expenses even if the building was untenable. Thus a reading of the lease found that a portion of the rent does in fact continue, but not the entire amount. The continuing portion was included and represented 10 percent of the historical annualized rent.

Employee Bonus

The claimant represented that these payments were for an employee incentive program for exceptional customer service based upon surveys submitted by patrons. Payments are generally made in periods subsequent to the completion of the survey. The explanation seemed likely since many service-oriented businesses make every effort to satisfy customers.

FRAUD THEORY APPROACH   An analysis of the general ledger account for employee bonuses would be the starting point of the inquiry. However, concerns regarding how the expense is paid could be:

1. What is the historical disbursement frequency?
2. How often are surveys given to customers?

DETERMINATION   An analysis of the general ledger account for employee bonuses turned up several entries payable to cash that were dated during the loss period. The payment to cash raised the question that perhaps someone other than an employee was receiving these funds. A copy or electronic image of the front and back of the canceled checks was requested. Examination of the canceled check revealed that the check was deposited in the account of a vendor that supplied food and other products used by DDD. To further prove the invalidity of the expense, invoices for the vendor were requested. Upon receipt of the requested invoices, it was discovered that these payments were for cost of goods sold incurred prior to the loss and therefore were a noncontinuing expense.

Discussion

The analytical gymnastics of attempting to make sense of a lost profits claim resulting from a business interruption demands that the damages analyst have a unique type of skill set in addition to being familiar with the quantitative techniques discussed in this book. Damages analysts performing these assignments should bring a breadth of aptitude that includes curiosity, persistence, creativity, common business sense, and a high degree of professional skepticism. Equally critical is the ability to include in the investigative dimension both deductive reasoning and deductive analysis.

For example, the adjustment and explanation for the additional revenue included in the claim appeared out of the ordinary. This adjustment represented exactly 25 percent of gross revenue—a material inclusion that should initiate further inquiry. There are two evident ways to validate the information: (1) request the claimant to retrieve the transcript of the tax return from the IRS, and (2) obtain a power of attorney from the claimant and retrieve it yourself.

The owners of a business receive their compensation through profits and/or compensation with an increase in one resulting in a decrease in the other. In the case of DDD, the position immediately preceding the loss was one of lower profits and no compensation for the officers. One way to uncover a potential deception in the payroll area is to review prior payroll tax reports and journals. This inspection should include a detailed examination of employee earnings reports that reconcile with the payroll tax returns with corresponding third-party evidence from the taxing authorities. This approach provides the appropriate confidence that the tax returns presented for the claim are, in fact, genuine.

Key employees of an ordinary, small, closely held company generally include management as well as the owners/officers who work in the business. In the restaurant business it is typical to consider the manager and chef as key employees. However, this topic should be approached with caution because when the manager or chef is not the owner of the restaurant or does not participate in the success of the business, the position could be transitory and therefore noncontinuing as these employees leave to seek new employment immediately after the date of loss.

The techniques in the verification of continuing rent and employee bonus were no more than asking for the correct documents. A basic reading of the entire lease usually remedies the issue of whether rent continues after a casualty.

The employee bonus issue required a bit more investigative analysis than the rent. The presentation of checks payable to cash was enough reason to raise the level of inquiry and analysis. Our investigative procedures were a comparison of the names listed on the back of the cleared checks to accounts payable and/or purchases before the loss. The check was eventually traced to the vendor who was paid for the delivery of goods in a prior period.

Conclusion

The intention of this case study was to broaden the outlook of the damages analyst when calculating lost profits. Explicitly, you should include other qualitative methods that may be important to avoid overstating the loss. As demonstrated, elements of the fraud triangle and professional skepticism can play an important role. The case of DDD exemplifies the red flags that call for further examination. The foregoing

TABLE 12.3

		Schedule of Loss Differences	

	Per Claimant	Recommended	Difference
Lost Revenue:	$ 6,000,000	$ 4,800,000	
Multiplied by:			
Business Interruption Value	× 35.16%	× 10.68%	
Business Interruption Loss:	$ 2,109,600	$ 512,640	$ (1,596,960)

narrative brings to light how compelling these factors can be in the determination of the loss.

As shown in Table 12.3 and Table 12.4, when the elements of pressure, opportunity, and rationalization are considered in conjunction with an approach that includes a questioning mind, dramatic results can be obtained. Critical assessment of the evidence submitted to support a claim for lost profits should be integrated

TABLE 12.4

	Schedule of Business Interruption Value					
	Amended Tax Return			**Initial Tax Return**		
	Profit & Loss Statement (adjusted) *12 Months Preceding Loss*	%	Net Income Plus Continuing Expenses as a % of Sales	Profit & Loss Statement *12 Months Preceding Loss*	%	Net Income Plus Continuing Expenses as a % of Sales
Revenue	$ 6,000,000.00	100.00%		$ 4,800,000.00	100.00%	
Cost of Goods Sold	3,600,000.00	60.00%		2,880,000.00	60.00%	
Gross Profit	$ 2,400,000.00	40.00%		$ 1,920,000.00	40.00%	
Expenses						
Officer's Compensation	300,000.00	5.00%	5.00%			
Salaries and Wages	575,000.00	9.58%	9.58%	575,000.00	11.98%	3.59%
Depreciation/Amortization	55,000.00	0.92%		55,000.00	1.15%	
Linens and Laundry	99,000.00	1.65%		99,000.00	2.06%	
Delivery	59,000.00	0.98%		59,000.00	1.23%	
Insurance	95,000.00	1.58%	1.58%	95,000.00	1.98%	1.98%
Rent	627,000.00	10.45%	10.45%	627,000.00	13.06%	0.01%
Telephone and Utilities	77,000.00	1.28%		77,000.00	1.60%	
Employee Bonus	88,000.00	1.47%	1.47%	88,000.00	1.83%	
Total Expenses	$ 1,975,000.00	32.92%		$ 1,675,000.00	34.90%	
Net Income	$ 425,000.00	7.08%	7.08%	$ 245,000.00	5.10%	5.10%
Business Interruption Value *Net Income Plus Continuing Expenses*			35.16%			10.68%

into the claim development process. That the potential for overstatement is evident is illustrated in Table 12.3. From a materiality perspective alone, it is sensible to conclude that the addition of these types of procedures should be a consideration in all claims for lost profits.

In the next chapter, we describe and implement a forecasting tool that requires no knowledge of statistical methods, but still accounts for trend and seasonality in the data.

CHAPTER **13**

Case Study 13—A Simple Approach to Forecasting Sales

In the introduction to this book, we briefly described a forecasting model under the heading of "More Complex Arithmetic Models." Well, they are that, but when compared to regression models that rely on statistical theory for their efficaciousness, these models offer a simpler approach to forecasting sales. In this case study, we delve deeper into the workings of one of these models and show how it can provide an excellent forecast solution when faced with declining sales during a recession.

Month Length Adjustment

Our subject company is a retail store located in a small city on the Gulf of Mexico. The store alleges that its sales were affected by the BP oil spill that started on April 20, 2010, and that those effects began on May 1 and ran through August 31, 2010. In column C in Table 13.1 we show 52 months of sales from January 2006 through April 2010. We then account for the length of month effect with the following formula found in column F: (365.25/12/number of days in a month). For example, cell F6 contains the following formula: (365.25/12/31) = .981855. Taking this adjustment factor and multiplying it by the actual sales for January 2006 of $34,565 gives us adjusted sales for that month of $33,938. At the end of our forecasting exercise we will have to reconvert forecasted adjusted monthly sales back to their natural state by dividing by each month's adjustment factor. A line chart of the 52 months of adjusted monthly sales is shown in Figure 13.1. Note the repetitive patterns, which indicate a high degree of seasonality.

Graph Your Data

We also present in Table 13.1 the same 52 months of both actual and adjusted monthly sales in tabular format, which we will use to create the charts shown in Figures 13.2 through 13.4. On the radar chart in Figure 13.2 we note that six of the 12 months' sales for 2006 (the most interior line) are below the range of the other five years, and that the shape of each year's line is the same as all the other years, indicating that seasonality is present. We note the same features in Figure 13.3, and

Table 13.1
Southern Retail Store
Monthly Actual and Adjusted Sales

Month	Actual Monthly Sales	Annual Totals	# of Days in Month	Adjusted Factor	Adjusted Monthly Sales	Annual Totals
Jan-06	34,565		31	0.981855	33,938	
Feb-06	35,917		28	1.087054	39,043	
Mar-06	67,655		31	0.981855	66,428	
Apr-06	75,809		30	1.014583	76,914	
May-06	83,810		31	0.981855	82,289	
Jun-06	113,746		30	1.014583	115,405	
Jul-06	96,623		31	0.981855	94,869	
Aug-06	63,227		31	0.981855	62,080	
Sep-06	59,431		30	1.014583	60,298	
Oct-06	63,462		31	0.981855	62,310	
Nov-06	67,686		30	1.014583	68,673	
Dec-06	84,076	846,007	31	0.981855	82,550	844,799
Jan-07	39,368		31	0.981855	38,654	
Feb-07	45,150		28	1.087054	49,081	
Mar-07	110,924		31	0.981855	108,911	
Apr-07	106,249		30	1.014583	107,798	
May-07	119,117		31	0.981855	116,956	
Jun-07	136,620		30	1.014583	138,612	
Jul-07	131,422		31	0.981855	129,037	
Aug-07	83,864		31	0.981855	82,343	
Sep-07	69,188		30	1.014583	70,197	
Oct-07	78,585		31	0.981855	77,159	
Nov-07	68,882		30	1.014583	69,886	
Dec-07	92,769	1,082,138	31	0.981855	91,086	1,079,720
Jan-08	33,910		31	0.981855	33,294	
Feb-08	46,669		29	1.049569	48,983	
Mar-08	94,823		31	0.981855	93,102	
Apr-08	93,977		30	1.014583	95,348	
May-08	109,603		31	0.981855	107,614	
Jun-08	115,601		30	1.014583	117,287	
Jul-08	124,704		31	0.981855	122,442	
Aug-08	82,145		31	0.981855	80,655	
Sep-08	66,466		30	1.014583	67,435	
Oct-08	69,339		31	0.981855	68,081	
Nov-08	67,886		30	1.014583	68,876	
Dec-08	64,085	969,208	31	0.981855	62,922	966,038
Jan-09	44,765		31	0.981855	43,953	
Feb-09	53,888		28	1.087054	58,579	
Mar-09	92,277		31	0.981855	90,603	
Apr-09	108,345		30	1.014583	109,925	
May-09	117,889		31	0.981855	115,750	
Jun-09	124,942		30	1.014583	126,764	
Jul-09	122,989		31	0.981855	120,757	
Aug-09	81,421		31	0.981855	79,944	
Sep-09	60,231		30	1.014583	61,109	
Oct-09	66,006		31	0.981855	64,808	
Nov-09	55,815		30	1.014583	56,629	
Dec-09	85,460	1,014,026	31	0.981855	83,909	1,012,729
Jan-10	43,963		31	0.981855	43,165	
Feb-10	50,645		28	1.087054	55,054	
Mar-10	90,741		31	0.981855	89,094	
Apr-10	90,033		30	1.014583	91,346	
May-10						

Actual Monthly Sales

	2006	2007	2008	2009	2010
January	34,565	39,368	33,910	44,765	43,963
February	35,917	45,150	46,669	53,888	50,645
March	67,655	110,924	94,823	92,277	90,741
April	75,809	106,249	93,977	108,345	90,033
May	83,810	119,117	109,603	117,889	
June	113,746	136,620	115,601	124,942	
July	96,623	131,422	124,704	122,989	
August	63,227	83,864	82,145	81,421	
September	59,431	69,188	66,466	60,231	
October	63,462	78,585	69,339	66,006	
November	67,686	68,882	67,886	55,815	
December	84,076	92,769	64,085	85,460	
Total	846,007	1,082,138	969,208	1,014,026	275,381

Adjusted Monthly Sales

	2006	2007	2008	2009	2010
January	33,938	38,654	33,294	43,953	43,165
February	39,043	49,081	48,983	58,579	55,054
March	66,428	108,911	93,102	90,603	89,094
April	76,914	107,798	95,348	109,925	91,346
May	82,289	116,956	107,614	115,750	
June	115,405	138,612	117,287	126,764	
July	94,869	129,037	122,442	120,757	
August	62,080	82,343	80,655	79,944	
September	60,298	70,197	67,435	61,109	
October	62,310	77,159	68,081	64,808	
November	68,673	69,886	68,876	56,629	
December	82,550	91,086	62,922	83,909	
Total	844,799	1,079,720	966,038	1,012,729	278,659

Actual Sales During Period of Interruption

May-10	92,953
Jun-10	114,215
Jul-10	120,487
Aug-10	86,801

in addition we perceive that each succeeding year is not necessarily higher in the chart than the year before, indicating a definite lack of trend in the data. Finally, in Figure 13.4 we see that all three features are explicitly shown—much of 2006 is below average, and there is much seasonality and very little trend in the data. This is confirmed mathematically in Table 13.2 with an analysis of variation (ANOVA) two-factor without replication calculation, and the same results are shown graphically in Figure 13.5.

Worksheet Setup

With our preliminary analysis behind us, we can now create the forecasting work-sheet shown in Table 13.3. Each of the past four years, 2006, 2007, 2008 and 2009, has three columns of data: monthly adjusted sales, the percentage that each month represents of the annual total, and a cumulative percentage column that sums the percentage for each month with all the months previous to it in that year. The 2010

Figure 13.1
Southern Retail Store
Line Chart
Adjusted Monthly Sales

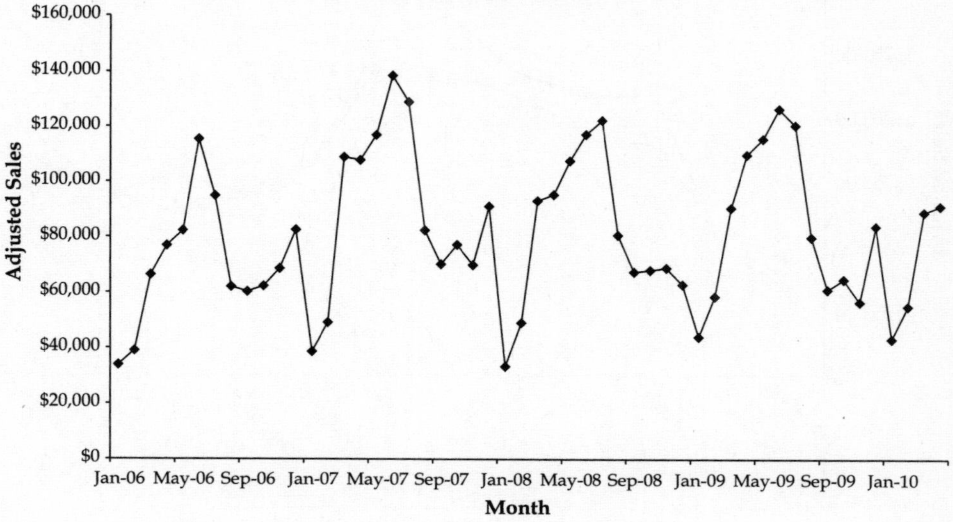

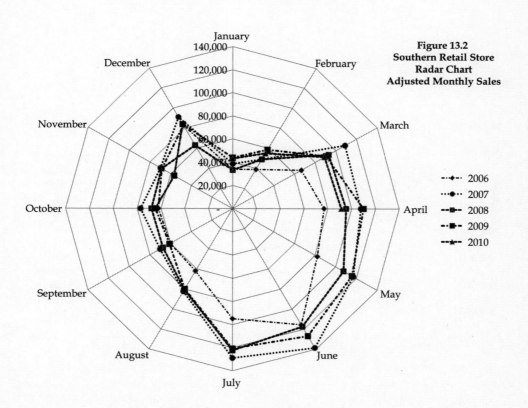

Figure 13.2
Southern Retail Store
Radar Chart
Adjusted Monthly Sales

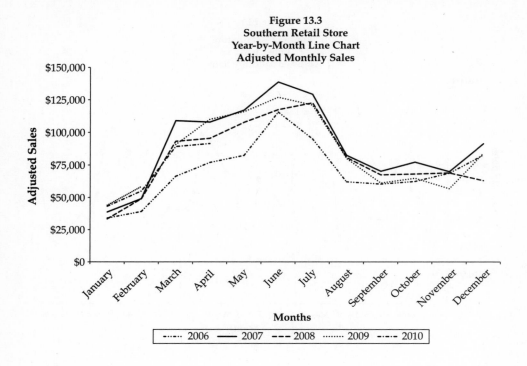

Figure 13.3
Southern Retail Store
Year-by-Month Line Chart
Adjusted Monthly Sales

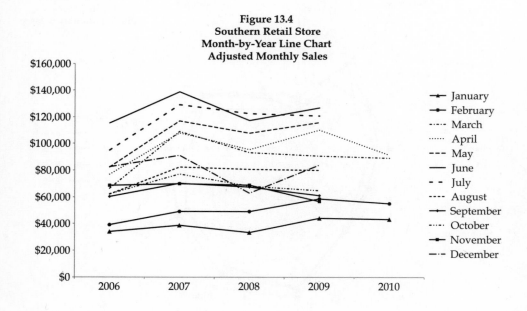

Figure 13.4
Southern Retail Store
Month-by-Year Line Chart
Adjusted Monthly Sales

Table 13.2
Southern Retail Store
ANOVA: Two-Factor Without Replication

SUMMARY	Count	Sum	Average	Variance
January	4	149,840	37,460	24,445,670
February	4	195,686	48,922	63,624,459
March	4	359,043	89,761	307,678,320
April	4	389,986	97,496	229,619,510
May	4	422,609	105,652	259,800,148
June	4	498,068	124,517	113,005,092
July	4	467,105	116,776	226,063,650
August	4	305,021	76,255	90,318,993
September	4	259,039	64,760	23,317,144
October	4	272,358	68,090	42,142,222
November	4	264,064	66,016	39,444,093
December	4	320,467	80,117	145,428,694
2006	12	844,799	70,400	502,163,469
2007	12	1,079,720	89,977	965,479,110
2008	12	966,038	80,503	747,056,026
2009	12	1,012,729	84,394	800,879,801

ANOVA

Source of Variation	SS	df	MS	F	p-value	F crit
Rows	30,928,331,589	11	2,811,666,508	41.366	0.000000	2.093
Columns	2,451,633,107	3	817,211,036	12.023	0.000018	2.892
Error	2,243,030,879	33	67,970,633			
Total	35,622,995,575	47				

Seasonality	86.82%
Trend	6.88%
Noise	6.30%
Total	100.00%

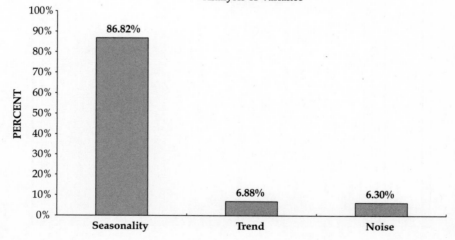

Figure 13.5
Southern Retail Store
Monthly Adjusted Sales
Analysis of Variance

Table 13.3
Southern Retail Store
Two-Way Analysis and Forecast of Monthly Adjusted Sales

Annual Weights —>

		2007	2008	2009	
Annual Weights		1.0372E+42	3.3146E+41	-166.84	

Month	2006 $	2006 %	2006 Cum %	2007 $	2007 %	2007 Cum %	2008 $	2008 %	2008 Cum %	2009 $	2009 %	2009 Cum %	2010 $	2010 %	MIN	MAX	2006
January	33,938	4.0%	4.0%	38,654	3.6%	3.6%	33,294	3.4%	3.4%	43,953	4.3%	4.3%	43,165	3.5%	3.4%	4.3%	4.0%
February	39,043	4.6%	8.6%	49,081	4.5%	8.1%	48,983	5.1%	8.5%	58,579	5.8%	10.1%	55,054	4.7%	4.5%	5.8%	4.6%
March	66,428	7.9%	16.5%	108,911	10.1%	18.2%	93,102	9.6%	18.2%	90,603	8.9%	19.1%	89,094	10.0%	8.9%	10.1%	7.9%
April	76,914	9.1%	25.6%	107,798	10.0%	28.2%	95,348	9.9%	28.0%	109,925	10.9%	29.9%	91,346	10.0%	9.9%	10.9%	9.1%
May	82,289	9.7%	35.3%	116,956	10.8%	39.0%	107,614	11.1%	39.2%	115,750	11.4%	41.4%		10.9%	10.8%	11.4%	9.7%
June	115,405	13.7%	49.0%	138,612	12.8%	51.9%	117,287	12.1%	51.3%	126,764	12.5%	53.9%		12.7%	12.1%	12.8%	13.7%
July	94,869	11.2%	60.2%	129,037	12.0%	63.8%	122,442	12.7%	64.0%	120,757	11.9%	65.8%		12.1%	11.9%	12.7%	11.2%
August	62,080	7.3%	67.6%	82,343	7.6%	71.4%	80,655	8.3%	72.3%	79,944	7.9%	73.7%		7.8%	7.6%	8.3%	7.3%
September	60,298	7.1%	74.7%	70,197	6.5%	77.9%	67,435	7.0%	79.3%	61,109	6.0%	79.7%			6.0%	7.0%	7.1%
October	62,310	7.4%	82.1%	77,159	7.1%	85.1%	68,081	7.0%	86.4%	64,808	6.4%	86.1%			6.4%	7.1%	7.4%
November	68,673	8.1%	90.2%	69,886	6.5%	91.6%	68,876	7.1%	93.5%	56,629	5.6%	91.7%			5.6%	7.1%	8.1%
December	82,550	9.8%	100.0%	91,086	8.4%	100.0%	62,922	6.5%	100.0%	83,909	8.3%	100.0%			6.5%	8.4%	9.8%
	844,299	100.0%		1,079,720	100.0%		966,038	100.0%		1,012,729	100.0%		278,659				

Right-side weighted averages:

	2010 $	2010 %	
3 YEAR WEIGHTED AVERAGE, JAN	43,165	3.5%	
3 YEAR WEIGHTED AVERAGE, FEB	55,054	4.7%	
3 YEAR WEIGHTED AVERAGE, MAR	89,094	10.0%	
3 YEAR WEIGHTED AVERAGE, APR	91,346	10.0%	
3 YEAR WEIGHTED AVERAGE, MAY		10.9%	
3 YEAR WEIGHTED AVERAGE, JUNE		12.7%	
3 YEAR WEIGHTED AVERAGE, JULY		12.1%	
3 YEAR WEIGHTED AVERAGE, AUG		7.8%	
3 YEAR WEIGHTED AVERAGE, JAN - APR		28.2%	-2.87%

278,659

989,735   PROJECTION MADE FROM 4 MONTHS SALES

CHANGE FROM AVERAGE OF TWO PRIOR YEARS =

PERIOD OF INTERRUPTION: MAY, JUNE, JULY & AUGUST

MAY PROJECTION BASED ON AVERAGE MONTHLY PRO-RATA SHARE OF ANNUALIZED SALES — 989,735 X 10.91% — Solver

MAY PROJECTION BASED ON COMPARISON WITH PRIOR YEAR'S MONTHLY SALES — 115,750 X (1 -.0287) — 4,564

AVERAGE

- 109,941
- 114,505
- 112,223

JUNE PROJECTION BASED ON AVERAGE MONTHLY PRO-RATA SHARE OF ANNUALIZED SALES — 989,735 X 12.67%

JUNE PROJECTION BASED ON COMPARISON WITH PRIOR YEAR'S MONTHLY SALES — 126,764 X (1 -.0287) — (2,232)

AVERAGE

- 123,588
- 121,356
- 122,472

JULY PROJECTION BASED ON AVERAGE MONTHLY PRO-RATA SHARE OF ANNUALIZED SALES — 989,735 X 12.13%

JULY PROJECTION BASED ON COMPARISON WITH PRIOR YEAR'S MONTHLY SALES — 120,757 X (1 -.0287) — (2,777)

AVERAGE

- 122,236
- 119,459
- 120,847

AUGUST PROJECTION BASED ON AVERAGE MONTHLY PRO-RATA SHARE OF ANNUALIZED SALES — 989,735 X 7.80%

AUGUST PROJECTION BASED ON COMPARISON WITH PRIOR YEAR'S MONTHLY SALES — 79,944 X (1 -.0287) — 445

AVERAGE

- 78,639
- 79,084
- 78,862

SUM OF AVERAGES — 434,403 — (0)

CHANGE FROM PRIOR 4 YEARS:
JAN-APR CURRENT YEAR	278,659
JAN-APR 4 YEAR AVERAGE	273,639
DOLLAR CHANGE	5,020
PERCENTAGE CHANGE	1.83%

CHANGE FROM PRIOR 3 YEARS:
JAN-APR CURRENT YEAR	278,659
JAN-APR 3 YEAR AVERAGE	292,744
DOLLAR CHANGE	(14,085)
PERCENTAGE CHANGE	-4.81%

CHANGE FROM PRIOR 2 YEARS:
JAN-APR CURRENT YEAR	278,659
JAN-APR 2 YEAR AVERAGE	286,893
DOLLAR CHANGE	(8,234)
PERCENTAGE CHANGE	-2.87%

CHANGE FROM PRIOR YEAR:
JAN-APR CURRENT YEAR	278,659
JAN-APR 1 YEAR AVERAGE	303,060
DOLLAR CHANGE	(24,401)
PERCENTAGE CHANGE	-8.05%

226

year, the year that contains our forecast, has only two columns: monthly adjusted sales and a percentage column.

The first percentage in the 2010 column is a three-year weighted average of cumulative percentage for the months January through April. The weights used are found in cells G5, J5, and M5, which are initially seeded with the number 1 as a placeholder. We will explain shortly how these weights were developed using Solver. The reason we have chosen a three-year weighted average instead of four years is for the reasons we noted when we reviewed the charts in Figures 13.2 through 13.5—2006 is different from the other three years. This deduction from charts is further substantiated by the information contained in cells T7:V19—except for January and February, the monthly percentages for 2006 lie outside the range of the other three years. In addition, the cumulative percentage through April 2006 in the amount of 25.6 percent is also outside the range of the other three years, 28.0 percent to 29.9 percent. Therefore, we have dropped 2006 from all our computations—expounding the point that just because you have the data, it doesn't mean it's relevant. The percentages in cell P12:P15 are also three-year weighted averages, and these four cells show how much May, June, July, and August (the months of the period of interruption) each represent of annual sales.

Dividing the three-year weighted average cumulative percentage of 28.2 percent for the months January through April located in cell P17 into cumulative sales through April of $278,659 found in cell O19, we produce expected annual sales for 2010 in the amount of $989,735 in cell O20.

First Forecasting Method

Knowing expected sales for 2010, we can develop one of our two monthly forecasting methods. For May 2010, the three-year weighted average of monthly sales as a percentage of annual sales is 10.91 percent, which when applied to expected sales of $989,735 produces a monthly forecast of $107,946. This number is then divided by .981855, the month of May adjustment factor necessary to reconvert adjusted sales back to actual sales. The resultant quotient of $109,941 is found in cell O23 and represents expected seasonal sales for May 2010.

Second Forecasting Method

The second method of forecasting monthly sales is to take May sales for 2009 in the amount of $115,750 and multiply it by the percentage by which 2010's cumulative sales differs from some previous period's January to April sales. We have chosen, for reasons explained in the next paragraph, to use the previous two-year average percentage difference of –2.87 percent. Therefore, $115,750 * (1 – .0287) = 112,428, which amount is then divided by .981855, the month of May adjustment factor necessary to reconvert adjusted sales back to actual sales. The resultant quotient of $114,505 is found in cell O24. This amount is then averaged with the $109,941 found in cell O23 to give us May's average forecast of $112,223 in cell O25, and accounts for trend. This process is repeated for the remaining three months in the forecast period, with the four-month forecast total of $434,403 shown in cell O39.

Selection of Length of Prior Period

We now explain how we choose the percentage by which 2010's forecasted monthly sales will be different from the prior year(s). At the bottom of Table 13.3 there are four boxes, each presenting the dollar amount and percentage difference by which cumulative sales through April 2010 differ from the same period for the immediate prior year and the averages of the prior two-, three- and four-year periods. For reasons given above, since it includes 2006 data, we will not be considering the four-year average difference. To help us choose which one of the three remaining percentage differences to use, we turn to Excel's Solver add-in.

In column S, cells S24:S39, we have calculated the difference between the two forecasting methods for each month and the sum of those differences. For example, cell S24 shows $4,564, which is the difference between May's two forecasted amounts, $114,505 and $109,941. The other three forecast months are treated accordingly, and the sum of the monthly differences is computed in cell S39. For each of three possible percentage differences—one year, two-year, or three-year average, which we place recursively in cell U21—we run Solver, telling it to minimize cell S39 with the constraint that its value be equal to or greater than zero, while changing cells G5, J5, and M5 (this is how the weights are developed). We compare the three results and choose the one that produces both a zero value in S39 and the smallest differences between monthly forecasting methods. In this case the best results were obtained with the two-year average difference of −2.87 percent, shown in cell U21.

Reasonableness Test

An overall test of reasonableness is found in Table 13.4, where we show the ratio of May to August sales to January to April sales for the prior four years, our forecast

	A	B	C	D	E	F	G	H	I	J	K	L	M
1						Table 13.4							
2						Southern Retail Store							
3						Ratio of Comparative Periods							
4													
5				Forecast Period		Immediate Prior Period							
6		Year		May–Aug		Jan–Apr		Ratio		3-Year Average		4-Year Average	
7		2006		357,406		213,946		1.67					
8		2007		471,023		301,692		1.56					
9		2008		432,054		269,379		1.60					
10		2009		447,240		299,275		1.49		1.55		1.58	
11		Forecasted 2010		434,403		275,381		1.58					
12		Actual 2010		414,455		275,381		1.51					
13													

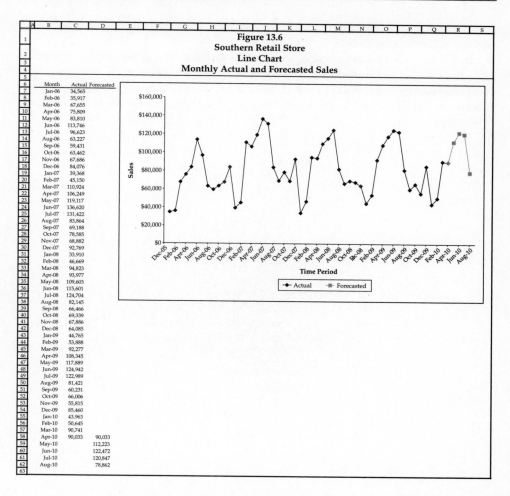

period for 2010 and 2010's actual results. The ratio for the forecast period falls well within the range of both the three-year and four-year periods, and it is very close to the average for both periods.

Figure 13.6 presents a chart of actual and forecasted sales for the 56-month period January 2006 through August 2010. A visual inspection of the chart leads us to conclude that our simple forecasting method has produced reasonable results.

Conclusion

As we stated in the opening paragraph of this case study, we like this model because it adapts itself very nicely to declining sales situations such as that exhibited in this case. Without some way for regression models to give the immediate past some additional weight, they usually overstate expected sales in these circumstances.

While this presentation used 52 months of historical sales, 12 months in each of the past four years and four months in the forecast year, we use models with five, three, and even two years of historical sales. We recommend that the minimum number of historical sales data in the forecast year should never be less than three, and we set no upper limit.

In the next chapter we present some more sophisticated and complex analytical tools than those we introduced in Chapters 2 and 3. These tools help to determine stationarity, independence of observations, autocorrelation among the observations, and test for trend and seasonality so that the proper forecasting tool can be selected.

CHAPTER 14

Case Study 14—Data Analysis Tools for Forecasting Sales

An average monthly sales figure derived from 12 months of annual sales is not useful for a seasonal business, as it overstates sales for a peak summer season business that has a loss period in midwinter, and it will understate the loss for that same business in midsummer. Even for a nonseasonal business, monthly average sales computed from earlier years' data can be misleading if there has been an upward or downward trend over time. If the measure of damages is the lost value of the business, then forecasting sales using a five-year simple or weighted average of past sales will misstate next year's expected revenue if historical sales have exhibited a trend in either direction. So, are there any situations that allow for the use of averaging techniques in determining damages?

Need for Analytical Tests

Yes, there are such techniques that are appropriate for stationary time series, that is, sales over time that exhibit no significant upward or downward trend, and that have equality of means and variances throughout the length of the series. First, though, in this chapter we will present some more sophisticated and complex analytical tools than those we introduced in Chapter 2 to determine stationarity, independence of observations, autocorrelation among the observations, and test for trend and seasonality. In subsequent chapters, we will describe the techniques for forecasting with random models, introduce techniques for modeling seasonal patterns in those models, and acquaint you with various measures of forecast accuracy.

Graph Your Data

In this case, an urban food store suffered a fire loss in its produce section at the end of February 2011, causing the section to be shut down for three months because of reconstruction, starting March 1, 2011. We gathered 38 months of sales history and present it in tabular form in Table 14.1 and graphical form in Figure 14.1. Note that the line chart in Figure 14.1 suggests neither an upward nor downward trend nor any seasonality in the data. The line chart indicates that monthly sales randomly fall

	A	B	C	D	E	F
1			**Table 14.1**			
2			**Urban Food Store Sales**			
3			**January 2008–February 2011**			
4						
5	**Month**	**2008**	**2009**	**2010**	**2011**	
6	Jan	13,026	13,644	12,870	12,565	
7	Feb	13,339	15,318	10,418	12,367	
8	Mar	10,513	14,290	14,381	-	
9	Apr	13,635	14,031	11,202	-	
10	May	12,597	12,516	13,996	-	
11	Jun	13,505	11,870	12,036	-	
12	Jul	10,107	15,234	13,716	-	
13	Aug	12,808	13,529	12,791	-	
14	Sep	12,480	12,755	13,612	-	
15	Oct	14,867	13,689	10,348	-	
16	Nov	13,020	13,979	12,192	-	
17	Dec	10,856	10,348	15,984	-	
18		152,761	163,215	155,554	26,943	
19						

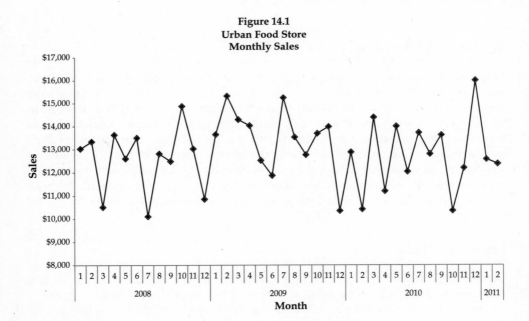

Figure 14.1
Urban Food Store
Monthly Sales

between \$10,000 and \$16,000 with no continuing pattern or regularity from month to month. At this point you might be asking why, with inflation affecting prices, isn't there an upward trend? The answer is that the food store is likely showing its age, and within the past five years has faced new competition from both Whole Foods and Trader Joe's, which have opened nearby stores. Therefore, inflationary price increases have been offset by either fewer customers and/or lower sales per customer so that monthly sales over the 38 months are essentially flat.

Statistical Procedures

But appearances can be deceiving, so let's present some statistical procedures in Table 14.2 to test our assumptions of neither trend nor seasonality in the time series data, as well as equality of means and variances. The first procedure is a simple regression model in which monthly sales is the dependent variable and a trend sequence of 1 to 38 is the independent variable. If there is some meaningful trend in the data, then the trend coefficient will be statistically significant. Rather than use

	Year	Month	Trend	Monthly Sales	Variance	Mean			
							Table 14.2		
							Urban Food Store		
							Monthly Sales		
							Various Statistical Procedures		
	2008	1	1	13,026			**Testing for Trend**		
		2	2	13,339			Slope		0.889
		3	3	10,513			Standard Error		21.945
		4	4	13,635			t-Statistic		0.040
		5	5	12,597			p-value		0.968
		6	6	13,505					
		7	7	10,107			Cannot reject the null hypothesis that the slope is		
		8	8	12,808			equal to zero		
		9	9	12,480					
		10	10	14,867			**Testing For Equal Variances**		
		11	11	13,020			F-Test Two-Sample for Variances		
		12	12	10,856				Periods 20–38	Periods 1–19
	2009	1	13	13,644			Mean	12,778	13,035
		2	14	15,318			Variance	2,206,824	2,159,761
		3	15	14,290			Observations	19	19
		4	16	14,031			df	18	18
		5	17	12,516			F	1.022	
		6	18	11,870			P(F >=f) two-tail	0.964	
		7	19	15,234	2,159,761	13,035	F Critical two-tail	2.596	
		8	20	13,529			Alpha in Analysis Tool dialog box = .025		
		9	21	12,755					
		10	22	13,689			Cannot reject the null hypothesis that the variances		
		11	23	13,979			are equal		
		12	24	10,348					
	2010	1	25	12,870			**Testing For Equal Means**		
		2	26	10,418			t-Test: Two-Sample Assuming Equal Variances		
		3	27	14,381				Periods 20–38	Periods 1–19
		4	28	11,202			Mean	12,778	13,035
		5	29	13,996			Variance	2,206,824	2,159,761
		6	30	12,036			Observations	19	19
		7	31	13,716			Pooled Variance	2,183,293	
		8	32	12,791			Hypothesized Mean Difference	0	
		9	33	13,612			df	36	
		10	34	10,348			t Stat	(0.536)	
		11	35	12,192			P(T<=t) one-tail	0.298	
		12	36	15,984			t Critical one-tail	1.688	
	2011	1	37	12,565			P(T<=t) two-tail	0.595	
		2	38	12,367	2,206,824	12,778	t Critical two-tail	2.028	
							Cannot reject the null hypothesis that the means are equal		

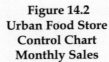

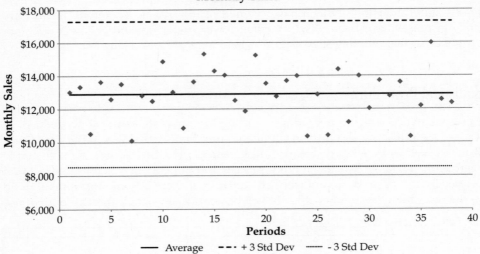

Figure 14.2
Urban Food Store
Control Chart
Monthly Sales

the regression tool or the LINEST array function, let's build our significance test from scratch.

Below are the key cell formulas used in this significance test on Figure 14.2.

Function	Cell	Formula
Slope	K7	=SLOPE(E7:E44,D7:D44)
Standard Error	K8	=STEYX(E7:E44,D7:D44)/SQRT(DEVSQ(D7:D44))
t-statistic	K9	=K7/K8
p-value[1]	K10	=T.DIST.2T(ABS(K9),COUNT(D7:D44)-2)

With a p-value of .968 in cell K10, we cannot reject the null hypothesis that the slope of the line is essentially zero. In fact, sales only increase at the rate of 89¢ per month, an amount that is practically no different from zero.

The second test in Table 14.2 is the test for equal variances using Excel's data analysis tool, the F-Test Two-Sample for Variances. The variances we are testing are that of the first 19 observations versus the second 19 observations. With a p-value in cell J23 of .964, we cannot reject the null hypothesis of equal variances.

The third and final test in Table 14.2 is the test for equal means using Excel's data analysis tool, the t-Test: Two-Sample Assuming Equal Variances. The means we are testing are that of the first 19 observations versus the second 19 observations. With a p-value in cell J42 of .595, we cannot reject the null hypothesis of equal means.

While these three tests, along with the chart in Figure 14.1, confirm our assumptions of constant mean and variance and no obvious time series patterns, we turn now to more sophisticated checks for randomness, all of which, in one form or another, we have seen before when we presented tests of residuals for a regression model.

Tests for Randomness

The first of these is to plot the time series on a control chart. In Figure 14.2 the individual 38 observations are plotted, the centerline is the average of the observations, and the control limits are plus or minus three standard deviations from the centerline. Then if the series is random, it should be "in control" as the term is used in the statistical process control environment. Specifically, there should not be any points beyond the control limits, and there should not be any pattern to the data. We note that in Figure 14.2 the data appear to be "in control" as no one data point lies beyond the control limits, and the data points appear to be randomly distributed within the control limits.

A second check is the runs test. For each observation in a time series, we associate a 1 if an observation is greater than the average or median of all the observations in the series, and a 0 if an observation is less than the average. Thus, the time series has an associated series of 0s and 1s. For example, suppose that the successive observations are 87, 69, 53, 57, 94, 81, 44, 68, and 77, with an average of 70. Then the sequence of 0s and 1s is 1; 0 0 0; 1 1; 0 0; and 1; four of the nine observations are above the mean and five are below it. A run is a consecutive sequence of 0s or 1s. The preceding sequence has five runs: 1; 0 0 0; 1 1; 0 0; and 1. The runs test checks whether this is about the right number of runs for a random series. Below are the key cell formulas used in the runs test in Figure 14.3.

Function	Cell	Formula	Copied to
Count Below Average	G6	=IF(E6<AVERAGE($E$6:$E$43),1,0)	G7:G43
Count Above Average	H6	=IF(E6>AVERAGE($E$6:$E$43),1,0)	H7:H43
Number of Runs	I6	1	–
Number of Runs	I7	=IF(H7=H6,"",1)	I8:I43
Expected Runs	Q40	=2*M38*Q38/M37+1	–
Standard Deviation	Q41	=SQRT(((2*M38*Q38)/(M37*(M37-1)))* (((2*M38*Q38)/M37)-1))	–
Z	Q42	=((M40-Q40+0.5)/Q41)	–
p-value[2]	M41	=2*(1-NORMSDIST(Q42))	–

The rest of the output in Figure 14.3 is fairly straightforward. The number of observations below and above the mean is the sum of columns G and H, respectively, while the number of runs is the total of column I. The area chart in Figure 14.3 also depicts the number of runs. The factor 2 in the p-value calculation in cell M41 is used to obtain the probability in both tails, that is, that the number of expected runs is different from the actual number of runs, not just more or fewer runs.

The output in Figure 14.3 shows that there is some evidence of too many runs. The expected number of runs under randomness is 20, and there are 24 runs for this series. However, the evidence is certainly not overwhelming—the p-value is only .1388. If we ran this test as a one-tailed test, checking only for too many runs, then the appropriate p-value would be .0694, half of the value shown in cell M41. The

Figure 14.3
Urban Food Store
Runs Test for Randomness

Year	Month	Period	Urban Food Store	Count Below Average	Count Above Average	Number of Runs
2008	1	1	13,026	0	1	1
	2	2	13,339	0	1	0
	3	3	10,513	1	0	1
	4	4	13,635	0	1	1
	5	5	12,597	1	0	1
	6	6	13,505	0	1	1
	7	7	10,107	1	0	1
	8	8	12,808	1	0	0
	9	9	12,480	1	0	0
	10	10	14,867	0	1	1
	11	11	13,020	0	1	0
	12	12	10,856	1	0	1
2009	1	13	13,644	0	1	1
	2	14	15,318	0	1	0
	3	15	14,290	0	1	0
	4	16	14,031	0	1	0
	5	17	12,516	1	0	1
	6	18	11,870	1	0	0
	7	19	15,234	0	1	1
	8	20	13,529	0	1	0
	9	21	12,755	1	0	1
	10	22	13,689	0	1	1
	11	23	13,979	0	1	0
	12	24	10,348	1	0	1
2010	1	25	12,870	1	0	0
	2	26	10,418	1	0	0
	3	27	14,381	0	1	1
	4	28	11,202	1	0	1
	5	29	13,996	0	1	1
	6	30	12,036	1	0	1
	7	31	13,716	0	1	1
	8	32	12,791	1	0	1
	9	33	13,612	0	1	1
	10	34	10,348	1	0	1
	11	35	12,192	1	0	0
	12	36	15,984	0	1	1
2011	1	37	12,565	1	0	1
	2	38	12,367	1	0	0
			Totals	19	19	24

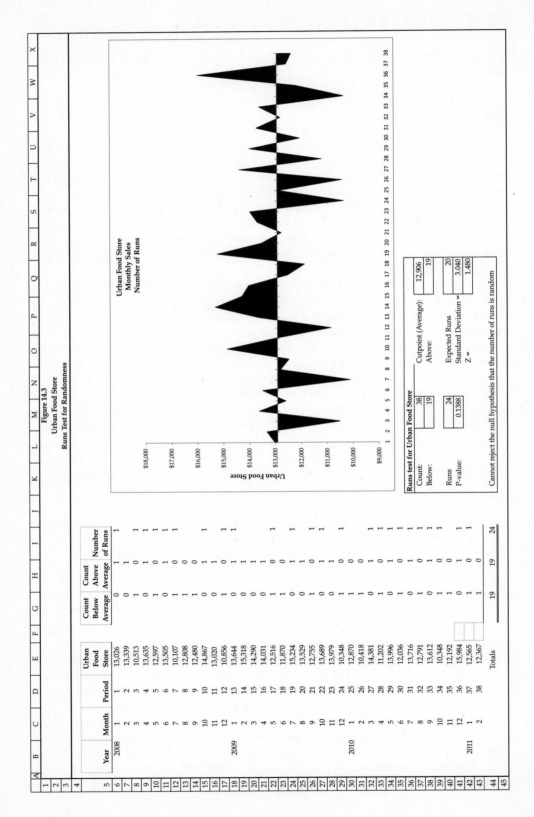

Urban Food Store
Monthly Sales
Number of Runs

Runs test for Urban Food Store			
Count:	38	Cutpoint (Average):	12,906
Below:	19	Above:	19
Runs	24	Expected Runs	20
P-value:	0.1388	Standard Deviation =	3.040
		Z =	1.480

Cannot reject the null hypothesis that the number of runs is random.

236

conclusion in either case is that although sales tend to "zigzag" more than a random series, there is not enough evidence to reject the null hypothesis of randomness at the 5 percent level.

The third check is a test for autocorrelation. The successive observations in a random series are probabilistically independent of one another. Many time series violate this property and are instead autocorrelated. The term "auto" means that successive observations are correlated with one another. For example, in the most common form of autocorrelation, positive autocorrelation, large observations tend to follow large observations, and small observations tend to follow small observations. While the runs test may pick it up, another way to check for the same nonrandomness property is to calculate the autocorrelations of the time series.

To understand autocorrelation it is first necessary to understand what it means to lag a time series. Since this concept is easy to grasp with a spreadsheet, let's take a look at Table 14.3. In the first section on the left, titled lag 1, in column (3) we have simply pushed down the series by one row, and the first period's sales of $13,026 now appears in cell D10. Note that there is a blank cell at the top of the lagged series (in cell D9). We continue to push the series down one row at a time to obtain the other lags. For example the lag 3 version of the series appears in the section on the far right of Table 14.3. Now there are three missing observations at the top of column (3)—cells T9:T11. You can readily see that lags are merely prior observations removed by a certain number of periods from the present time. Table 14.3 shows lags 1, 2, and 3 and their autocorrelation functions. The autocorrelation function of lag k indicates the strength of the relationship between observations k periods apart. For example, the autocorrelation of lag 3 in Table 14.3, −.211, indicates that there is very little relationship between observations separated by three months. We have computed lags 4 to 12 and their autocorrelation functions elsewhere, but do not show them in Table 14.3. We leave that as an exercise for the reader to perform.

Below are the key cell formulas used in the creation of the autocorrelation functions for Lag 1 in Figure 14.6.

Function	Cell	Formula	Copied to
Average Sales	C48	=AVERAGE(C9:C46)	–
Monthly Sales—Average Sales	E9	=C9-$C$48	E10:E46
Lag 1 Monthly Sales—Average Sales	F10	=D10-$C$48	F11:F46
(Monthly Sales—Average Sales)³	G9	=E9^2	G10:G46
Column (4) * Column (5)	H9	=E9*F9	H10:H46
Total Column (6)	G47	=SUM(G9:G46)	–
Total Column (7)	H47	=SUM(H9:H46)	–
Autocorrelation Lag 1	G50	=H47/G47	–

We continue this process for lags 2 and 3 as shown in Table 14.3, each time pushing down the series by one row. For lags 4 to 12, the process just repeats itself, with each succeeding lag being pushed down the series by one row. Other than that difference, all the computations stay the same throughout the 12 lags, as we can see when we examine lags 2 and 3 and compare them with lag 1's calculations. Once we have computed the 12 autocorrelation functions (ACF) for each of the lags, we bring them forward to Figure 14.4.

Table 14.3
Urban Food Store
Autocorrelation Function
Lags 1, 2, and 3

Lag 1

(1) Period	(2) Monthly Sales	(3) Lag 1 Monthly Sales	(4) Monthly Sales - Average Sales	(5) Lag 1 Monthly Sales - Average Sales	(6) (Monthly Sales - Average Sales)²	(7) Column (4) * Column (5)
1	13,026		120		14,371	-
2	13,339	13,026	433	120	187,787	51,949
3	10,513	13,339	(2,393)	433	5,726,620	(1,037,008)
4	13,635	10,513	729	(2,393)	531,144	(1,744,035)
5	12,597	13,635	(309)	729	95,473	(225,189)
6	13,505	12,597	598	(309)	358,151	(184,916)
7	10,107	13,505	(2,799)	598	7,832,849	(1,674,915)
8	12,808	10,107	(99)	(2,799)	9,710	275,784
9	12,480	12,808	(426)	(99)	181,844	42,020
10	14,867	12,480	1,960	(426)	3,843,338	(835,995)
11	13,020	14,867	114	1,960	13,062	224,058
12	10,856	13,020	(2,051)	114	4,204,817	(234,357)
13	13,644	10,856	738	(2,051)	545,129	(1,513,991)
14	15,318	13,644	2,412	738	5,815,748	1,780,544
15	14,290	15,318	1,384	2,412	1,916,264	3,338,339
16	14,031	14,290	1,125	1,384	1,266,237	1,557,705
17	12,516	14,031	(390)	1,125	152,189	(438,985)
18	11,870	12,516	(1,036)	(390)	1,073,479	404,193
19	15,234	11,870	2,328	(1,036)	5,420,968	(2,412,322)
20	13,529	15,234	623	2,328	388,199	1,450,660
21	12,755	13,529	(151)	623	22,745	(93,967)
22	13,689	12,755	783	(151)	613,311	(118,110)
23	13,979	13,689	1,072	783	1,150,178	839,891
24	10,348	13,979	(2,558)	1,072	6,541,867	(2,743,047)
25	12,870	10,348	(36)	(2,558)	1,317	92,816
26	14,381	12,870	1,475	(36)	6,192,755	90,305
27	11,202	14,381	(1,704)	1,475	2,904,265	(3,670,284)
28	13,996	11,202	1,090	(1,704)	1,187,434	(2,513,482)
29	12,036	13,996	(871)	1,090	757,879	(1,857,047)
30	13,716	12,036	809	(871)	655,223	(948,647)
31	12,791	13,716	(116)	809	13,351	(704,684)
32	13,612	12,791	706	(116)	498,212	(93,530)
33	10,348	13,612	(2,558)	706	6,543,304	(81,557)
34	12,192	10,348	(714)	(2,558)	510,452	(1,805,534)
35	15,984	12,192	3,078	(714)	9,473,131	1,827,579
36	12,565	15,984	(342)	3,078	116,719	(2,198,995)
37	12,367	12,565	(539)	(342)	290,692	(1,051,521)
38		12,367		(539)		184,199
Totals					79,225,498	(16,022,078)
Average	12,906					

Auto correlation lag 1 = H47/G47   -0.202

Lag 2

(1) Period	(2) Monthly Sales	(3) Lag 2 Monthly Sales	(4) Monthly Sales - Average Sales	(5) Lag 2 Monthly Sales - Average Sales	(6) (Monthly Sales - Average Sales)²	(7) Column (4) * Column (5)
1	13,026		120		14,371	-
2	13,339		433		187,787	-
3	10,513	13,026	(2,393)	120	5,726,620	(286,875)
4	13,635	13,339	729	433	531,144	315,820
5	12,597	10,513	(309)	(2,393)	95,473	739,418
6	13,505	13,635	598	729	358,151	436,153
7	10,107	12,597	(2,799)	(309)	7,832,849	864,770
8	12,808	13,505	(99)	598	9,710	(58,971)
9	12,480	10,107	(426)	(2,799)	181,844	1,193,464
10	14,867	12,808	1,960	(99)	3,843,338	(193,180)
11	13,020	12,480	114	(426)	13,062	(48,737)
12	10,856	14,867	(2,051)	1,960	4,204,817	(4,020,017)
13	13,644	13,020	738	114	545,129	84,383
14	15,318	10,856	2,412	(2,051)	5,815,748	(4,945,114)
15	14,290	13,644	1,384	738	1,916,264	1,022,063
16	14,031	15,318	1,125	2,412	1,266,237	2,713,690
17	12,516	14,290	(390)	1,384	152,189	(540,032)
18	11,870	14,031	(1,036)	1,125	1,073,479	(1,165,881)
19	15,234	12,516	2,328	(390)	5,420,968	(908,302)
20	13,529	11,870	623	(1,036)	388,199	(645,541)
21	12,755	15,234	(151)	2,328	22,745	(351,144)
22	13,689	13,529	783	623	613,311	487,942
23	13,979	12,755	1,072	(151)	1,150,178	(161,745)
24	10,348	13,689	(2,558)	783	6,541,867	(2,003,048)
25	12,870	13,979	(36)	1,072	1,317	(38,918)
26	14,381	10,348	1,475	(2,558)	6,192,755	6,364,918
27	11,202	12,870	(1,704)	(36)	2,904,265	(53,522)
28	13,996	14,381	1,090	1,475	1,187,434	4,240,920
29	12,036	11,202	(871)	(1,704)	757,879	1,607,172
30	13,716	13,996	809	1,090	655,223	1,483,605
31	12,791	12,036	(116)	(871)	13,351	882,062
32	13,612	13,716	706	809	498,212	100,590
33	10,348	12,791	(2,558)	(116)	6,543,304	571,349
34	12,192	13,612	(714)	706	510,452	295,567
35	15,984	10,348	3,078	(2,558)	9,473,131	(504,295)
36	12,565	12,192	(342)	(714)	116,719	(7,873,092)
37	12,367	15,984	(539)	3,078	290,692	244,089
38		12,565				(1,659,447)
Totals					79,225,498	(1,809,888)
Average	12,906					

Auto correlation lag 2 = P47/O47   -0.023

Lag 3

(1) Period	(2) Monthly Sales	(3) Lag 3 Monthly Sales	(4) Monthly Sales - Average Sales	(5) Lag 3 Monthly Sales - Average Sales	(6) (Monthly Sales - Average Sales)²	(7) Column (4) * Column (5)
1	13,026		120		14,371	-
2	13,339		433		187,787	-
3	10,513		(2,393)		5,726,620	-
4	13,635	13,026	729	120	531,144	87,367
5	12,597	13,339	(309)	433	95,473	(133,898)
6	13,505	10,513	598	(2,393)	358,151	(1,432,129)
7	10,107	13,635	(2,799)	729	7,832,849	(2,039,698)
8	12,808	12,597	(99)	(309)	9,710	30,447
9	12,480	13,505	(426)	598	181,844	(255,201)
10	14,867	10,107	1,960	(2,799)	3,843,338	(5,486,738)
11	13,020	12,808	114	(99)	13,062	(11,262)
12	10,856	12,480	(2,051)	(426)	4,204,817	874,426
13	13,644	14,867	738	1,960	545,129	275,618
14	15,318	13,020	2,412	114	5,815,748	1,447,452
15	14,290	10,856	1,384	(2,051)	1,916,264	(2,838,581)
16	14,031	13,644	1,125	738	1,266,237	830,821
17	12,516	15,318	(390)	2,412	152,189	(940,795)
18	11,870	14,290	(1,036)	1,384	1,073,479	(1,434,249)
19	15,234	14,031	2,328	1,125	5,420,968	2,619,968
20	13,529	12,516	623	(390)	388,199	(243,063)
21	12,755	11,870	(151)	(1,036)	22,745	156,259
22	13,689	15,234	783	2,328	613,311	1,823,387
23	13,979	13,529	1,072	623	1,150,178	668,205
24	10,348	12,755	(2,558)	(151)	6,541,867	385,743
25	12,870	13,689	(36)	783	1,317	(28,419)
26	14,381	13,979	1,475	(2,558)	6,192,755	(2,668,852)
27	11,202	10,348	(1,704)	(2,489)	2,175,281	(3,772,320)
28	13,996	12,870	1,090	(36)	2,904,265	61,843
29	12,036	14,381	(871)	1,475	1,187,434	(2,711,732)
30	13,716	11,202	809	(1,704)	757,879	(1,283,979)
31	12,791	13,996	(116)	1,090	655,223	(1,379,471)
32	13,612	12,036	706	(871)	498,212	(125,910)
33	10,348	13,716	(2,558)	809	6,543,304	(614,479)
34	12,192	12,791	(714)	(116)	510,452	(2,070,585)
35	15,984	13,612	3,078	706	9,473,131	82,553
36	12,565	10,348	(342)	(2,558)	116,719	2,172,470
37	12,367	12,192	(539)	(714)	290,692	873,916
38		12,367				385,207
Totals					79,225,498	(16,695,678)
Average	12,906					

Auto correlation lag 3 = X47/W47   -0.211

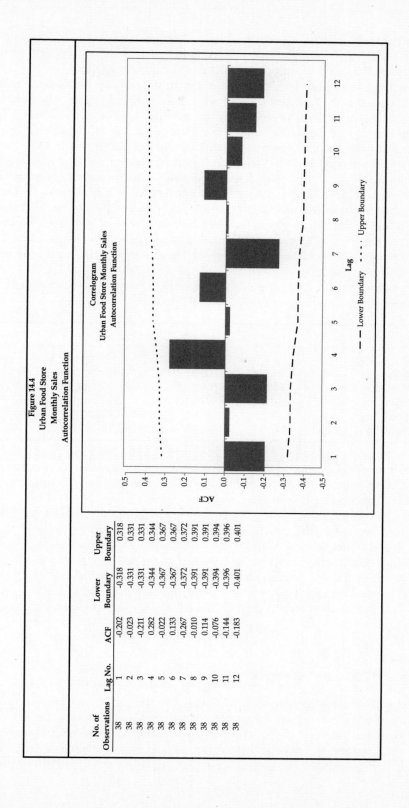

Figure 14.4
Urban Food Store
Monthly Sales
Autocorrelation Function

Correlogram
Urban Food Store Monthly Sales
Autocorrelation Function

No. of Observations	Lag No.	ACF	Lower Boundary	Upper Boundary
38	1	-0.202	-0.318	0.318
38	2	-0.023	-0.331	0.331
38	3	-0.211	-0.331	0.331
38	4	0.282	-0.344	0.344
38	5	-0.022	-0.367	0.367
38	6	0.133	-0.367	0.367
38	7	-0.267	-0.372	0.372
38	8	-0.010	-0.391	0.391
38	9	0.114	-0.391	0.391
38	10	-0.076	-0.394	0.394
38	11	-0.144	-0.396	0.396
38	12	-0.183	-0.401	0.401

The runs test on monthly sales suggests that the pattern of sales is not completely random. Large values tend to follow large values, and small values tend to follow small values. Do autocorrelations support this conclusion?

How large is a "large" autocorrelation? Under the assumption of randomness, it can be shown that the standard error of any autocorrelation is approximately $1/\sqrt{N}$, where N is the number of observations. In this case $1/\sqrt{38} = .162$, though as we shall see shortly, we use a calculation for the confidence levels that accounts for the cumulative R^2 of the autocorrelation functions. If the series is truly random, then only an occasional autocorrelation should be larger than two standard errors in magnitude. Typically, the first few lags are the most important, as intuitively, if there is any relationship between successive observations it is likely to be between nearby observations. The June 2010 observation is more likely to be related to the May 2010 observation than to the October 2008 observation. The one exception to this is a seasonal lag, where monthly data will show an autocorrelation at lag 12 that corresponds to a relationship between observations a year apart, such as December 2008 and December 2009.

Below are the key cell formulas used in the creation of the upper and lower boundaries for autocorrelation functions in Figure 14.4.

Function	Cell	Formula	Copied to
Lower Boundary	E7	=-1.96/SQRT(B7)	–
Lower Boundary	E8	=-1.96*SQRT((1/B8)*(1+2*SUMSQ($D$7)))	–
Lower Boundary	E9	=-1.96*SQRT((1/B9)*(1+2*SUMSQ($D$7:D8)))	E10:E18
Upper Boundary	F7	=1.96/SQRT(B7)	–
Upper Boundary	F8	=1.96*SQRT((1/B8)*(1+2*SUMSQ($D$7)))	–
Upper Boundary	F9	=1.96*SQRT((1/B9)*(1+2*SUMSQ($D$7:D8)))	F10:F18

The numerical output in Figure 14.4, along with the associated correlogram, indicates that none of the 12 autocorrelation functions exceeds the upper or lower boundary. This finding is consistent with randomness.

As lag 4 in Figure 14.4 approaches its upper boundary, indicating that perhaps there might be some small amount of seasonality and/or trend in the time series, we ran the 38 observations through Excel's Data Analysis tool, ANOVA: Two Factor Without Replication, and show the results in Figure 14.5. While we don't think that the seasonality and trend percentages are significant at 2.4 percent and 6.2 percent, respectively, we will perform some additional analysis and testing of the time series data in order to detect any trends and seasonal cycles that might exist.

Tests for Trend and Seasonality

Time series data displays a trend if the variance of the differences between adjacent observations, or observations a year apart if we are also accounting for seasonality, is less than the variance of the observations themselves. To understand why this is true, let's review the statistical definition of variance. Variance is a measure of

Figure 14.5
Urban Food Store
Monthly Sales
Analysis of Variance

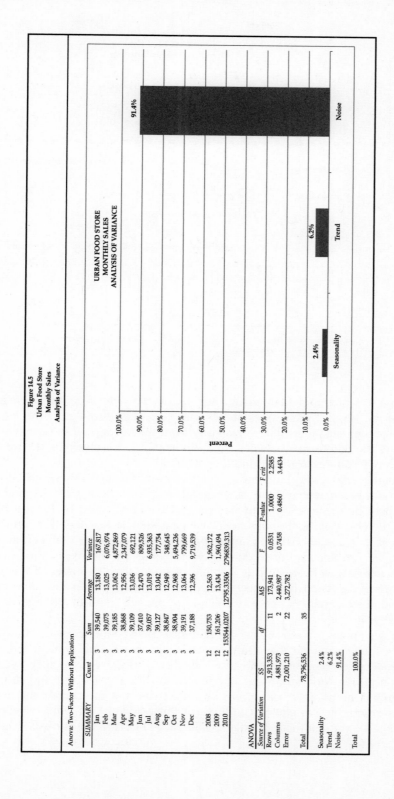

Anova: Two-Factor Without Replication

SUMMARY	Count	Sum	Average	Variance
Jan	3	39,540	13,180	167,817
Feb	3	39,075	13,025	6,076,974
Mar	3	39,185	13,062	4,872,869
Apr	3	38,868	12,956	2,347,079
May	3	39,109	13,036	692,121
Jun	3	37,410	12,470	809,526
Jul	3	39,057	13,019	6,935,363
Aug	3	39,127	13,042	177,754
Sep	3	38,847	12,949	348,645
Oct	3	38,904	12,968	5,494,236
Nov	3	39,191	13,064	799,669
Dec	3	37,188	12,396	9,719,539
2008	12	150,753	12,563	1,962,172
2009	12	161,206	13,434	1,960,494
2010	12	153544.0207	12795.33506	2796839.313

ANOVA

Source of Variation	SS	df	MS	F	P-value	F crit
Rows	1,913,353	11	173,941	0.0531	1.0000	2.2585
Columns	4,881,973	2	2,440,987	0.7458	0.4860	3.4434
Error	72,001,210	22	3,272,782			
Total	78,796,536	35				

Seasonality	2.4%
Trend	6.2%
Noise	91.4%
Total	100.0%

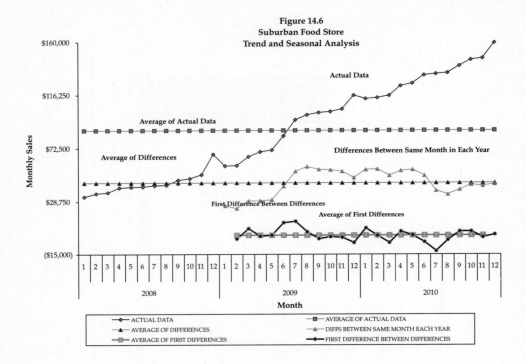

Figure 14.6
Suburban Food Store
Trend and Seasonal Analysis

the degree to which individual values in a set of data differ from the average of all values. If the original data series shows a trend, observations near the beginning and end of the data series differ drastically from the average of the data series. By computing the differences between data observations, we eliminate the trend, and the difference values cluster around their average.

To detect seasonality in the data, we compute the first difference between a given month or quarter and the same month or quarter in a previous year. When we compute differences, we eliminate the fluctuations caused by the seasonal cycle and thereby reduce the variance. The next step is to check for trend in the monthly sales data. Since there is no seasonality in differences between months or quarters, we can analyze those differences to see if a trend exists. First, we compute the differences between the monthly or quarterly differences. If this first set of differences between differences has a lower variance than the difference between months or quarters, there is at least a moderate trend in addition to thepgb seasonal cycle.

Next we compute a second set of differences between differences. If the second set has a lower variance than the first set, there is a strong trend in addition to a seasonal cycle. To demonstrate how all this works, we have time series data from a suburban food store that opened about three years ago and has shown strong growth in monthly sales along with, we suspect, some degree of seasonality. From an article by Everette S. Gardner Jr., PhD, in the May 1988 issue of *Lotus* magazine,[4] we present these calculations in Table 14.4 and the corresponding chart in Figure 14.6.

Table 14.4
Suburban Food Store
Monthly Trend and Seasonal Analysis:

		Actual	DBM	DBD-1	DBD-2
Variance		1,562,370,882	120,029,526	30,387,643	43,891,372
Index		100%	8%	2%	3%
Trend		None	None	Moderate	Strong
Seasonal?		No	Yes	Yes	Yes
Indicator				++++++	

Year	Month	Actual Data	Differences Between Same Month Each Year	First Difference Between Differences	Second Difference Between Differences
2008	1	32,791			
	2	35,461			
	3	36,290			
	4	40,296			
	5	40,802			
	6	41,126			
	7	42,137			
	8	42,461			
	9	46,466			
	10	47,801			
	11	50,977			
	12	67,653			
2009	1	58,159	25,368		
	2	58,483	23,022	(2,346)	
	3	65,664	29,374	6,352	8,698
	4	69,670	29,374	0	(6,352)
	5	71,005	30,203	830	830
	6	82,516	41,390	11,187	10,357
	7	95,867	53,731	12,340	1,153
	8	99,873	57,412	3,682	(8,659)
	9	101,714	55,247	(2,165)	(5,846)
	10	102,543	54,742	(506)	1,659
	11	104,708	53,731	(1,011)	(506)
	12	116,043	48,390	(5,341)	(4,329)
2010	1	113,225	55,066	6,676	12,016
	2	114,054	55,571	506	(6,170)
	3	115,895	50,231	(5,341)	(5,846)
	4	123,906	54,236	4,005	9,346
	5	126,071	55,066	830	(3,176)
	6	132,746	50,231	(4,835)	(5,665)
	7	133,758	37,890	(12,340)	(7,505)
	8	134,587	34,714	(3,176)	9,164
	9	140,433	38,720	4,005	7,181
	10	145,269	42,725	4,005	0
	11	146,604	41,896	(830)	(4,835)
	12	159,274	43,231	1,335	2,165

Below are the key cell formulas used in the creation of Table 14.4.

Function	Cell	Formula	Copied to
Variance	D6	=VAR(D17:D52)	E6:G6
Index	D7	=D6/$D6	E7:G7
Indicator	D11	=IF(D7=MIN($D7:$G7),"++++++","")	E11:G11
Differences Between Same Month	E29	=D29-D17	E30:E52
First Differences Between Differences	F30	=E30-E29	F31:F52
Second Differences Between Differences	G31	=F31-F30	G32:G52

The chart in Figure 14.6 graphically demonstrates the results shown in cells D7:G7 of Table 14.4—the variance of the differences between months and the variance of the first difference between differences is smaller than the variance of the actual data. In the chart, the actual data points do not cluster at all around their average, while the differences between the same months in each year do cluster around their mean, and the first difference between differences cluster even more so around their mean. As long as the variance in cell E6 in Table 14.4 is smaller than the variance in cell D6, we have seasonality. If the variances in cells F6:G6 are smaller than the variance in cell D6, we have varying degrees of trend, from moderate to strong. We will now apply these procedures to our Urban Food Store data series in Table 14.5 and Figure 14.7.

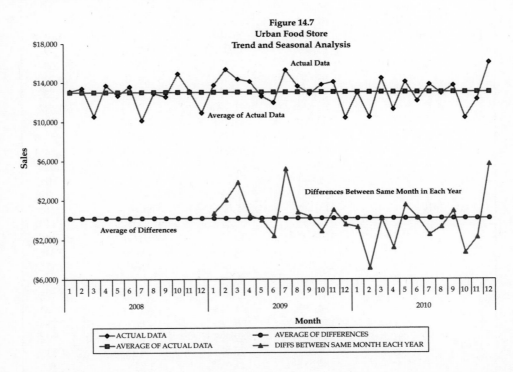

Figure 14.7
Urban Food Store
Trend and Seasonal Analysis

Table 14.5
Urban Food Store
Monthly Trend and Seasonal Analysis:

		Actual	DBM	DBD-1	DBD-2
Variance		2,251,330	5,872,336	11,097,707	29,769,660
Index		100%	261%	493%	1322%
Trend		None	None	Moderate	Strong
Seasonal?		No	Yes	Yes	Yes
Indicator		++++++			

Year	Month	Actual Same Month Data	Differences Between Each Year	First Difference Between Differences	Second Difference Between Differences
2008	1	13,026			
	2	13,339			
	3	10,513			
	4	13,635			
	5	12,597			
	6	13,505			
	7	10,107			
	8	12,808			
	9	12,480			
	10	14,867			
	11	13,020			
	12	10,856			
2009	1	13,644	618		
	2	15,318	1,978	1,360	
	3	14,290	3,777	1,799	439
	4	14,031	396	(3,381)	(5,180)
	5	12,516	(81)	(478)	2,903
	6	11,870	(1,635)	(1,553)	(1,076)
	7	15,234	5,127	6,762	8,315
	8	13,529	722	(4,405)	(11,167)
	9	12,755	276	(446)	3,959
	10	13,689	(1,177)	(1,453)	(1,007)
	11	13,979	958	2,135	3,588
	12	10,348	(507)	(1,465)	(3,601)
2010	1	12,870	(775)	(267)	1,198
	2	10,418	(4,900)	(4,125)	(3,858)
	3	14,381	91	4,991	9,116
	4	11,202	(2,829)	(2,920)	(7,911)
	5	13,996	1,480	4,309	7,229
	6	12,036	166	(1,314)	(5,624)
	7	13,716	(1,519)	(1,684)	(370)
	8	12,791	(739)	780	2,465
	9	13,612	857	1,595	815
	10	10,348	(3,341)	(4,198)	(5,793)
	11	12,192	(1,787)	1,554	5,752
	12	15,984	5,636	7,422	5,868

The output in Table 14.5 and Figure 14.7 confirms our earlier analysis—there is neither trend nor seasonality in the data. All the difference variances in cells E7:G7 are greater than the variance of the actual data as shown in Table 14.5. In Figure 14.7 the actual data cluster more tightly around their mean, while there is more dispersion about the average line for the data points for differences between the same month in each year. With the presentation of Figure 14.7, we are just about finished with our preliminary data analysis for forecasting. However, we have one more test to run on the Urban Food Store time series data.

Testing for Seasonality and Trend with a Regression Model

That final test consists of a multiple regression model that has trend and a seasonal index as its independent variables and monthly sales as its dependent variable. We have already run this test for trend as a bivariate model in Table 14.2, and we found that we could not reject the null hypothesis that the coefficient was essentially equal to zero. This time we wish to include trend in a multivariate model with seasonal index to make sure that our bivariate model results for trend do not change when another factor that might affect monthly sales is included along with it in a model. The first thing we need to do is create and then optimize the seasonal indexes in Figure 14.8.[5]

Below are the key cell formulas used in the creation of Figure 14.8.

Function	Cell	Formula	Copied to
Linear Trend	F8	=+$M$42+$L$42*D8	F9:F45
Actual as % of Trend	G8	=+E8/F8	G9:G45
Seasonal Forecast	H8	=F8*VLOOKUP(C8,$F$51:$J$62,5)	H9:H45
Unadjusted Seasonal Index	G51	=SUMIF($C$8:$C$45,F51,$G$8:$G$45)/ COUNTIF($C$8:$C$45,F51)	G52:G62
Normalizing Factor	H51	=12/$G$64	H52:H62
Adjusted Seasonal Index	I51	=+G51*H51	I52:I62
Optimized Seasonal Index	J51	=I51	J52:J62
LINEST Array	L37:M41	{=LINEST(E8:E45,D8:D45,TRUE,TRUE)}	–
Optimized Trend	L42	=L37	–
Optimized Intercept	M42	=M37	–
RootMean Squared Error (RMSE)	M44	=SQRT(SUMXMY2(E8:E45,$H$8:$H$45)/ (COUNT(E8:E45)-2))	–

Next we run Solver, instructing it to minimize cell P37 by changing cells L42:M42 and cells J51:J62, while constraining cell J64 to equal 1. The results are shown in Figure 14.8 and include in cells J51:J62 the optimized seasonal indexes that we will incorporate in our multivariate regression model in Figure 14.9.

Figure 14.8
Urban Food Store
Monthly Sales
Calculation of Optimized Seasonal Indexes

Year	Month	Trend	Actual Sales	Linear Trend	Actual as a % of Trend	Seasonal Forecast
2008	1	1	13,026	12,864	101.3%	12,986
	2	2	13,339	12,868	103.7%	12,819
	3	3	10,513	12,870	81.7%	13,037
	4	4	13,635	12,872	105.9%	12,928
	5	5	12,597	12,875	97.9%	13,011
	6	6	13,505	12,877	104.9%	12,444
	7	7	10,107	12,877	78.5%	12,995
	8	8	12,808	12,879	99.4%	13,016
	9	9	12,480	12,881	96.9%	12,923
	10	10	14,867	12,883	115.4%	12,938
	11	11	13,020	12,886	101.0%	13,036
	12	12	10,856	12,886	84.2%	12,374
2009	1	13	13,644	12,890	105.9%	13,012
	2	14	15,318	12,892	118.8%	12,845
	3	15	14,290	12,894	110.8%	13,064
	4	16	14,031	12,897	108.8%	12,954
	5	17	12,516	12,899	97.0%	13,037
	6	18	11,870	12,901	92.0%	13,022
	7	19	15,234	12,903	118.1%	13,042
	8	20	13,529	12,905	104.8%	12,950
	9	21	12,755	12,908	98.8%	12,965
	10	22	13,689	12,910	106.0%	13,063
	11	23	13,979	12,912	108.3%	13,039
	12	24	10,348	12,914	80.1%	12,399
2010	1	25	12,670	12,916	99.6%	12,872
	2	26	10,418	12,918	80.6%	13,091
	3	27	14,381	12,921	111.3%	12,981
	4	28	11,202	12,923	86.7%	13,064
	5	29	13,996	12,925	108.3%	12,495
	6	30	12,036	12,927	93.1%	13,048
	7	31	13,716	12,929	106.1%	13,069
	8	32	12,791	12,932	98.9%	12,976
	9	33	13,612	12,934	105.2%	12,991
	10	34	10,348	12,936	80.0%	13,090
	11	35	12,192	12,938	94.2%	12,425
	12	36	15,984	12,940	123.5%	13,066
2011	1	37	12,565	12,943	97.1%	12,898
	2	38	12,367	12,945	95.5%	

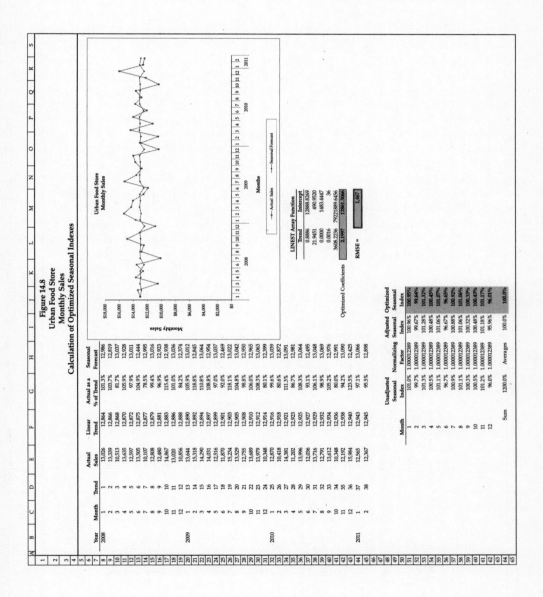

Urban Food Store Monthly Sales

— Actual Sales   — Seasonal Forecast

LINEST Array Function

	Trend	Intercept
	0.8886	12888.8269
	21.9451	490.9520
	0.0000	1483.4447
	3608.2236	36
	79221889.6456	12861.3066
Optimized Coefficients	2.1997	12861.3066

RMSE = 1,467

Month	Unadjusted Seasonal Index	Normalizing Factor	Adjusted Seasonal Index	Optimized Seasonal Index
1	101.0%	1.000012389	100.96%	100.95%
2	99.7%	1.000012389	99.67%	99.64%
3	101.3%	1.000012389	101.28%	101.32%
4	100.5%	1.000012389	100.48%	100.45%
5	101.1%	1.000012389	101.06%	101.07%
6	96.7%	1.000012389	96.67%	96.65%
7	100.9%	1.000012389	100.88%	100.92%
8	101.1%	1.000012389	101.06%	101.06%
9	100.3%	1.000012389	100.32%	100.39%
10	100.5%	1.000012389	100.48%	100.43%
11	101.2%	1.000012389	101.18%	101.17%
12	96.0%	1.000012389	95.96%	96.01%
Sum 1200.0%	Averages 100.0%		100.0%	100.0%

247

Figure 14.9
Urban Food Store
Monthly Sales
Significance Testing of Trend and Seasonal Factor

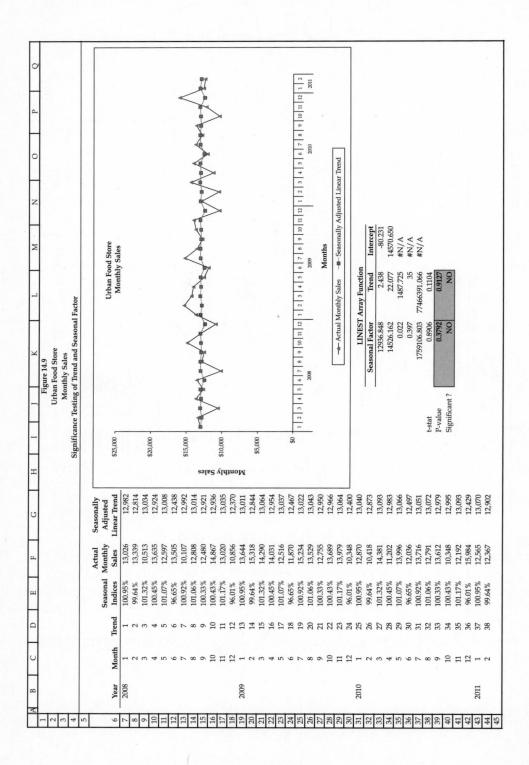

Urban Food Store
Monthly Sales

Year	Month	Trend	Seasonal Indices	Actual Monthly Sales	Seasonally Adjusted Linear Trend
2008	1	1	100.95%	13,026	12,982
	2	2	99.64%	13,339	12,814
	3	3	101.32%	10,513	13,034
	4	4	100.45%	13,635	12,924
	5	5	101.07%	12,597	13,008
	6	6	96.65%	13,505	12,438
	7	7	100.92%	10,107	12,992
	8	8	101.06%	12,808	13,014
	9	9	100.33%	12,480	12,921
	10	10	100.43%	14,867	12,936
	11	11	101.17%	13,020	13,035
	12	12	96.01%	10,856	12,370
2009	1	13	100.95%	13,644	13,011
	2	14	99.64%	15,318	12,844
	3	15	101.32%	14,290	13,064
	4	16	100.45%	14,031	12,954
	5	17	101.07%	12,516	13,037
	6	18	96.65%	11,870	12,467
	7	19	100.92%	15,234	13,022
	8	20	101.06%	13,529	13,043
	9	21	100.33%	12,755	12,950
	10	22	100.43%	13,689	12,966
	11	23	101.17%	13,979	13,064
	12	24	96.01%	10,348	12,400
2010	1	25	100.95%	12,870	13,040
	2	26	99.64%	10,418	12,873
	3	27	101.32%	14,381	13,093
	4	28	100.45%	11,202	12,983
	5	29	101.07%	13,996	13,066
	6	30	96.65%	12,036	12,497
	7	31	100.92%	13,716	13,051
	8	32	101.06%	12,791	13,072
	9	33	100.33%	13,612	12,979
	10	34	100.43%	10,348	12,995
	11	35	101.17%	12,192	13,093
	12	36	96.01%	15,984	12,429
2011	1	37	100.95%	12,565	13,070
	2	38	99.64%	12,367	12,902

LINEST Array Function

	Seasonal Factor	Trend	Intercept
	12936.848	2.438	-80.231
	14526.162	22.077	14570.650
	0.022	1487.725	#N/A
	0.397	35	#N/A
	1759106.803	77466391.066	#N/A
t-stat	0.8906	0.1104	
P-value	0.3792	0.9127	
Significant ?	NO	NO	

Below are the key cell formulas used in the creation of Figure 14.9.

Function	Cell	Formula	Copied to
Seasonally Adjusted Linear Trend	G7	=TREND($F$7:$F$44,$D$7:$E$44,D7:E7)	G8:G44
LINEST Array	K33:M37	{=LINEST(F7:F44,D7:E44,TRUE,TRUE)}	–
t-statistic	K38	=K33/K34	L38
p-value	K39	=T.DIST.2T(K38,$L$36)	L39
Significant?	K40	=IF(K39>0.05,"NO","YES")	L40

The results shown in Figure 14.9 confirm once again that the monthly time series data for the Urban Food Store are random, that is, they contain no trend or seasonal patterns. Both p-values are substantially greater than .05, forcing us to accept the null hypothesis that the trend and seasonal ·coefficients are effectively zero and therefore do not have to be considered when forecasting lost sales for the three-month loss period.

Conclusion

The purpose of all this analysis is more than just proving that monthly sales for the Urban Food Store are random; that is, they contain little or no trend or seasonality patterns. Indeed, the purpose is just the opposite—to provide you with the analytical tools necessary to not only detect trends and seasonal cycles in time series data, but to help determine the nature and strength of the trend. For example, if the amount of periodic growth in a trend is constant, then we have a linear trend. If the amount of periodic growth grows over time, then we have an exponential trend. If the amount of periodic growth in a trend slows down over time, then we have a damped-exponential trend.

The type and strength of a trend will determine what forecasting technique you use to get the best forecast results. For example, if your data shows no trend, like that of the Urban Food Store, averages, moving averages, or exponential smoothing are the best forecasting techniques.

If you are dealing only with annual data, a situation that is fairly uncommon in commercial damages, then you don't have to worry about seasonality. But if the period of loss is measured in months, then the issue of seasonality in the data needs to be investigated, otherwise your forecasted trend could be distorted. We urge you to get into the habit of testing your data before forecasting. While charts have a place in this testing, only statistical analysis will sufficiently detect and analyze trends and seasonal patterns.

In the next chapter we return to the Urban Food Store time series data and run through various forecasting techniques that are appropriate for random data.

Notes

1. The test statistic for the slope of the regression trendline follows the t distribution, while the test statistic for the expected number of runs follows the normal distribution. Hence, the different formulas for computing the respective p-values of each test statistic.

2. Ibid.
3. Ibid.
4. "How to Detect Trends and Seasonal Cycles," *Lotus*, Vol. 4, No. 5 (May, 1988), pp. 44–50.
5. Additional information can be found in J. M. Wooldridge, *Econometric Analysis of Cross Section and Panel Data*, 2nd ed. (Cambridge, MA: Massachusetts Institute of Technology, 2010), chap. 6.

CHAPTER 15

Case Study 15—Determining Lost Sales with Stationary Time Series Data

As promised in the previous chapter, we now return to the Urban Food Store time series data and run through various forecasting techniques that are appropriate for random data that are stationary. This chapter uses time series forecasting methods that analyze the past behavior of the time series variable so that we can predict its future behavior.

As discussed in the introduction, in commercial damages cases this variable would always be sales, rather than lost profits. If we can uncover some sort of systematic behavior in past sales, we can model this behavior to assist us in forecasting future sales. Techniques that analyze past behavior of a time series variable to predict the future are sometimes called extrapolation models. All these models search for patterns in the historical series and then extrapolate these patterns into the future. The time-series regression models that we have previously introduced demonstrate extrapolation techniques.

Prediction Errors and Their Measurement

After we build a model, we test it to see if it fits the historical data well; that is, how well does it "track" the known values of the time series? Specifically, we calculate the one-period-ahead predictions from the model and compare these to the known values for each observation in the historical time period. We attempt to find a model that produces small prediction errors, that is, small differences between the actual value and the prediction. We expect that if the model predicts the historical data well, it will also forecast future data well.

There are several summary measures of the prediction errors. In previous case studies, we have shown the use of RMSE (root mean square error). Two other widely used summary measures are MAD (mean absolute deviation), where the absolute errors are totaled and divided by the number of terms in the sum, and MAPE (mean absolute percent error), where each absolute error is divided by the actual value and then summed along with all the other quotients, with this total then divided by the number of terms in the sum. Most of the time, models that make any one of these measures small tend to make the others small, so that we can choose whichever measure we want to minimize. As we shall see, we are sometimes able to choose the best model from a given class of methods by minimizing RMSE, MAD, or MAPE. In any case, small values of these measures only guarantee that the model predicts the historical observations well. There is still no guarantee that the model will forecast future values accurately.

Moving Averages

The easiest extrapolation method to use and understand is the moving average technique. To implement the moving average method, we need to choose a span, the number of terms in each moving average. If the data are monthly and we choose a span of six months, then the prediction of next month's value is the average of the most recent six months. For example we average January to June to predict July, we average February to July to predict August, and so on. This procession of moving six-month spans is the reason for the term *moving averages*.

The role of the span is important because if the span is large—say, 12 months—then many observations go into each average, and extreme values have relatively little effect on the predictions. The resulting series of predictions will be much smoother than the original series. (For this reason, the moving average method is called a smoothing method.) In contrast, if the span is small—say, three months—then extreme observations have a larger effect on the predictions, and the prediction series will be less smooth. In the extreme, if the span is one, there is no smoothing at all. The method simply predicts next month's value to be the same as the current month's value. (This is often called the naïve predicting method.)

Let's turn to Table 15.1 and see how the spreadsheet is set up and what formulas are used in key cells by focusing first on the two-month moving average found in column F. Then we can deal with the question of span size.

Below are the key cell formulas used in column F in Figure 15.1.

Function	Cell	Formula	Copy To
2-Month Moving Average	F9	=AVERAGE(E7:E8)	F10:F44
Root Mean Squared Error (RMSE)	F46	=SQRT(SUMXMY2(E9:E44,F9:F44)/ COUNT(F9:F44))	–
Mean Absolute Deviation (MAD) (Array Function)	F47	{=SUM(ABS(E9:E44-F9:F44))/ COUNT(F9:F44)}	–
Mean Absolute Percent Error (MAPE) (Array Function)	F48	{=(SUM(ABS(E9:E44-F9:F44)/E9:E44))/ COUNT(F9:F44)}	–

Unfortunately, none of the above formulas can be copied across the spreadsheet to populate the three-month to 12-month moving average prediction columns. Instead, the formulas for each column must be entered individually. For example, the three-month moving average formula in cell G10 just extends the formula in cell F9 to =AVERAGE(E7:E9), which is then copied down to cell G44, and so on for each succeeding span of moving averages. The same holds true for the formulas for RMSE, MAD, and MAPE. In cells G46, G47, and G48 we would move the starting point of each range down by one row and substitute E10 and G10 for E9 and F9. This process would continue across the spreadsheet from columns H to P, each time lowering the starting point of each range by one row.

Table 15.1

Urban Food Store

Monthly Sales

2-Month to 12-Month Moving Averages

Year	Month	Time Period	Monthly Sales	2-Month Moving Average Predictions	3-Month Moving Average Predictions	4-Month Moving Average Predictions	5-Month Moving Average Predictions	6-Month Moving Average Predictions	7-Month Moving Average Predictions	8-Month Moving Average Predictions	9-Month Moving Average Predictions	10-Month Moving Average Predictions	11-Month Moving Average Predictions	12-Month Moving Average Predictions	Forecast 4-Month	Forecast 10-Month
2008	1	1	13,026													
	2	2	13,339													
	3	3	10,513	13,183												
	4	4	13,635	11,926	12,293											
	5	5	12,597	12,074	12,496	12,628										
	6	6	13,505	13,116	12,248	12,521	12,622									
	7	7	10,107	13,051	13,246	12,562	12,718	12,769								
	8	8	12,808	11,806	12,070	12,461	12,071	12,283	12,389							
	9	9	12,480	11,458	12,140	12,254	12,530	12,194	12,358	12,441						
	10	10	14,867	12,644	11,798	12,225	12,299	12,522	12,235	12,373	12,446					
	11	11	13,020	13,673	13,385	12,565	12,753	12,727	12,857	12,564	12,650	12,688				
	12	12	10,856	13,944	13,456	13,294	12,656	12,798	12,769	12,877	12,615	12,687	12,718			
2009	1	13	13,644	11,938	12,914	12,806	12,806	12,356	12,520	12,530	12,653	12,439	12,521	12,563		
	2	14	15,318	12,250	12,507	13,097	12,973	12,946	12,540	12,661	12,654	12,752	12,548	12,614		
	3	15	14,290	14,481	13,273	13,210	13,541	13,364	13,285	12,887	12,956	12,920	12,985	12,779		
	4	16	14,031	14,804	14,418	13,527	13,426	13,666	13,496	13,410	13,043	13,089	13,045	13,094		
	5	17	12,516	14,161	14,547	14,321	13,628	13,527	13,718	13,563	13,479	13,142	13,175	13,127		
	6	18	11,870	13,274	13,613	14,039	13,960	13,443	13,382	13,568	13,447	13,383	13,085	13,120		
	7	19	15,234	12,193	12,806	13,177	13,605	13,612	13,218	13,193	13,379	13,289	13,245	12,984		
	8	20	13,529	13,552	13,207	13,413	13,588	13,877	13,844	13,470	13,420	13,565	13,466	13,411		
	9	21	12,755	14,382	13,545	13,287	13,436	13,579	13,827	13,804	13,477	13,431	13,562	13,471		
	10	22	13,689	13,142	13,840	13,347	13,181	13,323	13,461	13,693	13,688	13,404	13,370	13,494		
	11	23	13,979	13,222	13,325	13,802	13,416	13,266	13,375	13,490	13,693	13,688	13,430	13,396		
	12	24	10,348	13,834	13,474	13,488	13,837	13,509	13,368	13,451	13,544	13,721	13,714	13,476		
2010	1	25	12,870	12,164	12,399	12,693	12,860	13,256	13,058	12,990	13,106	13,224	13,415	13,434		
	2	26	10,418	11,609	12,672	12,722	12,728	12,862	13,201	13,034	12,977	13,082	13,192	13,369		
	3	27	14,381	11,644	11,212	11,904	12,261	12,343	12,513	12,853	12,744	12,721	12,840	12,961		
	4	28	11,202	12,399	12,556	12,004	12,399	12,614	12,634	12,746	13,023	12,907	12,872	12,968		
	5	29	13,996	12,792	12,000	12,218	11,844	12,200	12,412	12,455	12,575	12,840	12,752	12,733		
	6	30	12,036	12,599	13,193	12,499	12,573	12,202	12,456	12,610	12,626	12,717	12,946	12,856		
	7	31	13,716	13,016	12,411	12,904	12,406	12,484	12,179	12,404	12,546	12,567	12,655	12,870		
	8	32	12,791	12,876	13,249	12,737	13,066	12,625	12,660	12,371	12,549	12,663	12,672	12,743		
	9	33	13,612	13,253	12,847	13,134	12,748	13,020	12,648	12,676	12,417	12,574	12,675	12,682		
	10	34	10,348	13,201	13,373	13,038	13,230	12,892	13,105	12,769	12,780	12,537	12,668	12,753		
	11	35	12,192	11,980	12,250	12,617	12,500	12,750	12,529	12,760	12,500	12,537	12,338	12,475		
	12	36	15,984	11,270	12,051	12,236	12,532	12,449	12,670	12,486	12,697	12,469	12,505	12,326		
2011	1	37	12,565	14,088	12,841	13,034	12,985	13,107	12,954	13,084	12,875	13,026	12,789	12,795		
	2	38	12,367	14,274	13,580	12,772	12,940	12,915	13,030	12,905	13,026	12,844	12,984	12,770		
	3	39													13,277	12,961
	4	40													13,548	12,857
	5	41													12,939	12,939
			RMSE	1,887.4	1,802.1	1,609.7	1,616.1	1,580.4	1,588.9	1,595.0	1,584.2	1,553.1	1,596.5	1,603.0		
			MAD	1,512.2	1,429.3	1,224.8	1,272.6	1,268.2	1,258.9	1,281.1	1,279.5	1,232.6	1,281.5	1,256.7		
			MAPE	12.04%	11.30%	9.75%	10.16%	10.13%	9.88%	10.05%	10.06%	9.77%	10.16%	9.86%		

Forecast Total: 39,764   38,757

Array Formulas

In addition, cells F47 and F48 are single-cell array formulas. To quote Excel's Help feature:

> *If you've done even a little programming, you've probably run across the term ar-*
> *ray. For our purposes, an array is a collection of items. In Excel, those items*
> *can reside in a single row (called a one-dimensional horizontal array), a*
> *column (a one-dimensional vertical array), or multiple rows and columns (a*
> *two-dimensional array). You cannot create three-dimensional arrays or array*
> *formulas in Excel.*
>
> *An array formula is a formula that can perform multiple calculations on one or*
> *more of the items in an array. Array formulas can return either multiple results*
> *or a single result. For example, you can place an array formula in a range of cells*
> *and use the array formula to calculate a column or row of subtotals. You can*
> *also place an array formula in a single cell and then calculate a single amount.*
> *An array formula that resides in multiple cells is called a multi-cell formula, and*
> *an array formula that resides in a single cell is called a single-cell formula.*

If you have ever used Excel's SUMPRODUCT formula, you have availed yourself of a ready-made single-cell array formula. For example, if we apply the SUMPRODUCT formula to the range A1:A5 that contains 5, 4, 3, 2, 1 and the range B1:B5 that contains 1, 2, 3, 4, 5, the result is 35. Using the array formula {=sum(A1:A5*B1:B5)} we obtain the same result. The trick to remember when using array formulas is to hold down the keys Control, Shift, and Enter simultaneously after creating the formula, rather than pressing just the Enter key. The benefit of array formulas is that we can do all the calculations in one cell. For example, for cell F48, rather than first calculating the absolute difference in one column, and then dividing it by the actual value in another column, and then summing that column of percentage errors, and then dividing the total percentage errors by the number of terms in the sum, we can perform all these functions in one cell with an array formula.

Since two of our summary measures of prediction error indicate that the four-month moving average best fits the historical data, and the remaining summary measure indicates that the 10-month moving average is the superior model, we have created three-month forecasts for both spans in columns Q and R of Table 15.1. Below are the key cell formulas used in columns Q and R in Table 15.1.

Function	Cell	Formula	Copy To
4-Month MA Forecast March 2011	Q45	=AVERAGE(E41:E44)	–
4-Month MA Forecast April 2011	Q46	=SUM((E42+E43+E44)+Q45)/4	–
4-Month MA Forecast May 2011	Q47	=SUM((+E43+E44)+Q45+Q46)/4	–
10-Month MA Forecast March 2011	R45	=AVERAGE(E35:E44)	–
10-Month MA Forecast April 2011	R46	=(SUM(E36:E44)+R45)/10	–
10-Month MA Forecast May 2011	R47	=(SUM(E37:E44)+R45+R46)/10	–

Notice that as we exhaust the historical data in each span, we substitute a forecasted value in the formula. With this technique we can forecast beyond one

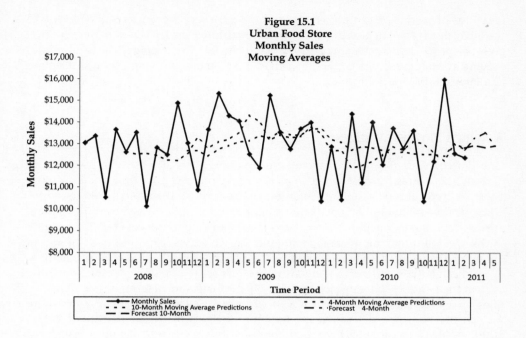

Figure 15.1
Urban Food Store
Monthly Sales
Moving Averages

period in the future. Of course, as we replace historical values with forecasted values the uncertainty surrounding the forecast increases.

Turning now to Figure 15.1, we can compare the effect of span size on the predictions and the forecasts. The predictions with the span 4 appear to track the data better, where the prediction series with the span 10 is considerably smoother—it reacts less to the ups and downs of the series. This is also true of the three-month forecast period—the 10-month moving average forecast is much smoother than the four-month forecast. The summary measures MAD and MAPE confirm that moving averages with span 4 predict the known observations better, but probably not enough to make a difference. Even if they were significantly better, there is no guarantee that a span of 4 is superior for forecasting future values. But why isn't the summary measure RMSE also the lowest for span 4 moving average predictions?

The answer to that question is included in the answer to this question: What span should we use? This requires some judgment. If we believe that the ups and downs in the series are random noise, then we don't want future forecasts to react too quickly to these ups and downs, and we should use a relatively large span. But if we want to track every little zigzag—under the belief that each up and down is predictable—then we should use a smaller span. We shouldn't be fooled by a plot of the (smoothed) predicted series superimposed on the original series. This graph almost always looks better when a small span is used, because the predicted series appears to track the original series better. Does this mean it always provides a better future forecast? Not necessarily. There is little point in tracking random ups and downs closely if they represent unpredictable noise.

Since we know from the tests we ran in Chapter 14 that the Urban Food Store monthly sales data contains little or no trend or seasonal patterns and therefore consists mainly of random noise, we should not be surprised that all three summary measures of prediction error are not in agreement. This is because the RMSE is more sensitive than other measures to the occasional large error: The squaring process gives disproportionate weight to very large errors. On average, the four-month moving average produces larger errors than the 10-month moving average, resulting in a larger RMSE for the former.

Weighted Moving Averages

One drawback of the moving average technique is that all past data used in calculating the average are weighted equally. However, we can often obtain a more accurate prediction by assigning different weights to each period included in the average. The weighted moving average technique is a simple variation on the moving average technique that allows for weights to be assigned to the data being averaged. In the weighted moving average technique the weights assigned to each period in the moving average are always a number between 0 and 1 and in total sum to 1.

Although the weighted moving average offers greater flexibility than the moving average, it is also a bit more complicated. In addition to determining a span, we must also determine values for each of the weights. However, for a given span, we can use Solver to determine the optimum weights that minimize either RMSE, MAPE, or MAD. In Table 15.2 we show the spreadsheet implementation of a series of weighted moving averages that range from a two-month span to a 12-month span for the Urban Food Store data. Let's begin to build some understanding of the technique by focusing first on the two-month weighted moving average prediction model.

Cells F53 and F54 represent the weights for the two months in the moving average. Cell F65 contains the sum of cells F53 and F54. Below are the key cell formulas used in column F in Table 15.2.

Function	Cell	Formula	Copy To
2-Month Weighted MA	F9	=$F$53*E8+$F$54*E7	F10:F44
RMSE	F46	=SQRT(SUMXMY2(E9:E44,F9:F44)/COUNT(F9:F44))	–
MAD	F47	{=SUM(ABS(E9:E44-F9:F44))/COUNT(F9:F44)}	–
MAPE	F48	{=(SUM(ABS(E9:E44-F9:F44)/E9:E44))/COUNT(F9:F44)}	–

Unfortunately, none of the above formulas can be copied across the spreadsheet to populate the three-month to 12-month weighted moving average prediction columns. Instead, the formulas for each column must be entered individually. For example, the three-month weighted moving average formula in cell G10 just extends the formula in cell F9 to pick up an additional weight to match the additional period (e.g., =$G$53*E9+$G$54*E8+$G$55*E7), which is then copied down to cell G44, and so on for each succeeding span of weighted moving averages. RMSE, MAD, and MAPE, located in cells G46, G47, and G48, have the starting point of each range moved down by one row and substitute E10 and G10 for E9 and F9. This process would continue across the spreadsheet from columns H to P, each time lowering the starting point of each range by one row. As discussed above in the section on moving averages, cells F47 and F48 are single-cell array formulas.

For the two-month weighted moving average, we can use Solver to optimize the weights in cells F53 and F54 and thereby minimize RMSE (or your summary measure of prediction error of choice). The Solver parameters would be to minimize cell F46 by changing cells F53:F54, subject to the following constraints: F53:F54 <=1, F53:F54 >= 0, F65 = 1.

If the weights in cells F53 and F54 were equal, that is, .5 each, then the RMSE value in cell F46 would be identical to the simple moving average method shown in cell F46 of Table 15.1. Notice that the optimal weights are now .425 and .575, which reduces the value of the RMSE only slightly, from 1887.4 to 1879.4.

We can use the weighted moving technique to forecast more than one time period into the future. However, as with the moving average technique, we must substitute forecasted values for unobserved actual values where needed. Since all three of our summary measures of prediction error indicate that a different moving average best fits the historical data, we have created three-month forecasts for the 6-month, 10-month, and 12-month spans in columns Q, R, and S of Table 15.2. Below are the key cell formulas used in those columns.

Function	Cell	Formula	Copy To
5-Month WMA Forecast March 2011	Q45	=$I$53*E44+$I$54*E43+$I$55*E42+ $I$56*E41+$I$57*E40	–
5-Month WMA Forecast April 2011	Q46	=$I$53*Q45+$I$54*E44+$I$55*E43+ $I$56*E42+$I$57*E41	–
5-Month WMA Forecast May 2011	Q47	=$I$53*Q45+$I$54*Q46+$I$55*E44+ $I$56*E43+$I$57*E42	–
10-Month WMA Forecast March 2011	R45	=$N$53*E44+$N$54*E43+$N$55*E42+ $N$56*E41+$N$57*E40+$N$58*E39+ $N$59*E38+$N$60*E37+$N$61*E36+ $N$62*E35	–
10-Month WMA Forecast April 2011	R46	=$N$53*R45+$N$54*E44+$N$55*E43+ $N$56*E42+$N$57*E41+$N$58*E40+ $N$59*E39+$N$60*E38+$N$61*E37+ $N$62*E36	–
10-Month WMA Forecast May 2011	R47	=$N$53*R45+$N$54*R46+$N$55*E44+ $N$56*E43+$N$57*E42+$N$58*E41+ $N$59*E40+$N$60*E39+$N$61*E38+ $N$62*E37	–
12-Month WMA Forecast March 2011	S45	=$P$53*E44+$P$54*E43+$P$55*E42+ $P$56*E41+$P$57*E40+$P$58*E39+ $P$59*E38+$P$60*E37+$P$61*E36+ $P$62*E35+$P$63*E34+$P$64*E33	–
12-Month WMA Forecast April 2011	S46	=$P$53*S45+$P$54*E44+$P$55*E43+ $P$56*E42+$P$57*E41+$P$58*E40+ $P$59*E39+$P$60*E38+$P$61*E37+ $P$62*E36+$P$63*E35+$P$64*E34	–
12-Month WMA Forecast May 2011	S47	=$P$53*S45+$P$54*S46+$P$55*E44+ $P$56*E43+$P$57*E42+$P$58*E41+ $P$59*E40+$P$60*E39+$P$61*E38+ $P$62*E37+$P$63*E36+$P$64*E35	–

Table 15.2
Urban Food Store
Monthly Sales
2-Month to 12-Month Weighted Moving Averages

Year	Month	Time Period	Monthly Sales	2-Month Weighted Moving Average Predictions	3-Month Weighted Moving Average Predictions	4-Month Weighted Moving Average Predictions	5-Month Weighted Moving Average Predictions	6-Month Weighted Moving Average Predictions	7-Month Weighted Moving Average Predictions	8-Month Weighted Moving Average Predictions	9-Month Weighted Moving Average Predictions	10-Month Weighted Moving Average Predictions	11-Month Weighted Moving Average Predictions	12-Month Weighted Moving Average Predictions	Forecast 5-Month	Forecast 10-Month	Forecast 12-Month
2008	1	1	13,026														
	2	2	13,339														
	3	3	10,513	13,159													
	4	4	13,635	12,139	12,491												
	5	5	12,597	11,839	12,133	12,680											
	6	6	13,505	13,194	12,496	13,032	13,284										
	7	7	10,107	12,983	13,127	11,657	11,732	11,978									
	8	8	12,808	12,062	12,339	12,951	12,647	12,772	12,709								
	9	9	12,480	11,254	11,770	12,242	12,483	12,219	12,199	12,209							
	10	10	14,867	12,668	11,976	12,916	13,107	13,257	13,165	13,169	13,314						
	11	11	13,020	13,493	13,214	11,555	11,574	11,715	11,884	11,885	12,130	12,153					
	12	12	10,856	14,083	13,712	13,200	12,383	12,400	12,380	12,371	12,206	12,190	12,230				
2009	1	13	13,644	12,101	12,944	12,524	12,630	11,982	11,971	11,971	12,168	12,214	12,223	12,208			
	2	14	15,318	12,040	12,203	13,757	13,489	13,564	13,450	13,448	13,276	13,236	13,320	13,262			
	3	15	14,290	14,355	13,329	13,323	13,700	13,341	13,277	13,274	13,153	13,194	13,176	13,089			
	4	16	14,031	14,881	14,580	12,489	12,291	12,640	12,838	12,836	12,110	13,132	12,065	12,233			
	5	17	12,516	14,180	14,503	13,972	12,962	12,832	12,831	12,813	13,040	13,022	13,063	13,248			
	6	18	11,870	13,388	13,694	14,535	14,566	13,677	13,500	13,502	12,985	13,030	13,136	13,168			
	7	19	15,234	12,242	12,759	13,544	14,238	14,303	14,294	14,296	14,284	14,285	14,281	14,131			
	8	20	13,529	13,299	12,955	13,690	13,770	14,334	14,348	14,339	14,051	14,011	14,012	13,918			
	9	21	12,755	14,510	13,849	13,135	13,424	13,456	13,493	13,498	12,732	12,764	12,744	12,839			
	10	22	13,689	13,201	13,790	12,614	12,350	12,690	12,847	12,853	13,144	13,131	13,074	13,126			
	11	23	13,979	13,152	13,220	14,372	13,826	13,516	13,431	13,426	14,146	14,112	14,179	14,190			
	12	24	10,348	13,812	13,510	13,565	14,053	13,516	13,455	13,467	13,390	13,440	13,435	13,328			
2010	1	25	12,870	12,437	12,920	12,676	13,131	13,651	13,756	13,751	13,967	13,947	13,892	13,914			
	2	26	10,418	11,419	12,027	12,955	12,847	13,288	13,301	13,294	13,112	13,065	13,098	13,011			
	3	27	14,381	11,828	11,515	12,882	13,637	13,512	13,377	13,392	12,923	12,934	12,980	12,948			

Forecast Comparison Table

Period	Actual	2-Month	3-Month	4-Month	5-Month	6-Month	7-Month	8-Month	9-Month	10-Month	11-Month	12-Month
4	11,202	12,101	12,161	11,230	11,482	12,145	12,350	12,367	13,061	13,039	12,905	12,686
5	13,996	13,031	12,433	12,673	12,366	12,574	12,514	12,506	13,277	13,239	13,236	13,407
6	12,036	12,389	12,830	11,485	11,324	11,071	11,193	11,207	11,296	11,333	11,280	11,181
7	13,716	13,163	12,698	13,656	13,134	12,963	12,797	12,790	13,444	13,411	13,474	13,625
8	12,791	12,749	13,028	12,005	12,303	11,840	11,913	11,914	12,053	12,110	12,054	11,901
9	13,612	13,323	13,004	13,580	13,125	13,378	13,315	13,304	12,808	12,773	12,841	13,020
10	10,348	13,139	13,267	12,577	12,755	12,346	12,378	12,374	12,199	12,247	12,227	12,157
11	12,192	12,226	12,506	13,072	13,148	13,361	13,332	13,331	12,684	12,667	12,721	12,855
12	15,984	11,131	11,743	12,306	12,635	12,733	12,752	12,752	13,029	13,019	13,005	12,817
2011 1	11,131	13,802	12,708	13,448	13,189	13,352	13,267	13,274	12,811	12,790	12,830	12,827
2	13,802	14,532	14,018	11,923	12,269	12,031	12,156	12,160	12,582	12,643	12,526	12,594
3	12,565											
4	12,367											

Out-of-sample forecasts

	10-Month	11-Month	12-Month
	11,730	12,407	12,553
	14,207	13,259	13,385
	13,800	12,840	12,681
Forecast Total	39,737	38,506	38,619

Error Measures

	2-Month	3-Month	4-Month	5-Month	6-Month	7-Month	8-Month	9-Month	10-Month	11-Month	12-Month
RMSE	1,879.4	1,784.6	1,502.2	1,470.9	1,448.3	1,428.8	1,452.3	1,408.2	1,402.3	1,417.1	1,413.7
MAD	1,466.6	1,400.8	1,164.7	1,127.5	1,213.7	1,196.2	1,231.8	1,151.7	1,133.3	1,145.2	1,136.6
MAPE	11.67%	11.05%	9.28%	9.04%	9.73%	9.46%	9.74%	9.11%	9.03%	9.14%	8.97%

Weights

	2-Month Weights	3-Month Weights	4-Month Weights	5-Month Weights	6-Month Weights	7-Month Weights	8-Month Weights	9-Month Weights	10-Month Weights	11-Month Weights	12-Month Weights
Weight 1	0.425	0.270	0.162	0.021	0.000	0.000	0.000	0.000	0.000	0.000	0.000
Weight 2	0.575	0.455	0.188	0.167	0.039	0.034	0.032	0.033	0.046	0.043	0.090
Weight 3		0.275	0.086	0.000	0.009	0.036	0.034	0.000	0.000	0.000	0.007
Weight 4			0.565	0.526	0.443	0.381	0.378	0.301	0.295	0.331	0.336
Weight 5				0.286	0.247	0.256	0.259	0.068	0.082	0.073	0.025
Weight 6					0.262	0.294	0.292	0.295	0.279	0.267	0.275
Weight 7						0.000	0.000	0.000	0.000	0.000	0.000
Weight 8							0.004	0.000	0.000	0.000	0.000
Weight 9								0.302	0.000	0.286	0.267
Weight 10									0.298	0.000	0.000
Weight 11										0.000	0.000
Weight 12											0.000
Total	1.0	1.0	1.0	1.0	1.0	1.0	1.0	1.0	1.0	1.0	1.0

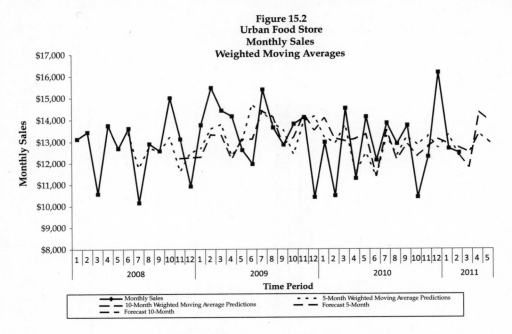

Figure 15.2
Urban Food Store
Monthly Sales
Weighted Moving Averages

In Figure 15.2, we can compare the effect of span size on the predictions and the forecasts. The predictions with the span 5 appear to track the data better, whereas the prediction series with the span 10 (we have excluded the span 12 data as it is almost identical to the span 10 data) is considerably smoother—it reacts less to the ups and downs of the series. This is also true of the three-month forecast period—the 10-month moving average forecast is much smoother than the five-month forecast. The same discussion concerning choice of span that was included in the section above on moving averages also applies to weighted moving averages.

Simple Exponential Smoothing

A possible criticism of both moving average methods is that they put equal weight on each value in a typical moving average when making a prediction. Even the weighted moving average method, which weights the individual observations in the weighted moving average, still places equal weight on the oldest weighted moving average as it does the newest. Most people would argue that if next month's forecast is to be based on the previous 12 months' observations, then more weight ought to be placed on the more recent observations.

Exponential smoothing is a method that addresses this criticism. It bases its predictions on a weighted average of past observations, with the ability to place more weight on the more recent observations. Since we are dealing in this chapter with data that exhibits no pronounced trend or seasonality in the series, simple exponential smoothing is a method of choice. In the next chapter, we will introduce more complicated exponential smoothing methods, such as Holt's, that deals with trend, and Winter's, which deals with both trend and seasonality.

Stated in basic terms, the predicted value for time period $t + 1$ in a simple exponential smoothing model is equal to the predicted value for the previous period plus an adjustment for the error made in predicting the previous period's value. The equation looks like this:

$$\hat{Y}_{t+1} = \hat{Y}_t + \hat{Y}\alpha(\hat{Y}_t - \hat{Y}_t)$$

where $\hat{Y}$ represents a predicted value, Y represents an actual value, and α is an adjusting factor.

The adjusting factor is called the smoothing constant, which is always between 0 and 1. Simple exponential smoothing has a single smoothing constant denoted by α. Small values of α tend to produce sluggish predictions that do not react quickly to changes in the data. A value of α near 1 produces predictions that react more quickly to changes in the data. Therefore, a constant of .9, for example, closely follows the series, while a constant of .2 produces a rather flat trendline through the actual data.

We can use Solver to determine the optimal value for α when building an exponential smoothing model for a particular time series. In Table 15.3 we instruct Solver to minimize cell J9 by changing cell J7, while constraining cell J7 to a value between 0 and 1. The result of implementing the optimized exponential smoothing forecasting model for the Urban Food Store data is shown in Table 15.3.

Every exponential smoothing method requires initial values, in this case the initial prediction in cell F7. There is no way to calculate this value because the previous month's sales are unknown. While there are many ways to initialize an exponential smoothing model, we have chosen the simplest method, and that is to assume that the first predicted value equals the first actual value. The effect of initializing in different ways is typically minimal because any effect of early data is usually washed out as we forecast into the future. Below are the key cell formulas used in Table 15.3.

Function	Cell	Formula	Copy To
Prediction	F7	=E7	–
Prediction	F8	=F7+$J$7*(E7-F7)	F9:F44
Forecast March 2011	G45	=F44+J7*(E44-F44)	–
Forecast April 2011	G46	=G45+J7*(G45-G45)	–
Forecast May 2011	G47	=G46+J7*(G46-G46)	–
RMSE	J9	=SQRT(SUMXMY2(E7:E44,F7:F44)/ COUNT(F7:F44))	–

Notice the optimal value of alpha in given in cell J7 as .01. Actually, if you create this model and run Solver, the optimal value is 0—we have changed it to .01 to create some variability in the predictions. Otherwise, all the predicted amounts in column F would have the same value—$13,026. We address why this is so in a moment. Figure 15.3 charts the actual data as well as the predicted and forecasted amounts.

Forecasted sales for period 39 in cell G45 is calculated as:

$$\hat{Y}_{39} = \hat{Y}_{38} + \alpha(Y_{38} - \hat{Y}_{38}) = 12,994 + .01 * (1,367 - 12,944) = 12,988$$

	Year	Month	Time Period	Monthly Sales	Exponential Smoothing Prediction	Exponential Smoothing Forecast				
1					Table 15.3					
2					Urban Food Store					
3					Monthly Sales					
4					Simple Exponential Smoothing					
5										
6										
7	2008	1	1	13,026	13,026			alpha	0.01	
8		2	2	13,339	13,026					
9		3	3	10,513	13,029			RMSE	1,454.6	
10		4	4	13,635	13,004					
11		5	5	12,597	13,010					
12		6	6	13,505	13,006					
13		7	7	10,107	13,011					
14		8	8	12,808	12,982					
15		9	9	12,480	12,980					
16		10	10	14,867	12,975					
17		11	11	13,020	12,994					
18		12	12	10,856	12,995					
19	2009	1	13	13,644	12,973					
20		2	14	15,318	12,980					
21		3	15	14,290	13,003					
22		4	16	14,031	13,016					
23		5	17	12,516	13,026					
24		6	18	11,870	13,021					
25		7	19	15,234	13,010					
26		8	20	13,529	13,032					
27		9	21	12,755	13,037					
28		10	22	13,689	13,034					
29		11	23	13,979	13,041					
30		12	24	10,348	13,050					
31	2010	1	25	12,870	13,023					
32		2	26	10,418	13,021					
33		3	27	14,381	12,995					
34		4	28	11,202	13,009					
35		5	29	13,996	12,991					
36		6	30	12,036	13,001					
37		7	31	13,716	12,992					
38		8	32	12,791	12,999					
39		9	33	13,612	12,997					
40		10	34	10,348	13,003					
41		11	35	12,192	12,976					
42		12	36	15,984	12,969					
43	2011	1	37	12,565	12,999					
44		2	38	12,367	12,994					
45		3	39			12,988				
46		4	40			12,988				
47		5	41			12,988				
48										
49					Forecast Total	38,964				
50										

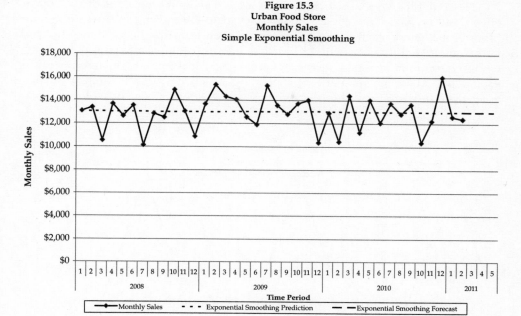

Figure 15.3
Urban Food Store
Monthly Sales
Simple Exponential Smoothing

An interesting property of the exponential smoothing technique becomes apparent when we try to use it to forecast more than one time period into the future. For example, suppose that at time period 38 we wish to forecast time periods 39 and 40. Because time period 39 is unknown at time period 38, we must substitute the forecasted value of time period 39 in the forecast equation. In fact, the forecast for all future time periods would equal that of time period 39, as can be seen in cell G45, G46, and G47 of Table 15.3. So when using exponential smoothing, the forecast for all future time periods equals the same value. This is consistent with the underlying idea of a stationary time series. If a time series is stationary (or has no trend), it is reasonable to assume that the forecast of the next time period and all future time periods should equal the same value, as the series is not really going anywhere but forward in a straight line, as can be seen in Figure 15.3.

In Figure 15.3 we see the obvious smoothing effect of a very small α level. The predictions don't track the series very well, but if the various zigzags in the original series are really random noise, then perhaps we don't want the predictions to track these random ups and downs too closely, as they would if we set α to .8. Maybe we instead prefer a prediction series that emphasizes the basic underlying pattern of no trend or seasonality.

Seasonality with Additive Effects

Many stationary time series variables exhibit seasonality, or a regular, repeating pattern in the data. For example, in time series data for monthly fuel oil sales, we would expect to see regular jumps in the data during winter months each year. Similarly, monthly or quarterly sales data for suntan lotion would likely show consistent peaks during the summer and valleys during the winter.

Two different types of seasonal effects are common in time series data: additive effects and multiplicative effects. Additive seasonal effects tend to be on the same order of magnitude each time a given season is encountered because the seasonal effects are added to each period's baseline amount. Multiplicative seasonal effects tend to have an increasing effect each time a given season is encountered because each period's baseline amount is multiplied by the seasonal effect. Figure 15.4 illustrates the difference between these two types of seasonal effects for stationary data.

Figure 15.4
Idealized Seasonal Effects

Additive Seasonal Effects

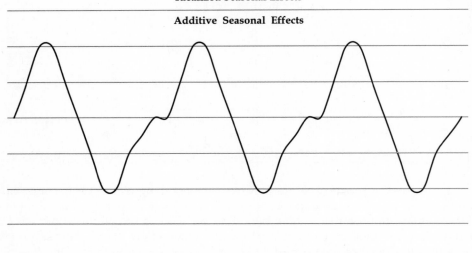

Time Period

Multiplicative Seasonal Effects

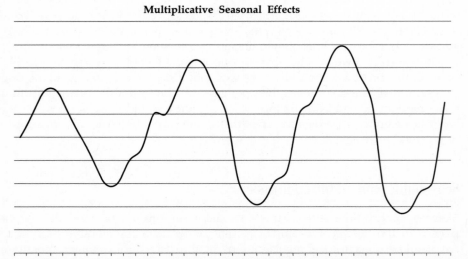

Time Period

Cumberland Climate Control sells and services residential and commercial heat pumps. Sales of heat pumps tend to be higher than average in winter and summer quarters when temperatures are more extreme. Similarly, sales tend to be lower than average in the spring and fall when temperatures are less extreme and property owners can put off replacing inoperable heat pump units. In early January 2011 the business suffered a fire that severely impacted its ability to sell and service heat pumps during the period of interruption that is expected to last through September 30, 2011. The first step in computing lost business income is to determine what sales would have been during quarters one, two, and three of 2011, absent the fire.

As always, we first graph our data in Figure 15.5, which chart indicates that sales tend to be high in quarters one and three, and low in quarters two and four, with no trend in the data. We can confirm these observations with the autocorrelation function, the runs test, and a significance test of the slope of the regression trendline. If we were to present their outputs, you would see that the autocorrelation function indicates that there is a strong correlation between observations one period apart, such that if we know one, we can predict the other. The runs test would show more runs than expected, indicating a lack of independence among the observations, and the slope of the regression line would not be statistically significant, confirming that there is no trend in the data. We leave it to our readers to perform these tests on their own.

We can now take the quarterly seasonal effects that the data exhibit and incorporate them into a model to make more accurate forecasts. The following equations generate the values in columns E, F, and G of the model shown in Figure 15.6.

The prediction equation in column G, beginning with cell G10, is:

$$\hat{Y}_{t+n} = L_t + S_{t+n-p}$$

The level equation in column E, beginning with cell E10, is:

$$L_t = \alpha(Y_t - S_{t-p}) + (1 - \alpha)L_{t-1}$$

And the seasonal factor equation in column F, beginning with cell F10, is:

$$S_t = \beta(Y_t - L_t) + (1 - \beta)S_{t-p}$$

In this model, L_t represents the expected level of the time series in period t if there were no random noise in the data, and S_t represents the seasonal factor for period t. The constant p represents the number of seasonal periods in the data. Thus, for quarterly data, $p = 4$ and for monthly data, $p = 12$. As usual, α and β can take on values between 0 and 1, but need not sum to 1. As customary, Y_t and $\hat{Y}_{t+n}$, represent, respectively, an actual value and a predicted value.

The prediction for time period $t + n$ is simply the expected level of the time series at period t adjusted upward or downward by the seasonal factor S_{t+n-p}. The expected level for period t is a weighted average of the deseasonalized data for period t $(Y_t - S_{t-p})$ and the previous period's level (L_{t-1}). The seasonal factor for period t is the weighted average of the estimated seasonal effects in period t $(Y_t - L_t)$ and the previous seasonal factor for that same season (S_{t-p}).

In order to kick start the model, we must initialize the estimated levels and seasonal factors for the first p time periods. There are numerous ways to do this, but let's take a simple approach and just use the average value of the first p time periods as the initial expected levels for each of these time periods. Then, let's use the difference between the actual values and expected levels as the initial seasonal

Figure 15.5
Stationary Data with Additive Seasonal Effects

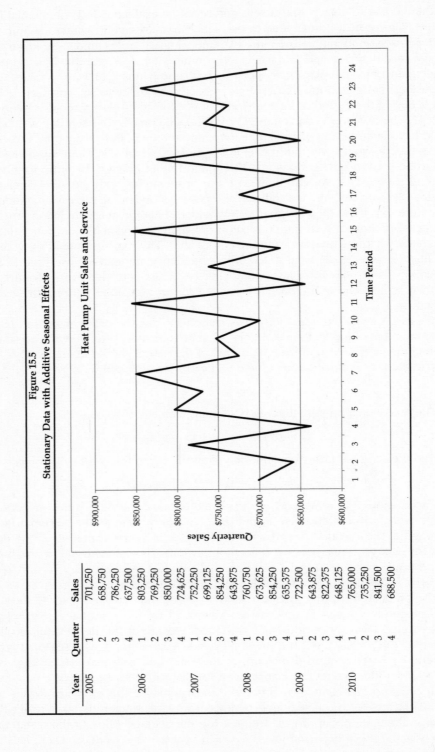

Heat Pump Unit Sales and Service

Year	Quarter	Sales
2005	1	701,250
	2	658,750
	3	786,250
	4	637,500
2006	1	803,250
	2	769,250
	3	850,000
	4	724,625
2007	1	752,250
	2	699,125
	3	854,250
	4	643,875
2008	1	760,750
	2	673,625
	3	854,250
	4	635,375
2009	1	722,500
	2	643,875
	3	822,375
	4	648,125
2010	1	765,000
	2	735,250
	3	841,500
	4	688,500

Figure 15.6

Stationary Data with Additive Seasonal Effects
Equal Level and Seasonal Factor Weights

alpha	0.5
beta	0.5

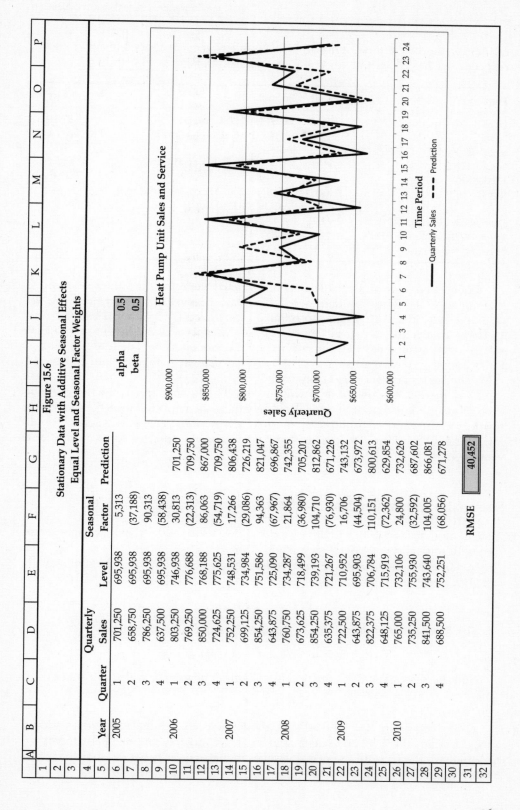

Heat Pump Unit Sales and Service

—— Quarterly Sales   ---- Prediction

Time Period

Quarterly Sales

Year	Quarter	Quarterly Sales	Level	Seasonal Factor	Prediction
2005	1	701,250	695,938	5,313	
	2	658,750	695,938	(37,188)	
	3	786,250	695,938	90,313	
	4	637,500	695,938	(58,438)	
2006	1	803,250	746,938	30,813	701,250
	2	769,250	776,688	(22,313)	709,750
	3	850,000	768,188	86,063	867,000
	4	724,625	775,625	(54,719)	709,750
2007	1	752,250	748,531	17,266	806,438
	2	699,125	734,984	(29,086)	726,219
	3	854,250	751,586	94,363	821,047
	4	643,875	725,090	(67,967)	696,867
2008	1	760,750	734,287	21,864	742,355
	2	673,625	718,499	(36,980)	705,201
	3	854,250	739,193	104,710	812,862
	4	635,375	721,267	(76,930)	671,226
2009	1	722,500	710,952	16,706	743,132
	2	643,875	695,903	(44,504)	673,972
	3	822,375	706,784	110,151	800,613
	4	648,125	715,919	(72,362)	629,854
2010	1	765,000	732,106	24,800	732,626
	2	735,250	755,930	(32,592)	687,602
	3	841,500	743,640	104,005	866,081
	4	688,500	752,251	(68,056)	671,278

RMSE	40,452

factors for the first p time periods. Cells J6 and J7 contain the values of α and β, respectively. Below are the key cell formulas used in Figures 15.6 and 15.7.

Function	Cell	Formula	Copy To
Level—1st 4 quarters	E6	=AVERAGE($D$6:$D$9)	E7:E9
Level	E10	=$J$6*(D10-F6)+(1-$J$6)*E9	E11:E29
Seasonal Factor—1st 4 quarters	F6	=D6-E6	F7:F9
Seasonal Factor	F10	=$J$7*(D10-E10)+(1-$J$7)*F6	F11:F29
Prediction	G10	=E9+F6	G11:G29
RMSE	G31	=SQRT(SUMXMY2(G10:G29,D10:D29)/ COUNT(D10:D29))	–
Forecast 1st Quarter 2011	H30	=$E$29+F26	–
Forecast 2nd Quarter 2011	H31	=$E$29+F27	–
Forecast 3rd Quarter 2011	H32	=$E$29+F28	–

Once again, we can use Solver parameters to determine the values of α and β that minimize RMSE for this data series. We instruct Solver to minimize cell G31 by changing cells J6 and J7, while constraining cells J6 and J7 to values between 0 and 1. These results are shown in Figure 15.7, along with a chart showing the actual sales plotted against the values predicted by the model, as well as forecasted sales for quarters one, two, and three of 2011. Note that the predicted and forecasted values fit the actual data reasonably well.

Since there is no upward or downward trend in the time series, the forecasts for each of the quarters in 2011 is calculated by taking the expected level for the fourth quarter of 2010 and adjusting it by the relevant seasonal factor for each succeeding quarter. Therefore, the forecast for 2011 is also the forecast for 2012 and any year beyond.

Seasonality with Multiplicative Effects

A slight modification to the additive model allows us to model stationary time series data with multiplicative effects. See Figure 15.8.

In particular, the predicting function in column G of Figure 15.8, beginning with cell G10, becomes:

$$\hat{Y}_{t+n} = L_t * S_{t+n-p}$$

The level equation in column E, beginning with cell E10, becomes:

$$L_t = \alpha(Y_t/S_{t-p}) + (1 - \alpha)L_{t-1}$$

And the seasonal index equation in column F, beginning with cell F10, is:

$$S_t = \beta(Y_t/L_t) + (1 - \beta)S_{t-p}$$

All the other aspects of the additive model hold, except that rather than adding and subtracting the level and seasonal indexes, we multiply and divide by them. We also initialize the level and seasonal indexes in the same way we did in the additive model. Below are the key cell formulas used in Figures 15.8 and 15.9.

Figure 15.7

Stationary Data with Additive Seasonal Effects

Optimized Level and Seasonal Factor Weights

Year	Quarter	Quarterly Sales	Level	Seasonal Factor	Prediction	Forecast
2005	1	701,250	695,938	5,313		
	2	658,750	695,938	(37,188)		
	3	786,250	695,938	90,313		
	4	637,500	695,938	(58,438)		
2006	1	803,250	749,910	12,222	701,250	
	2	769,250	779,821	(33,358)	712,722	
	3	850,000	769,168	88,949	870,133	
	4	724,625	776,520	(57,496)	710,730	
2007	1	752,250	757,210	9,750	788,742	
	2	699,125	744,126	(35,033)	723,852	
	3	854,250	755,331	90,383	833,075	
	4	643,875	726,779	(61,152)	697,835	
2008	1	760,750	739,595	11,391	736,529	
	2	673,625	723,225	(37,129)	704,562	
	3	854,250	744,730	93,136	813,608	
	4	635,375	719,224	(64,417)	683,579	
2009	1	722,500	714,930	10,841	730,615	
	2	643,875	696,978	(39,427)	677,801	
	3	822,375	714,049	95,322	790,115	
	4	648,125	713,251	(64,519)	649,632	
2010	1	765,000	734,897	13,612	724,093	
	2	735,250	755,946	(36,732)	695,470	
	3	841,500	750,778	94,660	851,268	
	4	688,500	751,964	(64,367)	686,259	
2011	1					765,576
	2					715,231
	3					846,624

RMSE 39,138

Forecast Total 2,327,431

alpha 0.529141
beta 0.143871

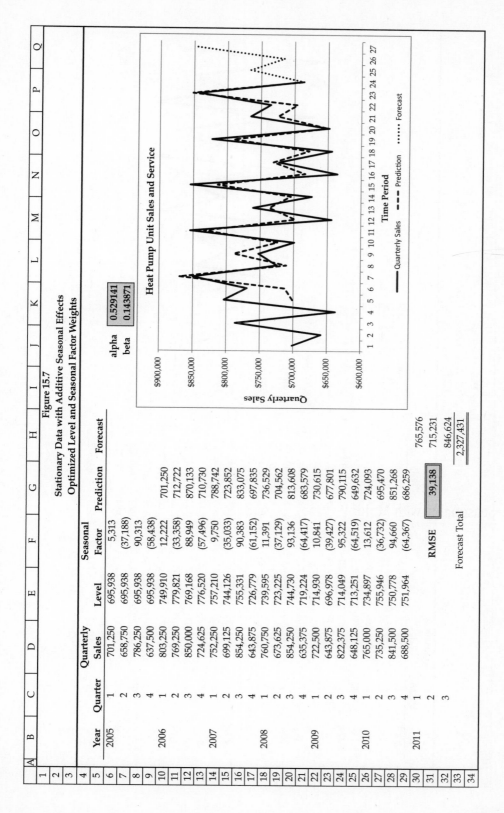

Heat Pump Unit Sales and Service

— Quarterly Sales   - - - Prediction   ······ Forecast

Time Period

Quarterly Sales

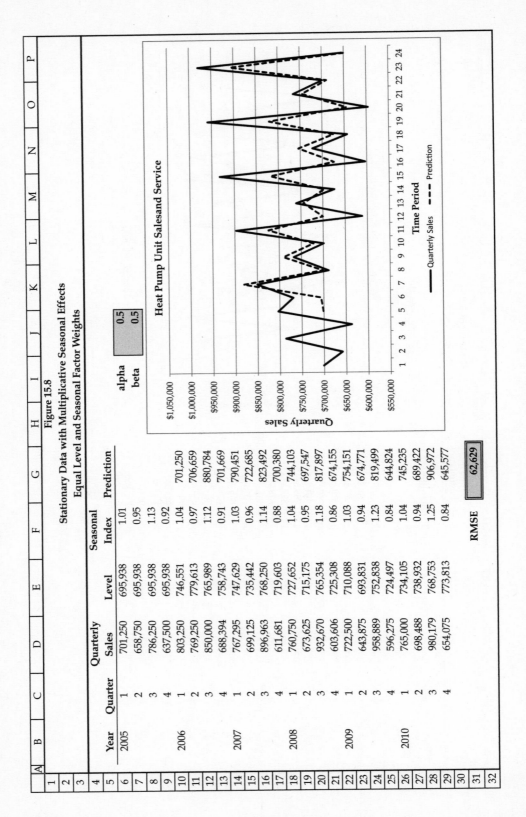

Figure 15.8
Stationary Data with Multiplicative Seasonal Effects
Equal Level and Seasonal Factor Weights

Year	Quarter	Quarterly Sales	Level	Seasonal Index	Prediction
2005	1	701,250	695,938	1.01	
	2	658,750	695,938	0.95	
	3	786,250	695,938	1.13	
	4	637,500	695,938	0.92	
2006	1	803,250	746,551	1.04	701,250
	2	769,250	779,613	0.97	706,659
	3	850,000	765,989	1.12	880,784
	4	688,394	758,743	0.91	701,669
2007	1	767,295	747,629	1.03	790,451
	2	699,125	735,442	0.96	722,685
	3	896,963	768,250	1.14	823,492
	4	611,681	719,603	0.88	700,380
2008	1	760,750	727,652	1.04	744,103
	2	673,625	715,175	0.95	697,547
	3	932,670	765,354	1.18	817,897
	4	603,606	725,308	0.86	674,155
2009	1	722,500	710,088	1.03	754,151
	2	643,875	693,831	0.94	674,771
	3	958,889	752,838	1.23	819,499
	4	596,275	724,497	0.84	644,824
2010	1	765,000	734,105	1.04	745,235
	2	698,488	738,932	0.94	689,422
	3	980,179	768,753	1.25	906,972
	4	654,075	773,813	0.84	645,577

alpha 0.5
beta 0.5

RMSE 62,629

270

Figure 15.9
Stationary Data with Multiplicative Seasonal Effects
Optimized Level and Seasonal Factor Weights

Year	Quarter	Quarterly Sales	Level	Seasonal Index	Prediction	Forecast
2005	1	701,250	695,938	1.01		
	2	658,750	695,938	0.95		
	3	786,250	695,938	1.13		
	4	637,500	695,938	0.92		
2006	1	803,250	715,662	1.11	701,250	
	2	769,250	734,566	1.04	677,421	
	3	850,000	738,034	1.15	829,891	
	4	688,394	740,657	0.93	676,062	
2007	1	767,295	730,549	1.05	825,083	
	2	699,125	719,205	0.98	759,661	
	3	896,963	731,032	1.22	827,160	
	4	611,681	716,960	0.86	678,730	
2008	1	760,750	717,770	1.06	756,365	
	2	673,625	712,253	0.95	701,290	
	3	932,670	722,265	1.29	869,913	
	4	603,606	718,502	0.84	620,188	
2009	1	722,500	711,372	1.02	761,267	
	2	643,875	705,094	0.92	674,421	
	3	958,889	712,973	1.34	906,887	
	4	596,275	712,126	0.84	599,931	
2010	1	765,000	719,670	1.06	725,553	
	2	698,488	728,068	0.96	659,023	
	3	980,179	728,666	1.34	976,062	
	4	654,075	738,839	0.88	610,345	
2011	1					782,990
	2					706,461
	3					993,617
						2,483,068

alpha 0.194856
beta 0.926802

RMSE 50,477

Forecast Total

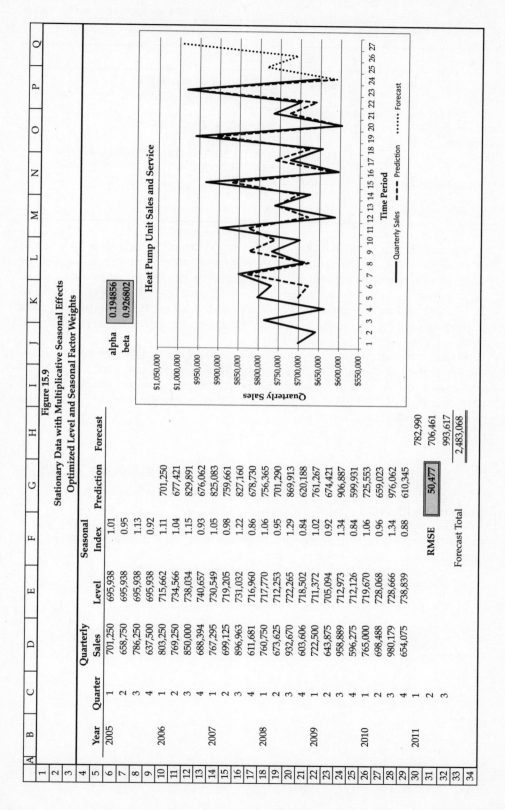

Heat Pump Unit Sales and Service

— Quarterly Sales   - - - Prediction   .... Forecast

Quarterly Sales

Time Period

Function	Cell	Formula	Copy To
Level—1st 4 quarters	E6	=AVERAGE($D$6:$D$9)	E7:E9
Level	E10	=$J$6*(D10/F6)+(1-$J$6)*E9	E11:E29
Seasonal Index—1st 4 quarters	F6	=D6/E6	F7:F9
Seasonal Index	F10	=$J$7*(D10/E10)+(1-$J$7)*F6	F11:F29
Prediction	G10	=E9*F6	G11:G29
RMSE	G31	=SQRT(SUMXMY2(G10:G29,D10:D29)/ COUNT(D10:D29))	–
Forecast 1st Quarter 2011	H30	=$E$29*F26	–
Forecast 2nd Quarter 2011	H31	=$E$29*F27	–
Forecast 3rd Quarter 2011	H32	=$E$29*F28	–

Once again, we can use Solver parameters to determine the values of α and β that minimize RMSE for this data series. We instruct Solver to minimize cell G31 by changing cells J6 and J7, while constraining cells J6 and J7 to values between 0 and 1. These results are shown in Figure 15.9, along with a chart showing the actual sales plotted against the values predicted by the model, as well as forecasted sales for quarters one, two, and three of 2011. Note that the predicted and forecasted values fit the actual data reasonably well.

Since there is no upward or downward trend in the time series, the forecasts for each of the quarters in 2011 is calculated by taking the expected level for the fourth quarter of 2010 and multiplying it by the relevant seasonal factor for each succeeding quarter. Therefore, the forecast for 2011 is also the forecast for 2012 and any year beyond.

Conclusion

This concludes our discussion and demonstration of the application of forecasting techniques to stationary time series data.

In the next chapter, we show you how to deal with time series data whose mean is not stationary, but which instead demonstrates a trend along with additive or multiplicative seasonal effects.

CHAPTER 16

Case Study 16—Determining Lost Sales Using Nonregression Trend Models

In the previous two chapters, we presented techniques for analyzing and then forecasting stationary time series data in which there was no significant trend in the data over time. However, simply because of inflation, it is usual for time series data, especially sales, to exhibit some type of upward trend over time. Trend is the long-term sweep or general direction of movement in a time series. It reflects the net influence of long-term factors that affect the time series in a fairly consistent and gradual way over time. In other words, the trend reflects changes in the data that occur with the passage of time.

When Averaging Techniques Are Not Appropriate

Because the moving average, weighted moving average, and exponential smoothing techniques use some average of the previous values to predict future values, they consistently underestimate the actual values if there is an upward trend in the data. For example, consider the time series data given by 2, 4, 6, 8, 10, 12, 14, 16, and 18. These data show a clear upward trend leading us to expect that the next value in the time series should be 20. But the forecasting techniques discussed in the previous two chapters would predict that the next value in the series would be less than or equal to 18 because no average or weighted average of the given data could exceed 18. In this chapter we consider several techniques that are appropriate for nonstationary time series involving a trend in the data over time and that do not rely on regression analysis for a solution to the forecasting problem.

Vestpack Corporation manufactures reinforced cloth fiber containers used in the removal of waste material in the oil refining industry. One of its vendors allegedly supplied it with substandard cloth fiber, which caused the containers used by one of its customers to collapse during the waste removal process at a refinery in January 2011. This incident caused many problems for Vestpack, including canceled orders from its customers over the next three quarters. We were hired to determine the extent of its lost business income during that period. Our first step was to gather the quarterly sales data shown in column E and the accompanying chart in Figure 16.1. The chart of the data suggests a relatively strong upward trend in the data over time, as the product line was introduced to the refining industry in the fall of 2005 and had enjoyed an excellent reception over the past five years.

Figure 16.1
Vestpack Corporation
Quarterly Sales
2-Quarter to 4-Quarter Moving Averages

Year	Quarter	Time Period	Quarterly Sales ($000's)	2-Quarter Moving Average Predictions	3-Quarter Moving Average Predictions	4-Quarter Moving Average Predictions
2006	1	1	684.2			
	2	2	584.1			
	3	3	765.4	634.15		
	4	4	892.3	674.75	677.90	731.50
2007	1	5	885.4	828.85	747.27	781.80
	2	6	677.0	888.85	847.70	805.03
	3	7	1,006.6	781.20	818.23	865.33
	4	8	1,122.1	841.80	856.33	922.78
2008	1	9	1,163.4	1,064.35	935.23	992.28
	2	10	993.2	1,142.75	1,097.37	1,071.33
	3	11	1,312.5	1,078.30	1,092.90	1,147.80
	4	12	1,545.3	1,152.85	1,156.37	1,253.60
2009	1	13	1,596.2	1,428.90	1,283.67	1,361.80
	2	14	1,260.4	1,570.75	1,484.67	1,428.60
	3	15	1,735.2	1,428.30	1,467.30	1,534.28
	4	16	2,029.7	1,497.80	1,530.60	1,655.38
2010	1	17	2,107.8	1,882.45	1,675.10	1,783.28
	2	18	1,650.3	2,068.75	1,957.57	1,880.75
	3	19	2,304.4	1,879.05	1,929.27	2,023.05
	4	20	2,639.4	1,977.35	2,020.83	

	2-Quarter	3-Quarter	4-Quarter
RMSE	318.8	319.6	322.5
MAD	280.3	291.5	279.3
MAPE	19.55%	19.74%	17.72%

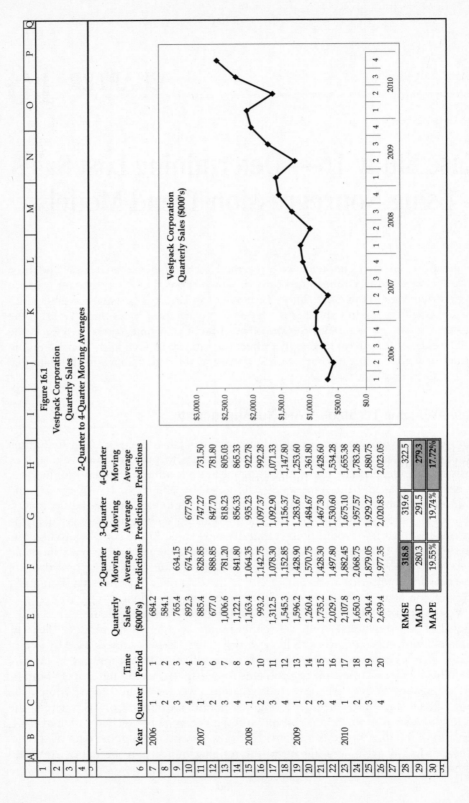

Vestpack Corporation
Quarterly Sales ($000's)

Double Moving Average

Since the first method introduced here is the double moving average technique, we first need to select the moving average span. In Figure 16.1 we employ summary measures of forecast error to help make that selection by calculating two-quarter, three-quarter, and four-quarter moving averages. As the four-quarter moving average enjoys the best ranking in two of the three metrics, let's choose that span on which to perform the double moving average technique.

As its name implies, the double moving average technique involves taking the average of averages. We know from the previous chapter that moving averages (MA) are calculated by adding the values in a span and then dividing by the length of the span. Column F, starting with cell F10 in Table 16.1, is calculated this way.

The same calculating principle applies to double moving averages (DMA). Column G, starting with cell G13 in Table 16.1, demonstrates this formula. The double moving average forecasting function is given by the following equation:

$$\hat{Y}_{t+n} = L_t + nT_t$$

where:

$$L_t = 2MA_t - DMA_t$$
$$T_t = 2(MA_t - DMA_t)/k - 1)$$

The values of L_t and T_t are basically derived by minimizing the sum of squared errors using the last k periods of data. In this case, since we are using a four-quarter moving average, $k = 4$. Note that L_t represents the estimated base or level of the time series at period t and is essentially where we think the series would be at time t if there were no random noise or seasonality in the data. T_t represents the estimated trend and is the expected rate of increase or decrease per period. Thus, at period t, the forecast n periods into the future would be $L_t + nT_t$ as indicated above. Below are the key cell formulas used in Table 16.1.

Function	Cell	Formula	Copy To
4-Quarter Moving Average	F10	=AVERAGE(E7:E10)	F11:F26
Double Moving Average	G13	=AVERAGE(F10:F13)	G14:G26
Level	H13	=2*F13-G13	H14:H26
Trend	I13	=2*(F13-G13)/(4-1)	I14:I26
Predicted Sales	J14	= +H13+I13	J15:J26
Forecast	K27	=$H$26+((D27-$D$26)*$I$26)	K28:K29
RMSE	G28	=SQRT(SUMXMY2(E14:E26,J14:J26)/ COUNT(J14:J26))	–
MAD	G29	{=SUM(ABS(E14:E26-J14:J26))/ COUNT(J14:J26)}	–
MAPE	G30	{=(SUM(ABS(E14:E26-J14:J26)/E14:E26))/ COUNT(J14:J26)}	–

The forecast amount of 2,525.23 for period 21 consists of the level for period 20 = 2,385.33 plus the trend value for period 20 = 139.9 * 1. Each succeeding

Table 16.1
Vestpack Corporation
Quarterly Sales
Double Moving Average

Year	Quarter	Time Period	Quarterly Sales ($000's)	4-Quarter Moving Average	Double Moving Average	Level	Trend	Predicted Sales	Forecast
2006	1	1	684.2						
	2	2	584.1						
	3	3	765.4						
	4	4	892.3	731.50					
2007	1	5	885.4	781.80					
	2	6	677.0	805.03					
	3	7	1,006.6	865.33	795.9	934.7	46.3		
	4	8	1,122.1	922.78	843.7	1,001.8	52.7	981	
2008	1	9	1,163.4	992.28	896.4	1,088.2	64.0	1,055	
	2	10	993.2	1,071.33	962.9	1,179.7	72.3	1,152	
	3	11	1,312.5	1,147.80	1,033.5	1,262.1	76.2	1,252	
	4	12	1,545.3	1,253.60	1,116.3	1,391.0	91.6	1,338	
2009	1	13	1,596.2	1,361.80	1,208.6	1,515.0	102.1	1,483	
	2	14	1,260.4	1,428.60	1,298.0	1,559.3	87.1	1,617	
	3	15	1,735.2	1,534.28	1,394.6	1,674.0	93.1	1,646	
	4	16	2,029.7	1,655.38	1,495.0	1,815.7	106.9	1,767	
2010	1	17	2,107.8	1,783.28	1,600.4	1,966.2	121.9	1,923	
	2	18	1,650.3	1,880.75	1,713.4	2,048.1	111.6	2,088	
	3	19	2,304.4	2,023.05	1,835.6	2,210.5	125.0	2,160	
	4	20	2,639.4	2,175.48	1,965.6	2,385.3	139.9	2,335	
2011	1	21							2,525
	2	22							2,665
	3	23							2,805
				RMSE	225.3				
				MAD	197.7				
				MAPE	12.50%			Forecast Total	7,995

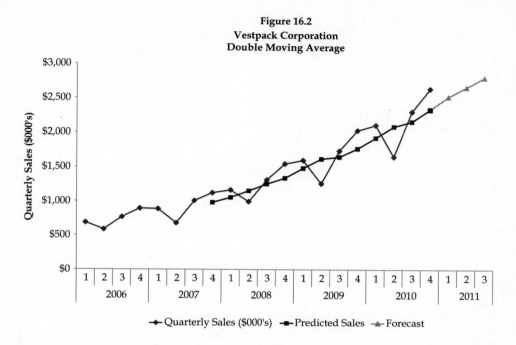

Figure 16.2
Vestpack Corporation
Double Moving Average

→ Quarterly Sales ($000's)   ■ Predicted Sales   ▲ Forecast

period increases by the trend value of 139.9. Figure 16.2 graphs the actual sales data against the values predicted by the double moving average model along with the three-quarter forecast period. Note that the predicted and forecasted values seem to follow the upward trend in the actual data reasonably well.

Double Exponential Smoothing (Holt's Method)

Another effective forecasting tool for time series data that exhibits a linear trend is double exponential smoothing, also known as Holt's Method. After observing the value of the time series at period t (Y_t), Holt's Method computes an estimated value of the base or expected level of the time series (L_t), and the expected rate of increase or decrease (trend) per period (T_t). The forecasting function in Holt's Method is represented by:

$$\hat{Y}_{t+n} = L_t + nT_t$$

where the level equation is:

$$L_t = \alpha Y_t + (1 - \alpha)(L_{t-1} + T_{t-1})$$

and the trend equation is:

$$T_t = \beta(L_t - L_{t-1}) + (1 - \beta)T_{t-1}$$

We can use the forecasting function to obtain forecasts n time periods into the future where $n = 1, 2, 3$, and so on. The forecast for time period $t + n$ (or $\hat{Y}_{t+n}$) is the base level at time period t (given by E_t), plus the expected influence of the trend during the next n time periods (given by nT_t).

The smoothing parameters α and β in the above equations can assume any value between 0 and 1, and do not have to add to 1.

Although Holt's Method might appear to be more complicated than the techniques discussed earlier, it is a simple three-step process:

1. Compute the base level L_t for time period t using the level equation.
2. Compute the expected trend value T_t for time period t using the trend equation.
3. Compute the final forecast $\hat{Y}_{t+n}$ for time period $t + n$ using the forecast function.

The application of Holt's Method to the Vestpack Corporation data is shown in Table 16.2.

Cells K8 and K9 represent the equally-weighted values of α and β, respectively. Column F implements the base levels for each time period as required in step 1 (that is, this column contains the Lt values). The level equation assumes that for any time period t the base level for the previous time period (Lt − 1) is known. It is customary to initialize column F by assuming that Lt = Yt, as reflected by the formula in cell F8.

	B	C	D	E	F	G	H	I	J	K
1				Table 16.2						
2				Vestpack Corporation						
3				Quarterly Sales						
4				Double Exponential Smoothing (Holt's Method)						
5				Equal Weighting of Alpha and Beta						
6										
7	Year	Quarter	Time Period	Quarterly Sales ($000's)	Base Level	Trend	Predicted Sales			
8	2006	1	1	684.2	684.2	-			alpha	0.500
9		2	2	584.1	634.2	(25.0)	684.2		beta	0.500
10		3	3	765.4	687.3	14.0	609.1			
11		4	4	892.3	796.8	61.8	701.3			
12	2007	1	5	885.4	872.0	68.5	858.6			
13		2	6	677.0	808.7	2.6	940.5			
14		3	7	1,006.6	909.0	51.4	811.4			
15		4	8	1,122.1	1,041.3	91.9	960.4			
16	2008	1	9	1,163.4	1,148.3	99.4	1,133.1			
17		2	10	993.2	1,120.4	35.8	1,247.7			
18		3	11	1,312.5	1,234.4	74.9	1,156.2			
19		4	12	1,545.3	1,427.3	133.9	1,309.2			
20	2009	1	13	1,596.2	1,578.7	142.6	1,561.2			
21		2	14	1,260.4	1,490.9	27.4	1,721.3			
22		3	15	1,735.2	1,626.7	81.6	1,518.3			
23		4	16	2,029.7	1,869.0	162.0	1,708.4			
24	2010	1	17	2,107.8	2,069.4	181.2	2,031.0			
25		2	18	1,650.3	1,950.4	31.1	2,250.6			
26		3	19	2,304.4	2,143.0	111.8	1,981.5			
27		4	20	2,639.4	2,447.1	208.0	2,254.8			
28	2011	1	21							
29		2	22		RMSE	264.9				
30		3	23							

Column G implements the expected trend values for each time period as required in step 2 (that is, this column contains the T_t values). The trend equation assumes that for any time period t the expected trend value at the previous time period (T_{t-1}) is known. So we assume as an initial trend estimate that $T_t = 0$ (although any other initial trend estimate could be used), as reflected in the formula in cell G8. Below are the key cell formulas used in Table 16.2.

Function	Cell	Formula	Copy To
Initialize Base Level	F8	=E8	–
Base Level	F9	=$K$8*E9+(1-$K$8)*(F8+G8)	F10:F27
Initialize Trend	G8	=0	–
Trend	G9	=$K$9*(F9-F8)+(1-$K$9)*G8	G10:G27
Predicted Sales	H9	=SUM(F8:G8)	H10:H27
RMSE	G29	=SQRT(SUMXMY2(E9:E27,H9:H27)/ COUNT(H9:H27))	–

Once again, we can use Solver parameters to determine the values of α and β that minimize RMSE for the Vestpack Corporation data series. In Table 16.3 we instruct Solver to minimize cell G29 by changing cells L8 and L9, while constraining cells L8 and L9 to values between 0 and 1.

The optimized results shown in Table 16.3 can be used to forecast sales for the first three quarters of 2011. The forecast value for period 21 is computed by taking the level value of 2,336.9 for period 20 and adding to it the product of 1 * 152.1, that is, one forecast period ahead times the trend value of period 20. Periods 22 and 23 are forecasted the same way but with the numbers 2 and 3, representing 2 and 3 forecast periods ahead, substituted for the number 1. These calculations are shown in cells I28, I29, and I30 of Table 16.3.

The chart that is Figure 16.3 shows the actual sales plotted against the values predicted by the model, as well as forecasted sales for quarters one, two, and three of 2011. Note that the predicted and forecasted values follow the trend in the data quite well.

Triple Exponential Smoothing (Holt-Winter's Method) for Additive Seasonal Effects

In addition to having an upward or downward trend, nonstationary data may also exhibit seasonal effects. Here again, the seasonal effects may be additive or multiplicative in nature. Holt-Winter's Method is another forecasting technique that we can apply to time series exhibiting trend and seasonality. In this section we concern ourselves with Holt-Winter's Method for additive seasonal effects.

To demonstrate Holt-Winter's Method for additive seasonal effects, let p represent the number of seasons in the time series (for quarterly data, $p = 4$; for monthly data, $p = 12$). The forecasting function is then given by:

$$\hat{Y}_{t+n} = L_t + nT_t + S_{t+n-p}$$

Table 16.3
Vestpack Corporation
Quarterly Sales
Double Exponential Smoothing (Holt's Method)
Optimized Weights for Alpha and Beta

Year	Quarter	Time Period	Quarterly Sales ($000's)	Base Level	Trend	Predicted Sales	Forecast			alpha	0.119
										beta	1.000
2006	1	1	684.2	684.2	-	684.2					
	2	2	584.1	672.3	(11.9)	684.2					
	3	3	765.4	672.9	0.6	660.4					
	4	4	892.3	699.5	26.6	673.5					
2007	1	5	885.4	745.0	45.5	726.0					
	2	6	677.0	777.0	32.0	790.5					
	3	7	1,006.6	832.5	55.5	809.0					
	4	8	1,122.1	915.8	83.3	888.0					
2008	1	9	1,163.4	1,018.6	102.8	999.1					
	2	10	993.2	1,106.2	87.6	1,121.4					
	3	11	1,312.5	1,207.9	101.7	1,193.8					
	4	12	1,545.3	1,337.6	129.7	1,309.6					
2009	1	13	1,596.2	1,482.6	145.0	1,467.2					
	2	14	1,260.4	1,584.0	101.4	1,627.6					
	3	15	1,735.2	1,691.3	107.3	1,685.4					
	4	16	2,029.7	1,826.0	134.8	1,798.6					
2010	1	17	2,107.8	1,978.3	152.2	1,960.8					
	2	18	1,650.3	2,073.5	95.2	2,130.5					
	3	19	2,304.4	2,184.8	111.3	2,168.6					
	4	20	2,639.4	2,336.9	152.1	2,296.1					
2011	1	21					2,489				
	2	22					2,641				
	3	23					2,793				
				RMSE	218.8						
						Forecast Total	7,923				

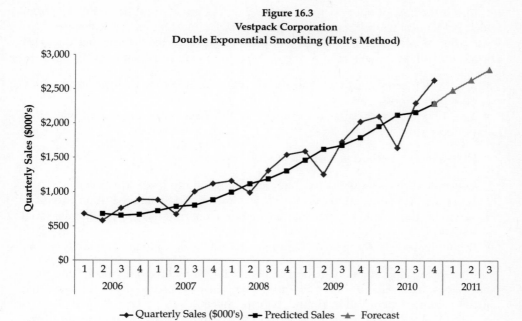

Figure 16.3
Vestpack Corporation
Double Exponential Smoothing (Holt's Method)

◆ Quarterly Sales ($000's) ■ Predicted Sales ▲ Forecast

where the level equation is:

$$Lt = \alpha(Y_t - S_{t-p}) + (1 - \alpha)(L_{t-1} + T_{t-1})$$

and the trend equation is:

$$Tt = \beta(L_t - L_{t-1}) + (1 - \beta)T_{t-1}$$

and the seasonal equation is:

$$S_t = \gamma(Y_t - L_t) + (1 - \gamma)S_{t-p}$$

We can use the forecasting function to obtain forecasts in time periods into the future where $n = 1, 2, \ldots, p$. The forecast for time period $t + n$ (or $\hat{Y}_{t+n}$) is obtained by the forecast function by adjusting the expected base level at time period $t + n$ (given by $L_t + nT_t$) by the most recent estimate of the seasonality associated with this time period (given by S_{t+n-p}). The smoothing parameters α, β, and γ (gamma) in the level, trend, and seasonal equations above can assume any value between 0 and 1, and do not have to add to 1.

The expected base level of the time series is updated in time period t (L_t) by the level equation, which takes a weighted average of the following two values:

- $L_{t-1} + T_{t-1}$, which represents the expected base level of the time series at time period t before observing the actual value at time period t (given by Y_t).
- $Y_t - S_{t-p}$, which represents the deseasonalized estimate of the base level of the time series at time period t after observing Y_t.

The estimated per-period trend factor T is updated using the trend equation, which is identical to the trend equation used in Holt's Method. The estimated seasonal adjustment factor for each time period is calculated using the seasonal equation above, which takes a weighted average of the following two quantities:

- S_{t-p}, which represents the most recent seasonal index for the season in which time period t occurs.
- $Y_t - L_t$, which represents an estimate of the seasonality associated with time period t after observing Y_t.

Holt-Winter's Method is basically a four-step process:

1. Compute the base level Lt for time period t using the level equation.
2. Compute the estimated trend value T_t for time period t using the trend equation.
3. Compute the estimated seasonal factor S_t for time period t using the seasonal equation.
4. Compute the final forecast $\hat{Y}_{t+n}$ for time period $t + n$ using the forecast function.

The spreadsheet implementation of Holt-Winter's additive method for the Vestpack Corporation data is shown in Table 16.4. Cells L9, L10, and L11 represent the equally weighted values of α, β, and γ, respectively.

The level and trend equations assume that at time period t an estimate of the seasonal factor from time period $t - p$ exists or that there is a value for S_{t-p}. Thus, our first task in implementing this method is to estimate values for $S_1, S_2, \ldots S_p$ (or, in this case, S_1, S_2, S_3, and S_4). While there are many ways to initialize the seasonal factor, we have chosen to do so by subtracting the average quarterly sales of periods 1 to 4 from actual sales for periods 1, 2, 3, and 4.

The first L_t value that can be computed using the level equation occurs at time period $p + 1$ (in our case, time period 5) because this is the first time period for which S_{t-p} is known. However, to compute L5 using the level equation, we also need to know L_4 (which cannot be computed using the level equation because S_0 is undefined) and T_4 (which cannot be computed using the trend equation because L_4 and L_3 are undefined). Thus, we assume that $L_4 = Y_4 - S_4$ (so that $L_4 + S_4 = Y_4$) and $T_4 = 0$. Below are the key cell formulas used in Table 16.4.

Function	Cell	Formula	Copy To
Initialize Seasonal Factor	H9	=E9-AVERAGE($E$9:$E$12)	H10:H12
Seasonal Factor	H13	=$L$11*(E13-F13)+(1-$L$11)*H9	H14:H28
Initialize Base Level	F12	=E12-H12	–
Base Level	F13	=$L$9*(E13-H9)+(1-$L$9)*(F12+G12)	F14:F28
Initialize Trend	G12	=0	–
Trend	G13	=$L$10*(F13-F12)+(1-$L$10)*G12	G14:G28
Predicted Sales	I13	=+F12+G12+H9	I14:I28
RMSE	G30	=SQRT(SUMXMY2(I13:I28,E13:E28)/ COUNT(I13:I28))	–

Before making a forecast using this method, we want to identify optimal values for α, β, and γ. We can use Solver to determine the values for α, β, and γ that minimize the RMSE. We choose Solver parameters that minimize cell G30 by

Table 16.4
Vestpack Corporation
Quarterly Sales
Triple Exponential Smoothing (Holt-Winter's Method)
Additive Seasonal Effects
Equal Weighting of Alpha, Beta, and Gamma

Year	Quarter	Time Period	Quarterly Sales ($000's)	Base Level	Trend	Seasonal Factor	Predicted Sales
2006	1	1	684.2			(47.3)	
	2	2	584.1			(147.4)	
	3	3	765.4			33.9	
	4	4	892.3	731.5	-	160.8	
2007	1	5	885.4	832.1	50.3	3.0	684.2
	2	6	677.0	853.4	35.8	(161.9)	735.0
	3	7	1,006.6	931.0	56.7	54.8	923.1
	4	8	1,122.1	974.5	50.1	154.2	1,148.4
2008	1	9	1,163.4	1,092.5	84.1	37.0	1,027.6
	2	10	993.2	1,165.8	78.7	(167.3)	1,014.6
	3	11	1,312.5	1,251.1	82.0	58.1	1,299.3
	4	12	1,545.3	1,362.1	96.5	168.7	1,487.3
2009	1	13	1,596.2	1,508.9	121.7	62.1	1,495.6
	2	14	1,260.4	1,529.1	70.9	(218.0)	1,463.3
	3	15	1,735.2	1,638.6	90.2	77.3	1,658.1
	4	16	2,029.7	1,794.9	123.2	201.8	1,897.5
2010	1	17	2,107.8	1,981.9	155.1	94.0	1,980.3
	2	18	1,650.3	2,002.7	87.9	(285.2)	1,919.1
	3	19	2,304.4	2,158.8	122.1	111.5	2,168.0
	4	20	2,639.4	2,359.3	161.2	241.0	2,482.7

alpha	0.500
beta	0.500
gamma	0.500

RMSE 132.4

283

Table 16.5
Vestpack Corporation
Quarterly Sales
Triple Exponential Smoothing (Holt-Winter's Method)
Additive Seasonal Effects
Optimal Weighting of Alpha, Beta, and Gamma

Year	Quarter	Time Period	Quarterly Sales ($000's)	Base Level	Trend	Seasonal Factor	Predicted Sales	Forecast
2006	1	1	684.2			(47.3)		
	2	2	584.1			(147.4)		
	3	3	765.4			33.9		
	4	4	892.3	731.5	-	160.8		
2007	1	5	885.4	776.1	44.6	109.3	684.2	
	2	6	677.0	821.5	45.4	(144.5)	673.3	
	3	7	1,006.6	890.4	68.9	116.2	900.9	
	4	8	1,122.1	959.7	69.3	162.4	1,120.1	
2008	1	9	1,163.4	1,034.6	74.9	128.8	1,138.3	
	2	10	993.2	1,115.7	81.1	(122.5)	964.9	
	3	11	1,312.5	1,196.8	81.0	115.7	1,313.1	
	4	12	1,545.3	1,301.1	104.3	244.2	1,440.1	
2009	1	13	1,596.2	1,419.2	118.1	177.0	1,534.2	
	2	14	1,260.4	1,503.0	83.9	(242.6)	1,414.7	
	3	15	1,735.2	1,594.1	91.1	141.1	1,702.6	
	4	16	2,029.7	1,707.4	113.3	322.3	1,929.4	
2010	1	17	2,107.8	1,845.1	137.7	262.7	1,997.8	
	2	18	1,650.3	1,962.9	117.8	(312.6)	1,740.2	
	3	19	2,304.4	2,099.0	136.1	205.4	2,221.8	
	4	20	2,639.4	2,253.3	154.3	386.1	2,557.4	
2011	1	21						2,670.2
	2	22						2,249.2
	3	23						2,921.5

RMSE 92.4

alpha 0.222
beta 1.000
gamma 1.000

Forecast Total 7,841.0

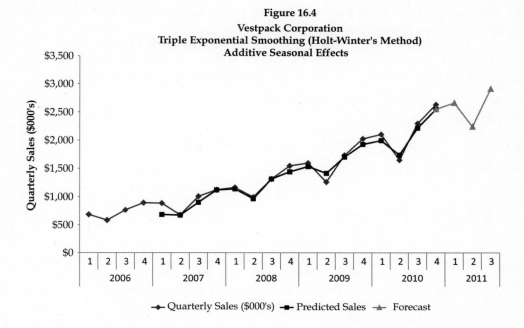

Figure 16.4
Vestpack Corporation
Triple Exponential Smoothing (Holt-Winter's Method)
Additive Seasonal Effects

changing cells L9, L10, and L11, while constraining cells L9, L10, and L11 to values between 0 and 1. Table 16.5 shows the Solver solution to the optimization problem. Also shown in Table 16.5 are the forecasted values for the first three quarters of 2011.

The quarterly forecasts shown in cells J29, J30, and J31 in Table 16.5 are calculated in the following manner:

$$\hat{Y}_{21} = L_{20} + 1 \ ^* T_{20} + S_{17} = 2253.3 + 1 \ ^* 154.3 + 262.7 = 2{,}670.2$$
$$\hat{Y}_{22} = L_{20} + 2 \ ^* T_{20} + S_{18} = 2253.3 + 2 \ ^* 154.3 - 312.6 = 2{,}249.2$$
$$\hat{Y}_{23} = L_{20} + 3 \ ^* T_{20} + S_{19} = 2253.3 + 3 \ ^* 154.3 + 205.4 = 2{,}921.5$$

where 1, 2, and 3 represent the number of forecast periods in the future.

Figure 16.4 displays a chart of the predicted and forecasted values obtained using Holt-Winter's Method along with the actual data. This chart indicates that the forecasting function fits the data reasonably well. However, it does appear that the seasonal effects in the data may be becoming more pronounced over time—suggesting perhaps that a model with multiplicative seasonal effects may be more appropriate in this case.

Triple Exponential Smoothing (Holt-Winter's Method) for Multiplicative Seasonal Effects

As noted above, Figure 16.4 indicates that the seasonal effects in the Vestpack Corporation data may be becoming more pronounced over time. As a result, it may be more appropriate to model this data with Holt-Winter's Method for multiplicative seasonal effects. Fortunately, this technique is very similar to Holt-Winter's Method for additive seasonal effects.

To demonstrate Holt-Winter's Method for multiplicative seasonal effects, we again let p represent the number of seasons in the time series (for quarterly data, $p = 4$; for monthly data, $p = 12$). The forecasting function is then given by:

$$\hat{Y}_{t+n} = (L_t + nT_t)S_{t+n-p}$$

where the level equation is:

$$L_t = \alpha(Y_t/S_{t-p}) + (1 - \alpha)(L_{t-1} + T_{t-1})$$

and the trend equation is:

$$T_t = \beta(L_t - L_{t-1}) + (1 - \beta)T_{t-1}$$

and the seasonal equation is:

$$S_t = \gamma(Y_t/L_t) + (1 - \gamma)S_{t-p}$$

Here, the forecast for time period $t + n$ $(\hat{Y}_{t+n})$ is obtained from the forecast function by multiplying the expected base level at time period $t + n$ (given by $L_t + nT_t$) by the most recent estimate of the seasonality associated with this time period (given by S_{t+n-p}). The smoothing parameters α, β, and γ (gamma) in the level, trend and seasonal equations above again can assume any value between 0 and 1 and need not add together to 1.

The expected base level of the time series at time period t (L_t) is updated in the level equation, which takes a weighted average of the following two values:

- $L_{t-1} + T_{t-1}$, which represents the expected base level of the time series in time period t before observing the actual value at time period t (given by Y_t).
- Y_t/S_{t-p}, which represents the deseasonalized estimate of the base level of the time series at time period t after observing Y_t.

The estimated seasonal adjustment factor for each time period is calculated using the seasonal equation, which takes a weighted average of the following two quantities:

- S_{t-p}, which represents the most recent seasonal index for the season in which time period t occurs.
- Y_t/L_t, which represents an estimate of the seasonality associated with time period t after observing Y_t.

The spreadsheet implementation of Holt-Winter's multiplicative method for the Vestpack Corporation data is shown in Table 16.6. Cells L9, L10, and L11 represents the equally weighted values of α, β, and γ, respectively.

The level and trend equations assume that at time period t an estimate of the seasonal factor from time period $t - p$ exists or that there is a value for S_{t-p}. Thus, our first task in implementing this method is to estimate values for $S_1, S_2, \ldots S_p$ (or, in this case, S_1, S_2, S_3, and S_4). While there are many ways to initialize the seasonal factor, an easy way to do this is to subtract the average quarterly sales of periods 1 to 4 from actual sales for periods 1, 2, 3, and 4.

Table 16.6
Vestpack Corporation
Quarterly Sales
Triple Exponential Smoothing (Holt-Winter's Method)
Multiplicative Seasonal Effects
Equal Weighting of Alpha, Beta, and Gamma

Year	Quarter	Time Period	Quarterly Sales ($000's)	Base Level	Trend	Seasonal Index	Predicted Sales
2006	1	1	684.2			0.935	
	2	2	584.1			0.798	
	3	3	765.4			1.046	
	4	4	892.3	731.5	–	1.220	
2007	1	5	885.4	839.1	53.8	0.995	684.2
	2	6	677.0	870.3	42.5	0.788	712.9
	3	7	1,006.6	937.4	54.8	1.060	955.2
	4	8	1,122.1	956.1	36.7	1.197	1,210.4
2008	1	9	1,163.4	1,080.9	80.8	1.036	988.1
	2	10	993.2	1,210.9	105.4	0.804	915.6
	3	11	1,312.5	1,277.2	85.9	1.044	1,395.3
	4	12	1,545.3	1,327.2	67.9	1.181	1,631.2
2009	1	13	1,596.2	1,468.0	104.4	1.062	1,445.0
	2	14	1,260.4	1,569.8	103.1	0.804	1,264.6
	3	15	1,735.2	1,667.6	100.4	1.042	1,746.3
	4	16	2,029.7	1,743.7	88.2	1.172	2,087.3
2010	1	17	2,107.8	1,908.7	126.7	1.083	1,944.7
	2	18	1,650.3	2,044.6	131.2	0.805	1,635.5
	3	19	2,304.4	2,193.5	140.1	1.046	2,267.6
	4	20	2,639.4	2,292.5	119.6	1.162	2,735.6

alpha 0.500
beta 0.500
gamma 0.500

RMSE = 102.1

287

The first L_t value that can be computed using the level equation occurs at time period $p + 1$ (in our case, time period 5) because this is the first time period for which S_{t-p} is known. However, to compute L_5 using the level equation, we also need to know L_4 (which cannot be computed using the level equation because S_0 is undefined) and T_4 (which cannot be computed using the trend equation because L_4 and L_3 are undefined). Thus, we assume that $L_4 = Y_4/S_4$ (so that $L_4 * S_4 = Y_4$) and $T_4 = 0$. Below are the key cell formulas used in Table 16.6.

Function	Cell	Formula	Copy To
Initialize Seasonal Factor	H9	=E9/AVERAGE($E$9:$E$12)	H10:H12
Seasonal Index	H13	=$L$11*E13/F13+(1-$L$11)*H9	H14:H28
Initialize Base Level	F12	=E12/H12	–
Base Level	F13	=$L$9*E13/H9+(1-$L$9)*(F12+G12)	F14:F28
Initialize Trend	G12	=0	–
Trend	G13	=$L$10*(F13-F12)+(1-$L$10)*G12	G14:G28
Predicted Sales	I13	=SUM(F12:G12)*H9	I14:I28
RMSE	G30	=SQRT(SUMXMY2(I13:I28,E13:E28)/ COUNT(I13:I28))	–

Before making a forecast using this method, we want to identify optimal values for α, β, and γ. We can use Solver to determine the values for α, β, and γ that minimize the RMSE. We choose Solver parameters that minimize cell G30 by changing cells L9, L10, and L11, while constraining cells L9, L10, and L11 to values between 0 and 1. Table 16.7 shows the Solver solution to the optimization problem. Also shown in Table 16.7 are the forecasted values for the first three quarters of 2011.

The quarterly forecasts shown in cells J29, J30, and J31 in Figure 16.7 are calculated in the following manner:

$$\hat{Y}_{21} = (L_{20} + 1 * T_{20}) * S_{17} = (2217.5 + 1 * 137.3) * 1.152 = 2,713.7$$
$$\hat{Y}_{22} = (L_{20} + 2 * T_{20}) * S_{18} = (2217.5 + 2 * 137.3) * .849 = 2,114.8$$
$$\hat{Y}_{23} = (L_{20} + 3 * T_{20}) * S_{19} = (2217.5 + 3 * 137.3) * 1.103 = 2,900.4$$

where 1, 2, and 3 represent the number of forecast periods in the future.

Figure 16.5 displays a chart of the predicted and forecasted values obtained using Holt-Winter's multiplicative method along with the actual data. This chart indicates that the forecasting function fits the data reasonably well. Comparing this chart to the one in Figure 16.4, it seems that the multiplicative model produces a forecasting function that may fit the data better.

Conclusion

This concludes our presentation of nonregression trend models. As to which model to use in any given situation, that is up to you. Begin, as always, by graphing your data and looking for evidence of trend and seasonality. If trend and seasonality are

Table 16.7
Vestpack Corporation
Quarterly Sales
Triple Exponential Smoothing (Holt-Winter's Method)
Multiplicative Seasonal Effects
Optimal Weighting of Alpha, Beta, and Gamma

Year	Quarter	Time Period	Quarterly Sales ($000's)	Base Level	Trend	Seasonal Index	Predicted Sales	Forecast
2006	1	1	684.2			0.935		
	2	2	584.1			0.798		
	3	3	765.4			1.046		
	4	4	892.3	731.5	-	1.220		
2007	1	5	885.4	783.8	52.3	1.087	684.2	
	2	6	677.0	838.9	55.1	0.805	667.5	
	3	7	1,006.6	910.5	71.6	1.092	935.4	
	4	8	1,122.1	967.0	56.5	1.173	1,198.1	
2008	1	9	1,163.4	1,034.9	67.9	1.116	1,112.5	
	2	10	993.2	1,134.6	99.7	0.860	887.9	
	3	11	1,312.5	1,226.3	91.7	1.075	1,348.4	
	4	12	1,545.3	1,317.7	91.4	1.173	1,546.5	
2009	1	13	1,596.2	1,414.3	96.6	1.126	1,572.4	
	2	14	1,260.4	1,499.9	85.6	0.845	1,299.2	
	3	15	1,735.2	1,592.4	92.5	1.086	1,704.8	
	4	16	2,029.7	1,696.0	103.6	1.192	1,976.2	
2010	1	17	2,107.8	1,817.2	121.2	1.152	2,026.0	
	2	18	1,650.3	1,942.2	125.0	0.849	1,637.3	
	3	19	2,304.4	2,080.2	138.0	1.103	2,245.9	
	4	20	2,639.4	2,217.5	137.3	1.191	2,643.1	
2011	1	21						2,713.7
	2	22			RMSE **71.8**			2,114.8
	3	23						2,900.4
							Forecast Total	7,729

alpha	0.243
beta	1.000
gamma	0.780

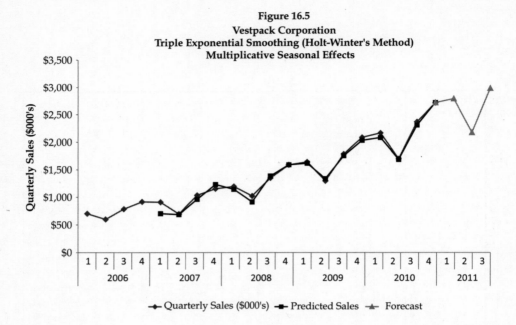

Figure 16.5
Vestpack Corporation
Triple Exponential Smoothing (Holt-Winter's Method)
Multiplicative Seasonal Effects

obvious, then default to the models demonstrated in this chapter. If trend and/or seasonality are not obvious from the graph, then run some of the tests we showed you in other chapters. Of course, you can also run all the models and select that model with the lowest summary measure of forecast error that you have chosen to use, be it RMSE, MAD, or MAPE. If you think past facts and circumstances will continue into the future, the model selected in this manner will probably produce the most reliable forecast.

The Next Frontier in the Application of Statistics

Although this book focused on statistical applications using Excel, some readers may decide to move on to a software product that is specifically designed for the same procedures we have outlined and has more advanced statistical techniques.

There are many software packages in the marketplace that can accommodate an array of statistical methods. One could write a book just on all of the software available. We are limiting the coverage to the programs most familiar to the authors. The following statistical software is highlighted in this appendix: EViews, Minitab, NCSS, R, SAS, SPSS, Stata, and WINKS.

The Technology

Computing usage is getting easier, faster, and more pervasive with statistical software making complicated procedures painless. The purpose of this appendix is to present an overview and inform readers of a limited universe of the statistical software available to perform more complex analyses. The authors are not recommending any of the reviewed software packages.

EViews

EViews provides a broad range of statistics and econometric analysis with powerful modeling tools. The data-handling feature includes a conversion between Excel and EViews. An important aspect of this software is the time series data handling. EViews supports exponential smoothing (single, double) and Holt-Winters. In addition, it also supports linear models with autoregressive integrated moving average (ARIMA), seasonal autoregressive, and seasonal moving average errors. EViews utilizes the Windows operating system.

The maximum observations per series is 4 million. Pricing for single commercial use ranges from $1,075 to $1,175. For more information, refer to the EViews web site: http://www.eviews.com/EViews7/ev7main.html.

EViews has a point and click menu for ease of use in addition to programming capabilities. The individual commands assist in immediate execution and future replication. According to the web site, training seminars for using EViews are provided by third parties at various locations. In addition, for EViews version 7, a book titled *EViews Illustrated for Version 7* is available. The book presents pointers and instructions for users at every level of experience.

Please see http://www.eviews.com/illustrated/illustrated.html. *EViews Illustrated* is "filled with examples, step-by-step instructions, and screen-shot images." *EViews Illustrated* is bundled with new single-user copies of EViews 7, and can also be purchased separately for the price of $40 per copy.

Minitab

Minitab prides itself on being simple to learn with an instinctive design. Minitab has an effortless export to PowerPoint and Word. Minitab software also has a unique feature referred to as the StatGuide. The Minitab StatGuide provides an explanation to the user on how to interpret the statistical tables and graphs in a readable format. This element is different from using the Help feature (which just provides guidance). The StatGuide spotlights the interpretation of the Minitab results. In addition to standard basic statistics/graphics for regression analysis and time series forecasting, Minitab also includes the following:

- Linear regression.
- Nonlinear regression.
- Orthogonal regression.
- Binary, ordinal, and nominal logistic regression.
- Partial least squares (PLS).
- Stepwise and best subsets.
- Residual plots.
- Easy creation of indicator variables.
- Confidence and prediction intervals.
- Trend analysis.
- Decomposition.
- Moving average.
- Exponential smoothing.
- Winters's method.
- Auto, partial auto, and cross correlation functions.
- ARIMA.

A single-user license is currently priced at $1,395. For more information on Minitab, the Web address is http://www.minitab.com/en-US/. Minitab also incorporates a command structure to automate statistical processes.

Minitab has several different options for learning how to use the software. Options include live instructor–led training at locations worldwide; webcasts, including the e-learning "Quality Trainer"; and a personal statistical support trainer.

NCSS

NCSS was founded over 26 years ago and offers technology in statistical analysis, power analysis, and microarray data analysis in a user-friendly format that easily imports/exports all major spreadsheets/file formats. The software runs on 32-bit and 64-bit systems with Windows 7, Vista, XP, 2000, NT, ME, 98, or 95.

The foremost statistical procedures available in NCSS are:

- Appraisal methods, binary diagnostic tests, charts and graphs.
- Cross tabulation, curve fitting, descriptive statistics.
- Design of experiments, forecasting, general linear models.
- Meta-analysis, mixed models, multivariate I, multivariate II.
- Proportions, quality control, regression analysis.
- Reliability analysis, repeated measures, ROC curves.
- Survival analysis, time series analysis, t-tests.

NCSS has a feature integrated within the software that can be functional for valuation professionals. There are three techniques developed purposely for appraisal work. The methods are the comparables procedure, the sales ratio procedure, and the hybrid (feedback) model procedure. NCSS provides common descriptive data in addition to statistics that are of particular interest to appraisers. These include the coefficient of dispersion (COD), the weighted mean (W mean), and the price-related differential (PRD). The methods utilized in this element of the software are prominent in real estate appraisals. However, applying the market method in business valuation would be analogous.

According to the NCSS, the three appraisal procedures are described as follows.

SALES RATIO REPORTS NCSS has a sales ratio procedure that automatically provides the specialized statistics used in appraisal. The output includes the mean, median, W mean, COD, and PRD. These statistics may be broken down by category variables such as property type and/or neighborhood.

COMPARABLES REPORTS NCSS has a comparables procedure that uses special computer algorithms to find a set of comparables for a subject property, adjust their sales prices appropriately, and output a report that summarizes results for a few of the closest properties. You have complete control over which variables are used and how market value adjustments are applied.

HYBRID APPRAISAL MODEL NCSS has a nonlinear regression procedure that lets you apply special multiplicative-adjustment models. It also has an easy-to-use implementation of the hybrid appraisal model designed specifically for appraisal work.

Pricing for a single-user commercial license is $795. NCSS does not offer training, but publishes user guides and a quick start manual. For more information, please see http://www.ncss.com/.

The R Project for Statistical Computing

The R Foundation is a not-for-profit organization working in the public interest. It has been founded by the members of the R Development Core Team in order to provide support for the R project and other innovations in statistical computing.

R is a free software system for statistical computing and graphics. R runs on a wide variety of UNIX platforms, Windows, and Mac OS. R was initially written by Robert Gentleman and Ross Ihaka of the Statistics Department of the University of Auckland. Since the late 1990s, there has been a core group of additional contributors with write access to the R source.

R provides a range of statistical and graphical procedures. R is an open source route to participation in the software. According to "Introduction to R" (available at http://www.gnu.org/software/r), "One of R's strengths is the ease with which well-designed publication-quality plots can be produced, including mathematical symbols and formulae where needed. Great care has been taken over the defaults for the minor design choices in graphics, but the user retains full control." Sounds too good to be true? Well, R has been referred to as having a capacious learning curve because it requires programming.

SAS

SAS refers to its software as "business analytics." The software is geared toward applications used in business intelligence, customer intelligence, data management, financial intelligence, fraud and financial crimes, risk compliance, human capital intelligence, risk management, and sustainability management. The supported operating systems for SAS are Windows, UNIX, z/OS, IBM mainframe, Linux, and OpenVMS Alpha. The SAS application consists of separate software components, which are separately licensed and too numerous to list. The SAS base seemingly covers a vast body of statistical procedures. According to the SAS web site, http://www.sas.com/technologies/analytics/statistics/stat/, the features in the newest version of the software include:

- Analysis of variance (ANOVA).
- Regression.
- Least squares regression with nine model selection techniques, including stepwise regression.
- Diagnostic measures.
- Robust regression and Loess regression.
- Nonlinear regression and quadratic response surface models.
- Partial least squares.
- Quantile regression.
- Categorical data analysis.
- Contingency tables and measures of association.
- Logistic regression.
- Multivariate analysis.
- Factor analysis.
- Principal components.
- Nonparametric analysis.
- Nonparametric analysis of variance.
- Kruskal-Wallis, Wilcoxon-Mann-Whitney, and Friedman tests.
- Power and Sample Size application, which provides interface for computation of sample sizes and characterization of power for t-tests, confidence intervals, and linear models, tests of proportions, and rank tests for survival analysis.

The SAS software utilizes the components of the DATA step, procedure steps, and a micro language.

The DATA step segment uses a default file structure by automating the process of identifying files to the operating system, opening the input file, reading the records, opening the output file, writing the next record, and closing the files. Additional tasks are completed by procedures using SAS terminology. SAS also has an extensive SQL procedure, allowing SQL programmers to use the system with little additional knowledge. SAS uses macro programming extensions that allow for replication and automation.

SAS software is licensed annually. Customers have the option to renew the software. The first-year fee reflects the fee owed for use of the software. The charge for subsequent years is approximately 28 percent of the first-year license fee. Pricing based upon component need can be completed online at https://www.sas.com /order/product.jsp?code=PERSANLBNDL.

SAS has a training and bookstore resource site located at http://support.sas.com /training/us/.

SPSS

SPSS was initially released in 1968 after being developed by academics at Stanford University. In 2009, SPSS was acquired by IBM and it is now part of the company's business analytics software brands. Current operating systems supported are Windows, Mac, and Linux. The SPSS environment uses two main windows, the data editor and the viewer. The data editor has both a data view and a variables view. The viewer is a window for the output of results of the analysis. SPSS is a modules source package. The software has a base system and dedicated modules. SPSS base software has the ability to perform the following:

- Descriptive statistics.
- Cross tabulation.
- Frequencies.
- Descriptive ratio statistics.
- Bivariate statistics: means, t-test, ANOVA, correlation (bivariate, partial, distances), nonparametric tests.
- Linear regression.
- Automatic linear models to build powerful linear models in an easy, automated manner.
- Prediction for identifying groups.
- Factor analysis.
- Cluster analysis.
- Generalized linear mixed models.

SPSS has pull-down menus to perform tasks in addition to a command syntax window. The pull-down menu also creates syntax upon completion. This allows for future replication without writing syntax. SPSS has many module add-ons for particular statistical application. Some of the available modules are:

- SPSS Regression—logistic regression, ordinal regression, multinomial logistic regression, and mixed models.

- SPSS Advanced Models—multivariate GLM and repeated measures ANOVA.
- SPSS Forecasting (time series).

SPSS reads and write data from ASCII text, Excel files, and other statistics packages data files.

Pricing for IBM SPSS 19 (the latest version) base system starts at $2,249. Each module is $1,249. The software is also available in bundles, which include the base system and specific modules. For more information, please see: http://www-01.ibm.com/software/analytics/spss/statistics/buy/.

In addition to the numerous books on how to use SPSS, IBM SPSS offers an array of training modes to learn SPSS. The options available are:

- Public courses taught at IBM/SPSS training facilities.
- Private training.
- On-site training.
- One-to-one.
- Live instruction via the Web for individuals or groups.
- Web-based training for on-demand learning.

IBM SPSS also offers statistics certification for the software upon completion of a sequence of courses.

Considering the investment required for statistical software, there is good news for anyone interested in SPSS. There is a free replacement program available, PSPP. The software currently highlights a high-quality output formatting, an easy-to-use graphical interface, and a command line interface. PSPP has the ability to perform t-tests, ANOVA, linear regression, reliability analysis, factor analysis, nonparametric tests, and other analyses. This software runs on many operating systems including Windows and Mac OS X. For more information, the Web address is http://www.gnu.org/software/pspp/faq.html.

Stata

Stata is an inclusive, integrated statistical package that offers data analysis, data management, and graphics. Stata is not module based. The software has its entire statistical collection in one package. Stata has a point-and-click interface, easy-to-use command syntax, and PDF documentation within the program environment. A partial listing of the statistical techniques available in Stata are:

- Data management.
- Basic statistics: summaries, cross-tabulations, correlations, t-tests, equality-of-variance tests, tests of proportions, confidence intervals, factor variables.
- Linear models: regression; bootstrap, jackknife, and robust Huber/White/sandwich variance estimates; instrumental variables; three-stage least squares; constraints; quantile regression.
- Binary, count, and limited dependent variables; logistic, probit, tobit; Poisson and negative binomial; conditional, multinomial, nested, ordered, rank-ordered,

and stereotype logistic; multinomial probit; zero-inflated and left-truncated count models; selection models; marginal effects; and more.

- ANOVA/MANOVA: balanced and unbalanced designs; factorial, nested, and mixed designs; repeated measures; marginal means; contrasts; and more.
- SEM (structural equation modeling): graphical model builder, standardized and unstandardized estimates, modification indexes, direct and indirect effects, path diagrams, factors scores and other predictions, estimations with groups and tests of invariance, goodness of fit, handling of MAR data by FIML, survey data, clustered data, and more.
- Multivariate methods.
- Cluster analysis.
- Generalized linear models (GLMs).
- Nonparametric methods.
- Resampling and simulation methods.
- Time series: ARIMA, ARFIMA, ARCH/GARCH, VAR, VECM, multivariate GARCH, unobserved components model, dynamic factors, state-space models, business calendars, correlograms, periodograms, forecasts, impulse-response functions, unit-root tests, filters and smoothers, rolling and recursive estimation.
- Survey methods.
- Survival analysis.
- Contrasts and pairwise comparisons.

Stata has a very vibrant user community that has written many commands integrated within Stata. Updates are automatically downloaded each time the software is used. Technical support is free for registered users.

Different types of training are offered for the software in the form of:

- NetCourses—Web-based courses available in a standard scheduled format or on demand.
- On-site training—Stata experts on site.
- Public training—two-day courses led by StataCorp personnel at sites across the country.
- Short courses—offered by independent sources.

Stata Press (a division of StataCorp, LP) publishes many books on using the software. *The Stata Journal* is a quarterly publication containing articles about statistics, data analysis, teaching methods, and effective use of the command language.

Stata has three different packages based upon user needs. Stata/IC allows data sets with as many as 2,047 variables. The number of observations is limited only by the amount of RAM in your computer. Stata/IC can have at most 798 right-hand-side variables in a model. Stata/SE and Stata/IC differ only in the data set size that each can analyze. Stata/SE and Stata/MP can fit models with more independent variables than Stata/IC (up to 10,998). Stata/MP is the fastest and largest version of Stata.

Pricing for Stata depends upon the version (IC, SE, MP). As of this writing, the price for a single IC user with a perpetual license and PDF documentation is $1,195. Stata 12 is the current version. The web site is www.stata.com.

WINKS SDA 7 Professional

WINKS SDA 7 Professional requires Windows XP or higher to be fully functional. No programming is needed to perform any analysis and to open data from Excel files. The WINKS interface resembles the Excel data handling and graphs. The program is designed to help users learn and use statistics, from basic analysis to more advanced topics. A new feature in version 7 is optional extended explanations, including write-up suggestions for results tested, and summarized information that can be pasted into a report.

Some of the procedures the software can perform are:

- T-tests (paired t-test, independent group t-test/unpaired t-test).
- ANOVA.
- Regression.
- Pearson's correlation coefficient (and Spearman).
- Chi-square.
- Nonparametric.
- Multiway analysis of variance (including repeated measures).
- Analysis of covariance (ANCOVA).
- Stepwise and all possible regression analysis.
- Logistic regression.
- Bland-Altman plots, Mantel-Haenszel tests, kappa (interrater-reliability), time series (ARMA).
- Pareto charts.
- Grubbs and Tukey tests for outliers.
- Kruskal-Wallis.
- Mann-Whitney.
- Odds ratios.
- Data entry and manipulation.
- Comparison of proportions.
- Point biserial correlation.
- Wilcoxon signed rank test and the sign test for paired group comparisons.
- Friedman's test for repeated measures with post hoc nonparametric multiple comparisons.
- Cochran's Q test for comparison of dichotomous data.
- McNemar's test for paired dichotomous data.
- Frequency tables.
- Goodness-of-fit analysis.
- Post hoc, nonparametric multiple comparisons (Dunn's test).
- Calculated p-values for normal, t-, chi-square, and F statistics.
- Tests for normality: Lilliefors/Kolmogorov-Smirnov, Anderson-Darling
- Box-Cox transformation.
- Time series: selecting best model using several AIC criteria.

WINKS has statistical tutorials available. The WINKS SDA reference guide is a primer tutorial for using the software with precise directions, screen shots, and output. WINKS provides an index to the statistical tutorials. For more information, please see http://www.texasoft.com/tutindex.html. Pricing for the professional version of the software is $299, with free updates. WINKS also has online technical support service.

The general database limitations for WINKS are:

- Maximum number of fields per database: 250.
- Maximum length of a character field: 65.
- Maximum width for a numeric variable: 15.
- Maximum number of records per database: 32,000.

Conclusion

The objective of this appendix was merely to inform readers of the statistical software options available, rather than to advocate for a particular brand. If the choice is to venture out from Excel and use proprietary statistical software, the answer is simple: It depends on the user's needs. Although Excel performs fantastic statistical applications, the possibility exists that a data set could be too large. This is just one reason one may decide to migrate to one of these statistical software products. The universe of statistical products is not limited to the software highlighted in this appendix. Since most programs offer a trial version, the best advice would be to give the software a test drive before making the investment. Furthermore, as financial litigation experts make persuasive use of applying statistical analysis to reports and testimony, this alters the practice landscape, requiring that incremental leap to the next level of knowledge.

Bibliography of Suggested Statistics Textbooks

Achen, Christopher. *Interpreting and Using Regression*. Newbury Park, CA: Sage, 1982.

Allen, Michael Patrick. *Understanding Regression Analysis*. New York: Plenum Press, 1997.

Anderson, D.A., D.J. Sweeney, and T.A. Williams. *Statistics for Business and Economics*. 11th ed. Madison, OH: South-Western Cengage Learning, 2011.

Berk, Kenneth and Patrick Carey. *Data Analysis with Microsoft Excel*. 3rd ed. Boston, MA: Brooks/Cole Cengage Learning, 2009.

Bowerman, Bruce L., Richard O'Connell, and Anne Koehler. *Forecasting, Time Series, and Regression*. 4th ed. Pacific Grove, CA: Duxbury, 2004.

Brightman, Harvey. *Data Analysis in Plain English with Microsoft Excel*. Pacific Grove, CA: Duxbury, 1998.

Chatterjee, Samprit and Ali S. Hadi. *Regression Analysis by Example*. 4th ed. Hoboken, NJ: John Wiley & Sons, 2006.

De Veaux, Richard D., Paul F. Velleman, and David E. Bock. *Stats: Data and Models*. 2nd ed. Boston, MA: Addison Wesley, 2007.

Gonick, Larry and Wollcott Smith. *The Cartoon Guide to Statistics*. New York: Collins, 1993.

Hamilton, Lawrence. *Regression with Graphics: A Second Course in Applied Statistics*. Belmont, CA: Duxbury, 1991.

Lewis-Beck, Michael. *Applied Regression: An Introduction*. Newbury Park, CA: Sage, 1980.

Makridakis, Spyros, Steven Wheelwright, and Rob Hyndman. *Forecasting: Methods and Applications*. 3rd ed. New York: John Wiley & Sons, 1998.

Mendenhall, William and Terry Sinicich. *A Second Course in Statistics: Regression Analysis*. 7th ed. Upper Saddle River, NJ: Pearson Education, Inc. 2011.

Middleton, Michael. *Data Analysis Using Microsoft Excel*. 3rd ed. Belmont, CA: Thompson, 2003.

Moore, David and William Notz. *Statistics: Concepts and Controversies*. 7th ed. New York: W.H. Freeman & Company, 2008.

Neter, John, Michael Kutner, Christopher Nachtsheim, and William Wasserman. *Applied Linear Regression Models*. 3rd ed. Chicago, IL: Irwin, 1996.

Neufeld, John. *Learning Business Statistics with Microsoft Excel 2000*. Upper Saddle River, NJ: Prentice Hall, 2001.

Pardoe, Iain. *Applied Regression Modeling: A Business Approach*. Hoboken, NJ: John Wiley & Sons, 2006.

Pindyck, Robert and Daniel Rubinfeld. *Econometric Models and Economic Forecasts*. 4th ed. Boston, MA: Irwin, 1997.

Schleifer, Arthur and David Bell. *Data Analysis, Regression, and Forecasting*. Cambridge, MA: Course, 1994.

Schroeder, Larry, David Sjoquist, and Paula Stephan. *Understanding Regression Analysis: An Introductory Guide*. Newbury Park, CA: Sage, 1986.

Tatum, Toby. *Transaction Patterns*. Reno, NV: Self-Published, 2000.

Wang, George and Chaman Jain. *Regression Analysis: Modeling and Forecasting*. Flushing, NY: Graceway Publishing, 2003.

Glossary of Statistical Terms

adjusted R-square Since we can raise R^2 to 1.0 simply by adding more predictor variables to the regression model, we want to be sure that the predictor variables we do add are statistically significant and, in fact, improve the goodness of fit of the model. Thus, another goodness-of-fit measure known as adjusted R^2 has been suggested that accounts for the number of predictor variables included in the regression model. If we add statistically insignificant predictor variables to the model, we would expect to see adjusted R^2 decrease for the same reasons described in Chapter 3. Therefore, a predictor variable with an absolute t-statistic greater than 1 will increase adjusted R^2 as well as lowering the standard error of the estimate.

alternative hypothesis The alternative hypothesis, H_a, is a statement of what a statistical hypothesis test is set up to establish. For example, in a clinical trial of a new drug, the alternative hypothesis might be that the new drug has a different effect, on average, compared to that of the current drug. We would write H_a: The two drugs have different effects, on average. The alternative hypothesis might also be that the new drug is better, on average, than the current drug. In this case we would write H_a: The new drug is better than the current drug, on average. The final conclusion once the test has been carried out is always given in terms of the null hypothesis. We either "Reject H_0 in favor of H_a" or "Do not reject H_0." We never conclude "Reject H_a" or even "Accept H_a." If we conclude: "Do not reject H_0," this does not necessarily mean that the null hypothesis is true, it only suggests that there is not sufficient evidence against H_0 in favor of H_a. Rejecting the null hypothesis, then, suggests that the alternative hypothesis *may* be true, as when a verdict of "not guilty" does not necessarily imply that the accused is innocent. It just means that (1) he may be and (2) the prosecutor did not present enough evidence to convince the jury to reject the null hypothesis of "not guilty" and to accept the alternative hypothesis of "guilty."

ANOVA Analysis of variance (ANOVA) consists of calculations that provide information about levels of variability within a regression model and form a basis for tests of significance. The values from which r^2 and RMSE are calculated are derived from the ANOVA table in the regression summary output.

autocorrelated errors When the error terms remaining after application of a forecasting method show autocorrelation, it indicates that the forecasting method has not removed all of the pattern from the data. There are several hypothesis tests for autocorrelated errors. One of them is the Durbin-Watson test that checks only for first-order autocorrelations after fitting a regression model.

autocorrelation   This term is used to describe the correlation between values of the same time series at different time periods. It is similar to correlation but relates the series for different time lags. Thus there may be an autocorrelation for a time lag of 1, another autocorrelation for a time lag of 2, and so on.

autocorrelation function   The pattern of autocorrelations for lags 1, 2, . . . , is known as the autocorrelation function or ACF. A plot of the ACF against the lag is known as the correlogram. It is frequently used to identify whether or not seasonality is present in a given time series (and the length of that seasonality), to identify appropriate time series models for specific situations, and to determine if data are stationary.

back-transformation   If the dependent or response variable has been transformed, the regression results will be expressed in terms of the transformed variable, that is, the coefficients will be in the language necessary to calculate predicted values in the transformed language. For example, if the response variable is 2, and it is transformed into 4 by squaring it, then the coefficients when applied will produce a fitted value that equals or approximates 4. To reexpress the results in natural language, that is, 2, it is necessary to back-transform the equation in this case by raising it to the power of .5, or $\frac{1}{2}$. If only the predictor variables are transformed, there is no need to back-transform the model's results.

box plot   A box and whisker plot is a way of summarizing a set of data measured on an interval scale. It is often used in exploratory data analysis. It is a type of graph that is used to show the shape of the distribution, its central value, and variability. The picture produced consists of the most extreme values in the data set (maximum and minimum values), the lower and upper quartiles, and the median. A box plot (as it is often called) is especially helpful for indicating whether a distribution is skewed and whether there are any unusual observations (outliers) in the data set. Box and whisker plots are also very useful when large numbers of observations are involved and when two or more data sets are being compared.

causal model   Some forecasting methods use the assumption that it is possible to identify the underlying factors that might influence the variable that is being forecast. For example, sales of umbrellas might be associated with weather conditions. If the causes are understood, projections of the influencing variables can be made and used in the forecast. See *cross-sectional model*.

central limit theorem   Regardless of the shape of the population distribution, this theorem states that the sampling distribution of the mean of n independent sample values will approach the normal distribution as the sample size increases. In practice, when the sample size is sufficiently large (say, greater than 30), this theorem is invoked.

coefficient of variation   The coefficient of variation (CoV) is simply the SEE divided by the average of the dependent variable. It expresses the average degree of dispersion about the trendline in percentage form. It is a dimensionless metric that allows us to compare the goodness of fit of various regression models, because the standard deviation of the data must always be understood in the context of the mean of the data. Since it is a dimensionless number, when comparing between data sets with different units or widely different means, one should use the coefficient of variation for comparison instead of the standard deviation. In a nonregression setting, the CoV is computed by dividing the standard deviation by the average.

composite regression model   A linear combination of individual forecasts to assist in obtaining a more accurate forecast. As such, the dependent variable is actual sales, and the independent variables are the predicted values from the individual forecasts. The usual rules concerning adjusted r^2 and individual t-statistics for the X coefficients apply in this case as well.

confidence interval, or level   Based on statistical theory and probability distributions, a confidence interval, or set of confidence limits or levels, can be established for population parameters such as the mean. For example, a 95 percent confidence interval will contain the true value of the population parameter with probability 95 percent.

correlation coefficient   A standardized measure of the association or mutual dependence between two variables, say, X and Y. Commonly designated as r, its values range from -1 to $+1$, indicating strong negative relationship, through zero, to strong positive association. The correlation coefficient is the covariance between a pair of standardized variables.

correlation matrix   Most computer programs designed to perform multiple regression analysis include the computation of the correlation coefficients between each pair of variables. The set of these correlation coefficients is often presented in the form of a matrix, referred to as the correlation matrix.

covariance   This is a measure of the joint variation between variables, say, X and Y. The range of covariance values is unrestricted (large negative to large positive). However, if the X and Y variables are first standardized, then covariance is the same as correlation, and the range of covariance (correlation) values is from -1 to $+1$.

critical value   In hypothesis testing, the critical value is the threshold for significance. A test statistic beyond the critical value gives a significant result. See *hypothesis testing* and *p-value*.

cross-sectional model   A form of regression analysis where the observations are measured at the same point in time or over the same time period but differ along another dimension. For example, an analyst may regress stock returns for different companies measured over the same period against differences in the companies' yields for the period. See *causal model*.

curve fitting   One approach to forecasting is simply to fit some form of curve, perhaps a polynomial, to the historical time series data. Use of a linear trend is, in fact, a curve-fitting method. Higher forms of curve fitting are also possible, and they frequently provide better results.

curvilinear   A nonlinear trendline that curves upward or downward as it extends out over the x-axis.

degree of freedom   Degrees of freedom are a way of keeping score. Assume a data set contains a number of observations, say, n. They constitute n individual pieces of information with n degrees of freedom. These pieces of information can be used to estimate means and standard deviations. In general, each item, the mean and the standard deviation, being estimated costs one degree of freedom. The remaining degrees of freedom are used to estimate the remaining observations that contribute to the data set's average or degree of variability. All we have to do is count properly. For example, given 10 observations in a sample data set, if we know the mean, then nine observations can vary freely, but one observation must be fixed to produce the given mean. Therefore, the degrees of freedom for the data set are $n - 1$, or 9 degrees of freedom. In regression analysis, we lose 1 degree of freedom to compute the intercept and an additional degree of freedom for each independent variable we put into the model.

dependent or response or predicted variable A dependent variable is what you measure in the experiment and what is affected during the experiment. The dependent variable responds to the independent variable. It is called dependent because it "depends" on the independent variable. In a scientific experiment, you cannot have a dependent variable without an independent variable.

descriptive statistics Descriptive statistics are used to describe the main features of a collection of data in quantitative terms. Descriptive statistics are distinguished from inferential statistics (or inductive statistics) in that descriptive statistics aim to quantitatively summarize a data set, rather than being used to support inferential statements about the population that the data are thought to represent. Even when a data analysis draws its main conclusions using inductive statistical analysis, descriptive statistics are generally presented along with more formal analyses.

dimensionless A dimensionless quantity is a quantity without a physical unit and is thus a pure number. Such a number is typically defined as a ratio of quantities. Typical examples or applications are common-sized financial statements, standardized variables, and r and r^2.

distribution A distribution shows the number of observations falling into each of several ranges of values, which are typically portrayed as histograms. Distributions can show either the actual number of observations falling in each range or the percentage of observations. For example, if we asked the students in a classroom to line up on a line marked off by segments that define height, for example, greater than $5'6''$ up to $5'8''$, and so on, we would expect the student heights to be distributed normally, or in a bell-shaped manner. Another typical distribution is the uniform, which results when we roll one die over and over again and record the results. Distributions that are near–bell shaped but not symmetrical are skewed either to the left or right, such as the lognormal distribution that is characteristic of stock market returns.

double moving average When a moving average is taken of a series of data that already represents the result of a moving average, it is referred to as a double moving average. It results in additional smoothing or the removal of more randomness than an equal-length single moving average.

dummy variable In regression analysis, a dummy variable (also known as indicator variable or just dummy) is one that takes the values 0 or 1 to indicate the absence or presence of some categorical effect (month, quarter, strike, fire loss) that may be expected to shift the outcome. For example, in time series analysis, dummy variables may be used to capture seasonal effects.

Durbin-Watson statistic The Durbin-Watson (DW) statistic, named after its creators, tests the hypothesis that there is no autocorrelation of one time lag present in the errors obtained from forecasting. By comparing the computed value of the Durbin-Watson test with the appropriate values from a table of values of the DW statistic, the significance can be determined.

econometric model   An econometric model is a set of equations intended to be used simultaneously to capture the way in which endogenous (within the system) and exogenous (outside the system) variables are interrelated. Using such a set of equations to forecast future values of key economic variables is known as econometric forecasting. The value of econometric forecasting is intimately connected to the validity of the assumptions underlying the model equations.

empirical rule   For data sets having a normal, bell-shaped distribution, approximately 68 percent of the data values are within 1 standard deviation of the mean; approximately 95 percent are within 2 standard deviations of the mean; and approximately 99.7 percent (nearly all) are within 3 standard deviations of the mean.

error   A forecast error is calculated by subtracting the forecast value from the actual value to give an error value for each forecast period. In forecasting, this term is commonly used as a synonym for residual.

estimation   Estimation consists of finding appropriate values for the parameters of an equation in such a way that some criterion will be optimized. The most commonly used criterion is that of root mean squared error. Often, an iterative procedure is needed in order to determine those parameter values that minimize this criterion.

exponential smoothing   Exponential smoothing methods provide forecasts using weighted averages of past values of the data and forecast errors. They are commonly used in inventory control systems where many items are to be forecast and low cost is a primary concern. The simplest exponential smoothing method is single exponential smoothing (SES), suitable for data with no trend or seasonal patterns. For trended data, Holt's Method is suitable, and for seasonal data, Holt-Winter's Method may be used.

F ratio   The F ratio or F statistic is calculated by dividing MSR (mean squared regression) by MSE (mean squared error), or explained variance by unexplained variance. If the F ratio is small, then the explained variation is small relative to the unexplained variation, and there is evidence that the regression equation provides little explanatory power. But if the F ratio is large, then the explained variation is large relative to the unexplained variation, and we can conclude that the equation does have some explanatory power.

function   A function is a statement of relationship between variables. Virtually all of the quantitative forecasting methods involve a functional relationship between the item to be forecast and either previous values of that item, previous error values, or other explanatory variables.

goodness of fit   The goodness of fit of a statistical model describes how well it fits a set of observations. Measures of goodness of fit typically summarize the discrepancy between actual or observed values and the values predicted by the model in question. Typical goodness-of-fit metrics for regression are r^2, RMSE, the F ratio, and the t-statistic.

histogram   A histogram is a way of summarizing data that are measured on an interval scale (either discrete or continuous). It is often used in exploratory data analysis to illustrate the major features of the distribution of the data in a convenient form. It divides up the range of possible values in a data set into classes or groups. For each group, a rectangle is constructed with a base length equal to the range of values in that specific group and an area proportional to the number of observations falling into that group. This means that the rectangles might be drawn of nonuniform height.

heteroscedasticity   This condition exists when the errors do not have a constant variance across an entire range of values. For example, if the residuals from a time series have increasing variance with increasing time, they would be said to exhibit heteroscedasticity.

homoscedasticity   This condition exists when the variance of a series is constant over the entire range of values of that series. It is the opposite of heteroscedasticity. When a series of residuals exhibits constant variance over the entire range of time periods, it is said to exhibit homoscedasticity.

hypothesis testing   The procedure for deciding if a null hypothesis should be accepted or rejected in favor of an alternate hypothesis. A statistic is computed from a survey or test result and is analyzed to determine if it falls within a preset acceptance region. If it does, the null hypothesis is accepted otherwise rejected.

independent or predictor or explanatory variable   A variable that you believe might influence your outcome measure. For example, in an agronomy experiment, this might be a variable that you control, like a fertilizer treatment, or a variable not under your control, like the amount of rainfall. In other fields, it also might represent a demographic factor like age or gender.

inferential statistics   Inferential statistics are used to draw inferences about a population from a sample.

intercept, or constant   In an XY scatterplot, the point where the trendline intercepts the Y-axis. Note that this value usually doesn't make much sense. In fact, the intercept is usually not interpreted, especially if a value of zero for the predictor variable can't really be obtained in practice. Since the regression intercept is not determined by the value of the x variable, it represents the amount of the total model-derived value not determined by the x variable (i.e., the amount of y not determined by x).

KURT   KURT is the Excel function that calculates the kurtosis of a data set's distribution. Kurtosis characterizes the relative peakedness or flatness of a distribution compared to the normal distribution. Positive kurtosis indicates a relatively peaked distribution, while negative kurtosis indicates a relatively flat distribution. A kurtosis of 0 indicates a bell-shaped peakedness.

lag   A difference in time between an observation and a previous observation. Thus $Yt-k$ lags Yt by k periods.

least squares estimation   This approach to estimating the parameter values in an equation minimizes the squares of the deviations that result from fitting that particular model. For example, if a trend line is being estimated to fit a data series, the method of least squares estimation could be used to minimize the mean squared error. This would give a line whose estimated values would minimize the sum of the squares of the actual deviations from that line for the historical data.

Lilliefors test   The normality assumption is at the core of a majority of standard statistical procedures, and it is important to be able to test this assumption. In addition, showing that a sample does not come from a normally distributed population is sometimes of importance per se. Among the many procedures used to test this assumption, one of the most well known is a modification of the Kolmogorov-Smirnov test of goodness of fit, generally referred to as the Lilliefors test for normality (or Lilliefors test, for short). The null hypothesis for this test is that the error is normally distributed (i.e., there is no difference between the observed distribution of the error and a normal distribution). The alternative hypothesis is that the error is not normally distributed.

log scale   You can have the Y-axis on a logarithmic scale instead of a linear one. On a logarithmic axis, equal distance along it represents an equal percentage change. It is very useful if you want to present data with large differences in scale on the same chart. A logarithmic scale is also widely used for showing stock price changes over a longer period of time.

mean   measure of location, especially central tendency, for a batch of data values. It is the sum of all data values divided by the number of observations in the distribution. Its accompanying measure of spread is usually the standard deviation. Unlike the median and the mode, it is not appropriate to use the mean to characterize a skewed distribution.

mean absolute percentage error (MAPE)   The mean absolute percentage error is the mean or average of the sum of all of the percentage errors for a given data set taken without regard to sign. (That is, their absolute values are summed and the average computed.) It is one summary measure of accuracy commonly used in quantitative methods of forecasting.

median   Another measure of location, especially central tendency, just like the mean. It is the value that divides the distribution in half when all data values are listed in order. It is insensitive to small numbers of extreme scores in a distribution. Therefore, it is the preferred measure of central tendency for a skewed distribution (in which the mean would be influenced by extreme values).

model   A model is the symbolic representation of reality. In quantitative forecasting methods a specific model is used to represent the basic pattern contained in the data. This may be a regression model, which is explanatory in nature, or a time series model.

moving average   For a time series we can define the moving average of order K as the average (mean) value of K consecutive observations. This can be used for smoothing or forecasting.

multicollinearity   In multiple regression, computational problems arise if two or more explanatory variables are highly correlated with one another. The regression coefficients associated with those explanatory variables will be very unstable. In larger sets of explanatory variables, the condition of multicollinearity may not be easy to detect. If any linear combination of one subset of explanatory variables is nearly perfectly related to a linear combination of any other subset of explanatory variables, then a multicollinearity problem is present.

multiple correlation coefficient   If a forecast variable Y is regressed against several explanatory variables $X1$, $X2$, . . , Xk, then the estimated Y value is designated $\hat{Y}$. The correlation between $\hat{Y}$ and Y is called the multiple correlation coefficient and is often designated R. It is customary to deal with this coefficient in squared form (i.e., R^2).

multiple regression   The technique of multiple regression is an extension of simple regression. It allows for more than one explanatory variable to be included in predicting the value of a forecast variable. For forecasting purposes a multiple regression equation is often referred to as a causal or explanatory model.

naive forecast   Forecasts obtained with a minimal amount of effort and data manipulation and based solely on the most recent information available are frequently referred to as naive forecasts. One such naive method would be to use the most recent observation available as the future forecast. A slightly more sophisticated naive method would be to adjust the most recent observation for seasonality.

noise   The randomness often found in data series is frequently referred to as noise. This term comes from the field of engineering where a filter is used to eliminate noise so that the true pattern can be identified.

nonlinear estimation   If parameters have to be estimated for nonlinear functions, then ordinary least squares estimation may not apply. Under these circumstances certain nonlinear techniques exist for solving the problem. Minimizing the sum of squared residuals is one common criterion. Another is maximum likelihood estimation. Nonlinear estimation is an iterative procedure, and there is no guarantee that the final solution is the global minimum.

nonparametric tests   Nonparametric or distribution-free tests are so called because the assumptions underlying their use are fewer and weaker than those associated with parametric tests. To put it another way, nonparametric tests require few if any assumptions about the shapes of the underlying population distributions. For this reason, they are often used in place of parametric tests if/when one feels that the assumptions of the parametric test have been too grossly violated (e.g., if the distributions are too severely skewed).

nonstationary   A time series exhibits nonstationarity if the underlying generating process does not have a constant mean and/or a constant variance. In practice, a visual inspection of the plotted time series can help determine if either or both of these conditions exist, and the set of autocorrelations for the time series can be used to confirm the presence of nonstationarity or not.

normal distribution   This is a probability distribution that is very widely used in statistical modeling. It is the distribution of many naturally occurring variables and the distribution of many statistics. It is represented by a bell-shaped curve.

normal probability plot   A plot of the residuals versus a z value (or cumulative normal percentile) derived from the normal probability distribution for the ranking location of the residual. This gives a visual look to determine if the residuals are actually normally distributed. The assumption of residuals being normally distributed is an important assumption. The p-values of the coefficients and coefficient confidence intervals are based on this assumption. If the plot is roughly a straight line, then the assumption is valid.

null hypothesis   The null hypothesis is a hypothesis that the researcher tries to disprove, reject, or nullify. The "null" often refers to the common view of something, that is, the "status quo" or a state of no difference. An experiment conclusion always refers to the null, rejecting or accepting H_0 rather than H_a. For example, in a criminal trial, the null hypothesis is that the defendant is no different from everyone else, that is, not guilty. It is up to the prosecution to present sufficient, credible evidence to the jury such that they reject the null hypothesis and accept the alternative hypothesis that the defendant is guilty as charged.

observation   An observation is the value of a specific event as expressed on some measurement scale by a single data value. In most forecasting applications a set of observations is used to provide the data to which the selected model is fit.

one-tailed t-test If you are using a significance level of .05, a one-tailed test allots all 5 percent to testing the statistical significance in the one direction of interest. This means that .05 is in one tail of the distribution of your test statistic. When using a one-tailed test, you are testing for the possibility of the relationship in one direction and completely disregarding the possibility of a relationship in the other direction. Let's return to our example comparing the mean of a sample to a given value x using a t-test. Our null hypothesis is that the mean is equal to x. A one-tailed test will test either if the mean is significantly greater than x or if the mean is significantly less than x, but not both. Then, depending on the chosen tail, the mean is significantly greater than or less than x if the test statistic is in the top 5 percent of its probability distribution or bottom 5 percent of its probability distribution, resulting in a p-value less than 0.05. The one-tailed test provides more power to detect an effect in one direction by not testing the effect in the other direction.

outlier An outlier is a data value that is unusually large or small. Such outliers are sometimes removed from the data set before fitting a forecasting model so that unusually large deviations from the pattern will not affect the fitting of the model.

parametric tests Conventional statistical procedures are called parametric tests in which a sample statistic, such as a mean or standard deviation, is obtained to estimate the population parameter. Because this estimation process involves a sample, a sampling distribution, and a population, certain parametric assumptions are required to ensure all elements are compatible with each other. For example, the most common assumptions are: (1) observations are independent; (2) the sample data have a normal distribution; and (3) scores in different groups have homogeneous variances.

p-value A p-value is the probability that the observed result, or a result more extreme, could be obtained if the null hypothesis is true. For example, in Case Study 2 the null hypothesis is that there is no correlation between sales and time. The probability of finding an absolute correlation as large as −.217, if the null hypothesis is true, is .203. The degree of correlation and its p-value move in opposite directions from each other, that is, large degrees of correlation have small p-values. Therefore, the probability of .203 is too high, that is, too far from zero, to be uncommon or unexpected. Since it is greater than .05, we can say that a correlation of −.217 is not significant at the 5 percent significance level, or, in effect, not different from zero.

pattern The basic set of relationships and the underlying process over time is referred to as the pattern in the data.

polynomial In algebra a polynomial is an expression containing one or more terms, each of which consists of a coefficient and a variable(s) raised to some power. Thus $a + bx$ is a linear polynomial, and $a + bx + cx^2$ is a quadratic polynomial in x. A polynomial of order m includes terms involving powers of x up to x^m. Regression models often involve linear and higher order polynomials.

polynomial fitting It is possible to fit a polynomial of any number of terms to a set of data. If the number of terms (the order) equals the number of data observations, the fit can be made perfectly.

population   A population is a collection of data whose properties are analyzed. The population is the complete collection to be studied; it contains all subjects of interest. For example, a classroom of 30 students can be a population if the inquiries we make concern only those specific 30 students.

quadratic or second-degree polynomial   A quadratic or second-degree polynomial trendline is a curvilinear trendline that is used when data fluctuates from a straight-line trend. It is useful, for example, for analyzing trends that are slowing down over time. The degree or order of the polynomial can be determined by the number of fluctuations in the data or by how many bends (hills and valleys) appear in the curve. A second-degree polynomial trendline generally has only one hill or valley.

RMSE   Root mean squared error. See *standard error of the estimate* for a definition.

R-square   R-square, or R^2, or r^2, indicates how much of the dependent variable's total variation is accounted for by the predictor variables. It equals, once more from the ANOVA section of any summary output, residualSS/totalSS. R-square measures the percentage of the variation in the dependent variable accounted for by the predictor variables(s) in the regression model. The range of possible values is 0 to 1.0 (or 0 percent to 100 percent). In the quarterly time series model of Case Study 4, R-square is .9904, which means that the two predictor variables, trend and seasonal index, account for 99.04 percent of the variation in the 12 quarters of sales. The remaining variation in the dependent variable, .06 percent, is due to all the predictor variables other than the present two and is still unaccounted for. If we could identify, locate, and add statistically significant predictor variables to the regression model, R-square would increase, the standard error would decrease, and so would the accuracy of the model as measured by the width of the interval surrounding the predicted values.

RSS, ESS, and TSS   Regression sum of squares, or RSS, is included in the ANOVA table, along with TSS, or total sum of squares, and ESS, or error sum of squares. The formula RSS + ESS = TSS represents the relationship between the actual data point, the predicted data point, and the average of the Y variable, in other words, how much of the variability in the Y data is accounted for by the model. TSS is total variability measured as the sum of the squared distances between each data point and the average of the Y variable. RSS is the amount of variability accounted for by the model, that is, the sum of the squared distances between the predicted data point and the average of the Y variable. ESS is the amount of variability that is not accounted for by the model, that is, the sum of the squared distances between the predicted data point and the actual data point.

random sampling   This statistical sampling method involves selecting a sample from a population in such a way that every unit within that population has the same probability of being selected as any other unit.

regression   The term *regression* dates back to Sir Francis Galton and his work with the heights of siblings in different generations. The heights of children of exceptionally tall (or short) parents "regress" to the mean of the population. Regression analysis today means any modeling of a forecast variable Y as a function of a set of explanatory variables X_1 through X_k.

regression coefficients   In regression, a forecast variable Y is modeled as a function of explanatory variables X_1 through X_k. The regression coefficients are the multipliers of the explanatory variables. The estimates of these regression coefficients can be used to understand the importance of each explanatory variable (as it relates to Y) and the interrelatedness among the explanatory variables (as they relate to Y).

residual It is calculated by subtracting the forecast value from the observed value to give a residual or error value for each forecast period. In forecasting this term is commonly used as a synonym for error, although in some cases we might distinguish the two.

S-curve An S-curve is most frequently used to represent a product's or business's life cycle. Several different mathematical forms, such as the logistics curve, can be used to fit an S-curve to actual observed data.

sample A sample is a part of the population of interest, a subcollection selected from a population. For example, a classroom of 30 students can be a sample if we use it to make inferences about a larger population of students.

sampling distribution The distribution of a statistic from a finite sample. If we could take many such samples, the collection of possible values of the statistic would follow its sampling distribution.

sampling error The sampling error is an indication of the magnitude of difference between the true values of a population parameter and the estimated value of that parameter based on a sample.

seasonality A characteristic of a time series in which the data experiences regular and predictable changes that recur every calendar year. Any predictable change or pattern in a time series that recurs or repeats over a one-year period can be said to be seasonal. Seasonality can be seen in many time series and is very common. For example, if one lives in a climate with cold winters and warm summers, one's home heating costs probably rise in the winter and fall in the summer. One would reasonably expect the seasonality of heating costs to recur every year. Similarly, a company that sells sunscreen and tanning products would see sales jump up in the summer, but drop in the winter.

SKEW SKEW is the Excel function that calculates the skewness of a data set's distribution. Skewness characterizes the degree of symmetry of a distribution around its mean. Positive skewness indicates a distribution with its long tail extending toward the right, or more positive values, while negative skewness indicates a distribution with its long tail extending toward the left, or more negative values. A skewness of 0 indicates a symmetrical distribution.

slope The slope quantifies the steepness of the trendline. It equals the change in Y for each unit change in X. It is expressed in the units of the Y-axis divided by the units of the X-axis, which is called the rise-over-run ratio. If the slope is positive, Y increases as X increases. If the slope is negative, Y decreases as X increases.

smoothing The technique of estimating a smooth trend, usually by taking weighted averages of observations. The term *smoothed* is used because such averages tend to reduce randomness by allowing positive and negative random effects to partially offset each other.

specification error A type of error often caused either by the incorrect choice of a functional form of a forecasting model or the failure to include important variables in that functional form or model.

standard deviation   The standard deviation is the average deviation, or degree of dispersion, about the mean of any data set. It is computed by taking the difference between each observation in the data set and the mean, squaring that difference (in order to deal with negative differences), summing the squared differences, dividing by the number of observations (if dealing with a population) or the number of observations minus 1 (if dealing with a sample), and then taking the square root of the result.

standard error   Given a population distribution (say, a normal distribution), a sampling plan (say, a simple independent random sampling plan), and a specific statistic (say, the mean), then the sampling distribution of the mean is a probability distribution with an expected value, a standard deviation, and various other properties. The standard deviation of the sampling distribution of a statistic is called the standard error of that statistic.

standard error of the estimate   The standard error of the estimate (SEE), also called root mean squared error (RMSE), is the square root of the mean squared residual term from the ANOVA table of the summary output. In Case Study 4, the SEE measures the impact on room sales due to all the predictor variables excluded from the regression model. In a perfect world, we would know all the predictor variables and would have located and included them in the model, thereby causing all the observations to lie on the trendline and the SEE to be 0.

There are only two ways to reduce the SEE. (1) Identify and add statistically significant predictor variables to the regression model. (2) Remove insignificant predictor variables from the regression model, for example, those predictor variables that have an absolute t-statistic less than 1. This requires an iterative process of predictor variable removing until the regression model stabilizes, and all remaining predictor variables have absolute t-statistics greater than 1.

standardize   Given a sample set of values for X, where the mean is $\overline{X}$ and the standard deviation is S, the ith value in the set X_i is standardized by subtracting the mean and dividing by the standard deviation.

stationary   If the underlying generating process for a time series is based on a constant mean and a constant variance, then the time series is stationary. More formally, a series is stationary if its statistical properties are independent of the particular time period during which it is observed.

statistic   Given a sample consisting of n values, a statistic is any summary number that captures a property of the sample data. For example, the mean is a statistic, and so are the variance, the skewness, the median, the standard deviation, and so on. For a pair of variables sampled jointly the correlation coefficient is a statistic and so is the covariance. The values of a statistic vary from sample to sample, and the complete set of values is called the sampling distribution of the statistic.

stem and leaf plot   A stem and leaf plot is a way of summarizing a set of data measured on an interval scale. It is often used in exploratory data analysis to illustrate the major features of the distribution of the data in a convenient and easily drawn form. A stem and leaf plot is similar to a histogram but is usually a more informative display for relatively small data sets (<100 data points). It provides a table as well as a picture of the data, and from it we can readily write down the data in order of magnitude, which is useful for many statistical procedures.

time-series analysis A time series is a set of ordered observations of a phenomenon at equally spaced time points. One of the main goals of time series analysis is to forecast future values of the series. In time series models we presume to know nothing about the causality that affects the variable we are trying to forecast. Instead, we examine the past behavior of a time series in order to infer something about its future behavior. The method used to produce a forecast can be as simple as a deterministic model such as linear extrapolation.

transformation Transformations turn lists into other lists, or variables into other variables. For example, to transform a list of temperatures in degrees Celsius into the corresponding list of temperatures in degrees Fahrenheit, you multiply each element by 9/5 and add 32 to each product. In statistics, transformation of variables deals with nonlinearity and nonnormality of the data points and nonhomogeneous variance. Typical transformations are taking logs or square or cube roots, squaring or cubing, and raising to a power, either positive or negative.

trend The tendency of monthly sales to move in a particular direction over time. Sales can trend upward, downward, or not at all. In all three cases, sales will fluctuate about the trendline because of seasonality and/or noise.

trend analysis Trend analysis (or trendline analysis) is a special form of simple regression in which time is the explanatory variable.

t-statistic A t-statistic (the t is for test) provides a way of determining if the slope of the regression line is different from 0. If it is not, then the coefficient of the predictor variable does not contain any statistically significant information. The t-statistic for this test is the predictor coefficient minus 0/the standard error of the predictor coefficient. For example, in the quarterly time series output summary of Case Study 5, the value of the coefficient for the seasonal index predictor is 75,726.07, the standard error for that coefficient is 2,566.89, and so the t-statistic is 29.501 (75,726.07/2566.89). This can be interpreted to mean that the predictor coefficient is 29.5 standard deviations from 0. If 3 standard deviations cover 99.7 percent of the area under the normal curve, then 29.5 standard deviations is off the charts, and we can conclude the seasonal index coefficient is very highly significant.

A complementary metric of the t-statistic is the p-value, which indicates the probability of obtaining an outcome that is more extreme than the observed test statistic value if the slope of the trendline is 0. In this case, the p-value is 0, indicating that there is virtually no chance that we will obtain an outcome as large as the observed value of 75,726.07 if the true value of the predictor coefficient is 0.

two-tailed t-test If you are using a significance level of 0.05, a two-tailed test allots half of the 5 percent to testing the statistical significance in one direction and half of the 5 percent to testing statistical significance in the other direction. This means that .025 is in each tail of the distribution of your test statistic. When using a two-tailed test, regardless of the direction of the relationship you hypothesize, you are testing for the possibility of the relationship in both directions. For example, we may wish to compare the mean of a sample to a given value x using a t-test. Our null hypothesis is that the mean is equal to x. A two-tailed test will test both if the mean is significantly greater than x and if the mean is significantly less than x. The mean is considered significantly different from x if the test statistic is in the top 2.5 percent or bottom 2.5 percent of its probability distribution, resulting in a p-value less than 0.05.

variance   The variance is another statistic for calculating the mean deviation of a group of scores from the mean, such as a classroom of 30 students. However, rather than using the absolute values, as when calculating the mean absolute deviation, each of the deviations is instead squared. Adding up these squared deviations gives us the sum of squares, which we can then divide by the total number of scores in our group of data (in other words, 30 because there are 30 students) to find the variance. It should be noted, however, that the formula that divides the sum of squares by n is only appropriate when we are working with a population. In other words, we are only interested in the performance of our 30 students. Additional considerations are required if we were using, for example, the performance of these 30 students to examine how 500 students taking the same piece of coursework had performed.

weight   The term *weight* indicates the relative importance given to an individual item included in forecasting. In the method of moving averages, all of those past values included in the moving average are given equal weight. In more sophisticated methods of time series analysis, the problem of model identification involves determining the most appropriate values of those weights.

z score   The z score, or z-value for an item, indicates how far and in what direction that item deviates from its distribution's mean, expressed in units of its distribution's standard deviation. Z scores are sometimes called "standard scores." The z score transformation is especially useful when seeking to compare the relative standings of items from distributions with different means and/or different standard deviations. It is computed by subtracting the mean from each item's value and dividing the difference by the standard deviation.

About the Authors

Mark G. Filler, CPA/ABV, CBA, AM, CVA, and James A. DiGabriele, PhD/DPS, CPA/ABV/CFF, CFE, CFSA, FACEI, CrFA, CVA, have spent the last 20 years of their respective practices concentrated in the areas of business valuation, commercial damages, personal injury, and, for DiGabriele, forensic accounting. They have participated in adjusting hundreds of business interruption claims apiece, and each has testified at deposition or trial over a hundred times. Both are founders and name partners of their respective CPA firms, Filler & Associates in Portland, Maine, and DiGabriele, McNulty, Campanella & Co. in Fairfield, New Jersey. Dr. DiGabriele is also an Associate Accounting Professor at Montclair State University in the Department of Accounting, Law, and Taxation at the School of Business Administration.

Index

319